THE TOWNSHIP LIBRARY
OF LOWER SOUTHAMPTON
1983 Bridgetown Pike
Feasterville, PA 19053

*Defenders of the Unborn*

# DEFENDERS
# OF
# THE UNBORN

*The Pro-Life Movement before*
Roe v. Wade

DANIEL K. WILLIAMS

OXFORD
UNIVERSITY PRESS

# OXFORD

UNIVERSITY PRESS

Oxford University Press is a department of the University of
Oxford. It furthers the University's objective of excellence in research,
scholarship, and education by publishing worldwide.
Oxford is a registered trade mark of Oxford University Press in the UK and in certain other
countries.

Published in the United States of America by
Oxford University Press
198 Madison Avenue, New York, NY 10016, United States of America

© Oxford University Press 2016

All rights reserved. No part of this publication may be reproduced, stored in
a retrieval system, or transmitted, in any form or by any means, without the prior
permission in writing of Oxford University Press, or as expressly permitted by law,
by license, or under terms agreed with the appropriate reproduction rights organization.
Inquiries concerning reproduction outside the scope of the above should be sent to the
Rights Department, Oxford University Press, at the address above.

You must not circulate this work in any other form
and you must impose this same condition on any acquirer.

Library of Congress Cataloging-in-Publication Data
Williams, Daniel K.
Defenders of the unborn : the pro-life movement
before Roe v. Wade / Daniel K. Williams.
pages cm
ISBN 978–0–19–939164–6 (hardback)
1. Pro-life movement—United States—History. 2. Abortion—Moral and ethical
aspects—United States—History. 3. Abortion—Government policy—United
States—History. 4. Abortion—Religious aspects—Christianity. I. Title.
HQ767.5.U5W556 2016
363.460973—dc23
2015017478

3 5 7 9 8 6 4
Printed in the United States of America
on acid-free paper

# Contents

*Photos follow page 178*

# *Acknowledgments*

THIS BOOK WOULD not have been possible without assistance and encouragement from numerous people.

I am especially grateful to Robby George and Brad Wilson, the directors of the James Madison Program at Princeton University, for giving me the opportunity to spend a year at Princeton researching and writing this book. The intellectually stimulating conversations that I had with some of the other scholars I met through the James Madison Program—including Andy Lewis, Chris Tollefsen, Ben Kleinerman, Nathan Schlueter, Ken Miller, Kathleen Brady, Andy Bibby, Melissa Moschella, and Matt Franck, among others—gave me a new perspective on my research subject and helped me refine my ideas about natural law, Catholic theology, utilitarianism, the meaning of human freedom, and the defense of human life. I am also grateful to Bob Wuthnow for encouraging me in my research and giving me the opportunity to attend the research presentations of some of his graduate students and postdoctoral fellows during my year at Princeton. My progress on this book would have been much slower—and its quality would not have been the same—if I had not had the opportunity to spend a year in the James Madison Program. For that reason, I owe a special debt of gratitude to my late friend and fellow Brown Ph.D. Alan Petigny for inviting me to apply to the James Madison Program and recommending me to the program's directors. I know that I would have enjoyed sharing this book with Alan, and I regret that he did not live long enough to see its completion.

I am grateful to several colleagues who read this manuscript in whole or in part. These people include Mary Ziegler, Matt Sutton, Ray Haberski, Michael de Nie, and Laura Gifford. I benefited greatly from their thoughtful suggestions for revision, as well as from the suggestions of my manuscript's anonymous peer reviewers. I am also grateful to my graduate research assistant Thadis Coley for reading through a full draft of the manuscript and offering helpful suggestions. The students in a graduate seminar that I taught in the spring of 2014 read an early version of my manuscript, and I am grateful to them for their comments. I would also like to thank Stacie Taranto for reading my introductory chapter and offering encouraging feedback. I am sure that not all of these readers would endorse everything that I have written in this book or share my perspective on the subject, but I very much appreciated their thoughtful critiques of my work, insightful suggestions, and supportive feedback.

I am grateful to Don Critchlow, David Courtwright, Phil Goff, Axel Schäfer, and Darren Dochuk for giving me the opportunity to publish my research in journals or books that they were editing and for encouraging me in this project. Numerous other scholars have shared conference panels or discussed my research with me. It would be difficult to provide a comprehensive list of all of my fellow conference panelists and colleagues in the field who encouraged me in my research along the way, so I will not try to do so, but if you met with me for lunch or coffee to discuss my research, gave an insightful conference presentation that furthered my thinking on the history of the abortion debate, or simply asked a thoughtful question after one of my conference paper presentations, I want you to know that I am grateful for your help, insights, or encouragement.

I am grateful to the University of West Georgia (UWG) for providing me with research funds—including a faculty research grant—that facilitated some of my archival research trips, and for offering me a sabbatical to spend a year of research and writing at Princeton. I appreciate the support that my colleagues in the UWG history department have given me in completing this research project and for offering me the opportunity to present some of my research in public forums at UWG. I would also like to thank Mark Tietjen, a colleague in the philosophy department, for his thought-provoking conversations and encouragement throughout this project.

I am grateful to the numerous archivists and librarians who have assisted me. I am especially thankful to the directors of several diocesan archives—including the archives of the archdioceses of Boston, Los Angeles, New York, and St. Paul-Minneapolis, as well as the diocese of Harrisburg—for locating collections that would have been impossible for me to find without their kind assistance. Msgr. Kujovsky, the director of the archives of the diocese of Harrisburg, gave me special permission to use the archives after closing hours and went out of his way to put me in touch with useful contacts and locate helpful material for me in addition to arranging a place for me to stay while I was in Harrisburg. I am also grateful to the staff at *First Things* for giving me access to the unprocessed papers of Fr. Richard John Neuhaus. I am grateful to the Sisters of Life in New York for giving me access to their collection of pro-life materials. And I am thankful to the staff at many other archives and libraries, including those at Brown University, Princeton University, Princeton Theological Seminary, UCLA, University of Kansas, Wichita State University, Catholic University of America, Saint Anselm College, Saint John's University, Duke Divinity School, Emory University's Candler School of Theology, Harvard Divinity School, the Library of Congress, the North Dakota State Historical Society, the Wisconsin Historical Society, the Bentley Historical Library, the John F. Kennedy Library, the Gerald R. Ford Library, the Jimmy Carter Library, and the Ronald Reagan Library, for helping me during my research visits. I have also benefited from the opportunity to do research at Harvard University's Schlesinger Library and Countway Library of Medicine, and am grateful to the staff at those libraries for their professionalism in maintaining the high quality of their collections. The friendly staff at the library of my own university, UWG, was very helpful in facilitating interlibrary loan requests. I am also grateful to several people in the pro-life movement—especially Juan Ryan and Mary Vanis, who agreed to telephone interviews—for supplementing my archival findings with their own personal recollections of pro-life activism in the late 1960s and early 1970s.

I would like to thank the Right to Life League of Southern California, Minnesota Citizens Concerned for Life, Right to Life-LIFESPAN of Michigan, Birthright International, the Diocese of Pittsburgh Archives and Records Center, Saint John's University archives, and *The Tidings* (the newspaper for the Archdiocese of Los Angeles) for their generosity in sharing photos with me from the pro-life movement's early years. I would also like to thank the late Dr. Jack Willke and the family of Edward Golden for generously allowing me to publish photographs from their personal collections. The staff at Religion News Service was very helpful in helping me locate relevant photos from their files.

I am deeply grateful to my editor at Oxford University Press, Theo Calderara, for his skilled editing work on my manuscript. This is the second time that Theo has edited a book for me, and I continue to be thankful for the many things that he has done to strengthen the quality of my writing and eliminate extraneous material.

# A Note on Terminology

To a greater degree than most other historical topics, the debate over abortion is an issue of current political controversy with deep convictions on both sides, which means that any terminology surrounding the issue of abortion is likely to be contentious and laden with political overtones. This book is an attempt to explain the history of one side of that controversy and the development of its ideas—ideas that some readers may find deeply objectionable. Thus, in tracing this history, I have made choices in wording that some readers may find disconcerting.

Some readers may object to my frequent use of the term "pro-life," a term that is politically charged today. *The Associated Press Stylebook* recommends that journalists should "use *anti-abortion* instead of *pro-life* and *abortion rights* instead of *pro-abortion* or *pro-choice*," and many news analysts have followed this advice.[1] Supporters of abortion rights often resent the implication that someone who supports a woman's right to terminate her pregnancy is "anti-life" or that opposition to abortion—which they view as opposition to women's rights—makes one a defender of life. They also frequently point out the hypocrisy of calling someone pro-life if that person also supports the death penalty, gun rights, or recent wars in Iraq and Afghanistan. Wouldn't the term "anti-abortion" be more accurate? they ask.[2]

I understand these objections but think that there are at least two reasons for a historian to use the term "pro-life." First, this term, along with the phrase "right-to-life," has been the term favored by almost all activists in the movement since the late 1960s. If we want to approach the study of the pro-life movement as historians, rather than as champions of a particular political opinion, it would probably be best to set aside our presuppositions and attempt to understand the movement's own use of terminology before passing judgment on it. But I think that there is an even more important reason for me to use the term "pro-life" in this historical account, and that is that the pro-life movement thought of itself from the very beginning not as a movement primarily devoted to oppos-ing abortion—though that is what it largely became—but as a move-ment to defend the legal protection of all human life from the moment of conception. Pro-lifers saw themselves as defenders of the "inalienable . . . right to life," a right championed in the Declaration of Independence and legally enshrined in the Fifth and Fourteenth Amendments of the Constitution. They argued that this right to life began at the moment of conception. Their opponents accused them of campaigning against abor-tion primarily because of their religious views or their discomfort with women's rights, but pro-lifers rejected those accusations. In their view, they were simply defending the value of all human life, as outlined in the nation's founding documents. Thus, in their view, the term "pro-life" was the most accurate descriptor of their political project.

In this book I also did not hesitate to use the term "pro-choice," even though *The Associated Press Stylebook* discourages the use of this word. The term "pro-choice," in addition to being the preferred self-designation of supporters of abortion rights after the early 1970s, accurately conveys the movement's emphasis on defending women's personal autonomy through their own reproductive choices. Just as pro-lifers viewed their cause as larger than merely restricting abortion, so pro-choice activists thought of their cause not primarily as a fight for the availability of safe, legal abortion for its own sake, but rather as part of a larger battle to secure reproductive choices for women. It thus seemed fair and accurate to use the term "pro-choice" when describing defenders of abortion rights over the past forty years.

However, the term "pro-choice" originated only in the early 1970s, so when discussing the abortion legalization movement prior to 1970, I gener-ally avoided using a term that would be historically anachronistic. Before 1970, the movement for legalized abortion focused not on defending wom-en's "right to choose"—a phrase that people in the 1960s would not have recognized—but on protecting women's health, preventing the birth of unwanted children (particularly if they were likely to be born with severe deformities), reducing population growth, and giving doctors greater legal protections in making choices that they thought would be in the best inter-ests of their patients. In its early years, the campaign for legalizing abortion was a medical or population control movement, not a women's rights cause.[3] Thus, readers will rarely see the term "pro-choice" used in the early chap-ters of this book, which focus on the abortion debate prior to the 1970s, but they will often encounter the term in the book's final chapters, which discuss the abortion debate after *Roe v. Wade*. When describing early advocates of abortion legalization, I used phrases such as "abortion law reformers," "advocates of abortion law liberalization," or similar nomenclature that was used at the time and that accurately conveyed the desire of reform advocates to modify abortion laws but not necessarily to legalize all abortions. Throughout the book, I attempted to use terminology that would accurately describe the beliefs of my subjects. In most cases, that meant using the self-designations that the historical subjects chose for themselves, even if they might seem surprising to some contemporary readers.

The language of the pro-life movement developed before the language of the pro-choice movement. Catholics argued even in the early 1950s that abortion violated the fetus's "right to life," while abortion rights advocates did not adopt the term "pro-choice"—or even the term "abortion rights"—until much later. Yet in order to avoid historical anachronism, I waited until discussing the events of the 1960s to describe my subjects as "right-to-life advocates," and I waited until a discussion of the late 1960s to describe them as "pro-life," because even though opponents of abortion used the phrase "right to life" before the 1960s, they did not employ the term as a movement label. I think that, had I chosen to do so, I could have used the word "pro-life" as a descriptively accurate term for the Catholics who spoke out against abortion in the 1930s and 1940s, because the Catholics who mobilized against abortion law reform proposals invariably grounded their arguments in claims that abortion legalization constituted a societal disrespect for human life. But because the terms "right-to-life" and "pro-life" were not used as movement descriptors in the 1930s and 1940s, I waited until the Catholic opponents of abortion had formed a grassroots movement in the 1960s—which now had its own labels—to begin applying those terms to their cause.

At times, my desire to avoid historical anachronism in terminology led to complications. Nowhere was this more evident, perhaps, than in the dilemmas I faced when searching for the right words to describe the removal of legal restrictions on abortion during the first two trimesters of pregnancy. Pro-lifers called this phenomenon "abortion on demand." Advocates of abortion rights called it "abortion law repeal." I had to decide which of these terms I should use, since both carried political connotations. I ultimately decided to split the difference by using the phrase "abortion on demand" when describing the pro-lifers' *perspective* on the legalization of abortion, and the phrase "abortion law repeal" when describing the actions of abortion rights proponents. I also tried, whenever possible, to use a more neutral term—the "legalization of elective abortion"—which was occasionally used at the time, even though participants in the debate commonly favored one of the more politically charged phrases.

Despite my attempt to be balanced and historically accurate in my use of terminology, it will be clear to readers that I have not written an even-handed treatment of both sides in the abortion debate. This is because my book is not primarily a study of the abortion controversy but rather a history of the pro-life movement. I have tried to be as fair as possible in representing the arguments and ideas of the pro-life movement's opponents and to provide an accurate and fair-minded explanation of their various motivations for advocating the legalization of abortion, but the primary focus of the book is on the pro-life activists and their reasons for mobilizing, not the abortion rights movement and its ideas. Several other historians have already written detailed studies of the abortion rights activists, but until now, no one has produced a comprehensive history of the early years of the pro-life movement, so that has been my focus in this work. In order to bring the pro-life activists' story to light and give readers a sense of their concerns, I have presented most of the narrative from their perspective. As a consequence, some readers who are familiar with the histories of abortion legalization that have been written from the perspective of the abortion rights advocates may find the perspective presented in this book unfamiliar, surprising, and perhaps even disconcerting. Some readers may strongly disagree with the reasoning of the abortion opponents that I describe. If you are a reader in this category, I do not assume that you will lay aside your philosophical and political commitments on this issue, but I would ask that for the purposes of historical inquiry, you would try to understand the mindset of the mid-twentieth-century opponents of abortion who were just as convinced as their feminist opponents that they were engaged in a campaign for human rights. You may think that they were wrong in their beliefs, but I think that as historians, we owe it to these subjects to accurately understand their thoughts, motivations, and actions. If we begin taking the political pronouncements and ideological rhetoric of the early pro-life activists seriously, we may discover that we have been mistaken in some of our assumptions about the political realignments of the late twentieth century, and that the pro-life movement that we have always labeled "conservative" was at one time much more deeply rooted in liberal rights-based values than we might have suspected.

# *Introduction*

ON SUNDAY, APRIL 16, 1972, ten thousand people gathered in New York's Central Park to protest New York's liberal abortion law. The Supreme Court's decision in *Roe v. Wade* was still nine months away, but the battle over abortion was already raging. Yet the divisions did not fall neatly along partisan or ideological lines.

In New York, the state with the highest number of legal abortions, the polarization was especially acute. It had been a Republican legislator and Republican governor who had been chiefly responsible for the legalization of abortion in the state two years earlier, and many of New York's Republicans—including Governor Nelson Rockefeller—were still strongly supportive of abortion rights. But it was also a Republican who was leading the charge to reverse their actions. Democrats were equally divided.

The media portrayed the pro-life movement as a Catholic cause, but by 1972, that stereotype was already outdated.[1] In Michigan, for instance, the fight against a referendum to legalize abortion was spearheaded by three Protestants—a gynecologist, a white Presbyterian mother, and an African American woman who was a liberal Democratic state legislator. In Minnesota, the leader of the state's pro-life campaign was a liberal Methodist whose physician husband was a member of Planned Parenthood. In Massachusetts, one of the leading pro-life activists was an African American Methodist physician who had been the first black woman to graduate from Harvard Medical School. And even in New York, where Catholics accounted for the vast majority of the movement's activists, there was more religious diversity than the media often acknowledged, partly because Catholics had joined forces with Orthodox Jews. In fact, one of the keynote speakers at the April 16 pro-life rally in Central Park was an Orthodox Jewish rabbi who served as president of the Rabbinical

Alliance of America.[2] One of New York City's most vocal pro-life advocates was a liberal Lutheran minister who was best known for his protests against the Vietnam War and his advocacy of civil rights.[3]

Perhaps most surprisingly, at the time the protest took place, the pro-lifers were winning. Only a few years earlier, their campaign had looked like a last-gasp battle against the forces of progress. They faced opposition from the women's rights movement, newspaper and television media, the medical and legal establishments, mainline Protestant denominations, ecumenical religious organizations such as the National Council of Churches, and political leaders in both major parties. Yet the pro-life movement had figured out a way to defy the international trend toward abortion legalization and defeat several efforts to liberalize state abortion laws.

The right-to-life movement had faced nearly insuperable challenges in the late 1960s, when a wave of sixteen states legalized at least some forms of abortion within a three-year period.[4] But then the pro-lifers regrouped, changed their strategies, and figured out how to win legislative battles. In 1971, twenty-five states considered abortion legalization bills. Every one of them failed to pass. In 1972, the pro-life movement went on the offensive and began campaigning for measures to rescind recently passed abortion legalization laws and tighten existing abortion restrictions. In the wake of the Central Park protest, the New York state legislature voted to repeal New York's liberal abortion law and was thwarted only by Governor Rockefeller's veto.[5]

The size of the backlash against abortion legalization surprised many supporters of abortion rights. What had happened? How did a small, beleaguered Catholic movement manage to create a massive ecumenical coalition of grassroots activists and stop the march of abortion legalization?

## Why We Need a History of Pro-Life Activism

Most histories of postwar American politics say almost nothing about the millions of Americans who opposed abortion before *Roe v. Wade*. They do not mention the African Americans in Detroit, the Lutheran wheat farmers in rural North Dakota, or the Catholics in Midwestern parishes who mobilized on behalf of the unborn at the beginning of the 1970s. They do not discuss the pro-life movement's success in defeating abortion liberalization proposals in dozens of state legislatures and ballot initiatives in 1971 and 1972. Nor do they include much information about the pro-life movement's failures in the late 1960s—or its quiet successes a few years earlier.[6]

Instead, most histories of postwar American politics treat the pro-life movement—if they mention it at all—only as a reaction against *Roe v. Wade*, the feminist movement, the sexual revolution, and the growth of federal power. As Rickie Solinger has written, "There was no organized anti-abortion movement in the United States until after 1973. In reaction to *Roe*, a growing number of people, identifying a pervasive 'values crisis,' called for laws and policies to restrain what they saw as an excess of equality."[7] Solinger, who is one of the nation's leading authorities on the history of abortion and reproductive rights in twentieth-century America, is hardly alone; her summary represents a widely accepted historical consensus on this topic, especially among historians of feminism and sexuality. "One might speculate that had there not been a feminist movement, abortion might have been decriminalized with less opposition," Linda Gordon declared.[8] This consensus has largely been established by historians of abortion rights activism, and the activists they study have almost invariably misunderstood the motives of their opponents. As a result, historians have mischaracterized both the chronology of the pro-life movement and its ideological origins.[9] Pro-life activism actually began decades before *Roe v. Wade* or the formation of the National Organization for Women. And it originated not as a conservative backlash against individual rights, but as a defense of human rights for the unborn.

Because historians have misunderstood the pro-life movement's origins, they have been unable to explain why it remains a potent political force today, long after other socially conservative, religiously inspired causes, from Prohibition to school prayer, have faded from the scene. If the opponents of abortion had based their opposition merely on religious teaching or the seemingly arcane principles of natural law—as Catholics had when campaigning against contraception—it is unlikely that the pro-life cause could have withstood the forces of the sexual revolution, the feminist movement, and the social changes of the 1960s. But because the pro-life movement grounded its arguments in the language of human value and constitutional rights, it was able to attract a politically and religiously diverse coalition that actually gained strength over time. The pro-life movement succeeded because it drew on the same language of human rights, civil rights, and the value of human life that inspired the struggle for African American freedom, the feminist movement, antiwar protests, and the campaign for the rights of gays and lesbians.

This book offers an intellectual and political history of the pro-life movement. I argue that the movement's origins and endurance can be explained by its rights-based paradigm and its utilization of the language of postwar American liberalism. The pro-life cause originated at a far earlier date than historians have previously thought, and its origins were not tied to a backlash against the women's movement, but instead to a concern about the consequences of the nation's disrespect for human life. This book also challenges conventional presuppositions about the pro-life movement by showing that it originated not among political conservatives, but rather among people who supported New Deal liberalism and government aid to the poor, and who viewed their campaign as an effort to extend state protection to the rights of a defenseless minority (in this case, the unborn). Only after *Roe v. Wade*, when the pro-life movement's interpretation of liberalism came into conflict with another rights-based movement—feminism—and it became clear that pro-lifers would not be able to win the support of the Democratic Party, did the movement take a conservative turn. Yet because of the movement's liberal origins, its position in the Republican Party remains an uneasy one even today.

## The Pro-Life Movement as a Campaign for Rights

The Catholics who launched the pro-life movement grounded their campaign not only in their Church's natural law theology, but also in the twentieth-century American liberal values of individual rights, legal protections for minorities, and societal recognition of human dignity. Many of the people who first began speaking against abortion in the 1930s, as well as those who created the first right-to-life organizations in the mid-1960s, were Catholic Democrats who were committed to New Deal liberalism. Their devotion to ideals such as a living wage and the legal recognition of workers' rights, both of which Pope Pius XI had endorsed, led them to give enthusiastic support to President Franklin Roosevelt and his Democratic successors from Harry Truman to Lyndon Johnson. American Catholics who came of age in the New Deal era believed that the principle of human dignity should be the foundation for government social policy—that both the government and the Church had a responsibility to care for the less fortunate, and that the law should respect human life.

In the 1930s and 1940s, the campaign against abortion was almost inseparable from the Catholic Church's fight against contraception, which

Catholics also viewed as an attack on the value of human life. But in the postwar period, Catholics began articulating their concern for fetal life in the language of both "inalienable" human rights and constitutional rights, broadening their appeal far beyond the walls of Catholic churches. For defenders of fetal rights, the idea that the law should protect the lives of all human beings—both born and unborn—was a fundamental American principle rooted in the Declaration of Independence and the Fourteenth Amendment. The fetus's right to life was thus not only an inalienable human right, but also a constitutional one.[10]

This message attracted many Catholic liberals and, after the late 1960s, won over a few left-leaning antiwar activists, civil rights advocates, and African American Democrats as well. It also attracted millions of people across the country who, regardless of partisan affiliation, accepted the basic liberal principle of equal rights under the law and were persuaded that this principle extended to fetuses. Because the pro-life movement used the language of liberal values and individual rights—a language that had widespread credence during the era of other rights-based movements—it was able to build a bipartisan, ecumenical coalition capable of exercising political power.[11]

But if the pro-life movement was a liberal cause in one respect, it also found itself in conflict with liberals who argued that the removal of certain restrictions on abortion would promote societal betterment by saving women's lives and fostering public health. In this conflict between two conflicting sets of liberal values, pro-life Catholics were able, for a while, to win the public debate by continually reiterating their argument for the personhood of the fetus, thereby keeping the focus on human rights. But that argument failed to resonate with Americans in the mid-1960s, largely because of Catholics' longstanding insistence on linking abortion with contraception, which alienated Protestants and Jews. For a while, the efforts of Catholics alone were sufficient to stop the threat of abortion law reform, but the Church's political influence dissipated rapidly after the mid-1960s. Two events that took place in 1965—the Supreme Court's decision in favor of birth control legalization in *Griswold v. Connecticut* and the conclusion of Vatican II, which emboldened lay Catholics to dissent from Church teachings—discredited the Church's campaign against contraception and diminished its influence in the abortion debate. By 1967, even a few Catholic politicians, including Senator Robert Kennedy, publicly supported abortion legalization. When sixteen states liberalized their abortion laws between 1967 and 1970—and when four of those states removed almost all restrictions on abortion before the second trimester, thus allowing several hundred thousand abortions to be performed legally in the United States each year—it was a sign that pro-life Catholics no longer had the upper hand.[12]

To turn the tide, Catholics decided to separate the issues of abortion and contraception and focus on the rights-based pro-life arguments that had long sustained their cause. In short, they portrayed themselves as American liberal human rights advocates rather than sectarian Catholics, and because of that they were able to win the support of Protestants and Jews, create large state and national organizations, and achieve legislative victories that had previously eluded them. By the summer of 1972, momentum had clearly swung toward the pro-life side. Both sides expected that some of the states that had recently legalized abortion might soon rescind those laws.[13]

The shift in strategy meant that there would now be no question that the pro-life movement would be solely about human rights, and not about sex. Prior to the 1960s, the Catholic Church had treated abortion as an issue of both human life and human sexuality; abortion was fundamentally wrong because it destroyed a human life, the Church argued, but this evil was a direct result of a prior sin—the desire for sex without consequences. After the late 1960s, most pro-lifers abandoned this argument; in public, they would talk only about the human rights that abortion violated, and not discuss sexual ethics or contraception. This move was critical to forging alliances with Protestants and other non-Catholics. It transformed what might have become a parochial, quixotic crusade into a vibrant, diverse movement of people across the religious and political spectrum. For a brief moment, it appeared to be a winning strategy. But because the pro-life movement's opponents viewed the issue of abortion as fundamentally related to sex (i.e., sexual freedom and sexual equality), it was not a strategy that could be maintained for long.

It was at this point that the pro-life movement came into conflict with two other key values of late twentieth-century American rights-based liberalism—personal autonomy and gender equality. Advocates of abortion legalization had initially called for the limited reform of abortion laws—a call that they had grounded in utilitarian arguments in favor of public health and societal betterment. But in the late 1960s, they began calling for the recognition of abortion as part of women's fundamental right to control their own bodies and fertility. Women, in other words, had an absolute right to choose not to be pregnant. The feminist movement of the late 1960s brought this argument to the forefront of the abortion debate. It soon gained widespread appeal among liberals who valued personal autonomy, individual rights, and human equality, and who accepted some of the values of the sexual revolution of the 1960s, including the idea that the state had no business regulating issues of sex and reproduction between consenting adults. The arguments of the "pro-choice" movement—a term that advocates of abortion rights began using in the early 1970s—seemed to force pro-lifers into conflict with some key liberal ideas.[14]

Pro-life Catholics met this challenge by drawing on arguments they had used since the early twentieth century. Human life, they argued, was ultimately more important than individual choice. Women in the pro-life movement took the lead in the debate with feminists, arguing that it was in women's best interests not to abort their babies. Instead, the government should provide financial assistance for women facing crisis pregnancies—an argument that linked their movement to the social welfare politics of New Deal liberalism—rather than leaving impoverished women to choose between abortion and poverty.[15] By grounding their arguments in the liberal values of the need to care for the less fortunate and protect the lives of all people, including the unborn, pro-lifers continued to win political victories until the moment *Roe v. Wade* was decided.

The conflict between these two strands of rights-conscious liberalism centered in part over a fundamental difference of opinion regarding pregnancy, equality, and womanhood. Pro-choicers believed that the right of women to choose whether to become pregnant was critical to their liberation; gender equality required full bodily autonomy. Pro-lifers, by contrast, viewed all pregnancies, planned or unplanned, as gifts of human life, and thought that women would only be hurt if they destroyed that life. They also thought that they were promoting women's long-term freedom and well-being by advocating government programs that would give women the resources necessary to bear children and care for them. While pro-choicers spoke of the right of women to control their own bodies and to be free from forced pregnancies, pro-lifers spoke of women's right to be mothers, a right that some of them argued the state had a duty to support by offering prenatal and maternal health programs. To make their case, they drew on an older strand of American liberalism that promoted the feminism of difference—the notion that men and women had biologically distinct roles that public law needed to protect, an idea that had been widely accepted in the nineteenth and early twentieth centuries—and the early twentieth-century political tradition of providing legal protections for women and government assistance for mothers. In the pro-lifers' view, their own values offered the path of true freedom for women: freedom from sexual exploitation and freedom to follow their maternal desires. This view of freedom accorded well with twentieth-century Catholic doctrine on the role of the state in protecting the family.[16] But it conflicted with the values of the pro-choice and second-wave feminist movements. The conflict between these views came to a head in *Roe v. Wade*.

*Roe v. Wade* ended the pro-lifers' winning streak, because it ruled that the Constitution did not protect the unborn child. *Roe* enshrined the values of the abortion rights movement while directly repudiating the pro-life movement's belief that the fetus was one of the defenseless minorities protected by the Constitution. *Roe* thus privileged one set of liberal arguments while ignoring another. This had a profound effect on American liberals. Prior to *Roe*, the Democratic Party had been divided over abortion, because both pro-life and pro-choice Democrats could legitimately claim that their arguments were grounded in the party's historic liberal tradition. But by making one particular set of arguments settled law, *Roe* bolstered the claims of one group of liberals and tipped the balance of power in the Democratic Party in favor of pro-choice advocates. Sensing the direction in which the debate was moving, several formerly pro-life Democratic leaders, such as Senator Ted Kennedy, became defenders of abortion rights, and in 1976, the party adopted a platform that opposed attempts to rescind *Roe* through a constitutional amendment. Many Democrats (including Kennedy) who endorsed abortion rights after *Roe* continued to insist that they were personally opposed to abortion, and some Democrats, such as Sargent Shriver, tried to conciliate pro-lifers with a promise to adopt measures to reduce abortion rates. But in the aftermath of *Roe*, these attempted reassurances counted for little; pro-lifers were willing to settle for nothing less than constitutional protection of the unborn. They wanted a full reversal of *Roe*'s declaration that the Constitution did not protect the fetus, which they viewed as a direct assault on the nation's traditional recognition of human rights.[17]

Most of the limited political support that pro-lifers found for a constitutional amendment to protect unborn life came from the political right. In 1980, they solidified a new alliance with conservatives by throwing their support to Ronald Reagan. But pro-lifers' alliance with the Republican Party was never a comfortable one, and it required them to make compromises that distressed some members of their movement. As they became more narrowly focused on reversing *Roe*, pro-lifers began to lose interest in some of the earlier human rights causes, such as anti-poverty efforts, that had once been important to them.

In spite of this political shift, pro-lifers' central human rights claim—the claim that the fetus has an inalienable right to life—remained their guiding principle, and it was the primary reason why the movement retained its political influence in the rights-conscious era of the early twenty-first century. Most pro-lifers today have long forgotten the Catholic New Deal liberals of the 1930s who first spoke out against abortion legalization, and they are ideologically distinct from their forebears in many respects. Yet they continue to believe that they are championing a foundational human right—the right to life for the unborn. That central idea has enabled the pro-life movement to broaden its appeal and build a new generation of supporters.

# *I*

# *A Clash of Values*

THE CATHOLIC DOCTORS who gathered in Atlantic City in 1937 for the annual meeting of the National Federation of Catholic Physicians' Guilds were worried about what they saw as an unprecedented societal assault on the value of unborn human life. The American Medical Association had just issued a statement in favor of birth control, which was bad enough, but some doctors were even beginning to argue for the acceptability of abortion in some cases. It was time, the Catholic doctors believed, to take a strong stance against all attempts to destroy human life before birth.

"Abortion," the Federation declared, was, along with contraception, sterilization, and euthanasia, one of the "pagan and irrational philosophies" based on "modern creeds of unlimited sex indulgence." It reduced human beings to the "level of a beast or to that of a cog in the social mechanism, thus destroying the essential dignity of man as a child of God and destined for God in heaven." The Catholic physicians therefore pledged that they would never cooperate with those who would "make the medical practitioner the grave-digger of the nation."[1]

The disagreement over the extent to which the law should protect fetal life was a symptom of a larger ideological divide. Proponents of "therapeutic abortion," as it was then called, took a utilitarian approach, arguing that they could improve societal well-being by allowing women to obtain abortions when pregnancies endangered their health. But many Catholics believed that allowing someone to kill a fetus in these circumstances would make anyone's right to life dependent on the will of the majority or calculations of societal happiness. The right to life would no longer be absolute. Abortion, therefore, threatened to usurp God's control over life and death, and replace the absolute protection of life under civil law with a relativistic set of calculations about which lives were worthy of protection. The clash over abortion was therefore a battle over the values that formed the basis for the nation's most fundamental rights and laws. It was a battle that eventually entered the political sphere in the 1960s, and it is still raging in the twenty-first century, seventy-five years after the National Federation of Catholic Physicians' Guilds first adopted its resolution.

## From a Societal Consensus against Abortion to a Debate over Contraception

The calls for legalized abortion that were first issued in the 1930s alarmed Catholic physicians precisely because they challenged a societal consensus that Catholics considered unassailable. Most state abortion laws had been in existence for at least half a century. Prior to the early nineteenth century, judges had generally interpreted the common law to allow for abortion prior to "quickening"—that is, the point at which a pregnant woman could feel her unborn child moving. But in the nineteenth century, a number of Protestant doctors convinced state legislatures that medical science proved that biological life began long before quickening, which meant, in their view, that abortion should be prohibited at any stage of fetal development. By the end of the nineteenth century, legislatures in nearly every state had enacted laws that allowed abortion only in cases in which the procedure was required to save a woman's life. At the same time, many states also passed laws against contraception as part of broader anti-obscenity measures.[2]

The physicians behind this effort also embarked on an educational campaign to convince the public of the value of fetal life. Armed with cases of glass slides showing the fetus at various stages of development, they traveled to libraries and civic groups across the country to spread the message that human development proceeds along a continuum, that quickening is a biologically meaningless stage, and that the embryo deserved protection from the moment of conception. "It is not enough merely to tell them that in producing an abortion in the early months they are taking a human life; they must be shown that at this period the child is already well along in its development," Dr. Frederick Taussig, a professor of obstetrics and gynecology at Washington University in St. Louis, stated in 1910. "I think pictures like that of the six weeks' embryo will keep many women from having an abortion done."[3]

Although most of the physicians who launched this campaign were Protestants, their message was most eagerly embraced by Catholics.

The Catholic Church seized upon the doctors' biological evidence as proof that human life began at conception and that abortion was therefore homicide. Attempts to limit procreation through artificial means, including abortion, had always been prohibited by Catholic teaching. An ancient Christian text from the early second century called abortion "murder" and equated it with infanticide, and other early Church fathers echoed this teaching. The Church never backed away from the idea that abortions in the later stages of pregnancy constituted the destruction of human life and were therefore to be treated as homicides. But in the medieval and early modern eras, many of the Church's leading theologians, including Thomas Aquinas, classified abortion during the first few weeks of pregnancy as a much lesser sin than killing a fully developed human. Following Aristotle, they did not believe that ensoulment occurred until forty days after conception in the case of males and eighty days in the case of females. Before that point, the fetus was only a *potential* human being. In the seventeenth century, a few Catholic physicians and theologians challenged this assumption by arguing that human life began at conception, which meant that abortion was always murder—a theory that gained increasing acceptance in the Church in the nineteenth century, when medical opinion, backed by the latest discoveries in embryology, was beginning to pinpoint conception as the point at which each human life began. In 1869, Pope Pius IX issued the papal bull *Apostolicae Sedis*, declaring that all abortions, performed at any stage of pregnancy, were excommunicable offenses, a declaration that brought the Church's teaching into line with the ancient Christian view that all abortions were murder. As Vatican rulings subsequently clarified, this meant that even abortions performed to save a woman's life were gravely sinful.[4]

The Catholic Church's position on this issue was more restrictive than the views of the Protestant physicians and legislators who had created the nation's first anti-abortion laws. Protestants often appealed to the right of self-defense to argue that abortion was justifiable if pregnancy threatened a woman's life, whereas the Catholic Church argued that an innocent unborn life could never be deliberately killed.[5] But since the law prohibited almost all abortions, these fault lines were dormant.

Indeed, there appeared to be a widespread societal consensus against abortion in the early twentieth century. Illegal abortion remained a thriving industry, but even if many law enforcement officials were reluctant to enforce the law unless criminal negligence resulted in a woman's death, there was no serious discussion of legalizing abortion during these years.

The nation's newspapers took it for granted that abortion was a dangerous, immoral activity, and that those who performed abortions were criminals.[6] Though most non-Catholics paid no attention to the pope's pronouncements against abortion, Protestants had their own reasons for opposing abortion: their regard for fetal life—a concern that the physicians' campaign of the late nineteenth century had highlighted—and their antipathy toward sex outside of marriage, which many of them believed abortion encouraged. At the time, Protestants, like Catholics, opposed contraception, and they saw a connection between abortion and birth control. The anti-obscenity crusader Anthony Comstock lumped birth control, sexual promiscuity, pornography, and abortion under the general category of obscenity, and the laws for which he campaigned in the 1870s attempted to limit all of these supposed vices by making it illegal to send advertisements for contraceptives or abortions through the mail. For fifty years, Comstock's prohibitions remained the law of the land.[7]

The first apparent challenge to this consensus came with the birth control campaigns of the 1920s and 1930s. The campaigns were not about abortion per se—they focused on contraception—but Catholics nevertheless viewed them as a dangerous assault on human life that would soon put the societal consensus against abortion in jeopardy. For decades, the two issues had been linked, in both Catholic teaching and public discussion. In addition to the national Comstock laws, there were state laws that restricted the sale or use of birth control devices. Neither Catholic nor Protestant churches approved of contraception; the Anglican Communion issued official condemnations of the practice in 1908 and 1920.[8]

In the early 1920s, Margaret Sanger and her American Birth Control League (which later became Planned Parenthood) challenged this taboo and quickly won widespread acceptance among middle-class Protestants for the use of contraceptive devices. The Anglican Communion reversed course in 1930 and declared that Christian married couples had a right to use artificial birth control, and other Protestant Church bodies quickly followed suit. The Federal Council of Churches' Committee on Marriage and the Home issued a report endorsing contraception in 1931. By the late 1930s, national committees of the American Episcopal, United Methodist, United Presbyterian, and Congregational Christian Churches had officially endorsed birth control. Several Jewish organizations, including the Central Conference of American Rabbis and the National Council of Jewish Women, did the same. Though many Protestant fundamentalists continued to oppose contraception for several decades, liberal Protestants and Jews embraced it as a progressive humanitarian measure. By 1946, 3,200 ministers were members of Planned Parenthood's Clergyman's Council.[9]

The nation's physicians—especially those who were not Catholic—also joined the cause. In 1947, 98 percent of American doctors approved of contraception for health reasons and 79 percent approved of it in cases when a family's economic situation required it. One Jesuit philosophy professor in Kansas lamented in the mid-1950s that it was almost impossible to find a non-Catholic doctor who would refuse to fit a patient with a birth control device in at least some circumstances. In less than a generation, a once-taboo (and often illegal) practice had become a positive good that was now used by most middle-class Protestant couples, prescribed by their doctors, and endorsed by their pastors. A few heavily Catholic states in the Northeast, including Massachusetts and Connecticut, continued to restrict the sale of birth control devices until the 1960s, but those states were in the minority. After the 1930s, the overwhelming body of Protestant opinion in the United States was in favor of birth control use, with 85 percent of Americans in 1943 believing that married women should have access to contraceptives, according to a *Fortune* magazine survey.[10]

There was also substantial support in some areas of the country for the eugenic use of birth control to limit the reproductive capabilities of poor, sexually promiscuous, or mentally disabled women—especially those who were African American—a project that Sanger and many of her allies in the birth control movement endorsed. Some birth control advocates hoped to reduce birth rates among the poor through the use of voluntary contraception, but others accepted the use of more coercive means in at least some circumstances. In the early twentieth century, more than half of America's forty-eight states passed laws allowing the forcible sterilization of criminals or the "feeble minded," a practice that the Supreme Court upheld in *Buck v. Bell* (1927). Sixty thousand Americans were forcibly sterilized under these programs.[11]

Catholics were aghast at the disrespect for human life that had given rise to the idea of eugenics. "Its propagandists talk much of the betterment of the race very much as the owners of stock farms talk of the betterment of stock," the Jesuit magazine *America* complained in 1924. This was a direct attack on the "law of God," the "law of nature," and "human life" itself.[12] A later generation of secular liberals would agree with the Catholic denunciation of eugenics programs, but disagree with Catholic proscriptions on voluntary contraception. Yet at the time, Catholics saw these issues as inseparable aspects of the same fundamental problem—a disrespect for the divine gift of human life.

With the exception of some Protestant fundamentalists, Catholics stood almost alone in their refusal to countenance artificial birth control and sterilization under any circumstances. While a sizeable minority of Catholics (a minority that included 30 percent of married, white Catholic women of childbearing age, according to a 1955 survey) quietly violated official Catholic teaching by using forbidden means of birth control and then abstaining from communion until they received absolution for their "sin" from a priest, the majority of Catholics continued to follow their church's teaching on this issue, and some launched public efforts to oppose the rapid liberalization of public attitudes toward contraception and sterilization.[13]

They believed that birth control was equally wrong for both Catholics and non-Catholics, because the use of contraception not only violated nearly two thousand years of Church teaching but was also an offense against natural law, which should have been accessible to anyone—whether or not they were Catholic—by reason alone. In their view, abortion, contraception, and sterilization were violations of the same natural law principles, so they were dismayed when Protestants, who for the most part still opposed abortion, nevertheless rejected natural law arguments against contraception and sterilization, thus jettisoning the philosophical principles on which, for Catholics, opposition to abortion rested. Protestants saw the matter differently, of course. Though nineteenth-century Protestants had often conflated contraception and abortion, Protestants of the mid-twentieth century separated the two issues, approving of one as a beneficial social good while condemning the other as the taking of a human life that should be performed only in extreme circumstances. But Catholics were convinced that a compromise on contraception would inevitably lead to an acceptance of abortion, and they became increasingly vocal in their defense of the natural law principles that condemned both practices. Indeed, in their successful campaign against a referendum to legalize birth control in Massachusetts in 1948, they claimed that birth control was "like abortion" and against "God's law."[14]

The Catholic idea of "natural law" came from the thirteenth-century theologian Thomas Aquinas, who was, if not the most influential theologian in Catholic Church history, a close second only to Augustine. His approach to theology and philosophy had shaped the intellectual tradition of the Dominican and Jesuit orders, and by the early twentieth century, his teachings not only provided the foundation for most Catholic moral reasoning, but had also shaped the philosophy of the most influential Catholic intellectuals of the era, such as the French philosopher Jacques Maritain. Aquinas taught that all moral truths are accessible via human reason, and he provided a model for deducing those moral truths through logical reflection on the natural function of human beings and human actions. Maritain and many of his Catholic contemporaries argued that because natural law was universally accessible to human reason, it offered a nonsectarian universal guide to morality that could not only shape civil law but also provide a foundation for a universal system of human rights. Human rights, Catholics like Maritain believed, had to be grounded in universal principles in order to be universally recognized, and natural law philosophy offered such a foundation. But natural law theology gained little traction among Protestants, who had longstanding suspicions of Catholic theology and who, by the mid-twentieth century, had become especially skeptical of Catholics' argument that contraception violated a universal natural law.[15]

Catholic theologians argued that contraception contravened natural law in several ways. First, it separated sex from its natural purpose of pro-creation. Second, by attempting to prevent the formation of new human life, it challenged God's authority as the Creator. Finally, it treated human life as something to be prevented rather than valued. Contraception intro-duced a "deadly . . . cheapening of human life," the Jesuit magazine *America* charged in 1924. Those who promoted contraception "would destroy the law of God and the law of nature by interfering with human life at its inception. For they would teach the custodians of human life how to frus-trate life before birth." In the views of Catholics, this was only a short step removed from abortion. "Does artificial prevention of life stand on any higher moral ground than the artificial taking of life?" Edward J. Heffron, executive secretary of the National Council of Catholic Men, asked in 1942.[16]

Birth control advocates, including Sanger, disagreed. They saw contra-ception as an anti-abortion measure, since women would likely have fewer illegal abortions if they had a more convenient and safer way to limit their fertility. Catholics disputed this claim. They argued that legalized birth control would actually increase the abortion rate, because people who had been encouraged to try to avoid pregnancy would resort to any means at their disposal—even an illegal abortion—if their contraceptive devices failed. Birth control had "created the mentality which abhors births,"

Jesuit priest Wilfrid Parsons declared in 1935. Its "inexorable outcome will be the killing by abortion of unwanted babies."[17]

It was thus not surprising that when Pope Pius XI issued his landmark anti-contraceptive encyclical *Casti Connubii* in 1930, he coupled his condemnation of artificial birth control with an injunction against "the taking of the life of the offspring hidden in the mother's womb." While most of the encyclical was devoted to the issue of contraception, which he viewed as the more immediate threat, he also believed that abortion was merely a more extreme manifestation of the same impulse: a general attack on the family. The individualism that had led some to attempt to prevent pregnancy by artificial means was leading others to justify the termination of pregnancies that had already begun. Although hardly anyone in the United States had yet dared to publicly claim the right to an abortion, the pope was aware that some in Europe were arguing for that right, and that in the Soviet Union, abortion was legal and widely practiced. Even in the United States, doctors were commonly performing legal abortions to save women's lives, which the pope viewed as "misguided pity." "What could ever be a sufficient reason for excusing in any way the direct murder of the innocent?" he asked.[18]

Many Protestants, by contrast, argued that contraception had nothing to do with abortion; they saw no reason why they could not accept the legitimacy of doing everything possible to prevent pregnancies before conception while continuing to condemn the taking of unborn human life afterward. In 1930, when the Anglican Communion became the first Protestant denomination to give birth control at least a cautious endorsement, it coupled the resolution with a firm declaration of its unequivocal opposition to abortion. Margaret Sanger insisted that she also was opposed to abortion.[19]

While the consensus against abortion held—at least momentarily—it had been weakened. The birth control campaigns created a religious divide in Americans' approach to reproductive issues. After the 1930s, few Protestants outside of fundamentalist circles preached against birth control, and many clerics from more progressive denominations joined campaigns to promote its use. By rejecting Catholic natural law-based arguments against birth control, Protestants made it more difficult to use those arguments against abortion. By the time that abortion policy became a matter of political controversy, most Protestant denominations had no consistent theological position on the subject.[20]

Catholics, by contrast, became more vocal in their denunciations of both birth control and abortion after the 1920s. American Catholic priests were preaching against birth control long before *Casti Connubii*, but the encyclical encouraged their efforts and gave renewed vigor to their campaign. Warnings against the use of contraception appeared in Catholic diocesan papers and Sunday homilies, and premarital counseling sessions for Catholic couples invariably included instruction on the subject. The discussions of birth control in the mid-twentieth century laid the natural law groundwork for later arguments against abortion. Some priests even preached directly about abortion as early as the 1930s.[21]

The Church's intense focus on issues of reproduction at a time when the medical community was becoming increasingly open to the idea of birth control forced Catholic doctors to make the difficult choice between the teachings of their Church and the views of their profession. In reaction to this crisis, Brooklyn physician Richard Rendich began to organize guilds of Catholic physicians who chose to remain faithful to Church teachings while carrying out their professional duties. In 1931, he consolidated these local societies into a national organization called the National Federation of Catholic Physicians' Guilds, whose chief purpose, according to the organization's Jesuit moderator Fr. Ignatius Cox, was to "form a powerful barrier of both science and Catholicism, against the loose morals and sex liberalism of the day."[22]

Nowhere were these "loose morals" more evident than in the area of birth control, the Federation's leaders believed. The Federation's organizational meeting featured a keynote address against birth control, and the organization's official journal, the *Linacre Quarterly*, devoted much of its space to contraception and sterilization, publishing detailed natural law arguments about why artificial birth control was not only "intrinsically evil" but also a violation of the Fifth Commandment's prohibition against the taking of human life. Conscientious Catholic physicians were aghast that their Protestant colleagues—including, as the Jesuit medical ethicist Fr. Gerald Kelly lamented, "even very competent and conscientious doctors, whose general attitude toward the child-bearing function is both wholesome and reverent"—failed to view contraception as an assault on human life, and even gave contraceptive assistance to their patients who requested it.[23]

The Federation argued that Americans' willingness to use contraceptives signaled a dangerous disrespect for human life that could compromise the entire Western legal tradition of respect for human dignity. When the American Medical Association endorsed contraception in 1937, Fr. Ignatius Cox viewed the resolution as a setback for a much larger program of human rights. "This action is closely connected with a long denial of a truly living wage and of social justice in our present economic order," he declared. "Those who advocate contraception . . . have a philosophy which in its cynical disregard of the dignity of human life is equivalent to the philosophy which accounts for the massacres of history."[24] If people began to view the formation of new human life as an impediment to societal progress, economic prosperity, and social well-being—something that they should try to prevent if it inconvenienced them in any way—then we should not be surprised, Catholics such as Fr. Cox thought, when they had little regard for the rights of workers, the poor, and other people whom they viewed as burdens on society.

The Catholics who opposed contraception and abortion were strong advocates of relief for the poor. Indeed, Catholic clerics of the 1930s, who had embraced a theology of social obligation and care for the less fortunate that papal encyclicals such as *Rerum Novarum* (1891) and *Quadragesimo Anno* (1931) had mandated, often outpaced the New Deal in their call for government social programs, aid to the impoverished, and a living wage for workers.[25] But in contrast to Protestant, Jewish, and secular liberals, Catholics believed that care for the poor was incompatible with the promotion of birth control or sterilization, whether voluntary or coerced. In their view, the entire Catholic program of social justice depended on a regard for human life that the contraceptive movement threatened.

The debate over birth control in the 1930s was thus a conflict between two factions of political progressives who both saw their stance on reproductive issues as a logical extension of their support for social reform and a welfare state. On the one side was an eclectic coalition of Protestant, Jewish, and secular progressives who believed that they could use state resources and the power of technology to improve society by reducing the number of unwanted children and hungry mouths to feed, especially in impoverished households. Some of these progressives were New Deal administrators who saw the promotion of birth control as an extension of government efforts to reduce poverty and advance human happiness through social reform. On the other side were Catholics who were also avid supporters of the New Deal, but who believed that the attempt to improve society through the artificial limitation of human reproduction signaled a dangerous disregard for human life. Their commitment to poverty relief equaled or exceeded that of many of the birth control promoters and political liberals; indeed, the pope, the National Catholic Welfare Conference, and politically progressive clerics such as Fr. John Ryan had been calling for the recognition of workers' rights and a living wage for years before Franklin D. Roosevelt's election in 1932. They believed that they were advancing the principles of the New Deal by protecting human life. Ryan, for instance, who had been campaigning for a living wage for decades and who served on Roosevelt's National Recovery Administration Appeals Board, was also an outspoken leader in the campaign against contraception.[26] Because the politics of reproduction had not yet become a partisan issue, Catholic opponents of contraception in the 1930s could happily join with birth control advocates in supporting the New Deal, unaware that their disagreement on the politics of reproduction would eventually split apart the liberal coalition.

The physicians' opposition to contraception prepared them to speak out against abortion as soon as the first calls for its legalization were sounded. Indeed, the arguments that they used against abortion—arguments that appealed to human dignity, natural law, social justice, and the value of human life—were the same arguments that they used against contraception in the 1930s. Thus, when the first books advocating abortion legalization were published in the early 1930s, Catholic doctors were ready for battle, because they already had a nationwide professional organization, a papal encyclical, and a bevy of natural law arguments at the ready.

## The Abortion Debate Begins

Catholics who opposed the physician-led campaign for abortion law reform in the 1930s believed that they were defending the absolute values of natural law against moral relativism and utilitarian arguments that sought to justify "killing" for the sake of a higher social good. The first abortion law reformers conceded that abortion was morally problematic—likely even the taking of a human life—but they thought that its legalization was the lesser of two evils, given the public health crisis produced by illegal abortion. With the onset of the Great Depression, the nation's birthrates plunged to record-low levels, and numerous women terminated their pregnancies illegally in a desperate attempt to avoid having additional mouths to feed. The most reliable estimates suggested that the abortion rate likely more than doubled during the early years of the Great Depression and that perhaps as many as 700,000 abortions occurred annually during the early to mid-1930s.[27] Since several thousand women died each year from these illegal operations, a few doctors decided that the most humane response to the crisis would be to provide a way for these women to terminate their pregnancies legally—and safely—in hospitals.

The doctors who issued this call harbored a deep antipathy toward Catholic moral teaching on the subject, with one calling the Church's proscriptions on abortion a "resuscitated relic of the Dark Ages."[28] In fact, their disagreement with the Church's moral doctrine went far beyond the narrow subject of abortion. Most of them were liberal or secular Jews who believed that Catholic attempts to use public law to enforce the Church's own standards of sexual morality violated people's personal freedoms and impeded social progress. They had been at the forefront of the contraceptive campaign of the 1920s. Indeed, one of the physicians writing in favor of abortion legalization wanted to separate sex not only from procreation but also from marriage itself—a radical idea at the time. Some of them were also eugenicists who believed that society would be better off if certain people were discouraged from reproducing. And all of them, despite their regard for fetal life and their moral squeamishness about abortion, justified the loosening of abortion restrictions on utilitarian grounds—that is, they claimed that legalizing abortion would produce fewer social evils than the prohibitions on abortion had already caused.

One of these doctors, William J. Robinson, had already established himself as one of the leading advocates of birth control in the United States. He was a self-identified humanist "freethinker" who had written tracts against religion and had spent the previous two decades trying to convince the public to accept eugenics (including forced sterilization of "morons and imbeciles"), pacifism (a view that got him arrested during the First World War), and non-monogamous sex. After years of campaigning for contraception, he called for legalized abortion in a book on sexual morality published in 1928, and then argued his case in much greater detail five years later in *The Law against Abortion: Its Perniciousness Demonstrated and Its Repeal Demanded*, which the Eugenics Publishing Company released in 1933. Robinson's advocacy of legalized abortion did not mean that he thought that the practice was moral. In fact, despite his strong endorsement of contraception and his approval of non-monogamous sexual relations in a variety of contexts, including adultery and incest, he still viewed abortion as "an evil." It is "not a *nice* thing," he wrote, because "it does mean the destruction of a commencing life." He hoped that the universal use of contraceptives would eventually make it a "rare occurrence." In the meantime, though, he argued that it was better to legalize abortion than to drive a desperate woman into the hands of an "incompetent midwife" whose abortion methods might kill her.[29]

Robinson did not present himself as a women's rights advocate, and he frequently made statements that, even by the standards of his own time, could hardly have been considered feminist. His argument, for instance, that the penalties for rape should be reduced on the grounds that some women "perhaps did not mind the assault so terribly much" or his statement that a man was "justified in having extramarital relations if he can do so without causing his wife any suffering" seemed more indicative of a commitment to sexual freedom than to women's rights. But Robinson also had a deep sympathy for women who experienced lifelong health complications or even death after botched abortions. Early in his medical career, he had watched a twenty-five-year-old woman die from the after-effects of an illegal abortion obtained from a midwife, and he wanted to do everything possible to prevent such unnecessary and untimely deaths. "The anti-abortion law is a stupid senseless law, which does not abolish or diminish abortion, but in addition causes endless suffering and anguish, chronic invalidism, death and suicide—and even murder," he declared. It was best, he argued, to repeal all laws against abortion during the first three months of pregnancy, provided that they were performed by a licensed physician.[30]

Robinson freely admitted his utilitarianism and his willingness to sacrifice fetal life for the sake of a higher social good. There was no "divine origin of morality," he thought, and thus no fixed standard of value that transcended human society; instead, a moral "code" would have to be "based upon the greatest happiness of the greatest number." The good that abortion legalization would produce for the women involved far outweighed the harm that would come to their fetuses, he believed. "Yes, abortion is an evil, and always will be one," he declared. "But very often ... it is so much the lesser of two evils, that there cannot be a moment's hesitation as to the choice."[31]

Robinson's proposal for the repeal of all laws against abortion during the first trimester did not receive much support until the late 1960s, thirty years after his death. But even if Robinson's ideas seemed radical at the time he published them, a few of his fellow physicians in the 1930s sympathized with his argument that prohibitions on abortion drove some women to their deaths, and the idea gradually gained a larger hearing. In the late twentieth and early twenty-first centuries, decades after Robinson himself had largely been forgotten, his claim that laws against abortion would not prevent the practice and would instead only cause desperate women to die remained one of the pro-choice movement's central arguments.[32]

In the same year in which Robinson published his book, A. J. Rongy, another New York physician who identified with the political left, made a related argument in his book *Abortion: Legal or Illegal?* (1933). Abortion laws should be repealed, he said, because nearly two million illegal abortions were occurring in the United States each year, which meant that the laws were as useless as Prohibition had been. Just as the Eighteenth Amendment had not stopped drunkenness and had instead given rise to violent gangs, so too, Rongy argued, laws against abortion had not stopped women from terminating their pregnancies and had instead encouraged the growth of criminal abortion rings and rampant bribery of law officers. Anti-abortion legislation had also encouraged "a contempt for the law" on the part of doctors and pregnant women. Rongy's estimate of the number of illegal abortions was almost certainly too high, but there was strong evidence that at least a few hundred thousand women obtained illegal abortions each year, and that the number was rapidly increasing. One New York criminal syndicate alone accounted for nearly 250,000 illegal abortions annually, and it was by no means the only such organization that provided the procedure.[33] In addition, Rongy claimed that, as a gynecologist, he knew many colleagues in the profession who routinely offered ostensibly legal "therapeutic" abortions that were not necessary to save women's lives.

Though Rongy's views were diametrically opposed to the pope's in most respects, he concurred with Pius XI in seeing a link between public acceptance of contraception and increased demand for abortion. "Now that the tide of public opinion is swelling in favor of greater freedom in the matter of childbearing," he wrote, more women were requesting abortions. It was therefore time, Rongy argued, for Americans to follow the example of the Soviet Union and legalize abortion "under circumstances justified by the health of the parent, her economic condition, the danger of a social stigma, or any one of a number of valid reasons."[34]

For the next thirty-five years, the abortion law reform movement continued to make the arguments that Robinson and Rongy had first posited. Yet almost no one in the movement cited either of these doctors as the source of his or her views or lauded them as pioneers for the cause. Though both were leading medical professionals, Robinson was a Russian Jewish immigrant and pacifist with an open antipathy to religion and a penchant for provocative statements on matters of sex, and Rongy was a Jewish Lithuanian immigrant and socialist who made no secret of his admiration for the Soviet Union.[35] Their political, ethnic, and religious backgrounds would not have endeared them to most socially conservative American Christians in the early 1930s. It was thus left to others to pick up their arguments.

Three years after Robinson and Rongy published their books, another doctor, the former anti-abortion lecturer Frederick Taussig, published a defense of abortion legalization. Taussig's book was more widely distributed than Rongy's, and it set the terms of the abortion debate partly because, as a 500-page, exhaustively detailed study of the medical and legal aspects of abortion, it was by far the most comprehensive analysis of abortion published up to that point. Taussig was, like Rongy, both a Jew and a gynecologist, but in contrast to his slightly younger colleague, the sixty-four-year-old Taussig was careful to distance himself from any direct approval of the Soviet Union's abortion policy. Unlike Rongy, he had once been active in the fight against abortion. In 1910, he had boldly declared that "life begins with conception," and that "each fertilized ovum ... is a precious object, that we must, by every effort in our power, save from premature destruction." He had called for more stringent abortion laws to prevent the "slaughter of the innocents."[36]

But Taussig found that none of this had succeeded in reducing the abortion rate. Through a series of detailed calculations, he determined, in an estimate that was probably accurate at the time, that between 8,000 and 10,000 women died from abortions each year—approximately one out of every eighty women who sought an illegal abortion. Taussig decided that it was best to give women the legal right to obtain what they wanted in a safe facility rather than force them to risk their lives by seeking abortions from unskilled criminal operators. "I know of no other instance in history in which there has been such frank and universal disregard for a criminal law," Taussig wrote.[37] In this respect, Taussig's argument was similar to Rongy's.

Taussig also presented another argument that would ultimately have far-reaching effects on the abortion debate: he redefined the value of life in relative, rather than absolute, terms. Already, he argued, physicians commonly performed abortions when they were necessary to save a woman's life. Why not also perform abortions when they were necessary to effect a higher social good, such as preventing the further impoverishment of a family through the birth of another child or saving the health of a pregnant woman? Unlike Robinson and Rongy, Taussig did not favor allowing women to obtain abortions whenever they desired, but he did suggest that it would be in society's best interest to allow abortion in carefully circumscribed cases—rape or incest, dangers to the health or life of the mother, suspected fetal deformity, and socioeconomic disadvantage. As a strong believer in both contraception and eugenics, Taussig was convinced that society would benefit from planned fertility. No good would come from women being forced to give birth to badly deformed or mentally defective babies. Nor would it be in society's best interest to force women to bear children they could not properly care for. It would be uncompassionate to require a woman who had been raped or whose health was in peril to bring her pregnancy to term, he argued. Taussig had previously insisted that the value of fetal life was paramount, but now he decided that women's health and larger societal considerations were more important.[38]

Taussig suggested that Americans could have the best of all worlds: they could reduce the illegal abortion rate, save women's lives, protect women's health, adopt a compassionate policy, and promote social well-being, while simultaneously recognizing the value of fetal life and avoiding a policy of indiscriminate abortion legalization. Rongy and Robinson had been well outside of the mainstream of public opinion when they had suggested that Americans should permit abortions in almost all cases. Taussig offered a middle ground that was more appealing. Like most Americans, Taussig was still personally uncomfortable with abortion; he viewed it as "probably the most wasteful of known ills in its expenditure of human life and human health." He hoped that free birth control clinics and better contraceptive devices would eventually make the practice almost obsolete. But in the meantime, he believed, doctors had a duty to campaign for the liberalization of abortion laws in order to prevent the "needless wreckage of human lives" that resulted from illegal abortions. "Saving the mother's life or health," he declared, "is more laudable than the observance of theoretical ideas regarding the viability and rights of the fetus." He recognized that this pronouncement was a direct affront to Catholic views of morality, but he believed that the Church's prohibition on abortion had been responsible for "much unnecessary suffering, disease and death" and therefore should be given no consideration in making public policy. The only "fixed standard of morality," he said, was the Golden Rule; "antiquated" laws and doctrines would therefore have to give way to "progress and reform."[39]

Taussig's book was not enough to cause most doctors to reject a half-century of professional medical opinion vilifying abortion practitioners, but some influential physicians found his arguments persuasive, a sign that the longstanding medical consensus against abortion was beginning to crack. In 1936, the president of the Medical Society of the County of New York announced his support for a liberalized abortion policy that would prevent the birth of the "unwanted and unloved child, to be raised in poverty and ignorance."[40] While Taussig's ideas were not widely accepted in his own lifetime, his argument that abortion law liberalization was a public health issue became the central platform of reform activists for the next three decades. In the mid-1960s, abortion law reformers were still repeating Taussig's arguments and citing his claim that more than five thousand women died from illegal abortions each year, even though by that time, improvements in medical care had greatly reduced the number.[41]

Behind this argument, of course, was the assumption that the loss of fetal life was a price worth paying in order to save the lives of women. To Taussig, Rongy, and other abortion law reformers, this was obvious, and it accorded well with longstanding legal doctrine. But to Catholic doctors, it threatened to set a dangerous precedent. In 1937, the National Federation of Catholic Physicians' Guilds declared that the demand for abortion was a direct result of the assumption that humans had the right to attempt to improve society by deciding who should live and who should die, a right that Catholic physicians believed belonged only to God. If the fetus was a human being, which even some advocates of liberalized abortion laws had conceded might be the case, no one had the right to take its life for any reason. One simply could not kill an innocent person for the sake of a greater social good.

The problem, Catholic physicians believed, was that Americans had decided that they had a right to sex without consequences. It was a small step from preventing pregnancy to terminating it. Catholic physicians thought that an incorrect view of sex had led to disrespect for human life and a new willingness to dispose of it for utilitarian reasons.[42] The calls for abortion legalization were an affront to the Church's core moral and social values: its teachings on sexuality, the family, the creation of human life, the value of human persons, natural law, and human rights. They were therefore a threat of the highest order.

By 1942, the Federation had moved abortion to the top of its list of stated concerns. In passing a resolution reaffirming the organization's "allegiance to all Catholic and moral principles which have a bearing on the practice of medicine," the Federation particularly noted its "abhorrence of the assaults on the sanctity of human life which arise from the advocacy of abortion, sterilization and planned parenthood through positive contraception."[43]

The conflict between two opposing viewpoints was launched. On the one side stood secularists such as Taussig who adopted a relativistic value system based on utilitarianism—whatever would accomplish the greatest good for the greatest number—and who believed that humans had the right to improve social happiness by controlling the creation and termination of life. On the other side stood socially conservative Catholics who believed in an absolute value system, viewed the creation of life as a divine blessing, and considered life's premature termination—except for divinely ordained reasons—an immense evil. In the 1930s, most of the active participants on both sides of the debate were doctors, because doctors, especially obstetricians and gynecologists, were the ones who were regularly confronted with women's requests for abortion or with the injuries women sometimes sustained when they attempted to self-abort.

The debate was a religious conflict because nearly all of the doctors speaking out against abortion were Catholic, while the most vocal proponents of abortion legalization were Jewish. It was hardly surprising that politically liberal or leftist-leaning Jewish doctors were some of the earliest proponents of abortion law reform. American Judaism had a strong progressive tradition that sought social betterment through economic justice, and Judaism, unlike Christianity, explicitly differentiated between the value of the fetus and that of a pregnant woman (with the Mishnah allowing for abortion in cases when it was necessary to save a woman's life). These doctors framed their arguments around concerns that were important to many liberal American Jews of the mid-twentieth century—concerns such as saving women's lives, promoting societal betterment, and aiding the poor.[44] Catholics shared Jews' interest in economic justice and human rights, but their view of the humanity of the fetus differed from rabbinic tradition, putting them on the opposite side of the debate.

Protestants, who made up the vast majority of the medical profession, occupied the middle ground. Some physicians, believing that the fetus was a human life—but that its right to life was not inviolable—argued that in extreme cases of medical necessity, abortion was warranted, but that Taussig and Rongy had gone too far in accepting it. In 1940, H. Close Hesseltine, a professor of obstetrics and gynecology at the University of Chicago School of Medicine, joined other Chicago physicians in reiterating this traditional view, asserting that "therapeutic abortion" was justified only in cases when "the procedure is necessary to preserve the life or health of the mother or, rarely, to prevent the perpetuation of hereditary defects." This was still a more liberal stance than the law allowed, but it stopped well short of the sweeping changes that Robinson, Rongy, and Taussig had advocated. As Hesseltine said, "The physician who termi- nates a pregnancy before the fetus is viable assumes a heavy responsibil- ity. He sacrifices one life on behalf of another." Yet in the 1940s, medical journals also published more liberal opinions on the subject, with some obstetricians and gynecologists encouraging fellow members of their pro- fession to take a woman's "socioeconomic status" or "future health" into consideration when deciding whether to perform a requested abortion.[45]

As Protestant doctors debated the acceptable grounds for an abor- tion, the ministers in their churches mostly stayed out of the controversy. With the exception of the Anglican Communion's 1930 declaration of its "abhorrence" of abortion, no Protestant denomination passed an offi- cial resolution on abortion before the 1960s, though when the bishops of the Episcopal Church passed a resolution endorsing birth control in 1934, one of the chief sponsors of the measure expressed the hope that the promotion of contraception would reduce the number of illegal abor- tions and thus save women's lives. For a while, fundamentalist Protestants vehemently denounced abortion. In 1930, Bob Jones Sr. condemned abor- tion as "murder," and several of his fellow fundamentalists continued to issue occasional denunciations of abortion for years. The fundamental- ist Baptist evangelist John R. Rice declared in 1945 that abortion, which he considered "the murder of the little one where conception has already taken place," was "a crime prohibited by law and condemned by all decent people." But most Protestant ministers who were not fundamentalists said nothing. While Catholic clergy and physicians considered liberalized abortion laws a direct attack on the nation's most fundamental values, Protestants were more likely to describe abortion as an unfortunate prob- lem that could be solved by better access to contraception.[46]

In the midst of this silence, the abortion law liberalization movement continued to advance. It received an important boost in 1938 from the British court decision *Rex v. Bourne*, which popularized the idea that rape constituted an acceptable ground for abortion and that a woman's men- tal well-being should be considered when deciding whether an abortion was justified. At the time, British law, like that of most American states, prohibited abortion except when it was necessary to preserve a woman's life. The *Bourne* case focused on the question of whether a doctor who had performed an abortion for a fourteen-year-old rape victim had broken the law. On the surface, it appeared that he had. Though the public might sympathize with the teenage girl, who had become pregnant after being gang-raped by a group of soldiers, and though some might decide that she had the right to an abortion after such an ordeal, the law did not allow for this, since the girl's pregnancy did not endanger her life. But the judge acquitted the doctor by reinterpreting the meaning of the word "life." Life, he declared, amounted to more than mere physical existence; it also encompassed a person's health and well-being. Forcing a teenage rape victim to bear an unwanted child would be devastating for her mental health and would likely ruin her life, the judge declared. Thus, the doctor had saved the woman's life by performing the abortion.[47]

This liberal interpretation of the word "life" was exactly what advocates of abortion liberalization wanted to hear, because it directly echoed Taussig's arguments. Abortion was permissible, Taussig had said, when it was necessary to advance the well-being of society or an individual woman. Now a British judge had essentially said the same thing. That same year, Sweden legalized abortions in cases of rape or pregnancies that endangered a woman's health, and Denmark adopted similar legislation the following year.[48] A few Americans argued that American states should follow suit.

As the Depression gave way to a wave of postwar prosperity, economic justifications for abortion became less common, but other arguments became even more powerful. Medical experts enjoyed enormous public respect, and since the abortion law reformers had framed their cause as a doctors' campaign to protect women's health and physicians' autonomy, their cause continued to gain ground, even during the Baby Boom when popular media celebrated motherhood and female domesticity.

The foremost advocate of abortion law reform in these years was Alan Guttmacher, a New York gynecologist who would become director of Planned Parenthood in the 1960s, but who began his public campaign for abortion liberalization as a hospital physician and medical school professor in the early 1940s. As a doctor—and eventually as director of obstetrics and gynecology at Mt. Sinai Hospital in New York—Guttmacher performed a few therapeutic abortions himself and arranged clandestine international abortions for other clients whose cases were not strictly medically necessary. Yet Guttmacher also saw firsthand the pain of poorer women who were unable to travel overseas for abortions and were thus left with no legal recourse. He felt compassion for these patients, including, in one case, an eleven-year-old victim of incest. Most of the women who sought out abortions did not conform to the popular stereotypes of the "fallen" woman, he argued. At least 85 percent were married. He was particularly upset that no state abortion law allowed abortion in cases of fetal deformity. The last thing the nation needed, he said, were additional "imbeciles." Echoing Taussig's arguments, he told his audiences on the lecture circuit that it was time to legalize abortion in cases of fetal deformity and danger to a woman's health. Doing so, he claimed, would reduce the number of illegal abortions and save women's lives.[49]

Guttmacher's views on abortion stemmed from his secular perspective on the creation of human life. In contrast to the Catholic physicians who opposed him, he viewed the moment of conception not as a divinely wrought miracle, but as the product of human choice. In 1933, he predicted that in the distant future, conception would become "an impersonal process" that would take place in laboratory test tubes. For Guttmacher, this was a prospect not to be feared, but rather embraced. Although he did not live to see the full development of in vitro fertilization (IVF), he was a pioneer in artificial insemination. His primary goal was to give women the power to control their own fertility, so he became a passionate advocate for contraception, abortion, and fertility treatments—what was called "planned parenthood."[50] For many Catholics, by contrast, these were frightening manifestations of a devaluation of human life and an attempt to "play God."

Despite his belief in reproductive freedom, Guttmacher shrank from suggesting that women should be given unrestricted access to abortion. Although he occasionally conceded in private that he could not see the difference in value between a fertilized egg and an unfertilized one, he believed that the fetus, as it developed, was more than simply a cellular mass and that to take its life unnecessarily was wrong. Yet as a self-described humanist and liberal Jew, he did not believe, as many Catholic physicians did, that the fetus's life was just as valuable as that of an adult woman. In extreme cases, it was far better to perform an abortion than to allow a woman to suffer, he thought. By defining "life" to include mental well-being—just as the British judge in the *Bourne* case had done— Guttmacher claimed that there were instances in which it was appropriate to protect a pregnant woman's "life" by taking the life of the fetus. "I don't like killing," Guttmacher stated in a public lecture in 1961, two decades after he began his campaign for the liberalization of abortion laws. "I don't like to do abortions, but many of you people probably fought in World War II and killed because you wanted to preserve something more important. I think a mother's life is more important than a fetus."[51]

Catholics who opposed abortion were alarmed at Guttmacher's attempt to relativize the value of human life. "The issue is really one of protecting the absolute right of the innocent human being to his life as against direct and deliberate destruction of it," one Jesuit priest told Guttmacher.[52]

## Catholic Physicians' Response

Though liberalization advocates drew a parallel with Prohibition and said that it was time to end the "hypocrisy" of unenforceable laws, Catholics who were concerned about abortion claimed that what was needed was not surrender but better enforcement. Blaming public "apathy" and bureaucratic corruption for the prevalence of illegal abortions, Jesuit professor J. Gerard Mears issued a plea in *America* magazine in 1942 for greater public vigilance. "Sporadic raids on abortion mills seem to satisfy the public that the situation is well in hand and that everything possible is being done to stamp out the evil," Mears complained. "Few people bother to follow up the cases and find out if those arrested were ever convicted. And yet out of one hundred cases reported in a year to the police of one city, fifty were thrown out for lack of sufficient evidence to make a *prima facie* case. Of the cases that reached the courts, only three convictions were obtained."[53]

Abortion prosecutions were notoriously difficult, because conviction depended on the willingness of clients to testify against an abortionist, which most abortion patients had no interest in doing. A few police agents tried to use sting operations in which a woman who claimed to be pregnant would attempt to trap an abortion provider into offering her an illegal abortion, but these operations were difficult to pull off successfully and therefore infrequent. In most cases, a conviction was likely only if a botched abortion sent an unfortunate client to the hospital or the morgue. But a skilled illegal abortionist might operate for years without getting caught, and licensed physicians had even less to worry about, because doctors who performed illegal abortions as part of their licensed medical practice were almost never prosecuted.[54]

Prior to the advent of the abortion liberalization campaign, few people had given much thought to the hundreds of thousands of illegal abortions that were occurring each year, but once advocates of abortion liberalization began publicizing their prevalence, concerned Catholic physicians decided to do something about the problem. They pushed for better enforcement of existing abortion laws in order to drive illegal abortionists out of business, and they also, for the first time, turned their attention to licensed physicians in public hospitals. Now that Rongy, Taussig, and Guttmacher had publicized the fact that hospital physicians were routinely stretching the limits of state law in order to perform "therapeutic" abortions, Catholic doctors decided to close the loopholes that allowed for this practice.

In 1944, two Catholic physicians—Samuel Cosgrove, who helped to create the Seton Hall College of Medicine and who also served as director of the Margaret Hague Maternity Hospital in Jersey City, and Patricia Carter, an ob-gyn from Charleston, South Carolina, who later became known as a pro-life advocate and who received a papal award for her medical work—coauthored a detailed study of abortion rates at East Coast hospitals in order to demonstrate that many hospitals were probably performing numerous abortions that were not necessary to save a pregnant woman's life. Because Margaret Hague Maternity Hospital, under Cosgrove's direction, limited abortion only to those cases in which a woman's physical life was in imminent danger, it had performed only four abortions in the previous twelve years, during which time it had performed 67,000 deliveries—a ratio of one abortion to every 16,750 live births. Any hospital that strictly followed the law should have a similarly low abortion rate, Cosgrove and Carter believed, because abortion was rarely required to save a woman's life. But the Johns Hopkins University (JHU) Hospital had an abortion rate of nearly three abortions for every one hundred deliveries, a rate that suggested that the JHU physicians were willing to perform abortions with slim justification. Such indiscriminate abortion, Cosgrove and Carter said, was "murder of the fetus," and it was almost indistinguishable from the "criminal" abortions that most physicians decried as the product of unscrupulous quacks.[55]

Some hospitals responded to these critiques by tightening their abortion policies and establishing committees to examine requests for abortion in order to ensure compliance with state law. "Formerly it was not difficult for any one who wanted to do a therapeutic abortion to get one or two doctors to agree with him," Albert Catherwood, a physician at Detroit's Harper Hospital, wrote in 1940, in an explanation of the effects that his hospital's recently formed therapeutic abortion committee—one of the first in the nation—had had on the practices of the hospital's physicians. "Since the appointment of this permanent committee, the number of therapeutic abortions in Harper Hospital has been greatly reduced." The idea of a therapeutic abortion committee quickly spread to other hospitals that were eager to secure the "medico-legal protection" that committee approval offered to their doctors. By the mid-1950s, hospital abortion committees were the norm throughout the United States.[56]

Despite their promise, therapeutic abortion committees did not accomplish their founders' objective of regularizing the review process for abortion procedures, because each committee's criteria for determining the legitimacy of a proposed abortion varied according to the views of the particular doctors who happened to be serving on the committee at the time. In some places, especially in California, hospital committees routinely approved abortions for reasons of mental health that went well beyond what a strict interpretation of their state's abortion law permitted. In many hospitals, if a psychiatrist certified that a woman was at risk of committing suicide if she were forced to carry her pregnancy to term, an abortion committee would approve the abortion on the grounds that pregnancy termination would save her life—thus satisfying the wording, if not the spirit, of strict abortion laws. But hospital administrators knew that what they were doing was probably not strictly legal; one survey of the abortion practices of twenty-six California hospitals between 1952 and 1956 found that at 75 percent of the hospitals, the administrators "thought their practices did not conform to the law." Physicians in other parts of the country made similar admissions. The therapeutic abortion committee that Guttmacher established at his own hospital approved 147 abortions between 1953 and 1958, but only 12 of those were necessary to save a woman's life—which, by Guttmacher's own admission, made more than 90 percent of the abortions "illegal" according to the "strictest interpretation of the law." "The law makes hypocrites of us all," he confessed.[57]

In other places, hospital committees were much less lenient, especially if a significant number of the committee members were Catholics. For instance, the abortion rate at Sloane Hospital in New York fell by two-thirds after the hospital created an abortion committee in 1955. Advocates of more liberalized abortion policies believed that, on average, despite the permissive practices of some hospital abortion committees, the establishment of these committees reduced the availability of hospital abortions, and they pointed to statistical evidence to prove their case. In 1940, approximately 30,000 legal abortions were performed in the United States each year, but by 1953, that figure had fallen to 18,000, and by 1966, it was only 8,000. Seventy percent of doctors who responded to a survey on the subject in the mid-1960s attributed the decline in the number of hospital abortions to the "Roman Catholic Church or religious pressure," which they believed had prompted the hospital abortion committees to adopt a cautious approach.[58]

Catholic physicians saw the issue differently. In their view, a strict interpretation of existing abortion laws should have produced a far lower abortion rate, and they accused hospital abortion committees of permitting a greater number of abortions than the law allowed. Abortion, Massachusetts physicians Roy Heffernan and William Lynch asserted in 1953, was "very probably the most poorly regulated procedure in medicine." The "therapeutic abortion" that hospital committees routinely permitted was "a direct violation of the fundamental ideals and traditions of medical practice."[59]

This had not been the case only a short time earlier. In the 1930s, most hospital abortions, according to the studies published in medical journals, were performed only in cases in which a doctor had concerns about a woman's ability to survive a pregnancy—that is, in cases in which the pregnant woman suffered from tuberculosis, heart conditions, or other physical ailments that directly threatened her life or prevented her from giving birth successfully.[60]

But medical advances of the early 1940s changed this situation. The invention of penicillin, combined with better anesthetic practices and new surgical techniques for Cesarean sections, resulted in a rapid reduction in maternal mortality. In the nineteenth century, C-sections were nearly always fatal, primarily because of the risk of infection, and even in the early twentieth century, they were highly dangerous. After penicillin dramatically reduced the complications of infection, doctors began performing far more C-sections, with much better results. Between 1943 and 1953, the rate of C-sections increased by more than 200 percent, while during the same period, the maternal mortality rate fell by 400 percent.[61]

This not only made childbirth less dangerous; it also obviated the need for many abortions. Prior to the discovery of a safe C-section, a pregnant woman who experienced complications and found herself unable to give birth vaginally faced a grim choice. She could lose her own life in a risky surgical operation or else allow a doctor to crush the skull of her late-term fetus so that its remains could be safely extracted, giving the woman herself a chance to live. But safe C-sections put an end to this and allowed pregnant women who were experiencing serious health complications to carry their pregnancies to term without risk of maternal or fetal death.[62]

Ironically, these same medical advances—especially penicillin—made abortions far safer as well, and they resulted in a dramatic reduction in the death rate for illegal abortions. In the early 1930s, thousands of women died each year from complications related to illegal abortions, and doctors warned that even hospital abortions performed in the best of conditions carried the risk of death. By 1950, according to statistics compiled by the Guttmacher Institute, the annual number of reported abortion-related deaths had fallen to just over 300, and by 1965, it would be only 200.[63] Some physicians now saw little reason to avoid abortions, since they were clearly safe.

The medical advances of the 1940s thus exacerbated the conflict between Catholic physicians and advocates of therapeutic abortion. Catholic doctors appealed to the new advances in childbirth to argue that hospital abortions were hardly ever needed and should thus be ended, while their opponents argued that since abortion was safer now than it had ever been before, restrictions on its use should be eased. In the 1950s, this debate took place in hospital abortion committees. Although liberalization advocates accused their Catholic opponents of using their positions on these committees to prevent doctors from performing needed abortions, Catholic physicians claimed that the non-Catholics on the committees were allowing far more abortions than a strict interpretation of the law should have permitted. Both charges were probably true; many doctors wanted to perform more abortions than the hospital committees allowed, but the hospital committees, in turn, often stretched the law to the breaking point for the abortions that they did permit.

Even as the number of hospital abortions declined, the percentage of hospital abortions that doctors performed solely for "psychiatric indications"—the most dubious of all therapeutic abortion categories, in the view of some Catholic physicians—increased rapidly, as doctors sought an acceptable classification for women who claimed that they would experience severe emotional distress if forced to give birth. As late as the mid-1940s, fewer than 14 percent of the therapeutic abortions performed at hospitals in New York City and only 13 percent of the abortions in Buffalo, New York, hospitals were performed because of psychiatric indications. But by 1963, psychiatric reasons accounted for nearly 88 percent of the abortions performed in Buffalo hospitals. A few doctors and hospital administrators privately admitted that they were assigning psychiatric indications to many women solely because that was the only way they could legally terminate their pregnancies. "The reason that psychiatric indications have become increasingly common, and form more than 60 per cent of the abortions done in my own institution is that we physicians are trying to find a way to do more legal abortions," Alan Guttmacher candidly admitted in a private letter to a physician friend in 1961.[64]

To halt this trend, Catholic physicians took their case to medical societies, hoping that if they could get a ruling from a professional body condemning this practice, hospital abortion committees—and maybe even state legislatures—would be shamed into tightening their abortion regulations. In 1951, Samuel Cosgrove and Roy Heffernan told the Clinical Congress of the American College of Surgeons that they favored outlawing all abortions since, in their view, the procedure was no longer required to save women's lives. Abortion, they believed, was encouraging either dishonesty or laziness on the part of doctors, because in the case of every pregnancy-related health emergency, they thought that a doctor could find a way to save a woman's life without deliberately destroying the life of the fetus. "Anyone who commits therapeutic (legal) abortion today, does so because he is either ignorant of the modern methods of treating the complications of pregnancy or is unwilling to take the time to treat them," Heffernan declared. Colorado lawyer T. Raber Taylor, a frequent contributor to the *Linacre Quarterly* and a specialist in litigation related to medical ethics, agreed. "In 1899 some competent and conscientious doctors did perform therapeutic abortions to save the life of the mother," he conceded in a 1959 article on the legality of abortion. But now, he said, childbirth was "eight to ten times safer than it was in 1930," so the concerns about saving a woman's life, which nineteenth-century legislators had written into the legal code on abortions, no longer applied. Doctors were abusing it, so it would be best to ban the procedure entirely.[65]

The Catholic physicians' call for a total ban on abortion received almost no support from Protestants, who believed that doctors should be free to make their own determinations about whether an abortion was medically necessary. An Episcopal priest in Charlottesville, Virginia, stated in 1952 that "the question of 'therapeutic' abortion is probably best decided among Episcopalians on the basis of the moral judgment of the individual, her family, the parish priest, and her physician." The pastor of one of Charlottesville's Southern Baptist churches concurred, declaring that abortion was "primarily a medical problem" rather than a theological one, and that "the advice of the physician should be followed." Protestant ministers continued to believe that abortions that were not medically necessary were "murder." But they trusted doctors to sort out those issues.[66] Catholics, by contrast, had spent the previous two decades opposing the medical profession over birth control, and they did not share Protestants' faith in doctors' ability to make the right decisions.

# A Human Rights Cause

Alarmed by the possibility that anyone might question the fetus's right to life, Catholics attempted to translate their natural law-based claims into concrete legal guarantees phrased in the language of international human rights, a new concern for many liberals at the time. In the late 1940s, the recent discovery of the full horrors of the Nazi atrocities, combined with the unearthing of ongoing human rights violations in totalitarian states, prompted the United Nations, with the support of American liberals such as Eleanor Roosevelt, to create a list of universal human rights that no state had the right to abrogate. Many American Catholic bishops supported the UN's project, especially since they believed that any unchanging standard of human rights must be divinely ordained and grounded in natural law. Foremost among universal human rights, they believed, was the right to life for all human beings, born and unborn. In 1947, the National Catholic Welfare Conference, the political and social justice organization of American Catholic bishops, presented the United Nations with its own model declaration of human rights, which began with the recognition of the "right to life and bodily integrity from the moment of conception." It also included the "right to a living wage" and "collective bargaining," along with the "right to education" and the "right to assistance from society," reflecting both the ideals of New Deal liberalism and the social tradition of the Church. None of these rights would be secure, the bishops believed, if the preeminent human right—the right to life—was not recognized. When the UN issued its Universal Declaration of Human Rights the next year, it did not include the bishops' suggested language, but that did not deter Catholic clerics. In 1948, the nation's leading Jesuit medical ethicist, Fr. Gerald Kelly, published a set of "Ethical and Religious Directives," designed to be posted in Catholic hospitals throughout the country, that made abortion a human rights issue by declaring, "Every unborn child must be considered a human person, with all the rights of a human person, from the moment of conception." Catholics renewed their efforts to obtain official recognition of this right from the UN. In 1950, the Catholic Association for International Peace asked the UN to amend its declaration by passing a resolution condemning abortion. Pope Pius XII also entered the fray in 1951 with a declaration that "every human being, even a child in the mother's womb, has a right to life directly from God," and that those who encouraged the destruction of so-called "life without value" in the case of therapeutic abortion were guilty of the same thinking that had led the Nazis to systematically kill those who had "some physical or mental defect."[67]

Within the next fifteen years, the comparison between abortion and Nazi eugenics or the Holocaust would become so common in the Catholic press that it would be hard to find a right-to-life advocate who did not make it. By introducing this, the pope solidified an argument that the National Federation of Catholic Physicians' Guilds had already foreshadowed and that his predecessor Pius XI had suggested in *Casti Connubii*—that public acceptance of abortion was a dangerous sign of disrespect for human life that would soon lead to the killing of any humans whose lives inconvenienced the majority. Catholics who had been speaking out against birth control and eugenics for several years before the rise of Adolf Hitler did not need to see reports of the horrors of Auschwitz and Buchenwald to believe the worst about the likely consequences of legalized abortion. But the hideous results of Nazi eugenics gave them new reasons to believe that if their fellow citizens ever removed the law's protection of an entire class of humans simply because those people had not yet been born, the consequences would be ghastly. As one might have expected, the proponents of abortion law reform were offended by this comparison, because they did not believe that by liberalizing the abortion law, they were removing legal protections for humans or showing disrespect for human life. In fact, they believed that they were saving human lives by protecting women who might otherwise die. Jewish proponents of legalization were especially upset by the suggestion that the cause they supported was comparable to the Holocaust.[68] But Catholics continued to make this comparison because they believed that any argument about the higher good that could be accomplished by legalizing abortion was tantamount to Nazi arguments about the greater societal good that would be accomplished if undesirable classes of people were exterminated.[69]

This made it impossible for Catholics to imagine compromising with their opponents. In their view, any removal of legal protection for the fetus was a step toward the eugenic and genocidal policies of the Nazis. They would fight each attempt to liberalize an abortion law as though the future of civilization depended on it. The debate over abortion had not even entered state legislatures, but already by the 1930s and 1940s, there were great chasms separating the two sides. When the conflict entered the realm of constitutional law at the end of the 1950s, the polarization would only become more pronounced.

## 2

# *The Political Fight Begins*

A HASTY VOICE vote at the 1959 convention of the American Law Institute (ALI) was all that it took to move the discussion of abortion out of hospitals and into state legislatures. The vote endorsed abortion law liberalization by making it a part of ALI's model penal code. Before 1959, the debate over abortion had mostly been restricted to doctors and Catholic theologians. Now there were lawyers involved.

At first, this seemed to be a major setback for anti-abortion Catholics; what had been little more than a hypothetical was now an imminent legislative possibility. But Catholic lawyers sprang into action. By translating their arguments for the protection of fetal life into the language of constitutional law, they created a nonsectarian defense of fetal rights that could reach a much broader audience than natural law-based arguments ever could. The campaign against abortion became a rights-based movement to defend the constitutional protection of the unborn.

## *Abortion Law Reform*

The ALI resolution was an attempt to address the gap between existing abortion laws and current medical practice. Doctors were already performing abortions for mental health reasons. It was time, the reformers said, to bring the law into line with this practice in order to protect both women and their doctors. Liberalized abortion laws, the reformers declared, could deter women from resorting to dangerous illegal methods to end their pregnancies, an argument that closely echoed claims made in the 1930s. There were now more data to support their case. In 1958, sex researchers who were expanding on Alfred Kinsey's work released a study showing that at least 20 percent of the pregnancies of white, educated, middle-class women ended in abortion.

With abortion so widespread, it was time, some argued, to change the law. Several Scandinavian countries had legalized abortion for "therapeutic" reasons. Why couldn't American states do the same? The model abortion code that ALI endorsed suggested that abortion should be legal in cases of rape or incest, dangers to a woman's physical or mental health, or suspected fetal deformity, as long as a committee of two doctors approved.[1]

Catholic lawyers were dismayed, because this seemed to directly contravene a growing recognition of the value of prenatal life in state, national, and even international law. Between 1939 and 1958, the state supreme courts of California, Kentucky, Minnesota, Ohio, and Oregon, along with the US District Court for the District of Columbia, had issued decisions recognizing the personhood of the fetus. The World Medical Association enjoined doctors in 1948 to "maintain the utmost respect for human life, from the time of conception" and enshrined this principle in the International Code of Medical Ethics that it adopted the following year. Even the United Nations, which had not included the National Catholic Welfare Conference's suggested language concerning the "right to life ... from the moment of conception" in its Universal Declaration of Human Rights, adopted the Declaration of the Rights of the Child in 1959, declaring that the child "needs special safeguards and care, including appropriate legal protection, before as well as after birth."[2] The ALI abortion resolution seemed to fly in the face of prevailing legal trends and to ignore a large body of international medical opinion.

T. Raber Taylor, a lawyer who frequently contributed to the National Federation of Catholic Physicians' Guilds' *Linacre Quarterly*, declared that if ALI wanted to engage in legal "advocacy" on abortion, it should call for the "outlawing of abortion" altogether; it should certainly not tell states to make their abortion codes more liberal. The editor of the *Catholic Lawyer* was similarly perturbed by the ALI resolution, and he urged the journal's readers to "register timely protest" and "offer constructive suggestions" to convince ALI to modify its statements. ALI had coupled its resolution with a proposal to make the death penalty more difficult to impose. The editor of *Catholic Lawyer* pointed out the incongruity of making it easier to "kill" the "innocent" unborn at the same time that the organization was attempting to protect the lives of adult offenders. But ALI ignored the pleas of Catholic lawyers, since, by their own admission, they comprised only "a very small group in the Institute."[3]

Armed with the ALI guidelines as a model, liberal-minded state legislators across the nation spent the next decade introducing bills that would legalize abortion for the exact reasons that ALI had laid out.[4] For almost three decades, the liberalization of American abortion laws had been a distant possibility, but not a direct threat. State legislators now had a set of guidelines that they could easily convert into bills. The fight moved to the statehouses.

The campaign for ALI-style abortion law reform began in California in 1960, when a Los Angeles county grand jury that had been charged with finding a solution to the problem of widespread illegal abortion recommended an ALI-style therapeutic abortion bill. Following that finding, a freshman Democratic state legislator from the Bay Area, John Knox, introduced the state's first abortion liberalization bill, also modeled on the ALI guidelines. Knox had entered the legislature with a passionate commitment to abortion reform because he had been moved by a news report about a rape victim who was denied an abortion. But his campaign was quickly stymied. Representatives from the Catholic Church made it clear that they would do everything in their power to stop the bill. In the pre-Vatican-II era, when politicians believed that the Church hierarchy could still deliver the votes of its parishioners, this frightened many legislators, and they voted to table the bill.[5]

The political fight over ALI-style abortion reform bills exacerbated the divisions between Catholics and Protestants on abortion. Mainline Protestants who had previously not supported the abortion law reform movement began to rethink the issue. In 1961, the National Council of Churches passed a resolution that condemned most abortions but that also explicitly allowed them in cases when a woman's life or health was in danger, and suggested continued study of the issue. In 1962, the United Presbyterian Church passed a resolution in favor of uniform state therapeutic abortion laws throughout the nation, though it left the specifics of those laws unstated.[6] It appeared that mainline Protestant Churches were open to at least some of the ALI guidelines, and that their invocation of the principle of self-defense to justify abortions in extraordinary situations had widened to include not only the necessity of preserving a woman's life, but also her health.

## Sherri Chessen Finkbine

The division between Catholics and Protestants became more evident in 1962 when Sherri Chessen Finkbine, a star of the children's television show "Romper Room" and a married mother of four, got pregnant again and sought an abortion. She and her husband initially wanted to have the child, but changed their minds after learning that a thalidomide-based tranquilizer that she had taken early in her pregnancy was likely to cause birth defects. Like most states, Arizona allowed abortion only in cases in which pregnancy endangered a woman's life, but like many upper-middle-class married women, Finkbine was able to gain a sympathetic hearing from her doctor and her hospital's abortion committee, which voted to approve the abortion on the grounds that the prospect of giving birth to a deformed child was causing Finkbine so much mental distress that she was in danger of becoming suicidal. Finkbine probably could have had the abortion quietly—as many women in similar situations did—if she had not informed a reporter of her intentions. When word got out, a hospital administrator who feared prosecution postponed the abortion until the hospital could obtain legal approval for the procedure from a judge. The judge, however, denied the request, which meant that Finkbine would be unable to get a legal abortion in Arizona. In fact, no state had an abortion law lenient enough to cover her situation, and now that her case had received national publicity, it was unlikely that any doctor in the United States would be willing to risk criminal prosecution by performing an abortion for her. Realizing that her options were limited, Finkbine decided to travel to Sweden to obtain a legal hospital abortion.[7]

Finkbine's case divided the nation and accelerated the demand for liberalized abortion laws. At first, Finkbine and her husband, Robert, insisted that they were "not crusading for abortion." But Finkbine's arguments in favor of her own abortion were very similar to those that advocates of liberalized abortion laws were making, and they resonated with people. Finkbine said she would have a mental breakdown if she were forced to give birth to a deformed child. Her husband insisted that "if we can prevent the bringing of a crippled child into this world, we feel it is our responsibility to do so." For years, abortion law reform advocates such as Frederick Taussig and Alan Guttmacher had argued that fetal deformity was a justifiable cause for abortion, but Finkbine's case gave the abortion law reformers' argument a human face and attracted an unprecedented amount of media coverage—much of it sympathetic. Her experience pushed her into the fray. She did not want other women to suffer as she had, she said. She had lost her job and received death threats, along with what she described as "thousands of pieces of hate mail." "You are a killer," someone had written. "Quit advocating death." Many Protestants and Jews viewed Finkbine as a hero. One New York rabbi applauded her for saving a deformed infant from a life of pain. "There is no greater sin than to condemn a helpless infant to the twilight world of living death," he declared.[8]

The public reaction to Finkbine's decision highlighted the emerging division between Catholics and non-Catholics over abortion. This division did not fall along gender lines. Women, in fact, were slightly more likely than men to oppose Finkbine's decision, with only 50 percent of women (compared to 54 percent of men) saying that she had done the "right thing." But there were stark religious differences. While 56 percent of Protestants said that Finkbine "did the right thing" in having an abortion, only 33 percent of Catholics agreed.[9] Many Catholics were horrified to learn that public opinion leaders such as journalists, television personalities, and Protestant and Jewish clergy—along with a sizeable number of Protestant and Jewish citizens—saw nothing wrong with aborting a deformed fetus.

Catholics who spoke out on the issue were especially upset that the press gave so little attention to whether the fetus was a person deserving of legal protection. Finkbine, who described herself as nonreligious, admitted to giving little consideration to the issue herself. "Did I think the fetus had a soul?" she asked four years later. "To tell you the honest truth, I had never even thought of it before." A Catholic doctor in Hawaii expressed outrage at Finkbine's apparently cavalier attitude toward unborn human life. "Is not the human life and soul sufficiently precious that *we* should 'think of it'?" he asked.[10]

Catholics were dismayed that even many people who did acknowledge the humanity of the fetus were willing to accept the utilitarian arguments in favor of the Finkbines' choice. Vatican Radio put it in stark terms: "If there be dangers to others, even the mother, from his existence and from the way he is formed, it is not his fault. It is therefore arbitrary to consider him an intruder and to condemn him to capital punishment."[11]

Some Catholics took direct action. A recently married Catholic couple offered to adopt Finkbine's child if only she would be willing to carry her pregnancy to term. The couple, Tim and Bonnie Orr of Los Angeles, both twenty-one years old, had not yet had any children of their own, but they both came from large families and were well aware of Catholic teaching on abortion. Tim was a student at Loyola Law School, a Jesuit institution. "We just don't believe in abortion," he said, "and would be glad to have the child even if it is born deformed." Other Catholic couples also came forward with similar offers.[12]

Catholic abortion opponents were especially concerned about Robert Finkbine's declaration that he and his wife had a "responsibility" to "prevent the bringing of a crippled child into this world." If the life of the Finkbines' unborn child could be ended on the grounds that it was physically deformed—if its humanity could be ignored—what would stop a state from allowing the killing of disabled children after birth? The abortion of deformed fetuses, one Burbank, California, resident wrote to the *Los Angeles Times*, was "opening the door to something worse than the kind of genocide practiced by Hitler."[13]

Some Catholics saw a parallel between Finkbine's situation and the case of a Belgian woman, Suzanne van de Put, who also took thalidomide-based medication while pregnant. Like Finkbine, van de Put could not bear the thought of letting a deformed child suffer, and she decided to end the child's life. The difference was that the child had already been born. Van de Put was tried in Belgium for murder but was acquitted. The Belgian public applauded the verdict. A few days later, another Belgian woman killed her three-year-old mentally retarded daughter for similar reasons. Van de Put's case, which occurred in the same year as Finkbine's, was covered in Catholic newspapers across the United States, as well as on Vatican Radio, and it provoked an outcry from the Catholic faithful. Both Europeans and Americans seemed to be losing respect for the lives of people with disabilities. The result, many Catholics believed, would be a cheapening of human life at all levels, as well as a lack of interest in providing genuine aid to those who needed it. "It seems fair to assume that neither the pharmaceutical firms nor the medical profession will become more responsible if the public at large adopts the attitude that the results of such mistakes can be scrapped like so many defective parts that fail to pass inspection at the end of a production line," Georgetown University philosophy professor Germain Grisez wrote.[14]

Catholics who opposed abortion began to illustrate their argument with a thought experiment. In the story, one doctor approaches another to ask what he would have advised in the case of a particularly unpromising pregnancy. "About the terminating of a pregnancy, I want your opinion," the first doctor says. "The father was syphilitic. The mother tuberculous. Of the four children born, the first was blind, the second died, the third was deaf and dumb, the fourth also tuberculous. What would you have done?" "I would have ended the pregnancy," replies the second doctor. "Then," says the first doctor, "you would have murdered Beethoven."[15]

This story was not historically accurate, but it resonated as a parable. Catholics began disseminating it in the early 1960s, and it soon became a staple of anti-abortion literature and diocesan newspapers. It seemed particularly effective because it pinpointed the weaknesses in arguments for a planned society. Abortion legalization advocates who had adopted a utilitarian social ethic thought they could calculate the benefit or cost that a potential member of society could bring. Many Catholics, on the other hand, believed that each child was a unique creation of God with a purpose that might be achievable only through suffering. Every life was valuable. If some were snuffed out before birth, people who were already born would never know the joys that these unborn children might have brought to the world. Imagine a world without Beethoven, the opponents of abortion implored.

Those on the opposite side of the debate responded that it might be equally profitable to imagine a world without various tyrants, criminals, and mental defectives. "It is plainly futile to make predications of the nonexistent," Garrett Hardin, a California biology professor, wrote in 1967. "Every child that is aborted (or not conceived) might have been a Beethoven—or, equally likely, a Hitler. Much more likely, it would simply have been another Caspar Milquetoast, of which the world already has an ample supply."[16] For advocates of liberalized abortion laws, this argument made sense, because to them, conceptions were merely random events. By contrast, many Catholics, as well as a few members of other religious faiths, viewed conceptions as divine blessings and believed that every human life was the product of a divine plan, even if that human life entered the world with severe handicaps or social disadvantages. For them, a human life had ultimate value not because it contributed something to society or because it was wanted by its parents, but because it was a unique creation of God. The ultimate measure of a life's worth was not individual happiness—as those who made arguments about a deformed infant's "quality of life" seemed to assume—but rather its inestimable valuation by its Creator. The two sides in the debate reasoned from very different premises, so compromise seemed impossible. The result was an intractable fight in state legislatures.

## *The Legislative Battle of 1962–63*

When the battle over abortion first entered the political arena, Catholics seemed to have the advantage. In spite of the emerging Protestant consensus in favor of a modest liberalization of the nation's abortion laws, legislators in heavily Catholic areas respected the Church's political influence and were reluctant to defy Church teaching. As long as bishops could convince state politicians that Catholics would vote en masse against any legislator who attempted to liberalize a state abortion law, the fear of political retaliation kept the abortion reform movement in check. But that did not mean that the church had an easy task. The 1962–63 legislative season was a challenging one for defenders of fetal life, as advocates of abortion law liberalization introduced new proposals in several states to create abortion laws based on the ALI framework.

Two months after Finkbine's abortion, an advisory committee headed by University of Minnesota law professor Maynard Pirsig recommended that Minnesota change its laws to allow for abortion in cases of rape and suspected fetal deformity, and the Minnesota legislature took up the bill for consideration. Compared to later abortion legalization bills, this one was quite modest in scope. It restricted abortion to a narrowly circumscribed set of circumstances. "A woman who has been humiliated by rape shouldn't be further humiliated by having an unwanted child," Pirsig said. But Pirsig was under no illusion that Catholics in his state would accept his proposed changes to the law. He predicted controversy, and his prediction soon came true.[17]

Catholic clergy in Minnesota viewed Pirsig's proposal as a utilitarian measure that devalued human life. The logic disturbed them as much as the bill itself. When Protestants had argued for the necessity of abortion in cases when a woman's life was in danger, they had generally done so by invoking the principle of self-defense, saying that it was legitimate for a woman to take the life of her unborn child in order to save her own. Catholics disagreed with the argument, but they understood why Protestants accepted it. Pirsig's proposal, in the view of many Catholics, invoked the utilitarian argument of Taussig, Guttmacher, and other abortion liberalization advocates that abortion was legitimate when it accomplished a greater social good—in this case, the mental well-being of a woman facing a crisis pregnancy. Why should an innocent unborn child be "executed" for a crime the child had not committed, merely because the death of that child would alleviate someone else's pain? This logic, if carried to the extreme, would endanger everyone's lives, Catholics said. "Once we claim the right directly to kill one innocent person in the name of a greater good there is left no moral grounds upon which to protest the killing of millions of innocent persons in the name of a greater good as the Nazis did," Msgr. Richard Doherty, director of the Catholic Action Committee for the Archdiocese of St. Paul and Minneapolis, wrote in October 1962. "Logic would lead us from abortion to the gas chamber."[18]

The Minnesota legislature let Pirsig's bill die in committee, but Catholics who might have rejoiced in this victory instead began to worry about California. In December 1962, three months after Finkbine's abortion, the California legislature held another round of hearings on John Knox's abortion liberalization bill. This time, the bill had the support of a bevy of doctors and lawyers who argued that it would protect doctors who were already performing abortions for therapeutic reasons, bringing law into line with practice. The California Medical Association endorsed the measure.[19]

California's bishops decided that it was best to leave the legislative testimony to lay professionals rather than official diocesan representatives, so each side had its own lineup of physicians and lawyers. All of those who testified against the bill were male, as were nearly all of those on the other side. Pro-liberalization lawyers met their match in Walter Trinkaus, a lawyer representing the Catholic Conference of California Hospitals. Described by his colleagues as an extremely self-disciplined young lawyer with an unflappable demeanor and a rigorously logical approach, Trinkaus quickly took Catholics' legal arguments out of the realm of natural law and into the arena of constitutional law.[20]

Trinkaus insisted that the question at stake in the debate was whether the fetus was a human person; if it were, it had a constitutional right to life under the Fourteenth Amendment that no state law could take away. It was a question that many liberalization proponents were unwilling to answer. Some felt conflicted about the issue, believing that the fetus probably deserved some legal protection, but that it did not have the same value as a full-grown woman. For example, the California legislative committee on criminal procedure that endorsed the legalization of therapeutic abortion expressed ambivalence about fetal life: "It should be clearly understood that the committee is not saying that a fetus is a blob of protoplasm, neither is it saying that a fetus is to be treated as a human being." But Trinkaus and the other Catholics who testified against liberalization insisted that the law did not allow for such ambivalence; there was no such thing as semi-personhood.[21]

Trinkaus was able to appeal to legal precedent because the weight of legal opinion had been shifting toward increased recognition of the rights of the unborn. After court decisions in many states during the 1930s and 1940s recognized the right of people to sue for prenatal injuries or for the wrongful death of an unborn child, the state supreme court of New Jersey explicitly extended that right to pre-viable fetuses in *Smith v. Brennan* (1960) on the grounds that "medical authority recognizes that an unborn child is a distinct biological entity from the time of conception, and many branches of the law afford the unborn child protection throughout the period of gestation." Four years later, in *Fitkin Memorial Hospital v. Anderson* (1964), the New Jersey high court ruled that a pregnant woman who was a Jehovah's Witness did not have the right to refuse a blood transfusion that doctors believed was necessary to preserve the life of the fetus she was carrying. The case quickly became a favorite of lawyers in the right-to-life campaign because of the court's unequivocal declaration of the fetus's status as a legal person with constitutionally protected rights. "The unborn child is entitled to the law's protection," the court declared.[22]

Anti-abortion Catholics in other states, hewing closely to Trinkaus's arguments, began making a legal case for the fetus's right to life. But they went a step further, arguing that the constitutional rights to which they appealed were a reflection of inalienable human rights that were given by God. In their view, natural law and constitutional law reflected the same unchangeable principles, which is why their testimony so frequently blended what sounded to outsiders like a combination of secular and religious arguments. As Catholic diocesan representatives in Kansas stated in the spring of 1963, "Every living being, born or unborn, is a creature of God possessed with an immortal soul and also the Creator-endowed inalienable rights guaranteed by our [state and national] Constitutions. . . . The direct taking of an innocent life . . . is an act clearly forbidden by the Laws of God and by our Constitutions." Catholics who opposed liberalization were sure that it would ultimately fail in the courts, if not the legislature, because they believed that proposed abortion reform legislation was blatantly unconstitutional—a fact that judges who had already recognized the legal personhood of the fetus would surely acknowledge.[23]

The proponents of abortion law reform in California disagreed with all of this. They dismissed the Catholics' arguments as the views of a religious minority that was attempting to violate the rights of the majority of Californians who did not subscribe to either natural law theory or the Catholic lawyers' interpretation of the Constitution. They had to acknowledge that courts had recognized the legal standing of the fetus in tort cases, but they did not believe that meant that an abortion reform bill was unconstitutional. The law already recognized the acceptability of abortion in cases when pregnancy endangered a woman's life, thus indicating, in the view of one of the leading lawyers in the abortion law reform movement in California, "a strong trend toward primary protection of the woman as opposed to the fetus." A liberalized abortion law would "only broaden this protection."[24]

Yet if proponents of liberalization dismissed Catholic legal arguments, they could not easily disregard the threat of Catholic voters. In California, John Knox, fearing that his own reelection might be in jeopardy, decided not to reintroduce his abortion liberalization bill. Another young legislator, Anthony Beilenson, took up the cause. Beilenson introduced a slightly modified version of Knox's bill in the spring of 1963, opening the issue up for public debate once again.[25]

As the representative of a legislative district carved out of posh suburban neighborhoods in Beverly Hills and West Los Angeles, Beilenson did not have to worry about the political challenges that concerned Knox. His district, which was the wealthiest in the state and one of the most liberal, did not contain enough Catholic opponents of abortion to threaten his political future. The letters that he received from his constituents were mainly in favor of abortion liberalization. After all, liberalization was a doctor's cause, and Beilenson knew a lot of influential doctors.

Beilenson, an articulate lawyer still in his early thirties, brought high levels of energy and talent to his campaign. Some journalists proclaimed him the most talented legislator in the state assembly. He had come from a wealthy, politically liberal family in New Rochelle, New York, and was educated at the best private schools on the East Coast, moving from Phillips Academy in Andover, Massachusetts, to Harvard University and then Harvard Law School. He had been active in liberal Democratic Party politics since he was old enough to vote, campaigning first for Adlai Stevenson and then for John F. Kennedy. Later, he would establish himself as a leader of the liberal wing of the California Democratic Party by making an early break with President Lyndon Johnson over the Vietnam War, but even before that, he was known as a man of the left, with an interest in both the population control movement and civil rights. When he moved to California, he joined a law firm whose partners included one of the state's leading advocates of the Knox bill. For Beilenson, abortion law reform was a progressive cause that was fully in keeping with his goal of creating a more humane society. And like many of the early pioneers of abortion law liberalization, such as A. J. Rongy, Frederick Taussig, and

Alan Guttmacher, he was a secular Jew, with no attachment to any theological tradition that linked the beginning of human personhood to the moment of conception. He was thus well suited to becoming the bill's new champion.[26]

Beilenson realized that the greatest obstacle to abortion law reform was a widespread feeling among politicians that it would damage their political careers. As long as legislators believed that Catholics would vote against them en masse if they supported abortion liberalization, they had a strong incentive not to do so. And even politicians who represented few Catholics shied away from what was seen as a controversial issue. Though a number of doctors supported abortion law reform, the American Medical Association did not, and its influence was sufficient to counter ALI's. Those who opposed abortion were quick to bring up the clause in the Hippocratic oath that required doctors to forswear their involvement in the procedure.[27] Many doctors had performed abortions to save a woman's life, but extending abortion legalization beyond this would be unethical, some thought.

Accordingly, all of the abortion liberalization bills that were proposed in various states during the 1962–63 legislative session were killed in committee.[28] It was a high-water mark for Catholics' effort to stop the abortion liberalization campaign. Without any official directives from the national church hierarchy, and without a direct lobbying campaign, Catholics had succeeded. Perhaps most remarkably, they succeeded in spite of the public support for abortion liberalization following the publicity surrounding Sherri Chessen Finkbine's experience. For the moment, the opponents of abortion seemed to have the upper hand.

Alan Guttmacher was in despair. "The Catholic Church is so well mobilized and makes up such a large percentage of the population that changing the law of any state in the Northeast of the U.S.A. is a virtual impossibility at least for the next several decades," Guttmacher wrote in April 1963. Three years earlier, when Guttmacher was attempting to interest politicians in a proposal to liberalize New York's abortion law, he had heard a priest tell a state senator in no uncertain terms that the Catholic Church was prepared to do everything in its power to block any abortion liberalization proposals, since the value of human life could not be compromised.[29] The successful Catholic mobilization in the wake of the Finkbine case seemed to bear this out.

These early victories probably made Catholics overconfident. After the victories of 1962–63, the National Catholic Welfare Conference (which was the national coordinating organization for Catholic bishops) made no effort to prepare for a new onslaught of abortion reform bills. Nor did most of the nation's bishops show much interest in the cause. In the midst of Vatican II and political debates about government funding for parochial schools and the distribution of contraception, the bishops found other matters far more pressing. The only abortion-related organizations in existence in 1964 were the ones that advocated legalization; abortion opponents were mostly silent and unorganized.

## *The Legislative Tide Begins to Turn*

While Catholic opponents of abortion law reform rested on their laurels, their foes regrouped and continued to fight. The leaders of Planned Parenthood, though still officially defending the organization's public stance that effective contraception would eliminate the need for abortion, began quietly working behind the scenes to advance the campaign for abortion law liberalization. After all, contraception would be of little help in the cases that the ALI-style abortion reform bills were designed to address, such as rape, suspected fetal deformity, and when a woman's health was endangered. Even if abortion was undesirable—as Margaret Sanger had suggested it was—it might be necessary when contraception could not help. When Planned Parenthood appointed Alan Guttmacher—perhaps the nation's most prominent advocate of abortion law liberalization—as its president in 1962, the move signaled the organization's willingness to rethink its official opposition to abortion. During the early 1960s, Guttmacher traveled the country giving public lectures in support of legalizing "therapeutic" abortion. Though Planned Parenthood's other staff members insisted that Guttmacher did not speak for the organization on this issue, it was increasingly difficult to maintain this distinction, especially when some of Planned Parenthood's other officers, such as its medical director Mary Calderone, were equally supportive of legalization. In addition, by the 1960s, some state directors of Planned Parenthood were routinely referring women to abortionists in Japan (which had legalized elective abortion in 1949), and they were dismayed that legal abortion was not available in the United States for those who did not have the money to travel abroad. As the executive director of Planned Parenthood's Massachusetts chapter told Guttmacher in 1966, "It breaks our hearts to be unable to help those (17 last month alone) who can't afford to use this legal resource."[30]

Thus, for several years before Planned Parenthood officially endorsed abortion legalization in 1968, the organization's leadership was already mobilizing in support of the cause. Because Planned Parenthood was a large, respected, and politically influential organization—in 1964, it enlisted former presidents Harry Truman and Dwight Eisenhower as honorary co-chairs of its fundraising campaign—the increasing support that its executive leadership gave to liberalization provided a significant boost to the movement.[31]

Liberalization advocates also formed new organizations specifically dedicated to their cause. In New York, a group of physicians and lawyers joined Guttmacher in forming the Committee for a Humane Abortion Law in 1964. The organization, which grew out of the Westchester Ethical Society in White Plains, represented a cross-section of upper-middle-class cultural liberals in suburban New York. Most of the members of its advisory board were doctors, though there were also a few attorneys (including birth control advocate Harriet Pilpel, who later served as the American Civil Liberty Union's general counsel) and an Episcopal priest. The group's work would be mainly educational, according to its charter document; the key would be changing the public's mind about the need for abortion law reform.

The Committee for a Humane Abortion Law, like almost all other advocates of abortion law reform in the early 1960s, saw the issue primarily as a public health measure. Criminalizing abortion, the committee believed, had led only to "illegal abortions"; it was time to give doctors the right to perform abortions whenever they thought that the "health and well-being of the woman" required it or whenever there was "serious risk of a defective child being born."[32]

Even though the goals of the liberalization movement were still relatively modest, Guttmacher expected fierce opposition. "None of us is optimistic enough to believe that there will be an immediate liberalization," he wrote to one supporter in April 1965. In 1962, he had glumly predicted that the fight for abortion law liberalization would not be won in his lifetime. Three years later, he was somewhat more optimistic, but he still envisioned his campaign as a long, drawn-out battle that would require many years of work.[33]

Meanwhile, on the opposite coast, Anthony Beilenson continued his fight for a liberalized abortion law. He was sure that the "hierarchy of the Roman Catholic Church" was the only thing standing in the way of his bill. "The moral philosophy of a single church is being imposed on all," he told the press in September 1964.[34]

Beilenson's assessment of Catholic influence was largely correct, though his belief that such opposition came only from the "hierarchy" was not. In a state that was 30 percent Catholic, the church had a lot of political power, and it used this influence to thwart Beilenson's efforts. But the opposition extended far beyond priests and bishops. At first, the bishops themselves stayed out of the fight, because they still thought the chance of the bill passing was remote, and therefore laymen's efforts would be sufficient to kill the measure. Thus, at the early hearings on the bill, there were hardly any Catholic clergy present; instead, most of the people who testified against the proposed legislation were lawyers and doctors, just like those on the other side.

Although Catholics were almost alone in speaking out against abortion liberalization at the earlier public hearings in California, two Protestant ministers testified against Beilenson's bill in 1964. One, a conservative Congregationalist who was concerned about the bill's effect on sexual morality, performed badly, but the other, a Bay Area Missouri Synod Lutheran pastor named Arnim Polster, amazed his allies with his testimony and quickly established himself as a leader in the state's fledgling right-to-life movement.[35]

Polster had worked as a lawyer before entering the ministry, and he brought to his task a set of legal skills that impressed even some of his opponents. He also took the subject of abortion out of the realm of Catholic natural law theory and into a realm of commonsense arguments that were more accessible to Protestants. The Bible did not define when human life begins, Polster quickly conceded, and even science had not been able to answer the question definitively. But since there was a good chance that human life began long before birth, why risk killing a full human being by performing abortion without just cause? Like many Protestants—and unlike his Catholic allies—he thought that if a woman had been raped or needed an abortion in order to protect her life, she was justified in terminating her pregnancy, but he also believed that abortion for reasons of fetal deformity, which Beilenson's bill would have allowed, was wrong. Here Polster used his personal story to maximum advantage. He himself had been disabled by polio, and he still walked with a severe limp. "My deformity was far worse than some of those for which abortions could be performed under this bill," he declared. "Yet I believe my life has been as purposeful as if I had not had polio."[36]

If deformed fetuses were allowed to be killed, Polster wondered, where would the line be drawn? Many of the damaged "thalidomide babies" had been born with missing limbs, but their brains functioned perfectly well. Was a missing leg or arm sufficient reason to terminate an unborn child's life? "How far is it from such destruction of life proposed in this bill to the destruction in force in Adolf Hitler's Nazi Germany under the guise of ridding society of the undesirable and defective?" Polster asked.[37]

Polster's testimony was aimed squarely at one of his leading opponents, Monterey County Episcopal priest Lester Kinsolving, who argued that society would benefit if abortions were allowed in cases of suspected fetal defects. The current abortion law "encourage[d] the progeny of rape, incest and venereal disease," Kinsolving declared. "Is society edified by the forced production of thalidomide monstrosities which differ intensely from the legion of comparatively mild defects?" he asked. "Is it sensible or sane to insist upon the permanent wrecking of a mother's health?"[38] Although many found Kinsolving's argument persuasive, Polster's opposing testimony gave a few Protestant supporters of abortion law reform reason to reconsider, especially when he argued that Kinsolving's reasoning bore an eerie similarity to Nazi eugenic programs. Polster's appearance at the hearing refuted the widespread argument that only Catholics opposed abortion law reform, and it paved the way for Protestants who did not accept most of the Catholic Church's natural law-based arguments to join the right-to-life movement on human rights grounds. And as director of public relations for the California and Nevada district of the Lutheran Church-Missouri Synod, Polster was able to speak in the name of an entire denomination. This represented an impressive coup for the Catholic Church, which up to that point had had no organizational allies among Protestants.

Nevertheless, Beilenson, Kinsolving, and their allies remained focused on the Catholic Church. By the mid-1960s, Kinsolving and Northern California Episcopal Bishop James Pike were issuing relentless attacks on the Catholic Church, claiming that it was misrepresenting its own theological history. Thomas Aquinas, Kinsolving pointed out, did not believe that ensoulment occurred until several weeks after conception, and the Catholic belief that life should be protected from the moment of fertilization was only a century old. No Protestant church taught this doctrine, Kinsolving claimed. It was a minority position within Christianity. It certainly did not belong in public law. While Kinsolving was correct about Aquinas's view of ensoulment, his argument glossed over a long tradition of Christian proscriptions against abortion that began well before the nineteenth century; the Catholic Church's teaching on the issue was not nearly as new or as anomalous as he claimed. Nevertheless, Kinsolving's argument appealed to many liberalization advocates. He showed up at every California abortion hearing after 1964, and gave impassioned testimony about the need to help rape victims and other women who were in dire need of therapeutic abortions. Only the intransigence of the Catholic Church prevented them from receiving such help, he argued.[39]

Polster's testimony notwithstanding, the fight against Beilenson's bill still depended almost entirely on the Catholic Church, so proponents of liberalized abortion laws believed they could win political victory if they discredited the Church's record. Some were only too ready to give voice to anti-Catholic stereotypes. "It is indeed a sad state of affairs when a self-proclaimed 'infallible' religious-political dictator sitting on a throne in a foreign land can give orders down through his chain of command, the Bishops and priests, to the governor of one of our supposedly free states," one California citizen wrote to Beilenson. "It is even sadder to think that so many of our elected officials who supposedly represent the people as a whole cower and cringe before the powerful Catholic Bishops and their blocs of controlled votes. For this reason the Roman Catholic church is far more dangerous to our freedom and liberties than Communism. How much longer will the people stand for it?"[40]

Catholic diocesan papers in California brought the anti-abortion message directly into Catholic homes. They trumpeted the arguments of the church's attorneys, charging that the legalization of therapeutic abortion would constitute an unprecedented attack on the nation's constitutional foundation and the promise of the Declaration of Independence. Like the lawyers who argued their case before state legislatures, the diocesan papers fused natural law arguments with appeals to constitutional law and rights-based ideology, a move that framed the campaign against abortion law reform as both a battle for the rights of the unborn and a defense of the nation's moral framework. "The unborn child is an individual person, endowed with a right to life by his Creator, and pointed to a destiny which it is beyond the prerogative of society to determine," Los Angeles's archdiocesan paper *The Tidings* declared in October 1964. "And once society presumes to dictate whether that life will be honored and preserved, the very foundation of human civilization crumbles. Surely the horrors of Dachau are still fresh enough in our memories to enable us to see the dark strain of inhumanity which touches this present question."[41]

The alleged genocidal consequences of legalizing abortion in cases of fetal deformities became a central issue in Beilenson's campaign for reelection in 1964. Beilenson's opponent, attorney David De Loach, charged that the legislator's attempt "to prevent the birth of potentially deformed infants . . . smacks of genocide" and was "the same goal desired by Hitler." Perhaps in another legislative district, those attacks would have had an effect, but in socially liberal Beverly Hills, De Loach's charges backfired. Beilenson won reelection by a landslide and returned to the legislature with a renewed determination to get his bill passed.[42]

For the first time, Catholic opponents of abortion realized that a large percentage of the public did not share their perspective on the value of fetal life. Their warnings about the logical consequences of liberalizing abortion law made little sense to many liberal Protestants and Jews, who saw the equation of abortion with the Holocaust as offensive and ridiculous. Catholics were puzzled by the unwillingness of the public to listen to their arguments, which they felt were well supported not only in natural law, but also in constitutional law. If the fetus was a person, then it was deserving of human rights.

Catholics continued to make this argument when testifying against Beilenson's therapeutic abortion bill in the spring of 1965, but they faced a difficult battle. More than 1,100 Protestant and Jewish clergymen had signed a petition in support of Beilenson's bill, as had more than 1,000 doctors. With the committee poised to approve the bill and send it to the assembly floor, where it was expected to pass, Bishop Alden Bell of Sacramento issued a last-minute call to his fellow bishops throughout the state to mobilize their parishioners and flood the desks of state legislators with letters and telegrams opposing the bill. The tactic seemed to work. A few legislators who favored Beilenson's bill decided that it was politically advantageous to vote against it, and by a vote of eleven to ten, the committee decided to refer Beilenson's bill for further study, effectively ending its consideration in the 1965 legislative session. As expected, Beilenson blamed the Catholic Church for his defeat and vowed to continue the fight. Catholics realized that it had been a close call. Bell warned his colleague in Los Angeles, Cardinal James McIntyre, that had it not been for their eleventh-hour efforts, the bill would have passed; the Church would have to be better prepared next time.[43]

The California bishops' near-defeat in 1965 jolted them into action and forced them to confront the possibility that their state might liberalize its abortion law, an outcome they had previously considered unthinkable. But now that they realized the threat they were facing, it was difficult to envision a path to victory. At the very moment when the bishops needed to rally support for their cause, the Church was rapidly losing its longstanding political influence even among its own members. Only a few days after the bishops' surprise victory over Beilenson, the Supreme Court delivered a crushing blow to Catholic political influence in *Griswold v. Connecticut*, which struck down state prohibitions on birth control for married couples. At the same time, the reforms of Vatican II brought a tsunami of cultural change within the Catholic Church. Laypeople quickly began defying clerical authority, especially on the issues of birth control and abortion. The days when a bishop could control the votes of his parishioners or defeat a legislative proposal with a telegram were over. The struggle over abortion that had begun as a clash of values had become, by the mid-1960s, a fierce conflict in which, for Catholic opponents of reform, nothing less was at stake than the value of human life in public law. And for the first time, it appeared that this was a fight they might lose.

# 3

# *Initial Losses*

THE CATHOLIC CHURCH'S close call in California—a state that was 30 percent Catholic—should have alerted opponents of abortion that their cause had much less public support than they had believed. Only two years earlier, a modest Catholic lobbying effort had been sufficient to easily defeat numerous abortion bills. By 1965, a herculean effort was required to squeak out a narrow victory. The Catholic Church was losing its political influence, and as a result, the campaign to save the unborn faced an unprecedented crisis.

## *The End of the Catholic Campaign against Birth Control*

The sudden loss of the Church's influence over abortion law resulted from a larger crisis in the Catholic Church over birth control politics. Since the 1930s, the Catholic Church had been the leading—indeed the only—force working to preserve state laws against birth control in the face of a concerted campaign to repeal them.[1] Two events that occurred in 1965—the conclusion of Vatican II and the Supreme Court's ruling in *Griswold v. Connecticut*—brought their efforts to an immediate halt.

Catholics were astonished when, in 1959, Pope John XXIII convened the Second Vatican Council, which no one had expected. Some were even more surprised by the dramatic changes the council wrought. In the political realm, that meant prodding Catholics to fight for social justice while prohibiting them from restricting the religious freedom of others. The Church, which had long sought to enforce personal morality through politics, now faced constraints. At the same time, Catholics who favored campaigns for social justice now had more reason than ever to engage in

them. Campaigns for tougher obscenity laws, an area of traditional interest for the American Catholic Church, gave way to liberal priests' protests against the Vietnam War. Anti-vice campaigns were out; civil rights
were in.[2]

Many Catholics quickly concluded that birth control fell into the area
of personal morality, making it off-limits politically. For decades, Catholic
bishops had argued that laws restricting birth control were necessary to
protect societal morality, an argument that should have been persuasive
to people of all religious faiths, they said, and therefore appropriate even
in a religiously pluralistic society. Catholic bishops changed their minds
about this immediately after Vatican II. In March 1965, Cardinal Richard
Cushing of Boston, who had established a reputation as a zealous crusader
against birth control, made an abrupt volte-face. "Catholics do not need
the support of civil law to be faithful to their religious convictions, and
they do not seek to impose by law their moral views on other members
of society," he declared. "It does not seem reasonable to me," he added,
"to forbid in civil law a practice that can be considered a matter of private
morality."[3]

The Supreme Court's ruling in *Griswold* three months later declared
anti-birth control laws unconstitutional, thereby rendering the Church's
position moot. Only a few weeks before the Court announced its decision
in *Griswold*, New York bishops had succeeded in getting a state legislative committee to kill a bill that would have legalized contraceptives. But
immediately after *Griswold*, legislators capitalized on the ruling to reintroduce the bill, and this time they managed to get it passed. There was
nothing the bishops could do.[4]

Catholic bishops did continue to try to prevent government funding
of birth control through foreign aid and social welfare programs, and
they also attempted to deny access to birth control for unmarried people,
a group that the *Griswold* decision did not cover. But even these modest
efforts usually failed, because Catholic bishops who opposed contraception faced an even more formidable obstacle than a Supreme Court decision: a massive shift in public opinion.

New polling data from the mid-1960s showed that the bishops had
been unable to hold the line on birth control even among their own
parishioners. A January 1965 Gallup survey showed that 78 percent of
American Catholics supported making birth control information available to anyone who requested it—an increase from only 53 percent two
years earlier. Many Catholics began using birth control themselves;

indeed, a survey conducted in 1965 revealed that 53 percent of Catholic wives in their late teens or twenties were using a form of contraception forbidden by the Church. While some Catholic couples had violated Church teaching on this doctrine for decades, they had done so quietly. Now many Catholics felt free to publicly voice their dissent from official Church teaching. And many priests decided that they were unwilling to stop them.[5]

Prior to Vatican II, nearly all American bishops—and indeed most of the Catholic laity—had viewed Catholic doctrine as unchanging, but in the wake of Vatican II, it became clear that the Church had modified its official position on important moral and religious questions. It seemed logical that the Church's proscription against birth control—the issue on which there was the greatest lay dissent in the Church—would be next. For those who no longer viewed prohibitions on birth control as an unchanging moral law, the newly available birth control pill, which millions of women began taking after the Food and Drug Administration approved it for public distribution in 1960, was a difficult temptation to resist. Many justified their noncompliance with Church teaching by claiming that they were only slightly ahead of the Church on the issue; indeed, 61 percent of Catholics in 1965 said that they expected the Church to change its stance on birth control in the near future. Some priests even began advising women in their parishes to go on the pill. Cushing himself now refused to say that birth control was a mortal sin.[6]

In 1964, when Pope Paul VI appointed a commission to study the issue of birth control in preparation for a possible papal pronouncement, it encouraged further speculation, which turned into open revolt. In the spring of 1967, the commission's findings, which were supposed to remain secret, were leaked to the American Catholic press. A majority of the commission's members had recommended that the Church allow the use of previously forbidden contraceptives.[7] What had seemed unthinkable only five years before now seemed all but guaranteed.

But in 1968, Pope Paul VI disregarded his commission's recommendations and issued the encyclical *Humanae Vitae*, which reiterated the strong condemnation of artificial methods of contraception. Yet conservatives in the Church who thought that the pope's pronouncement would reverse the damage that their cause had suffered were mistaken. A majority of Catholic couples of childbearing age continued to defy Church doctrine; in fact, more Catholics used forbidden methods of contraception after *Humanae Vitae* than had before.[8]

The beleaguered minority who tried to defend the Church's traditional teaching faced nearly insurmountable obstacles. Liberal Protestants who had long believed that birth control was acceptable began to champion it as a positive good and in many cases even a moral imperative. At the same time, evangelicals, who had been wary of contraception, began giving it their strong approval.[9]

The convenience of the pill, along with concerns about global over-population, led some Americans to become increasingly supportive of birth control. In 1965, President Lyndon Johnson called for, and Congress approved, funding for family planning as part of foreign aid. The administration also made efforts to curb the birth rate in the United States. In 1966, the secretary of Health, Education, and Welfare removed his department's restrictions on the offering of birth control pills and other contraceptive devices to unmarried women. Even devout Catholic Sargent Shriver, head of the Office of Economic Opportunity, championed his agency's sponsorship of birth control programs to combat poverty.[10]

The National Catholic Welfare Conference lobbied against these policy changes—saying that it was "a cruel thing to offer the poor as a remedy for their poverty what Theodore Roosevelt called 'race suicide'"—but the bishops' words fell on deaf ears. As the federal government championed "family planning" to alleviate social problems, millions of women turned to the pill, and young people in particular supported access to contraception. Catholic teaching on birth control now seemed to many Americans anachronistic, repressive, and harmful.[11]

Just as many Catholics had feared, public acceptance of contraception was quickly followed by an increasing acceptance of abortion. Only a year after *Griswold*, abortion law reformers capitalized on the public's support for birth control to argue that foolproof family planning required not only the availability of contraception, but the legalization of abortion to cover situations the pill could never address. "It is time we recognize that abortion is an integral part of birth control," abortion rights advocate Lawrence Lader argued in 1966. "In those cases of contraceptive failure or misuse, or in any case where pregnancy occurs against the will of the woman, I hold that abortion must be available as the 'backup' solution." This became a common refrain in the abortion rights movement. "Every contraception method, no matter how faithfully practiced, has an inherent failure rate," Joan Lamb Ullyot told the California State Assembly in 1970. "Compulsory pregnancy" was a "bizarre punishment for mechanical failure"; abortion was a humane and just way to give a woman "control over her own reproductive function."[12]

Having lost the birth control fight, and with it much of its credibility on sexual issues, the Catholic Church was unprepared to confront these arguments. Catholics had always coupled their arguments against abortion with arguments against contraception. Now legalization proponents such as Lader argued that if Catholics were willing to keep their opposition to birth control in the private realm, they should follow suit on abortion. He found that at least some Catholics were receptive to the idea. A National Opinion Research survey conducted in the spring of 1966 revealed that 64 percent of Catholic men and 58 percent of Catholic women supported legalizing abortion in cases where it was necessary to protect a woman's health. A similar survey conducted a few months earlier showed that 47 percent of Catholics said that abortion was acceptable in cases of rape, and 48 percent believed it was acceptable when a fetus was deformed. Abortion liberalization proponents were encouraged. "All studies we have show Catholics as much interested in moderate reform as any other faith," Lader declared.[13]

These poll results severely weakened the Church's lobbying influence. The bishops, it seemed clear, did not wield nearly as much influence over the faithful as they claimed. If they could not mobilize their own parishioners, bishops would have little sway over state legislators.

Despite the odds against them, theologically conservative Catholics resolved to continue their campaigns against both federal funding of birth control and abortion law liberalization. "I believe that the fight on the abortion and government birth control fronts can be won if there is the spine for it, the perceptiveness and the homework," William Ball, general counsel for the Pennsylvania Catholic Conference, told his friend Msgr. Paul Harrington in March 1966.[14] But they needed a way to counter their opponents' public relations advantage. A massive societal shift had given the abortion law liberalization movement a strength that had seemed unimaginable only two years earlier.

## *The Sudden Ascendancy of the Abortion Law Liberalization Movement*

New concerns about civil rights, poverty, and social justice made some liberal-minded Americans more sympathetic to the cause of abortion law reform than they had been previously. The arguments that no woman

should be forced to continue a pregnancy that endangered her health
or that had resulted from rape or incest, and that no woman should be
required to give birth to a severely deformed infant became increasingly
appealing in an era marked by increased stress on both social planning
and individual rights. At a time when the Johnson administration was
fighting a "war on poverty," the argument that legal abortion could be a
weapon in that war gained increasing currency. And as American liberals embraced the campaign for African Americans' civil rights, proponents of abortion law reform argued that their cause was a racial justice
issue. Between 1953 and 1962, African Americans in New York City were
nine times more likely than whites to die from illegal abortions. "The
white woman has the sophistication and the means to buy a safe abortion,
while the colored woman must abort herself or be aborted by some unsafe
para-medical abortionist," Alan Guttmacher wrote. "I deplore this class
privilege for survival," he told audiences.[15]

The news media sympathized with these arguments and, after Sherri
Chessen Finkbine's abortion, liberalization began to receive more favorable coverage. The *New York Times* had published fewer than ten articles
per year on abortion between 1950 and 1961, and most of those articles
were on the prosecution of abortion rings or the legalization of abortion
in the communist nations of Eastern Europe. But in 1962, the newspaper
published more than thirty articles on the subject, and their focus was
different. Instead of articles about criminally run abortion rings, there
were ministers and rabbis calling for reform of the abortion laws—and
editorials supporting their position.[16]

The *Times* was not alone. Throughout the 1960s, women's magazines
such as *Redbook* and general interest periodicals such as *Reader's Digest*
and *Look* reiterated the message that the nation's abortion laws were outdated. Television programs such as CBS's "Abortion and the Law" (1965)
gave abortion reformers a sympathetic hearing and presented a consistent
argument on behalf of abortion reform—namely, that existing abortion
laws, which were relics of the Victorian era, were inhumane because they
forced hundreds of thousands of women each year to seek out dangerous
illegal abortions. Women whose pregnancies carried a high risk of fetal
deformities should not be forced to bring "monsters" into the world, nor
should a rape victim or a teenage victim of incest be required to bear her
attacker's child.[17]

Americans who watched "Abortion and the Law" listened as Walter
Cronkite—the "most trusted man in America"—told viewers that "as

long as the abortion laws remain unchanged, abortion will continue to be a critical problem, and for those involved, may call for desperate decisions that may result in dangerous complications." "Eighty percent of the women who have abortions are married," he reminded viewers, citing a statistic that was probably not accurate, but that effectively framed abortion as a respectable, middle-class issue rather than the desperate refuge of the promiscuous. Every year, Cronkite reported, 5,000 women died from abortions. This statistic was now thirty years out of date—because of antibiotics, the number of maternal deaths due to abortion had fallen to less than 300 per year by 1965—but Cronkite was simply repeating the arguments that advocates of abortion law reform had been making since the 1930s.[18] Proposals that had seemed radical then had now become mainstream.

While a few doctors had been calling for liberalization since the 1930s, most had refrained from doing so, even if some who were silent on the issue were quietly performing abortions on the side. Now, beginning in the mid-1960s, large numbers of doctors began proclaiming that, in the interest of their patients' health, abortions should be allowed at doctors' discretion. According to a survey taken in 1965, a majority of final-year medical students supported abortion law liberalization. That same year, a *Medical Tribune* poll of 1,300 doctors revealed that 56 percent wanted to permit abortion for "justifiable medical, social or economic reasons." In some subfields of medicine, support for the liberalization of state abortion laws was even higher. A 1965 survey of 2,285 gynecologists in New York showed that 87 percent favored an abortion reform bill along the lines that ALI had proposed, and 80 percent of the nation's psychiatrists supported liberalization. While the American Medical Association (AMA) was still officially opposed to abortion, several state medical societies, including those in California and New York, supported liberalized abortion statutes.[19]

These doctors argued that in an era of modern medicine, existing abortion law, which had been enacted in the nineteenth century, was an "utterly unworkable legal anachronism."[20] Thanks to modern medicine, hospital abortions were now safer than ever, and the one legally permissible cause for an abortion—a pregnancy that endangered a woman's life—was now rare. Modern medicine also brought new knowledge about the genetic risks of incest and the ability to predict fetal deformities with some degree of certainty. It seemed a mistake not to allow doctors to make use of that knowledge to end pregnancies that seemed harmful to both women and society.

Liberal Protestant ministers also enlisted in the cause of abortion law reform, especially after 1965. Many were social liberals whose views of Christian ministry had been influenced by the civil rights movement. The civil rights march in Selma, Alabama, which attracted more than 400 clergy in March 1965, had been a defining event for many young ministers—both those who personally participated and the much larger number who experienced it vicariously through sympathetic articles in the *Christian Century*. Many reconceived of their ministerial calling as a prophetic one, in which they would "speak truth to power" and challenge laws they considered unjust.[21]

For a few, that included restrictive abortion laws. Protestants, they believed, had been far too quiescent on the issue. Protestant denominations and the National Council of Churches had occasionally passed resolutions in support of some forms of therapeutic abortion, and on a few occasions—such as the public discussion of the Finkbine case—some Protestant ministers had spoken out in support of liberalized abortion laws. But the younger ministers who entered the fray in 1965 and 1966 favored a more direct approach. In the course of ministry, they encountered families facing crisis pregnancies, and they thought it unconscionable that women who had gotten pregnant out of wedlock faced the choice between having their lives ruined by an "illegitimate" child and risking the dangers of an illegal abortion. They were even more upset by the statistics indicating that minority women faced a much higher rate of death from illegal abortion than their white counterparts did. Abortion laws, they decided, were biased against the poor and against women in general. Liberalizing those laws was therefore the only socially just course of action—indeed, the only Christian approach. They were ready to take on the Catholic Church, which they considered repressive, and the culture of sexual prudery, in order to usher in laws that were more humane toward women.

In 1965, James Pike, the Episcopal bishop of northern California, publicly called for the legalization of abortion in cases of rape or danger to a woman's health. Other Episcopal clergy, especially in California and New York, also supported abortion law reform, as did the Church's best-known ethicist, Episcopal Divinity School professor Joseph Fletcher. In fact, the Episcopal Church was so active in the campaign for abortion law liberalization that in March 1966, the Sunnen Foundation, a proponent of abortion rights, gave the Episcopal Diocese of California a donation of $100,000 specifically earmarked for the Church's abortion law reform efforts.[22]

Liberal ministers from other Protestant denominations also joined the campaign. In May 1967, twenty-one members of the clergy in New York formed an abortion counseling service that referred women facing crisis pregnancies to illegal abortion providers. The leader of the group was Howard Moody, the forty-six-year-old senior pastor of Judson Memorial Church, a liberal congregation that was part of the American Baptist Convention. Moody, who had worked for the civil rights movement in the South, saw himself as a crusader for justice, and thought that current abortion law was rank hypocrisy. "It's whom you know and how much money you have that makes the difference between a legal and an illegal abortion," he said. He believed he was leveling the playing field, helping poor women find competent doctors to perform the services previously available only to the well-connected rich. Moody's work caught on among liberal members of the mainline clergy. By 1969, several of the largest cities in the Northeast and on the West Coast (as well as Chicago and Detroit) had clergy abortion referral services, usually led by liberal American Baptists, Episcopalians, Methodists, or Unitarians. Moody's New York service, meanwhile, was receiving approximately 300 calls per week from women seeking help.[23]

Reform Jewish rabbis also became early leaders in the abortion law liberalization movement, a reflection of the fact that liberal Jews were far more supportive than most other Americans of abortion law reform. Judaism had always taught that personhood began at birth, they asserted. The fetus was a "nonperson, an undeveloped entity," the chair of the Conference of Presidents of Major American Jewish Organizations declared in the spring of 1967. It was therefore a "sin," some rabbis argued, to force women to carry problematic pregnancies to term. They assailed their Catholic pro-life opponents as "medieval-minded laymen and clerics" who wanted to impose their own religious beliefs on a public that did not share them.[24]

The entry of Protestant and Jewish clergy into the fight further marginalized Catholic pro-lifers and made it easier for proponents of abortion law liberalization to argue that the anti-abortion movement was an exclusively Catholic cause. With the exception of the Missouri Synod Lutherans in California, few Protestants, even from among the most theologically conservative denominations, were willing to affiliate publicly with the campaign against abortion before the late 1960s. Evangelical publications were mostly silent on the issue. *Christianity Today*, the flagship magazine of the evangelical movement, did not publish its first article on abortion until 1966. The first abortion resolution of the Southern Baptist Convention did not come until 1971.[25]

Evangelicals remained on the sidelines because they were suspicious of Catholics and because they lacked a clear theology of when human life began. Although the vast majority of evangelicals favored retaining most restrictions on abortion, many also thought that the Catholic Church's insistence that human life began at conception lacked clear biblical support. Though a previous generation of evangelicals had taken a harder line against abortion, by the late 1960s, many evangelicals had come to believe that abortion might be justified in cases of rape or medical necessity. They were unwilling to follow their liberal Protestant counterparts in campaigning for policies they thought might encourage promiscuity, but they saw no reason to oppose reforms that would allow a few women to obtain abortions for health reasons on the advice of their doctors. One could find at least a few evangelical scholars and leading pastors at all points along the spectrum, but a general consensus emerged: in favor of abortion in limited circumstances, but opposed to "abortion on demand." Twenty-five evangelical scholars gathered in August 1968 to discuss the abortion issue as members of the Protestant Symposium on Human Reproduction. The "human fetus" was either "an actual human life or at the least, a potential and developing human life," they declared, so physicians should "exercise great caution when prescribing an abortion" and should do so "only to safeguard greater values sanctioned by Scripture." Their approach echoed editorials that were appearing in evangelical magazines such as *Christian Life, Eternity,* and *Christianity Today,* which cautiously endorsed abortion legalization for a narrow range of cases: medically necessitated abortions or instances of rape or incest. This stance positioned evangelicals to the right of legalizers, but well to the left of pro-life Catholics. Hardly any evangelical Protestants joined Catholics in lobbying against the abortion law reform efforts of the late 1960s.[26]

A few Orthodox Jewish rabbis spoke out against abortion around this time, but their opinions, which were markedly different from those held by most other Jews, were marginal to the debate. Eastern Orthodox churches, guided by the ancient Christian tradition against abortion, also occasionally protested against the liberalization of abortion laws, but like Orthodox Jews, they lacked political influence.[27]

Catholics therefore stood almost alone. When they testified against abortion liberalization bills, they had to face off against members of the clergy who were prepared to argue—as Kinsolving often did—that the Catholic Church was out of step with the views of most American Christians. "With a growing body of public opinion in favor of revising the present abortion law ... this apparently minority position of Roman Catholics may eventually become private practice rather than public law—in the manner of Jehovah's Witnesses, regarding blood transfusions, Orthodox Judaism regarding pork or Christian Science regarding the medical profession," Kinsolving declared in 1966.[28]

He had reason to be optimistic. A Gallup poll taken in January 1966 showed that the majority of Americans supported an ALI-style abortion reform law: 77 percent believed that abortion should be legal when the "health of the mother is in danger" and 54 percent supported legalizing it in cases where "the child may be born deformed." Many Catholics were dismayed. Some blamed the media. "It is alarming how the American public is being barraged with propaganda from the mass media in support of more and more legalized abortions," A. J. Willinger, the bishop of Monterey-Fresno, California, lamented in early 1967, implicating "almost all the women's magazines, news publications, and some television shows."[29] It was certainly true that Catholic natural law arguments against abortion received little hearing (or sympathy) in the nation's major news outlets, let alone in mass-circulation women's magazines. Catholic priests and church periodicals continued to circulate the pro-life message, but these arguments rarely reached beyond the Catholic "ghetto."

Some Catholics began to realize that they probably would not be able to stave off the forces of liberalization much longer. "If three-quarters of the American people seriously want broader grounds for abortion written into the law, their wishes will eventually prevail," *America* magazine glumly predicted in February 1966.[30] They had a moral duty to continue the fight, they felt, but they expected to lose.

## *The Anti-Abortion Response to the Abortion Liberalization Movement*

In spite of the odds that Catholics now faced, most refused to acquiesce to public opinion as they had on birth control. They were firmly convinced that abortion, unlike contraception, destroyed a living baby. Indeed, they believed that they now had photographic proof.

Before 1965, most Americans had never seen a photograph of a fetus. But in April of that year, *Life* magazine published Lennart Nilsson's series of color photographs of embryonic and fetal life from conception to birth—the first such photographs ever taken. The pictures created a sensation; eight million copies of the magazine were sold within four days of its release. Opponents of abortion were delighted to have clear photographic evidence that even an eight-week-old fetus had fully developed eyes, fingers, and toes. For most people, Nilsson's photographs were far more persuasive than arguments from natural law. To abortion opponents, they proved that the abortion of even a first-trimester fetus destroyed a baby, not merely a lump of tissue or a "cellular growth." The arguments of abortion liberalization advocates therefore missed the point; the question was not whether hospital abortions were safe or socially advantageous, but whether abortion constituted the taking of a human life. Photographic evidence, they thought, now proved beyond a shadow of a doubt that it did. As one Wisconsin woman told her state legislator, "These pictures tell it like it really is—once you see them, you realize that a fetus is far from being a 'blob.'"[31]

The photographs also confirmed abortion opponents' belief that they were fighting for something even more important than the lives of unborn children. If the fetus was fully human—a proposition that they now thought no rational person could deny—then legalized abortion was the state-sanctioned destruction of innocent human life. In their view, what made abortion liberalization efforts so frightening was that, for the first time, a majority of Americans wanted to legitimize the killing of particular classes of people solely because they inconvenienced those who had the power to determine their fate. Once the nation accepted that principle, everyone would soon be subject to the whim of the majority or the will of the politicians in power. Moral law—based on Christianity, natural law, and the "inalienable right to life" promised by the Declaration of Independence—was the only protection citizens had against the tyranny of the state. "Once a state grants the right to murder the unborn, it is only a short step to the position where the state could order the killing of the unborn and a shorter step to commanding the death of living defectives, then healthy individuals," Msgr. Paul Harrington declared in 1965.[32] The campaign against abortion was thus an effort to preserve the lives and constitutional rights of defenseless minorities.

Harrington feared that most Catholics greatly underestimated the threat of the abortion liberalization movement, and he intended to rouse them to action. As the medico-moral counsel to the National Federation of Catholic Physicians' Guilds, he was well positioned to do it. The Federation had, since the 1930s, periodically passed resolutions against abortion, but Harrington wanted it to launch a more systematic campaign. That fall, he began a twelve-article series on abortion in the Federation's journal, the *Linacre Quarterly*. His central argument was that liberalized abortion laws were merely the first step in a systematic campaign for "abortion on demand," and that Catholics had a moral duty to oppose this effort with all their might. He insisted that Cardinal Cushing's statement that the Church should not impose its religious teachings on others through public law applied only to birth control, not abortion. He wrote letters to all the influential lay Catholics he could find who shared his views, carrying on a lengthy correspondence with doctors, lawyers, and law professors. In each case, he encouraged them to write articles in their professional journals alerting their colleagues to the dangers of liberalized abortion laws.[33]

In December 1965, Catholics squared off against Mary Calderone, a Planned Parenthood director who had become nationally known as an advocate of sex education, in a fight in the American Medical Association. The AMA's Committee on Human Reproduction had called for the legalization of abortion in cases of rape or incest or when a woman's health was in danger. Now, the AMA as a whole took up the resolution. Calderone cited women's emotional well-being as justification for the liberalization of abortion laws; unless women were granted abortions for reasons of "mental health," she argued, both the woman and her child would suffer severely. "A woman should not have to go through with having a baby she will shudder to see," Calderone declared.[34]

Catholic physicians seized on this issue and turned the tables. Psychiatrists generally opposed the idea of encouraging abortion for mental health reasons. Abortion, they believed, often worsened the conditions of women who suffered from depression or other mental health ailments. They sometimes experienced greater emotional distress than women who chose to bring an unwanted pregnancy to term. "One thing is certain, it is quite likely that there always will be some disagreement among psychiatrists about the psychiatric indications for abortion, and reform in the existing law will not ameliorate this," Catholic psychiatrist Frank Ayd Jr. declared, in a typical example of the Catholic case against "psychiatric" abortions. "Equally certain is the fear of the majority of psychiatrists that any liberalization of abortion legislation will lead to more abuses, as experience in countries like Japan has verified." In fact, Ayd predicted, allowing abortion for psychiatric reasons would, in essence, allow "abortion on demand," which few Americans wanted.

By forging an alliance with members of the psychiatric profession, Catholics won a rare victory, preventing an AMA endorsement of abortion law liberalization.[35]

But Harrington worried that this was not sufficient. He was discouraged by the low turnout at the educational forums he organized. His fellow Catholics showed little interest in the issue, and there was little sign of a Protestant awakening on the subject; most of the outspoken Protestant ministers were joining the opposing camp. The Catholic Church, Harrington believed, possessed the moral clarity that could save America from abortion legalization and moral anarchy, yet the bishops seemed afraid to speak up.[36]

In the early 1960s, several bishops had taken a leading role in the fight against the earliest abortion law reform proposals, but in 1965 and 1966, they were mostly silent. Perhaps they were too busy implementing the changes of Vatican II in their dioceses, certainly a formidable task. Perhaps they were still reeling from the Church's defeat on contraception. Perhaps they were worried about their waning political influence and were mindful of the potential dangers of opposing a cause that approximately three out of four Americans supported. Perhaps, in the midst of clerical division over the Vietnam War, taking on another controversial cause seemed too risky. Regardless of the reason, the National Catholic Welfare Conference (NCWC), the bishops' official lobbying organization on social and political issues, sat by as the abortion liberalization movement gained momentum, and in the absence of national leadership, few bishops or priests treated abortion as an urgent matter. "Unfortunately, the past history indicates that the Church usually stepped into these 'revolutions' only at the last moment—when the signs of death were already evident—and thus, did not have an influential position," Harrington lamented in March 1966. "I felt that in this battle the Church should be in the foreground."[37]

## *Losing the Battle in California*

The exception to this came in California, where Catholics were engaged in an unprecedented all-out effort to stop abortion law liberalization. The California bishops were better organized than their counterparts in most other states because they had been fighting abortion law reform attempts since 1962, years before most other bishops had taken notice of the issue. They also had considerable political influence. Nearly one-third of Californians were Catholic, making many state legislators reluctant to defy the Church. In June 1965, a campaign by the state's bishops had succeeded in derailing Anthony Beilenson's abortion bill at the eleventh hour. But it was a hollow victory, because several physicians in the state had already announced their intention to offer abortions in cases of suspected fetal deformity, regardless of state law.

The immediate cause of the controversy was a national outbreak of rubella (or German measles, as it was called at the time), a disease known to cause birth defects. A June 1965 *Life* cover story predicted that 20,000 women would give birth to deformed infants as a result of the rubella epidemic. Many pregnant women who had the disease panicked and demanded an immediate termination to their pregnancies. Several California hospitals began offering illegal abortions to women with rubella.[38]

Catholic physicians decided to put a stop to this practice. In early 1965, Richard Hayden, a forty-five-year-old Fordham University graduate and devout Catholic ob-gyn at Palm Harbor General Hospital in Garden Grove, California, reported several of his hospital colleagues to the district attorney's office. The doctors' willingness to flaunt the state's abortion law bothered the pious Hayden, who had put his faith into practice by abstaining from the use of birth control and fathering eleven children, and who made it a point to attend daily Mass in spite of his busy schedule. He was opposed to all abortion, he said, even when it met the strict guidelines of California law, but he was especially disturbed by the willingness of some doctors to violate the law by terminating pregnancies that did not even endanger a woman's health—let alone her life—merely because they suspected the possibility of fetal deformities.[39]

Rather than capitulate to Hayden's pressure, the Palm Harbor General Hospital administrator welcomed the threatened prosecutions as a test case for California's abortion law, which he believed was "antiquated." Doctors who performed abortions at Palm Harbor General were "willing to go to jail" if necessary, he said, because they believed that the state's abortion law was "not right."[40] The doctors at Palm Harbor General were not alone in taking this approach; throughout the state, numerous doctors performed abortions for women with rubella because they believed that such abortions, though illegal, were medically justifiable.

Many California Catholics were outraged at the physicians' act of civil disobedience. "These doctors can openly admit that they are violating the law and no one apparently is dismayed," an editorial in San Francisco's archdiocesan newspaper *The Monitor* lamented in May 1965. But abortion opponents were unable to stop the wave of public support for the doctors. *Life* magazine heralded the doctors' actions.[41]

This was too much for James McNulty, a Catholic obstetrician who had previously testified against Beilenson's bill. When district attorneys refused to prosecute doctors who performed illegal therapeutic abortions, McNulty decided to use his position as a member (and former president) of the California State Board of Medical Examiners to put a stop to the open evasion of California's abortion law. He brought the issue of illegal hospital abortions to the Board's attention, and then, as chair of its newly formed committee on therapeutic abortion, he presided over the investigation of more than forty physicians who were accused of performing illegal abortions for rubella patients, and pushed the Board to revoke their medical licenses. Several of the physicians readily admitted to performing illegal abortions, but they defended their actions as medically necessary and socially useful, since they prevented the births of deformed babies who would likely have become "public institutional charges."[42]

McNulty had heard this line of reasoning before, and as someone who had testified against abortion liberalization bills, he was well aware of the usual counter-arguments—namely, that the doctors' view of deformed infants as potential burdens on society reflected a tragic disregard for human life. Catholics had won their fight to prevent therapeutic abortion legalization in California. Now, at McNulty's direction, the State Board of Medical Examiners would try to prevent it in practice. In May 1966, the Board charged two physicians with performing illegal abortions and announced that it would revoke their licenses. The next month, it brought charges against seven other prominent, well-respected members of the profession.[43]

The move backfired. Several doctors expressed dismay that the Board had penalized some of the state's leading medical practitioners. California hospitals had been offering therapeutic abortions for years, they pointed out, and district attorneys had shown no interest in prosecuting the physicians who performed them. In the view of many physicians, the state's Board of Medical Examiners had acted unconscionably, and they were determined to mount a counteroffensive. Lester Kinsolving joined several doctors and prominent citizens in forming the California Committee on Therapeutic Abortions to defend the doctors. The new committee then set about trying to liberalize the state's abortion law. Their prospects of success now seemed better than they had ever been because, as Alan

Guttmacher predicted, the actions of the Board of Medical Examiners would likely "force liberalization of the laws since . . . the non-Catholic communities would rise up in horror."[44] Within a year, Guttmacher's predictions were fulfilled.

A July 1966 poll of California voters revealed a pattern of support for abortion liberalization that closely accorded with national sentiment. Fifty-six percent of Californians supported a moderately liberalized law, 9 percent wanted "unrestricted abortion," and only 25 percent favored retaining the state's restrictive law. Even a majority of Catholics supported abortion law reform: 46 percent favored abortion liberalization, and another 5 percent wanted "unrestricted abortion."[45] This survey gave the abortion liberalization movement the statistical proof it needed to press for reform. For years, politicians representing Catholic districts had been afraid to vote for abortion liberalization measures, but the survey data emboldened some of them. Catholics were almost as liberal on abortion as the general populace, they now realized; the clergy did not speak for them. And if the clergy could not deliver votes, their political sway over legislators would be sharply limited. With the release of the California poll in the summer of 1966, the Catholic lobbying campaign against abortion law reform may have lost its most potent weapon.

The time seemed right for Anthony Beilenson, who had just moved from the state assembly to the senate, to reintroduce his bill. This time, Beilenson came prepared with a coalition of allies across the political spectrum. Although he represented the liberal wing of his party, he found cosponsors of his bill among centrist Democrats, liberal Republicans, and even the conservative wing of the GOP.[46]

Catholic clergy in California knew that the battle against Beilenson's measure would be difficult, so they began preparing for it months before the 1967 legislative session began. In January 1966, Msgr. James Flynn, the director of Catholic Charities for the Archdiocese of San Francisco, wrote to his archbishop recommending a year-long, comprehensive, statewide educational program, directed on the diocesan level, to mobilize California Catholics against Beilenson's bill. If public opinion polls showed that half of the state's Catholics favored abortion law reform, that was not a reason for capitulation; it was a call to arms.[47]

The bishops took Flynn's advice, but decided to make the campaign national. In June 1966, Sacramento bishop Alden Bell wrote to the general secretary of the NCWC, urging the organization to issue an official statement on abortion law liberalization. The matter was urgent, he insisted, because some Catholics were not even aware of the Church's position. Perhaps even worse, some politicians were not either. If the national leadership of the Church did not issue an official statement, some bishops worried, state politicians would have no incentive *not* to capitulate to public demand.[48]

Until that time, the NCWC had paid little attention to abortion. In February 1966, it had taken its first tentative steps on the abortion issue by publishing a booklet on abortion policy and compiling a short bibliography for those who wanted to read more detailed arguments defending the humanity of the fetus. But few Catholics bothered to look at the materials. By the end of the summer, only 300 people had written to the NCWC to request an abortion information packet. Bell's letter prompted the NCWC to take action. The crisis in California was likely to be repeated in other states. It was therefore time to make abortion a national issue.[49]

After receiving Bell's letter, the NCWC mailed a questionnaire to bishops and theologians throughout the nation asking how the Church should address the abortion issue. The results of the survey surprised the NCWC. They had believed that only five state legislatures were currently considering proposals to liberalize their abortion laws, but the survey revealed that eight states had done so in the recent past, and thirteen were currently doing so. But there was also far more interest in opposing abortion than they had expected. An overwhelming number of the respondents wanted the NCWC to design an educational program on abortion that they could use in their dioceses. Many also suggested that the Church should ally with Protestants and other non-Catholics to form an ecumenical movement to defend the lives of the unborn, an idea the questionnaire had not mentioned, but that many respondents offered in response to the open-ended question, "What action do you think should be taken now?" They recognized that when the Church stood alone on a political issue, it almost never succeeded. They desperately wanted to win this time. As one bishop wrote, "I hope we can do better on it than we did on birth control."[50]

With newly released polls showing that approximately half of Catholics were opposed to the Church's position on abortion, the bishops realized that their lobbying campaign had to begin among their own parishioners. What was needed, many bishops believed, was a comprehensive educational campaign to convert their Church's laity into strong believers in the cause. California bishops launched such a campaign in the fall of 1966. The next April, the National Conference of Catholic Bishops, the successor organization to the NCWC, voted to spend $50,000 to launch a similar campaign on a national scale in order to promote "the dignity of the human person and the sanctity of human life as it applies to abortion."[51]

Even as the bishops campaigned throughout the country, they knew that California remained the most important battleground. Throughout the summer, Los Angeles archdiocesan attorneys Walter Trinkaus and J. J. Brandlin used their legal expertise to speak out against abortion liberalization. The Catholic Physicians' Guilds of California refined their arguments against abortion reform and encouraged the state's bishops to launch a comprehensive educational program in defense of fetal life. Still, the mood was grim. At a private meeting in September 1966, the bishops admitted that they would probably be unable to prevent a liberalization of their state's abortion law. The best they could realistically hope to do would be to secure amendments that might limit Beilenson's bill. They resolved to continue their campaign of outright opposition, but they were doubtful about their chances of success.[52]

Despite these fears, the California bishops engaged in an unprecedented level of activism to stop abortion liberalization. On December 8, 1966, they issued a collective pastoral letter entitled "Thou Shalt Not Kill." It grounded its arguments in the notion that the fetus was a human being entitled to the right to life and that abortion was therefore "murder."[53]

The letter attracted headlines, because a collective statement from all of the state's bishops was a rare event. But another event that occurred the same day had even greater significance for the campaign against abortion, even though the media did not cover it. On the evening of December 8, only a few hours after the pastoral letter was issued, Cardinal James McIntyre convened a meeting of the Right to Life League, the first organization in the state devoted to stopping the legalization of abortion.

McIntyre realized that, with liberalization activists labeling the right-to-life campaign a sectarian Catholic cause, it was vitally important to create a lobbying organization that was completely outside the control of the bishops. If he and his colleagues were the only ones speaking out against abortion, the cause was doomed. A lay-organized group might even attract a few Protestants to the cause.

By calling the new organization the Right to Life League, McIntyre and his associates gave the movement a label that would last for decades. "Right to Life" was an appropriate phrase because, from the very beginning, Catholics had defined their cause as protecting the "sanctity of human life."[54] Beginning in the early 1960s, when they began making constitutional arguments against abortion, Catholics had spoken of the fetus's right to life, invoking the Declaration of Independence.[55] But until 1966, they had never used the phrase as a formal name for their movement. In fact, prior to 1966, they had not viewed themselves as part of a movement at all. Now their cause had a name. Activists across the country quickly began identifying as part of the right-to-life movement and calling themselves right-to-life activists—a phrase that by 1970 was commonly shortened to "pro-life." By calling themselves "right-to-life" or "pro-life" rather than "anti-abortion," they signaled that their cause was about more than merely stopping an objectionable medical procedure.

Those whom McIntyre initially recruited to the Right to Life League were mainly trusted associates. The organization's first chair, J. J. Brandlin, was one of the attorneys for the archdiocese and a law partner of Walter Trinkaus, as well as a five-year veteran of the campaign against the proposed liberalization of California's abortion law. The vice-chair was Elizabeth Goodwin, a forty-four-year-old active church member who was president of the Los Angeles Archdiocesan Council of Catholic Women, mother of eight children, and wife of a physician who had already established himself as an outspoken opponent of abortion. The League's board of directors read like a "who's who" of the Catholic Church's five-year-long campaign against abortion in the state. Trinkaus was a founding member, as were several other lawyers and doctors who had already mobilized for the cause. For a group whose stated intention was to present a non-Catholic face of the right-to-life movement, the organization was remarkably Catholic. And for anyone who had been following the legislative hearings on abortion, the faces of its early board members would have seemed very familiar.[56]

Within days of the League's formation, McIntyre took steps to make it more religiously diverse—and thus more credible. He sent letters to his fellow bishops throughout the state, asking them to instruct the priests in their dioceses to recruit members for the League and start new chapters—making a special effort to recruit Protestants and Jews, particularly clergy. In an effort to broaden the League's appeal and increase its political influence, McIntyre put the organization under the administration of a full-time coordinator from the public relations firm Spencer Roberts, which had managed Governor Ronald Reagan's successful campaign only a few months earlier. McIntyre hoped that hiring a coordinator from this prestigious public relations agency would give the League the direction it needed to maximize its influence in the legislature. Spencer Roberts concurred with the bishops' assessment: to succeed, the public face of the League would have to be non-Catholic.[57]

Early in 1967, McIntyre found some of the non-Catholic leaders that he had been seeking. Two Episcopal priests who dissented from their denomination's support of abortion rights became directors of League chapters in Santa Barbara and Ventura Counties, and the Protestant megachurch pastor Robert Schuller—whose drive-in church in Orange Grove was already making him a national sensation—helped lead the League's Orange County chapter. The League's biggest coup came when John Fishburn, a Protestant who had recently retired as a Bank of America vice president and was a prominent figure in Los Angeles area financial circles, agreed to join J. J. Brandlin as co-chair.[58]

The northern California Right to Life League, a sister organization that started in the Bay Area four months after the Los Angeles-based League began meeting, was even more ecumenical. Led by the Missouri Synod Lutheran minister Arnim Polster, the northern California League did not initially include a single Catholic on its board. Instead, Polster recruited local non-Catholic educators and professionals, such as a Greek Orthodox psychiatrist and a Methodist biology professor, facts the group highlighted in order to convince state legislators that theirs was not merely a Catholic cause. Nevertheless, the northern California League cooperated very closely with Catholic right-to-life activists and the Church hierarchy, and when Polster and the other officers held public press conferences, they sometimes brought local Catholic allies, such as Berkeley law professor John Noonan, with them. Much like their southern California counterparts, the northern California League hired a San Francisco public relations firm that had managed several conservative Republican campaigns and that had close ties to Ronald Reagan's campaign—a useful contact, the League believed, if the Beilenson bill were to end up on the governor's desk.[59]

McIntyre believed that the League's most immediate priority should be a letter-writing campaign. Forty percent of the state's voters lived in the Los Angeles archdiocese, he reminded the League, so if right-to-lifers from the LA area urged their representatives to oppose the Beilenson bill, it would have an impact. McIntyre sent letters to priests under his direction, urging them to have their parishioners write letters to their state representatives. Other bishops in the state did the same. The bishop of Oakland took the unusual step of mailing his pastoral letter opposing the Beilenson bill to each of the 80,000 Catholics in his diocese, instead of merely having it read at Mass. The coordinator for the Right to Life League issued an urgent plea to flood the state capital with missives against the Beilenson bill. "Remember—human lives are at stake!" he wrote. "If you haven't written your letters, please do so today."[60]

The result was the greatest deluge of mail state legislators had ever seen. The state senate usually received 5,000 letters a day when it was in session, but for several weeks preceding the vote on the Beilenson bill, the volume of mail reached a record 15,000 to 20,000 letters per day. The state assembly received more than double its usual volume. One legislator reported that on one day, he personally received 2,000 letters—all but five of which were expressions of opposition to the Beilenson bill.[61]

The Right to Life League and the bishops encouraged parishioners to express their opposition to abortion in their own words, so legislators received many handwritten missives that occasionally included personal details designed to make the message more persuasive. The vast majority were written by women. Mothers discussed their own love of children. Nurses made a biological case for respecting fetal life. Young, unmarried women expressed their desire to eventually have a family and expressed horror that any woman would choose to kill her unborn child. Most of the letters made the argument that the Right to Life League had chosen as its signature message: abortion was the murder of an unborn baby. If California liberalized its abortion law, it would be legalizing murder, and the lives of the elderly and disabled would also be in jeopardy. They also stressed the importance of maintaining the nation's Christian values. Several identified themselves as Catholics, though nearly all insisted that theirs was a nonsectarian cause based on universal moral values. They expressed astonishment that someone of any faith would want to legalize abortion, because they viewed the move as an assault on the nation's foundational principles. "A human life, even if not yet born and able to live on its own, has a natural right to life," one of these women, Adele Vezeau, declared in her letter to Beilenson. "This country was founded to preserve our rights and freedom. No one has the right to act as judge and take an unborn life."[62]

Beilenson dismissed the record number of letters in opposition to his bill as the product of the Catholic Church's propaganda machine. "The great majority of women in this state support a slight modification of our existing laws such as is included in our bill, and I think that in these situations of great potential tragedy these women and their families should have some choice in the matter," Beilenson's standard response to these letters read. Public opinion polls still showed that he had overwhelming public support, regardless of what the letters said. When 450 California doctors signed a petition opposing the bill, advocates of abortion law liberalization pointed out that this number comprised only a small fraction of the 22,000 members of the California Medical Association, which had endorsed it.[63] No matter what the California right-to-life activists did, they could not overcome the public perception that they were merely a minority, and a Catholic minority at that.

What's more, the League's testimony against the bill was not effective. Although dozens of League members made the 400-mile journey from Los Angeles to Sacramento, few were given the opportunity to speak, and those who did take the floor did little more than repeat an argument that most state legislators were tired of hearing—namely, that the fetus was a human being with the right to life, and that it would be an abrogation of justice to legalize murder of the unborn. Cardinal McIntyre delivered a stinging message to the legislature, comparing politicians who supported the Beilenson bill to King Herod who ordered the slaughter of the "Holy Innocents" in Bethlehem. This comparison was so common in Catholic newspapers and homilies that it had almost become a cliché, and it served more to polarize than to win converts; though such rhetoric mobilized the Catholic faithful, it seemed strange and offensive to some Protestants and Jews.[64]

As the Church's efforts brought more attention to the right-to-life cause, California's newly elected governor, Ronald Reagan, tried to find a middle course that would allow him to come out in favor of moderate abortion reform without alienating too many conservative Catholics. Reagan, like many other Protestants, personally favored a few small-scale reforms in existing abortion law. Invoking the principle of self-defense, he argued that a woman had the right to terminate a pregnancy that endangered her physical or mental health, and he thought that no woman who became pregnant as a result of rape should be required to carry her pregnancy to term. Like many other Protestants at the time, he favored retaining most other restrictions on abortion.[65] In essence, his own views on abortion differed little from those of the vast majority (75 percent) of Americans.

Yet Reagan was not enthusiastic about Beilenson's bill, because he knew that it would be controversial among some of his socially conservative Catholic supporters, and because he had little interest in abortion law reform. The issue had not come up in his 1966 campaign. When first asked about the measure a few months into his first gubernatorial term, Reagan refused to take a public position. After repeated questioning about whether he would sign the bill, Reagan said that he recognized the need for legal abortion to cover extreme situations—particularly in the case of rape and incest, but also when a woman's health was in danger—but he had serious reservations about Beilenson's willingness to permit abortion in the case of fetal deformities. "The taking of the unborn life simply on the basis that it is going to be a somewhat less than perfect being," he said, was "no different than what Hitler tried to do." This argument was one that Catholic opponents of abortion had made for years, though Reagan insisted that in forming his opinion, he had not spoken to any representatives of the Catholic Church or the public relations firm managing the Right to Life League.[66]

Despite Reagan's reservations, when a journalist pressed him on the issue, he promised to sign a modified version of Beilenson's bill that eliminated the clause allowing abortion in cases of fetal deformity and that lowered the upper age limit for abortion in cases of statutory rape from sixteen to fourteen, a measure Reagan thought was needed to prevent sixteen-year-olds from obtaining easy abortions after premarital sexual activity. This was all the information that Beilenson needed. He made the modifications that Reagan had stipulated and prepared to send him the bill.[67]

Reagan was in a bind. He was personally conflicted about Beilenson's bill. On the one hand, as he said repeatedly, he believed that California's century-old abortion law was too strict and that rape victims should have the right to an abortion. On the other hand, like most Americans at the time, he opposed what the right-to-life movement called "abortion on demand," and he worried that, even with modifications, Beilenson's bill might be too permissive. Right-to-lifers argued that the bill's mental health provision would allow abortions based on the flimsiest of excuses. Furthermore, the lack of a residency requirement would turn the state into an "abortion center." When first questioned about this, Reagan admitted that he had not considered that possibility, but after right-to-life activists brought it to his attention, he began to reconsider his support for the bill.[68]

Reagan was also politically conflicted. Many Republicans in the state legislature, including members of the conservative wing of the party, supported the Beilenson bill. Indeed, the bill's sponsor in the assembly was the lower house's highest-ranking Republican, and he had consulted with Reagan throughout the process of shepherding the bill through the lower house. Many of the opponents of the bill were Democrats who would never have supported Reagan under any circumstances. Some of the strongest attacks on the bill in the assembly came from the liberal Democrat John Vasconcellos, whose impassioned statements against the bill also included a denunciation of the Vietnam War and the death penalty. Though Beilenson was a liberal Democrat, he had relied on a lot of conservative Republicans to secure his bill's passage, and Reagan could not afford to alienate them. On the other hand, he was also reluctant to alienate the many socially conservative Catholics who had voted for him only a few months earlier and who were urging him to veto the bill. Because Spencer Roberts, the public relations firm that was managing the southern California Right to Life League's activities, had managed his own gubernatorial campaign the previous year, some members of the press wondered if the firm was exerting influence on Reagan behind the scenes. The word on the street was that the Reagan administration was trying to figure out a way to keep the bill from getting out of the legislature.[69]

A few weeks before the Beilenson bill came up for a vote, there was a game-changing development: Colorado became the first state in the nation to adopt an ALI-style therapeutic abortion law. The situation was strikingly similar to the one in California: a liberal Democratic state representative, Richard Lamm, introduced an abortion bill with the support of conservative Republicans and shepherded it through a Republican-dominated legislature. Then a reluctant Republican governor decided, after some vacillation, to sign it. Advocates of the bill insisted, like their counterparts in California, that the bill was a conservative measure that would protect doctors and bring the law into conformity with current medical practices; it would never lead to unrestricted abortion. As in California, Catholics in Colorado protested against the bill, with a few picketing the state capital as the legislature debated the measure. The leading opponent of the bill in the state senate was the Catholic Democratic minority leader Sam Taylor, who called the proposal a "crime against motherhood" and warned that it would open the door to the creation of a massive abortion industry in the state. Catholic priests denounced the bill from their pulpits and, like their fellow church members in California, Colorado Catholics engaged in a massive letter-writing campaign to try to sway the state's political leaders. Governor John Love reported that of the 5,000 letters he received on abortion, approximately 75 percent expressed opposition to Lamm's bill. Yet in the end, both houses of the legislature passed the bill by strong margins, and the governor signed it into law.[70]

Lamm succeeded in getting his bill passed largely by relying on the line of argument that Lester Kinsolving had been using in California—that is, he branded the campaign against abortion as an exclusively Catholic cause and argued that for most of Christian history, even the Catholic Church had not taught that life begins at conception. It was an argument based on literature obtained from the American Lutheran Church, a liberal Protestant body that would soon officially endorse the cause of abortion liberalization, and it was similar to what many liberal Protestants had been saying for the previous year. If the pro-life cause were merely a matter of sectarian religious faith, it had no place in public law. After all, Lamm said, Cardinal Cushing had declared that Catholics should not impose their moral scruples on others through the legal system. Liberalized abortion laws had strong public support, especially from physicians. Using these arguments, Lamm broke Catholic opposition and convinced his fellow legislators to pass a bill legalizing hospital abortions in cases of rape, incest, suspected fetal deformity, and danger to a woman's health. *Time* magazine credited Lamm's success partly to his effective arguments against the Catholic Church. But it also helped, as the *New York Times* pointed out, that Colorado's Catholic population was very small and therefore easy to ignore. It would be more difficult to apply Lamm's strategy in California, where Catholics comprised a much greater percentage of the population.[71]

Seizing the opportunity to defer consideration of the issue, Reagan suggested that now that Colorado had adopted a liberalized abortion measure, it would be best to wait a while to see how Colorado's law worked in practice before passing a similar measure in California.[72] Beilenson ignored the suggestion. As Beilenson continued to gather support for his bill in the legislature, right-to-life advocates held out hope that they might be able to convince Reagan to veto the bill.

Hours before the scheduled vote in the senate, Reagan tried one last tactic to delay Beilenson's bill: he told the press that he was concerned that the bill's lack of a residency requirement and the provision allowing women to obtain abortions on grounds of mental health were "loophole[s]" that would lead to abuse. Reagan's potential allies in the legislature revolted, feeling that the governor had betrayed them. After carefully crafting a bill to meet his earlier specifications, they were livid that he was changing the rules of the game only hours before the bill was scheduled to reach his desk. Newspapers across the state denounced the governor's apparent ineptitude. Under pressure, Reagan backed down. He withdrew his objections and signed the bill as drafted. His earlier objections had succeeded in eliminating the clause allowing abortion for fetal deformity, so the bill was not quite as liberal as Beilenson had wanted.[73] But that was as far as

Reagan felt he could go. He was not yet ready to ally himself with the right-to-lifers and oppose all abortion liberalization. After years of work, the state's right-to-life movement had suffered a massive defeat.

The Right to Life League emerged from the fight angry, disappointed, and internally divided. Elizabeth Goodwin wrote an impassioned letter to Cardinal McIntyre outlining the mistakes that had led the Catholic Church to squander its opportunity to stop Beilenson's bill from becoming law. Despite its professed interest in an ecumenical pro-life coalition, the Church had insisted on orchestrating the right-to-life movement, and the results had been disastrous. Church officials wanted to entrust the right-to-life cause to Catholic professionals, especially lawyers and doctors who had worked with the Church for years and who, they thought, would have public credibility as legal and medical experts. A Catholic bureaucrat whom she described as "the Cardinal's man" had determined which speakers would testify against the Beilenson bill. When Goodwin brought one hundred Catholic women to Sacramento to testify against the bill, the church official did not allow any of them to enter the all-male lineup of speakers that he had created, leaving the women to look on in silence as the men delivered an embarrassing performance. Why hadn't a woman been allowed to testify about a matter that was surely a women's issue? Goodwin asked. And why wasn't the articulate Lutheran minister Arnim Polster given the task of organizing the pro-life speakers, thereby blunting the criticism that theirs was a strictly Catholic cause? Though she was a devout Catholic passionately devoted to her faith and the teachings of the Church, Goodwin was angry that Church officials had done so much damage to such an important cause. She had no intention of leaving the movement or even the Right to Life League. Stopping abortion was still as important as it ever was. But she believed that right-to-life activists needed a new strategy. The core of the Right to Life League was its female membership, but the cardinal had mostly ignored them and had given too much authority to a small coterie of male leaders whose credentials he hoped would impress the public. The move had backfired. It was time for Catholic women to take charge of the movement—and, they hoped, find the Protestant allies whose support was still so elusive.[74]

## *Other Legislative Fights of 1967*

The right-to-life movement suffered another defeat in the spring of 1967 when North Carolina passed an ALI-style abortion liberalization bill. The bill was even more liberal than the one that provoked a fight in California, because it allowed for abortion in cases of fetal deformity. Yet the bill provoked little dissension in the state, primarily because few socially conservative Protestants objected to it. The bill's chief sponsor was a retired Lutheran banker whom a local newspaper described as "very much on the conservative side" of most political issues. The North Carolina Baptist Convention issued no statement on the bill. Indeed, the state's most prominent evangelicals showed little interest in the issue. The state's best-known evangelist, Billy Graham, was willing to allow for abortion in cases of rape and incest, and Graham's father-in-law, the retired physician and Presbyterian magazine editor L. Nelson Bell, who also lived in North Carolina, later admitted that in his medical practice he had performed a few therapeutic abortions in extreme circumstances. Though a few lawmakers and doctors worried that the bill might be too loosely constructed and allow abortions for medically unnecessary reasons, most saw little reason for alarm. The bill sailed through the state senate, with more than 90 percent of the senators voting for it. The house of representatives likewise passed the bill by a margin of four to one.[75]

The main reason for the lack of controversy in North Carolina was the lack of Catholics in the state. At only 1 percent of the state's population, Catholics had little hope of influencing the legislative outcome, nor were they able to attract Protestant allies to their cause.[76]

Right-to-life advocates could take heart from a few major victories in the spring of 1967. All came in heavily Catholic states. In Connecticut, a state that was 50 percent Catholic, a bill to legalize abortion in the case of rape died in committee as soon as the state's three bishops condemned it. In Maryland, another state with a strong Catholic heritage, the archbishop of Baltimore, as well as the bishops of Wilmington and Washington, lobbied against a measure that would have legalized abortion in cases when a committee of two doctors determined that the procedure was necessary for a pregnant woman's physical or mental health. This vaguely defined rationale for abortion would "constitute a blank check in the hands of those among whom discretion is conferred," a diocesan lobbyist declared. The state house of delegates approved the bill, and the state's Republican governor, Spiro Agnew, endorsed the measured and promised to sign it. But when the bill reached the Maryland Senate, it was killed in committee after continued lobbying from the three dioceses.[77]

In New York, the church managed to stop an abortion law liberalization proposal primarily because two key Catholic politicians—the Republican senate majority leader and the Democratic assembly speaker—objected. They faced a formidable coalition of opponents, because some of New York's leading politicians, most notably Republican governor Nelson Rockefeller, supported the bill, as did New York's liberal Republican senator Jacob Javits and even Catholic Democratic senator Robert Kennedy. The bill had forty cosponsors. With support from liberal Democrats and Republicans, state medical and bar associations, and a bevy of Protestant and Jewish organizations, and with public opinion polls indicating majority support for abortion law liberalization, passage seemed assured. "Never before in the oppressive and often cruel 84-year history of abortion restriction in the state has there been such an interest in reform," the *New York Times* editorial page exulted.[78]

As expected, New York's eight Catholic bishops mobilized against the measure, but Kennedy's endorsement made their task especially difficult, because it signaled to other Catholic politicians that it was acceptable for Catholics to defy ecclesiastical authority. In the end, the continued opposition of the top-ranking members of both houses of the legislature, along with the church's concerted lobbying effort, induced an assembly committee to kill the bill.[79]

This was an important victory for right-to-lifers, but it came only because they had a few allies among the legislature's leaders, not because there was a groundswell of opposition to abortion. This did not bode well for the future. It appeared that right-to-life advocates could win only in states where pro-life Catholics controlled key legislative committees; otherwise, the efforts of Catholic bishops counted for little.

Several Catholic clerics decided to give up the fight. William Burke, the legislative representative and public relations counsel for California's Catholic education and welfare organizations, warned that it was already too late. Burke had been campaigning against abortion law liberalization in California since 1961, but having failed to defeat the Beilenson bill, he decided that it was time for Catholics in other states to admit defeat and move on. "Abortion may be a moot issue," he told the *National Catholic Reporter*. "It might be better if we addressed ourselves to the next obvious issues—infanticide and euthanasia."[80]

Some were even more willing to cut their losses. In February 1967, Msgr. William Magee, vice-rector of Immaculate Heart of Mary Seminary in Minnesota, published an editorial in his diocesan paper urging Catholics to support a liberalized abortion law that was "strictly written." Minnesota was a liberal Protestant state that had been one of the first in the country to consider abortion law liberalization, and such a law was certain to pass eventually, Magee reasoned. Catholics therefore faced a choice: they could support the most stringent of the proposed liberalization bills in the hope of maintaining the tightest possible controls over abortion, or they could continue to oppose all such bills, giving their opponents free rein to pass any bill for which they could gain a majority. With more than 75 percent of Americans favoring at least some liberalization, the choice seemed clear.[81]

Perhaps most alarmingly of all, one of the most prominent Jesuit legal experts in the Catholic right-to-life movement, Boston College Law School dean Robert Drinan, decided to abandon the cause and accept not only abortion law liberalization but even abortion law repeal. Drinan had joined the Catholic Church's campaign against abortion law reform in 1965 as a strong proponent of the fetus's right to life on natural law grounds, a view that he outlined in his widely circulated law review article "The Inviolability of the Right to Be Born." But as public opinion moved rapidly in the other direction, Drinan wondered whether he was ceding the debate to his opponents by insisting on an absolutist theological stand that would never be accepted as public policy. In the spring of 1967, he signaled his acceptance of limited liberalization. A few months later, he shifted his position yet again, declaring that liberalized abortion bills were worse than no controls on abortion at all, because they gave the state the power to decide which fetuses were worthy of protection and which were not. Giving doctors the right to terminate the lives of deformed fetuses because they might not conform to societal ideas of bodily perfection was particularly offensive. If abortion was going to be legalized in some cases, it would be better to avoid involving the state at all. Drinan preferred to legalize all abortion up to either twelve or twenty weeks of gestation rather than to let the state "establish standards as to who will live and who will die."[82]

Most pro-life Catholics thought that Magee and Drinan had given up the fight too quickly. Only a few weeks after Magee published his editorial, Minnesota's bishops issued a direct rebuttal. "Those who would weaken laws which protect human life are posing a threat both to society itself and to the fundamental moral principles upon which this society is based," they declared. "The proposals for direct abortion stand contrary to the law of God as well as to the laws of men."[83]

Yet the willingness of Magee and Drinan to cut their losses was a bad sign. States across the country were poised to take up abortion law reform, and pro-life Catholics did not have a strategy to stop them.

# 4

# *National Right to Life*

THE CATHOLIC THEOLOGIANS who gathered at the Church's Family Life Bureau in Washington, DC, to discuss abortion in March 1967 realized that the right-to-life campaign was in crisis. The Church would have to change its strategy. "Although the Church is clearly opposed to abortion, there is need for refinement in the statement of our position," they declared.[1]

Pro-life Catholics realized that they were losing for two reasons. First, their arguments were out of step with Protestant opinion. Second, the Church hierarchy no longer exercised much political influence, even among Catholics. With the exception of the Lutheran Church-Missouri Synod and a few small fundamentalist groups, no Protestant denomination supported the right-to-life movement en masse, and more than half of all Catholics disagreed with the Church's position.[2] Pro-life Catholics would have to win some Protestant allies while shoring up support among their own parishioners. Bishops had relied mainly on lobbying pressure, but once politicians realized that bishops no longer had much influence over their parishioners' voting preferences, the bishops' lobbying power collapsed. It was time for a new strategy.

Catholics who opposed abortion would have to sever the ties between the right-to-life cause and contraception, Church doctrine, and even the Church itself. Even this might not be enough, but it seemed to be their only hope. To launch this effort, the Church turned to the thirty-five-year-old priest who had convened the meeting—Fr. James McHugh.

## *Fr. McHugh's New Approach*

Young, intelligent, and ambitious, McHugh was the type of liberal social reformer that the right-to-life movement needed. As a young priest in northern New Jersey in the late 1950s, he had risen quickly through the clerical ranks and had combined his studies in theology with an interest in more secular topics. After pursuing graduate study in sociology at Fordham University and the Catholic University of America, he had been tapped to head the National Catholic Welfare Conference's (NCWC) Family Life Bureau in 1965 when he was still in his early thirties. He brought with him a firm commitment to the principles of Vatican II. The NCWC had long leaned to the left on questions of labor relations and social welfare, but McHugh's liberalism exceeded that of some of his predecessors. He was an associate and admirer of some of the liberal clergy who were calling for an end to the Church's ban on contraception, and he suggested that he himself might favor an end to this ban as well. Though he acquiesced to the Church's teaching after Pope Paul VI reiterated the Church's traditional stance, he evinced little enthusiasm for returning to the Church's fight for birth control legislation. At a time when some Catholic parents were campaigning against public school sex education, McHugh launched a campaign to bring sex education *into* Catholic schools.[3]

But for McHugh, abortion was a different matter—the taking of human life, which justice required him to oppose. Shortly after the NCWC was transformed into the NCCB in 1966, several California bishops called for a new right-to-life campaign.[4] McHugh made it his signature issue. He convened the meeting with Catholic theologians just as Colorado, North Carolina, and California were about to pass the nation's first liberalized abortion laws. The right-to-life movement was losing ground. It had to find arguments that could appeal to a larger audience.

Most radically, perhaps, it had to sever its connection with the Church's longstanding battle against contraception. Nothing had discredited the Church's right-to-life effort more than the campaign against birth control, McHugh believed. As long as arguments against abortion remained grounded in natural law, denunciations of contraception were never far from the surface, but if the right-to-life movement instead grounded its campaign in the constitutional arguments that lawyers such as Walter Trinkaus had advanced and in the international human rights tradition that McHugh favored, there was no need to discuss contraception at all. Abortion was a "separate matter," McHugh said, "a more serious threat to human life." It would be best to base arguments against abortion on the United Nations' Universal Declaration of Human Rights and its Declaration of the Rights of the Child—documents that appealed to non-Catholic politicians, especially political liberals. By citing the UN's declaration of a "right to life for all people" and its statement that children required "appropriate legal protection, before as well as after birth," McHugh invoked the rights-based language of secular liberalism and appealed to an audience that had little respect for the natural law theory of the Catholic Church. Secular liberals had been quite willing, in the era before abortion became a contentious political issue, to consider the unborn fetus a "child" that deserved "appropriate legal protection." McHugh hoped they could be brought back to that position.[5]

McHugh looked for inspiration to Jesuit theologian Richard McCormick, who had declared in a 1965 article in *America* that "one cannot put a price on human life." This would now become pro-lifers' primary argument. "As soon as one allows direct suppression of innocent human life in any form, he has priced human life," McCormick wrote. "That is, he has subordinated it to some temporal value: economic advantage, physical well being, the good life, protection of reputation or whatever it may be. Once he has done this, there is nothing *in principle* that prevents his destroying human life at other stages and in other circumstances: the aged, the infirm, the socially or economically burdensome, the crippled, the suffering. It is only a matter of waiting until the going price has been reached."[6] Catholics were going to wage a campaign against the utilitarian calculus of therapeutic abortion legislation by invoking the cause of universal human rights.

McCormick was certainly not the first to make this argument; at least two previous popes—Pius XI and Pius XII—had done so. Indeed, since most Catholics believed that all human rights were ultimately derived from natural law, it was not difficult for them to switch from the language of natural law to the language of universal human rights. Nevertheless, McHugh felt that Catholics had not been forceful enough in making human rights arguments against abortion, and they had therefore lost the support of liberal human rights advocates who should have been on their side. He sent a copy of McCormick's article to bishops throughout the nation so that they would have a "representation of current theological thinking on abortion."[7]

A few conservative Catholics disagreed with McHugh's approach, particularly with his declaration that bishops should stop talking about contraception. Germain Grisez, a philosophy professor at Georgetown who would soon become one of the American Catholic Church's leading intellectual defenders of the pro-life position on natural law grounds,

sent a letter to bishops across the nation warning them of the consequences of soft-pedaling the Church's teaching on contraception. "I have
seen no plausible effort at a new moral theology that would justify contraception which would not also, implicitly, justify abortion as well," he
wrote. When the bishops did not listen, Grisez took his case to the public. "The entire movement to legalize abortion is nothing more than an
extension of the contraceptive mentality to post-conceptive birth control," he insisted.[8]

Grisez's argument did not carry the day, but it did presage a division
in the pro-life movement between those who, like McHugh, wanted to
frame the fight against abortion as a human rights cause and those who,
like Grisez, believed that abortion was inextricably linked to larger debates
about sexual morality and procreation. Both believed that the fight to save
unborn life was a battle for the human rights of the fetus. But one group
believed that their movement should secularize its message, framing it
in the language of science, liberalism, and constitutional law. The other
group held to the more traditional Catholic view that abortion was simply
the end result of a decades-long shift away from God's standards of sexual
morality. To fight against it would require a much broader assault on sexual
liberalization, at the heart of which was contraception and the widespread
belief that people should have a right to risk-free sex. Thus, in the late
1960s and early 1970s, a small but vocal contingent of anti-contraceptive
Catholics—a group that included pro-life activists such as Randy Engel,
Charles Rice, and, eventually, Fr. Paul Marx (who had spoken in favor of
birth control in the late 1960s, but then changed course at the beginning
of the 1970s)—continued to speak out against the "contraceptive mentality" and the larger sexual revolution. Rice devoted an entire chapter in his
1969 book *The Vanishing Right to Live* to homosexuality, since he believed
there was a connection between sexual liberation, gay activism, and abortion. Some theologically conservative Catholics were upset with McHugh
for failing to recognize these links. McHugh was a "Trojan horse in the
pro-life camp," Engel declared.[9]

Opponents of contraception often argued that both the pill and
intrauterine devices (IUDs) blocked the implantation of fertilized ova,
which meant that they were "abortifacients." "Can we reject abortion and
embrace abortifacient contraception?" asked Eugene Diamond, a pediatrics professor at Loyola University's School of Medicine and future
president of the National Federation of Catholic Physicians' Guilds. "Can
we develop a pro-life program which implicitly excludes new life?" He

complained about the "agonizing inconsistencies" of those who vehemently denounced abortion while turning a blind eye to—or worse yet,
championing—the birth control pill, which, in his opinion, destroyed
human life during its first hours of existence. Even though he grudgingly
conceded that he could not make subscription to the Catholic Church's
teaching on contraception "a prerequisite for membership on the anti-
abortion team," he thought that pro-lifers should at least draw the line
at "abortifacient" methods of birth control, which he believed included
nearly all chemical contraceptives.[10]

But many other Catholics at the time—including such influential
voices as Berkeley law professor John Noonan, who had served on the
pope's birth control commission and worked closely with the northern
California branch of the Right to Life League—followed McHugh's lead
and welcomed the opportunity to dissociate themselves from what,
for many in the Church, had become an embarrassment.[11] With little
chance of getting even the Catholic faithful to follow Church doctrine
on birth control, McHugh and his allies knew that if the right-to-life
movement tried to link itself to the battle against contraception—as the
Church had done for decades—their cause was doomed. Although the
vast majority of pro-life activists in the late 1960s and early 1970s were
Catholics, and although an overwhelming number of them held conservative views on sexual morality—with many following Church teaching
on contraception in their own marriages—most refrained from talking
about contraception or sexual morality in their pro-life literature and
public presentations. It was far better, they thought, to concentrate on
what they believed was their most powerful argument—the need to protect human life.[12]

McHugh believed that local bishops and state Catholic conferences
should take the lead in directing pro-life campaigns in their own states,
but at the same time, he thought that a national educational campaign,
coordinated by the Family Life Bureau but carried out by local dioceses,
might be an ideal way to provide institutional support for the right-to-life
cause throughout the country. Accordingly, the NCCB voted in April 1967
to spend $50,000 on just such a campaign, overseen by McHugh.[13]

If the bishops thought that this would be sufficient to thwart liberalization, they were wrong. Three states liberalized their abortion laws within
weeks of the NCCB's vote, and the next year, two additional states followed
suit. By the spring of 1968, McHugh was beginning to rethink his strategy. Yet he took heart that liberalization legislation had been defeated in

six other states. McHugh thought he could detect a pattern in the results. In Georgia, where Catholics had little presence, the state legislature had passed its abortion liberalization bill with almost no debate: 144 to 11 in the house and 39 to 11 in the senate. And in Maryland, where bishops had mounted a strong offensive, but where they had lobbied through their official diocesan representatives rather than through lay-run organizations, the right-to-life cause had also suffered defeat.[14] On the other hand, most of the states in which abortion reform was defeated had strong lay-run Catholic conferences—political and legal advisory committees organized by bishops but operated by non-ordained Catholic professionals, including lawyers.

McHugh saw the value of state Catholic conferences but thought he could do even better by encouraging them to create independent pro-life organizations. These new state right-to-life committees could enlist lay Catholics, especially doctors and lawyers, in fighting liberalization measures, and their political lobbying efforts would be far more effective than the pronouncements of bishops or priests.[15] In other words, they would look very much like California's Right to Life League. That organization had failed in its attempt to defeat a liberalized abortion bill, but its continued growth and increasing political influence gave pro-lifers hope that similar organizations could succeed elsewhere.

New York offered another example. The organization had its genesis in late 1965, when Edward Golden, a thirty-one-year-old construction firm operator, faithful Catholic, and father of five, decided that the campaign to legalize abortion in his state must be stopped. With the help of three of his friends, as well as the encouragement of the secretary of the New York Catholic Conference, he launched the New York Right to Life Committee. At first it was, in Golden's words, "only a letter-writing operation" that had limited influence on the state legislature, partly because Golden and his allies had no previous lobbying experience. But Golden was dedicated to the cause and determined to acquire political skills. He also learned how to expand his network. In the late 1960s, he met Robert Byrn, a professor at Fordham University's School of Law who had been writing in opposition to abortion for several years and who had worked with Charles Rice to form a small right-to-life group. The Fordham professor was able to supply Golden's organization with needed legal expertise. Like the right-to-life campaign in California, the effort in New York represented a small beginning, but it suggested a model for the future.[16]

## The National Right to Life Committee

Until 1968, only a handful of independent state and local right-to-life organizations existed. Indeed, the movement was so decentralized that sometimes pro-life activists who led similar organizations in the same state
did not know of each other's existence until they met at legislative hearings. McHugh believed that the movement's leadership should continue
to come from state organizations, and he appreciated the flexibility that
a decentralized approach afforded, but he thought that some additional
degree of national coordination might be effective.

McHugh created the National Right to Life Committee (NRLC) in 1968
as an umbrella organization for state pro-life groups. He hoped to infuse
the movement with national direction but also make it at least nominally
independent from the NCCB and the United States Catholic Conference.
The NRLC began essentially as an adjunct of McHugh's office, with a leadership team made up entirely of his personal associates. Its first president was Juan Ryan, a Catholic lawyer and lifelong friend from McHugh's
home state of New Jersey. McHugh's personal assistant Michael Taylor, a
twenty-six-year-old employee of the NCCB, became the NRLC's executive
secretary. The operation had a shoestring budget, so the NRLC had no
paid staff in its early years; Taylor and Ryan were volunteers.[17]

McHugh envisioned the NRLC not as a national lobbying organization
but as a coordinating entity for state right-to-life organizations. To ensure
that every state would have such an organization, he wrote to the nation's
bishops in June 1968 urging each of them to create a state right-to-life
committee by September 15, in time for the upcoming legislative season.
Many state Catholic conferences failed to meet this tight deadline. The
Pennsylvania Catholic Conference, for instance, did not create a right-to-
life committee until 1970. Neither did North Dakota. Most southern states
waited even longer.[18] Nevertheless, McHugh's directive shaped the course
of the pro-life movement for at least the next five years. The pro-life movement would be led by laypeople, with the bishops playing a less public
role, and it would be organized primarily at the state level, with the NRLC
providing a limited degree of national coordination. While many of the
right-to-life organizations engaged in public educational efforts and other
activities, they were created for one central purpose: lobbying their state
legislatures to defeat all abortion law reform proposals.

McHugh recognized that even though bishops or Catholic conferences
would have to take the lead in launching state right-to-life organizations, it

would be best to sever those connections as quickly as possible, since such connections would undermine their influence and negate the primary reason for their existence. "It's best if this group has no structural link with the State Conference or Diocese," McHugh instructed, and pointed to the NRLC as a model. He had headquartered the NRLC in Alexandria, Virginia, rather than in the Family Life Bureau's office in Washington, DC, because he wanted to "shift attention away from the so-called 'exclusively Catholic opposition.'" The NRLC was thoroughly Catholic in its early days, and it was integrally connected with McHugh's Family Life Bureau, but McHugh thought it politically expedient not to highlight that fact.[19]

Opponents of the pro-life movement charged that the right-to-life committees were simply "the political front of the Catholic Church." Members of these organizations insisted that they were fully independent. The truth lay somewhere in between. In most states, the majority of the members of the right-to-life groups were Catholic, and in most cases, these organizations had their beginnings in state Catholic conferences. In some heavily Catholic states, such as New Jersey, where the Respect for Life Committee's letterhead described the organization as "a committee of the New Jersey Catholic Conference," the connection was especially obvious. In other places, it was less so. In a few states, such as Minnesota, Catholic conferences found preexisting grassroots, independent pro-life organizations and chose to partner with them, but in many other states, they simply sent letters to priests asking them to recruit interested members (particularly doctors, lawyers, and other influential community leaders) to start new organizations. The Catholic conferences provided the seed money and offered occasional financial help along the way, although usually not to the extent that the organizations wanted. In North Dakota, for instance, the state's Catholic conference provided a $5,000 startup grant but then required the organization to raise $3,800 on its own almost immediately. Collectively, Catholic bishops provided the NRLC with approximately $25,000 per year until 1973—an amount that did not go very far toward the goal of creating a lobbying presence in all fifty states.[20]

Although the right-to-life organizations depended on Catholic institutional support, there was a sense in which their claim to be independent was correct. By the early 1970s, many of the state organizations were led by Protestants who felt free to take positions that contradicted official Catholic teaching. And the relationships between organizations and local bishops varied. In Pennsylvania, the state right-to-life organization repeatedly received financial subsidies from the state Catholic conference and local bishops, and in Michigan, the state pro-life organization held its board meetings in the offices of the Michigan Catholic Conference. But in Arizona, right-to-life leaders claimed that their cash-strapped organization was reliant on its own meager fundraising efforts. When priests joined right-to-life organizations, they were discouraged from taking any positions of leadership or representing the organizations in public forums. Catholic clerics were happy to oblige; they wanted right-to-life organizations to remain under lay—and, when possible, non-Catholic—control. They felt it would help them get a hearing in places where the Catholic Church's official lobbying on abortion had been ignored.[21]

McHugh encouraged bishops to recruit doctors and lawyers to lead the right-to-life committees. This strategy seemed natural because, up to that point, organizations on both sides of the debate had consisted disproportionately of members of the medical and legal professions. On the side of abortion law reform were doctors such as Alan Guttmacher and lawyers such as Zad Leavy. Their pro-life counterparts were Catholic diocesan lawyers and doctors associated with the National Federation of Catholic Physicians' Guilds. Women had not yet become major players in the abortion debate. Feminists such as Betty Friedan had sought to make abortion a women's rights issue, and, on the other side, Elizabeth Goodwin had called for women to take the lead in the right-to-life movement, but the public debate still focused on medical issues rather than women's rights. By 1968, this was beginning to change, but the language of public health still dominated the debates on this topic in professional medical societies and state legislatures, so McHugh recruited experts who could beat the opposition's doctors and lawyers at their own game. He believed the campaign should rely on science and reason. Pro-lifers should "avoid emotional arguments and sensationalism," he instructed, "and emphasize a clear and reasoned presentation that accurately presents the Christian value on human life."[22]

Indeed, state Catholic conference attorneys had already been thinking along similar lines. "What we really need is a very strong front comprising the moralist, the scientist, the physician, and the constitutional lawyer," the Pennsylvania Catholic Conference's general counsel wrote in March 1966. "This, it seems to me, makes the complete team in these areas of civil concern which pertain to the right to life." The NRLC took this maxim to heart. By 1972, seventy-six lawyers were serving on the NRLC's legal advisory board, and doctors were heading several of its state organizational chapters.[23]

If McHugh was slow to recognize the important leadership that women could provide, he was quick to see the potential of recruiting Protestants to the cause, because a sectarian Catholic effort was bound to fail in most states where Catholics did not comprise a majority. He encouraged bishops to enlist Protestants in their pro-life campaigns, even if that required compromises on the permissibility of abortion in cases of rape and incest. "Efforts should be made to obtain non-Catholic participation," McHugh told the bishops in October 1967. "If non-Catholics will not totally oppose liberalization [of state abortion laws], the door should be kept open to join on those aspects of a bill that are unacceptable to all groups."[24] Protestant doctors who joined these organizations often rose quickly to positions of leadership, because right-to-life advocates realized the value of having a Protestant spokesperson.[25]

At first, most of the Protestant clergy who decided to join the movement were not evangelicals, but rather mainline Protestants who disagreed with their denominations' endorsement of abortion rights. At the time, mainline Protestantism had just experienced a political sea change. The civil rights movement and the Vietnam War had encouraged a new generation of liberal ministers to embrace social justice as a central mission and to make the political defense of human life and constitutional rights their primary message. Some of these young, socially conscious ministers joined the campaign for abortion rights, but several others who were just as socially conscious joined the right-to-life movement. Indeed, the right-to-life movement, now focused on defense of the unborn as a human rights cause, seemed ideally situated to appeal to liberal Protestant ministers who wanted to defend the rights of powerless minorities and promote respect for all human life. And in fact, most of the Protestant ministers who joined the right-to-life movement in the late 1960s shared the social justice vision of other liberal clergy in their denominations and viewed themselves as human rights advocates who wanted to help the poor and the disadvantaged. When the right-to-life campaign divorced itself from the birth control issue and became a human rights cause infused with the nonsectarian language of constitutional rights and social justice, they joined the movement.

One of the foremost liberal Protestant right-to-life advocates was California Episcopal priest Charles Carroll, an opponent of the Vietnam War who had participated in civil rights activism in Mississippi and had been an observer at the Nuremberg prosecutions. In 1967, he came to the conclusion that abortion was similar to the Holocaust and was part of a larger pattern of "denigration of life" in American society. Like several other Protestants who found their way into the right-to-life movement around this time, he had given abortion little thought for most of his clerical career and had, at first, sympathized with the argument that abortion should be legal in certain cases. But after becoming convinced that abortion was an assault on human life, he threw himself into the pro-life cause with abandon. He testified against the Beilenson bill in the spring of 1967, and then, when that effort ended in defeat, he extended his campaign to other places, speaking out against liberalized abortion bills in seven states in 1968 and adding others to his itinerary in 1969. In most cases, he came at the invitation of local Catholic bishops, who were delighted at their good fortune in finding a politically liberal Episcopal priest who endorsed their cause and lent credibility to their movement among Protestant liberals, who were generally supportive of abortion rights. "I am anxious to make some kind of impact on the local Iowa Council of Churches that endorsed the liberalized Abortion Bill during the past 1969 session," the Catholic bishop of Des Moines told Fr. Paul Marx when explaining why he had invited Carroll to Iowa in the summer of 1969. "It is my hope that Father Carroll can help in some way to influence the thinking of the local clergymen." Marx shared the bishop's confidence in Carroll's abilities. "I don't know anyone who is more effective, and his being an Episcopal priest makes him all the more effective," he told the Des Moines bishop.[26]

Pro-life Catholics had a similarly positive reaction when Paul Ramsey, a Methodist theologian and professor of religion at Princeton University who studied medical ethics, published an article concluding that abortion violated the divinely given "sanctity of life." Immediately, Catholic right-to-life activists sensed that Ramsey would be a useful ally and recruited him for their cause. They likewise rejoiced when Harvard Divinity School professor George Huntston Williams, a Unitarian, published an anti-abortion article in 1970. Williams, perhaps the only prominent Unitarian in the United States who opposed abortion legalization, quickly attracted the attention of pro-life Catholics, who convinced him to become the charter president of Americans United for Life in 1971. Some Catholics—particularly those on the left—were drawn to Richard John Neuhaus, a young, politically liberal Lutheran minister who strongly opposed the Vietnam War and who began speaking out against abortion in 1967 because he considered it another type of sinful killing. Neuhaus was sharply critical of the bishops for failing to denounce the Vietnam War, but he conceded that on the abortion issue, the Catholic hierarchy might have been right, while abortion rights activists in his own Protestant tradition were in error.[27] Yet these voices were a minority in the Protestant mainline, which, on the whole, was firmly behind the push for abortion legalization. The media continued to describe the lobbying effort against abortion law reform as a Catholic campaign—which it mostly was.[28]

Even those Protestants who did lend their support to the pro-life movement were sometimes less firmly devoted to the cause than Catholics. While Ramsey was willing to write against abortion, he showed little interest in getting involved in right-to-life activism. He refused an invitation to be the honorary chair of the New Jersey Right to Life Committee, saying that he was "really not an activist" and that he had other responsibilities that were more pressing. When the New Jersey state legislature considered an abortion liberalization bill, he politely declined an invitation to testify at the legislative hearings, despite the urgings of a local Catholic right-to-life activist who believed that Ramsey's academic credentials and Protestant faith would make him persuasive. Williams likewise found himself at odds with other pro-life activists, especially when his Unitarian views on personal freedom clashed with those of traditionalist Catholics in the movement. As a strong advocate of contraception, he testified before the Massachusetts state legislature in favor of a bill to repeal the last vestiges of the state's anti-birth control laws. He also believed that the law should allow abortion not only when a woman's life was in danger, but also in cases of rape, a stance that perturbed some Catholic purists. Similarly, Neuhaus was an ally, but his support for the movement was limited. While he strongly believed in the right to life, he devoted little time to pro-life organizations in the late 1960s and early 1970s because he considered opposition to the Vietnam War a more urgent priority. And, like most Protestants of the time, he believed that abortion might be allowable in cases of rape.[29]

Even though McHugh and other Catholics had made strenuous efforts to separate the right-to-life cause from the Catholic Church's unpopular stance on contraception and do whatever they could to recruit Protestants, they still found that very few Protestants were interested in joining their campaign. Unlike Catholics, most Protestants had not been fed a steady diet of anti-abortion sermons and articles, so even those who were sympathetic to the cause sometimes considered the issue less pressing than Catholics did. At a time when the war in Vietnam was resulting in thousands of deaths every year and race riots were engulfing America's cities, there were plenty of other social justice causes and political debates competing for their attention. As the abortion rights movement increasingly identified itself with the cause of women's rights, and as mainline Protestant denominations began officially endorsing abortion legalization as a social justice measure, liberal Protestants who believed in the equality of all people found it difficult to support the pro-life cause. Outside of Catholic circles, the fight against abortion generated only limited interest before the 1970s.

## Political Defeats in the Late 1960s

Plagued by a lack of widespread Protestant support, the right-to-life movement continued to lose legislative battles. In the South, North Carolina's liberalized abortion law became a model for other states. Georgia passed a similar law in 1968, followed by Arkansas in 1969 and South Carolina and Virginia in 1970. After Maryland adopted a liberalized abortion law in 1968, Delaware, Oregon, New Mexico, and Kansas followed suit the following year.[30]

Neither major political party supported the right-to-life cause. Most pro-lifers were Catholic Democrats who still believed in the principles of New Deal liberalism, but the Democratic Party showed little interest in embracing the right-to-life campaign. In the South, conservative Democratic legislators—invariably Protestants—pushed abortion liberalization bills through state assemblies, while in the North and West, the liberal wing of the Democratic Party was quickly making abortion law reform one of its favored political causes. In both California and New York, the chief legislative sponsors of liberalization proposals were liberal Democrats. Liberal Republicans were often equally supportive, if not more so. New York's liberal Republican governor, Nelson Rockefeller, a longtime birth control advocate, made the push for an abortion liberalization bill a central part of his political program in the late 1960s. Several Republicans in the Senate, including the liberal stalwart Jacob Javits (NY) and centrist Robert Packwood (OR), were likewise strong supporters of abortion rights. Some conservative Republicans also supported abortion rights on libertarian grounds, just as the GOP's conservative icon, Barry Goldwater, did. Goldwater, whose wife was a Planned Parenthood volunteer, had secretly arranged an abortion for his teenage daughter a decade earlier, and he was an early convert to the abortion legalization cause.[31]

Indeed, the right-to-life movement experienced some of its greatest defeats in the late 1960s at the hands of Republican politicians. In

both Colorado and California, Republican governors, responding to legislation supported by many Republican legislators, signed into law the
nation's first abortion liberalization bills. In Maryland, it was Republican
governor Spiro Agnew who pushed for abortion law reform and signed the
state's liberalized abortion bill in 1968. The next year, Delaware's liberal
Republican governor, Russell Peterson, signed into law another ALI-style
liberalized abortion bill that the Republican state legislature had passed.
The Republican governors of Oregon and New Mexico signed similar
legislation.[32]

In Kansas, Republicans pushed an abortion liberalization bill
through the state legislature in 1969, crushing the weak pro-life opposition in a state that was only 15 percent Catholic. All but two of the
twenty-one Catholics in the Kansas House of Representatives voted
against the bill, but they were no match for the Protestant majority;
the Republican-controlled house passed the liberalization measure by
seventy-six to forty-four, and the senate gave it overwhelming support.
Pro-life Catholics in Kansas wrote to their state legislators making the
standard pro-life arguments, but they had little effect on Republican
Protestants who believed that abortion liberalization measures would
protect the rights of the medical profession, expand personal freedom,
and promote social betterment.[33] Catholics were still only a small minority in the GOP, which was dominated by liberal Protestants and business interests, and the party was generally unsympathetic to the pro-life
movement—especially the argument that fetuses were a constitutionally
protected minority. A November 1969 Gallup poll showed that 46 percent of Republicans (compared to only 35 percent of Democrats) favored
legislation that would legalize elective abortion during the first trimester. Many young conservatives and college Republicans supported abortion law reform, especially if they identified with the libertarian wing of
the conservative movement. In one sign of this trend, the New York State
Association of Young Republicans passed a resolution in 1969 (by a vote
of thirty-three to twelve) that called for the liberalization of the state's
restrictive abortion law.[34]

In fact, the pro-life message contradicted key aspects of both parties'
ideologies. For liberal Democrats, the right-to-life campaign seemed badly
out of step with the tenor of President Lyndon Johnson's Great Society,
which sought to limit fertility in order to reduce poverty. It was no coin-
cidence that Johnson, the president who launched a "war on poverty,"
was the first president to publicly endorse federally funded birth control

distribution.[35] The pro-life message was antithetical to that goal. Similarly, at a time when many lawyers, doctors, and Protestant ministers supported the liberalization of abortion laws, the GOP—which was still the party of mainline Protestants and business interests, not Catholics—was not inclined to join the right-to-life cause either.

With dominant interests in both parties opposing them, pro-lifers' only hope seemed to be in appealing to Catholic politicians. Fortunately for the right-to-life movement, many devout Catholics in both parties still believed that they had a moral duty to oppose abortion law liberalization. In the heavily Catholic states of the Northeast, including Maine, Massachusetts, Connecticut, Rhode Island, and Pennsylvania, the state legislatures remained so firmly pro-life that all abortion liberalization proposals quickly failed. In other states, such as New York, pro-life Catholics held key state legislative leadership posts, so even if a near-majority of the legislature supported reform, pro-lifers had a legitimate chance of blocking it.[36] But elsewhere, they faced much more difficult challenges.

McHugh's new approach seemed to hold great promise, but he had not succeeded in stopping the wave of abortion law reform. Each year brought new legislative defeats, and the prospects for the future looked even worse. In 1970, pro-lifers faced the possibility that nearly all restrictions on first- and second-trimester abortions would be repealed—a phenomenon that right-to-life advocates called "abortion on demand." This was "tantamount to murder on demand," Cardinal Patrick O'Boyle declared.[37] But the new strategy and national organization that McHugh had created could not reverse the political momentum, nor could the American Catholic Church.

# 5

## "Abortion on Demand"

"THE LEGALIZATION OF limited Abortion is only the driving wedge for Abortion on demand," Msgr. Paul Harrington warned in 1967.[1] Although others in the right-to-life movement echoed his alarm, the warnings seemed far-fetched at the time. The legalization of elective abortion had the support of less than 20 percent of the population, and no state legislature was seriously considering a proposal to remove all restrictions on the procedure. But less than three years later, pro-lifers found themselves losing a fight that many had never expected to wage. What had happened?

### Pro-Lifers' Fight against the Legalization
### of Elective Abortion

For most of the 1960s, people on both sides of the debate generally believed that the law should restrict abortion to some extent; they disagreed only over how much. Early liberalization laws merely expanded the number of legitimate legal reasons for an abortion. Any woman who wanted an abortion still had to appeal to a hospital abortion committee for approval. These laws closely tracked public opinion. While in 1966, nearly three-fourths of Americans supported legalizing abortion in cases where pregnancy endangered a woman's health, only 15 percent said that a married woman should be able to obtain a legal abortion merely because she did not want to have any more children, and only 18 percent supported legalizing abortion for unmarried women.[2] The public supported laws that gave doctors greater freedom, but they did not favor giving women the right to simply choose to terminate their pregnancies.

Proponents of liberalized abortion bills gained popular support by insisting that the bills would not introduce any radical change in the abortion rate or encourage promiscuity. In 1967, as Colorado legislators prepared to pass the nation's first ALI-style abortion liberalization measure, the executive secretary of the Colorado Medical Society defended the bill from Catholic pro-life attacks by insisting that the new law "wasn't written for the secretary in Chicago who went out one night and had a good time.... It was written to fill what a great many people consider to be a legitimate need."[3]

Yet, in spite of such assurances, pro-lifers did not believe that liberalization advocates would stop with a minor revision of the law. A move in this direction, they argued, would only produce more demand for illegal abortions—and thus more pressure to further liberalize the law. Once abortion was allowed in cases of rape and incest, people would soon begin to accept abortion for a few other reasons as well, leading eventually to "abortion on demand."[4]

Pro-lifers thought they had good reason to believe that their opponents secretly favored much more sweeping measures. After all, if one of the chief goals of liberalization was to reduce the number of illegal abortions, allowing abortion in such limited circumstances would have little impact. Abortion law reformers claimed that one million women were resorting to illegal abortions each year; only a small minority of them would be helped by these laws. Right-to-life advocates were deeply skeptical that such laws were the liberalizers' ultimate goal.

As early as the 1930s, William Robinson, A. J. Rongy, and Frederick Taussig had suggested that abortion be allowed in far more circumstances than ALI-style laws permitted.[5] But it was not until the mid-1960s that a few activists began pushing for the legalization of all abortions. One of the first was Pat Maginnis. Maginnis had grown up in a large Catholic family and attended parochial schools in Oklahoma, but as an adult, she became sharply critical of the Church and began campaigning for women's reproductive rights. During her three-year stint as an army medic in the 1950s, she saw the life-threatening agony that women experienced when they were denied the opportunity to safely terminate their pregnancies, which first got her thinking seriously about abortion. She then had three dangerous illegal abortions herself—one in Mexico and two that she performed on herself using a catheter and Lysol.[6]

In 1961, when Maginnis was in her early thirties and finishing a degree at San Jose State College, she began lobbying for abortion law reform in

California. At the time, the vast majority of the activists in the movement were men, and none of them were working for the repeal of all restrictions on abortion. Although Maginnis suggested in her correspondence that she favored abortion law repeal as early as 1962, she was initially hesitant about proclaiming this idea too forcefully, and instead suggested that in the short term, she was willing to settle for modest changes that were "a step in the right direction," if also "very conservative." She lobbied the California state legislature in favor of John Knox and Anthony Beilenson's abortion reform bills, but by 1964, she was beginning to have second thoughts about that strategy. Abortion, she now declared, should be available to "any woman who has an unwanted pregnancy for any reason."[7]

Maginnis's organization, the Society for Humane Abortion (SHA), used the language of feminism to argue that access to abortion was a fundamental right. "Until women have the right to an abortion whenever they feel that they need one, they will not be fully free," one of the SHA's members, Louise Butler, declared in 1965. The society's treasurer, Robert N. Bick, was equally emphatic: "A woman's body is her own and she has a right to it," he stated.[8]

This was a new idea in 1965. Maginnis and her allies were the first to link the idea of abortion rights to the emerging second-wave feminist consciousness that Betty Friedan's bestselling book of 1963, *The Feminine Mystique*, had expressed. Women's freedom itself was at stake, Maginnis argued, but the male leaders of the movement were throwing women only a "token bone," passing laws that put physicians, rather than pregnant women, in control.[9]

Maginnis and the SHA opposed Beilenson's proposed abortion reform measure in 1965, calling it a "side step" instead of a "step forward." After the bill finally became law in 1967, the SHA continued to denounce it as inadequate; it covered only about 3 percent of the 100,000 California women who obtained illegal abortions every year, Maginnis claimed. There was no reason, she believed, for legislators to force 97,000 California women a year to risk their lives in illegal procedures when safe hospital abortions could be made available. Maginnis had no patience for moralizers. "It's no skin off the back of law, medicine, or religion if a woman decides to chuck a pregnancy she doesn't want," Maginnis said. For women, she had a simple message: "It's your right to end unwanted pregnancy."[10]

Maginnis positioned herself as a political radical, far more confrontational than the staid upper-middle-class doctors and lawyers who had been the face of the movement. She distributed abortion-related political literature outside Catholic churches and arranged to get arrested for teaching classes on abortion techniques. Such controversial tactics might not have seemed unusual in Maginnis's home city of San Francisco in the late 1960s, but in more conservative areas, few wanted to associate themselves with Maginnis's polarizing style. When the executive secretary of the SHA, Rowena Gurner, announced in 1967 that she was going to intentionally and repeatedly get pregnant in order to experiment on herself with new abortion techniques, it only confirmed the perceived radicalism of repeal advocates.[11]

Yet by the late 1960s, ideas that had once seemed radical were becoming mainstream. The rapid growth of Maginnis's SHA reflected the change in public sentiment. The organization, which had only 50 members on its mailing list in 1964, had 15,000 by the summer of 1970. "Our support seems to mushroom as we have gotten more radical," the SHA's treasurer observed in 1965.[12]

Others would follow her lead. Lawrence Lader, a freelance journalist whose pieces regularly appeared in the *New York Times* and popular women's magazines, published the first book-length defense of repeal in 1966. The next year, Harold Rosen, one of the early physician advocates for liberalized abortion laws, began advocating for repeal. Not just their positions, but their reasoning, had shifted—they argued that a woman should be able to choose whether or not to be pregnant.[13]

This was becoming a rallying cry in the rapidly growing feminist movement. In 1967, the National Organization for Women (NOW) passed a resolution calling for the repeal of all restrictions on abortion, saying that it was "a basic right of every woman to control her reproductive life." In 1968, Alan Guttmacher announced his own change of mind on the issue and joined the call for repeal. And in 1969, Lader and Friedan joined several others, including Maginnis and New York abortion doctor Bernard Nathanson, to create the National Association for the Repeal of Abortion Laws (NARAL). NARAL, which was structured very similarly to its nemesis, the National Right to Life Committee, began working for repeal of abortion restrictions throughout the nation, with special attention devoted to the two largest states, California and New York. Some members of the abortion rights movement, including the board members of the American Civil Liberties Union (ACLU), were not at first fully onboard, saying that a woman had an inviolable right to an abortion only up to the point at which a fetus became viable (which, given the state of medicine in the late 1960s, meant the very beginning of the third trimester), but others followed NOW and NARAL in advocating the repeal of all legal restrictions on abortion at any stage of pregnancy, insisting that only a woman and her doctor should have any say in the matter. Abortion, they thought, was a legitimate medical procedure that should be treated like any other; it had no place in the criminal code. By 1969, the leaders of the ACLU agreed, advocating the repeal of "all laws imposing criminal penalties for abortion" so that "any woman could ask a doctor to terminate a pregnancy at any time."[14]

Several factors—among them the rise of feminism and the sexual revolution—made longtime advocates of limited liberalization newly receptive to the idea of repeal, and not all embraced the position for precisely the same reasons. Lader, for instance, was concerned primarily about overpopulation, while for Friedan abortion was a women's rights issue. But for many, the most compelling argument was that the liberalization laws had not reduced the number of illegal abortions. The laws permitted abortions for only a small fraction of the women who wanted the procedure. In Colorado, for instance, most women who applied for abortions under the state's new law were refused, and even some of the ones who were accepted felt humiliated by the process. By 1970, Richard Lamm, the sponsor of the Colorado law, conceded that it had been a failure, and that it was time to "eliminate all laws on abortion and make it a private matter between a woman and her physician." "We tried to change a cruel, outmoded, inhuman law—and what we got was a cruel, outmoded, inhuman law," he said.[15]

The most humiliating cases, some thought, concerned rape. In North Carolina, a twelve-year-old rape victim was refused an abortion because she had not reported her assault to the police within seven days of the attack, as required by state law. Advocates of full repeal pointed to cases like this as examples of the injustice of the laws they had promoted only three years earlier.[16]

The hypocrisy of the early abortion liberalization bills was also evident to many observers. In theory, the laws allowed for abortion only in extreme situations, but as right-to-life advocates had predicted, many doctors were happy to stretch the definition of "mental health." Ninety-one percent of legal hospital abortions in California, Colorado, Georgia, and Maryland—four of the earliest states to liberalize their abortion laws— were performed for reasons of mental health during the first two years these laws were in effect. But because hospital abortion committees varied widely in their interpretation of what constituted a threat to mental health, abortions were far easier to obtain in some states than in others, even when the laws were nearly identical. In Georgia in 1968, there were only two legal abortions for every 1,000 live births; in California, there were thirty-five. The abortion laws of the two states were essentially the same, but the results were not.[17]

As the failures of liberalized abortion laws became evident, public opinion rapidly shifted in favor of the legalization of elective abortion—that is, abortions performed for any reason. A Gallup poll conducted in November 1969 revealed that 40 percent of Americans said that they would support a law that would "permit a woman to go to a doctor to end pregnancy at any time during the first three months." Fifty percent of Americans were opposed, but three years earlier, only 15 percent had been in favor. The abortion rights movement was quickly gaining ground.[18]

Protestant leaders underwent a similarly rapid transformation. In 1963, when the Unitarian Universalist Association (UUA) became the first denomination to officially endorse abortion law reform, it had called only for ALI-style liberalization bills. At the time, it was a bold move—the ALI guidelines were considerably more liberal than any existing abortion law. But only five years later, some abortion rights advocates thought it too conservative and the UUA passed a resolution calling for the repeal of all abortion laws. That same year, the American Baptist Convention advocated the removal of all restrictions on abortion during the first twelve weeks of pregnancy. Two years later, the United Presbyterian Church followed suit, drawing the line at the point of viability. The United Methodist Church went even further, backing the legalization of abortion "upon request." Although the national governing body of the Episcopal Church did not issue an official resolution on abortion prior to *Roe*, several local Episcopal dioceses committed themselves to the cause of abortion rights and abortion law repeal. The Episcopal Diocese of New York, for instance, called for the repeal of all legal restrictions on abortions performed by licensed medical practitioners, thus implying that abortion should be legal at every stage of pregnancy.[19]

They had allies among population control advocates. For the previous twenty years, a few academics and industrial magnates such as Hugh Moore and John D. Rockefeller III had been arguing that the world's population would soon outstrip the earth's resources. Overpopulation, they believed, was the root cause of poverty. During the economically vibrant 1950s, that message had appealed to only a few Americans, but it began to gain popular currency in the mid-1960s, partly because of widespread media coverage. Most middle-class white Americans of the 1960s were still enjoying an unprecedented degree of economic prosperity, but President Johnson's focus on poverty, combined with media coverage of riots and rising crime rates, led many people to wonder whether the United States could support all its people. Americans knew that the situation was even worse in the Third World. A worldwide baby boom in the early postwar years, along with medical advances that reduced childhood mortality, had caused the global population to double in less than half a century. If population growth was left unchecked, there would be at least six billion people on the planet by the year 2000, with some of the poorest countries, including India and China, among the most populous. Even in the United States, there was often a correlation between poverty and high fertility; women who had a lot of children—especially if they were not married, but sometimes even if they were—tended to be poor.[20]

Several of the leading proponents of abortion legalization, including Lawrence Lader, were also members of the population control movement. Garrett Hardin, a California biology professor who was an early member of the SHA, routinely invoked the dangers of overpopulation when arguing for unrestricted abortions. The California Committee to Legalize Abortion sent out fundraising letters asking people to "donate a meager amount to save ... California from overpopulation" by making abortion legal in the state. "Overpopulation is a greater threat than nuclear holocaust to continued human existence on this planet," one member of the SHA proclaimed in 1968. Overpopulation would lead to cannibalism within two generations, another abortion rights supporter told Anthony Beilenson.[21]

In the mid-1960s, these were fringe voices; by the end of the decade, they were much more prevalent. One reason was biologist Paul Ehrlich's bestselling book *The Population Bomb* (1968). Ehrlich's book predicted mass starvation as early as the 1970s, with worse consequences to follow. The planet, he believed, was incapable of supporting even its current population, let alone billions more. Among his proposed remedies was the legalization of elective abortion. Zero Population Growth (ZPG), an organization that Ehrlich cofounded in 1968, convinced many that this would be a cost-effective and humane way to reduce population pressures.[22]

Pro-lifers were dismayed, not only because this meant more support for repeal, but also because it seemed that an increasing number of Americans believed that the unborn were, in at least some cases, threats to societal resources and therefore legitimate targets for elimination. For pro-lifers, any willingness to sacrifice human life for future sustainability was a frightening manifestation of the utilitarian thinking and disregard for human dignity they had been fighting for years. When Anthony Beilenson tried to legalize all abortions performed by physicians so that, as he said, the "great problems of population and environment can be solved by free and uncoerced individual decision and choice," a California pro-life group called Voice for the Unborn castigated him for proposing what they considered the "extermination of man as a solution to over-population," which was "a negating of all those rights upon which our country was founded."[23]

Most pro-lifers argued that while the dangers of overpopulation were real, they were far less acute than ZPG activists believed, and they could be dealt with through technological innovation rather than efforts to reduce the birthrate. In 1959, when discussions of population control were still confined to a relatively small academic circle, the Catholic bishops of the United States issued a collective statement on population concerns, saying, "The logical answer [to the problem of overpopulation] would be, not to decrease the number of people but increase the food supply which is almost unlimited in potential." Most pro-lifers stuck to this line of argument through the 1960s and early 1970s. The real issue was a poor allocation of resources, not a surfeit of people, they said. They also pointed out that population growth was already beginning to level off in most countries, including the United States, so legalized abortion was hardly necessary. Anthony Zimmerman, a Catholic moral theology professor who had worked for several years as a missionary in Japan and who then used his experience in a country with an unrestricted abortion policy to argue against the claims of ZPG proponents, calculated that the earth could probably sustain up to 28 billion people, but predicted that based on current growth rates, the world population would likely never increase much beyond 11 billion. There was no genuine population crisis, he argued. Japan offered a case in point of the problems that could result from legalizing abortion in order to address a nonexistent population crisis. In 1970, after twenty years of legalized abortion, Japan had a labor shortage and a birthrate that some demographers considered too low, since it was below the replacement level. Pro-lifers also insisted that regardless of whether overpopulation was a worthy concern in the developing world, it was certainly not an issue in the United States. When a ZPG advocate in Kulm, North Dakota, wrote an impassioned plea for abortion legalization, the president of the state's Right to Life Association responded that there was no population crisis in North Dakota, and that legalizing abortion in the state would do nothing to reduce population growth in India, China, and the rest of the developing world.[24]

While population control advocates sought to reduce global poverty by curbing birthrates, pro-lifers cast themselves as the true defenders of the poor. They wanted to give impoverished women the resources to care for their children. Most of the poor did not want elites to limit their fertility, Randy Engel argued, but "wealthy industrialists, eugenics advocates, and elitist-oriented groups," such as John D. Rockefeller III's Population Council, had pressured them into accepting contraception and were on the verge of doing the same with abortion. Engel, a Catholic journalist and mother of five children in her early thirties, who had spent most of the previous decade working as an advocate for Vietnamese refugees, became the pro-life movement's most forceful opponent of population control. Her *Pro-Life Report on Population Growth and the American Future* quickly became the most widely circulated pro-life rebuttal of population control arguments. Her warnings resonated with a pro-life movement that already believed that the legalization of abortion would quickly lead to coercive abortion for the poor, and she became a sought-after speaker on the pro-life circuit and a leader in several local and national pro-life organizations.[25]

Pro-lifers emphasized the importance of aiding the poor rather than curbing population growth, but they faced opposition from both sides of the political aisle. Many liberals argued for loosening abortion laws in order to fight poverty and overpopulation. Some conservatives also invoked population concerns in support of abortion law reform, because they argued that the social welfare programs that liberals had created would bankrupt the nation if the population growth among the poor was not checked through abortion. The numbers of people enrolled in these programs had increased rapidly; in 1960, only one-third of those eligible for Aid to Families with Dependent Children (AFDC) were enrolled; by the end of the decade, 90 percent of eligible recipients were receiving benefits. Some states and municipalities with declining tax bases and escalating welfare rolls wondered if the AFDC program would bankrupt them. This was particularly true in New York City, where spending on public assistance quadrupled during the 1960s and became the city's largest budget item, surpassing public education by the end of the decade. At the same time, a growing number of whites saw poverty as an African American problem, one for which they had little sympathy at a time of urban race riots and a rising Black Power movement. Although the majority of AFDC recipients were white, many whites stereotyped welfare recipients as single African American women who had become pregnant out of wedlock and were "breeding children as a cash crop," as Alabama governor George Wallace said. Wallace eventually took a strong stance against abortion, but like some of his fellow conservatives, he supported legalization in the early 1970s.[26]

The idea that unwanted children were likely to become social problems and end up on the welfare rolls or in prison resonated with many middle-class conservatives. Legalized abortion, they thought, might reduce the crime rate in the long term and cut welfare costs in the short term. In 1970, a legislative analyst in California concluded that if his state legalized elective abortion, the state's welfare burden could be cut by $8.5 million per year. NARAL made a similar calculation, although it concluded that the potential savings might be even greater. There were nearly 225,000 "illegitimate children" on California's welfare rolls at the beginning of 1973. In each case, an abortion would have cost only $250, whereas the state would have to pay a total of $54,000 for each child who remained on the state's welfare rolls for eighteen years. "If we want to help our poor brethren and also slow our rapidly increasing welfare burden, we must help these people in their desires to control their childbearing," a Kentucky proponent of legalized abortion declared in state legislative hearings in 1972.[27]

Pro-lifers who heard these arguments feared that they signaled the beginning of coerced abortions for the poor, something they had predicted would happen once abortions were legalized. Already social workers from state family planning agencies were discussing family planning with impoverished mothers. Pro-lifers found it hard to believe that the women were not being encouraged to terminate their pregnancies. "Claims that no one is coerced, that the welfare client is merely 'informed' of her options have the ring of pious hypocrisy," John Noonan told a California State Assembly committee in 1970.[28] At a time when both the left and the right were trying to find ways to fight poverty by reducing the birthrates of the poor, pro-lifers positioned themselves as the true defenders of human dignity, because they were defending the right of the poor to bear children.

Pro-lifers also reacted sharply against the claim that abortion legalization would promote children's best interests by preventing the birth of children who were "unwanted" and thus unlikely to be given a loving, nurturing home. Abortion law reformers had made versions of this claim as early as the 1930s, but they gave it increasing emphasis in the late 1960s, and by the end of the decade, it was one of their most common arguments. "The right to abortion is the foundation of Society's long struggle to guarantee that every child comes into this world wanted, loved, and cared for," Lawrence Lader declared in 1966. "Every child has the right to be born into a loving environment—a wanted child, eagerly awaited by his parents," one of NARAL's brochures from the early 1970s proclaimed. "Psychological and sociological studies leave no doubt that unwanted children are a social danger.... Society suffers the consequences of ill-advised parenthood for decades and even generations." At a time when state legislatures were passing the first legislation to protect children from abuse, abortion rights proponents' claim that "unwanted" children were likely to be abused had persuasive power. Pro-lifers responded that there was no evidence that children who had been born through unwanted pregnancies were more likely to be abused; in fact, the opposite was true. They frequently cited the research of the University of Southern California professor of pediatrics Edward Lenoski, who conducted a study of more than 500 abused children in the early 1960s and found that 90 percent of them had been born as the result of planned pregnancies. For pro-lifers, this was clear evidence that reducing the number of unwanted pregnancies would do nothing to prevent child abuse. Furthermore, they were troubled by the implications of the assumption that only the "wanted" had a right to be born. As Juan Ryan argued, when advocates of abortion rights called for "every child [to] be a wanted child," they really meant that "no child who is unwanted should be allowed to survive."[29]

Pro-lifers also insisted that every child was indeed wanted—if not by its parents, then at least by another couple willing to adopt it. "Adoption, Not Abortion" became a popular sign at pro-life rallies in the early 1970s. And some pro-lifers did, in fact, practice what they preached. The president of Florida's Dade Right-to-Lifers, for instance, had adopted six children by the time she was elected to lead the organization in the fall of 1971. "We in Right to Life recognize that there are unwanted pregnancies, but we know that there are no unwanted babies," Margot Sheahan, the president of the Northern Region Chapter of Arizona Right to Life, wrote. "There are solutions and alternatives to abortion—adoption, strengthening the family unit, more emphasis on the marriage commitment, reaching out, caring. These are positive solutions. It is a negative element in our society that sees killing as a solution to a social problem." Thomas Hilgers, a young doctor in Minnesota who was a popular speaker at youth pro-life events, encouraged his fellow pro-lifers to make a commitment to adopt, and specifically, to be open to the "adoption of minority race and handicapped children."[30] Just as several Catholic couples had offered a decade earlier to adopt Sherri Chessen Finkbine's unborn child, so many pro-lifers of the early 1970s promoted adoption—and, in some cases, adopted children into their own families—in order to provide positive alternatives to abortion.

Pro-lifers were correct in their claim that there was no shortage of people willing to adopt. In fact, there was a shortage of children. The number of children available for adoption was falling rapidly, due partly to declining birthrates and the increased availability of legal abortion, but also to the increasing willingness of single women who became pregnant out of wedlock to raise their babies on their own. In 1970, 89,000 children were placed with nonrelated adoptive parents. The number fell to 50,000 in 1974.[31] Pro-lifers had good reason to believe that the number of parents trying to adopt was much greater than this, and that there were more than enough loving homes to care for all of the unwanted children in the United States.[32]

The focus on the "wanted child" seemed to confirm pro-lifers' longstanding belief that abortion rights supporters were willing to let the value of a human life be determined by social considerations. "If you start talking and thinking about a child as a 'wanted child' you cannot help but put the idea into people's heads that children exist and have a right to exist only because someone *wants* them," Sidney Callahan, a liberal Catholic who self-identified as both a feminist and a pro-life advocate, declared in the *National Catholic Reporter* in December 1971. "And, alas, the opposite conclusion is there waiting for us; if it's an 'unwanted child' it has no rights." After comparing the "unwanted child" to the "unwanted" black, "unwanted" Jew, or "unwanted" woman, she concluded, "The powerful (including parents) cannot be allowed to want and un-want people at will."[33]

## Competing Rights Claims in the Nation's Courts

The right-to-life movement had employed the language of inalienable rights for years, but supporters of abortion legalization had mostly relied on utilitarian arguments. In the early 1960s, Pat Maginnis and the handful of activists in the SHA had been almost alone in viewing abortion as a woman's right; none of the other leading abortion law reformers, including Alan Guttmacher and Anthony Beilenson, advocated removing all restrictions on abortion, and none of them used the language of rights. But in the late 1960s, Beilenson, Guttmacher, and a host of other advocates of abortion liberalization exchanged their longstanding utilitarian arguments for a new rights-based language. Though the advocates of abortion rights reached their new position for many reasons, all came to believe that abortion was a woman's absolute right, a claim that came directly from the feminist movement and the SHA.

A rights-based claim was ultimately a constitutional claim, to be decided by the courts, where the right-to-life movement had a longstanding advantage. A decades-long legal tradition established by a series of state court decisions, treated the fetus as a person with the right to sue, inherit property, and be provided with a court-appointed legal guardian, all of which helped establish the fetus's constitutional "right to life." The right-to-life movement was thus able to win several early court victories. In 1967, the New Jersey state supreme court ruled in *Gleitman v. Cosgrove* that women did not have a right to an abortion in cases of suspected fetal defects. "The right to life is inalienable in our society," the court declared. "A child need not be perfect to have a worthwhile life."[34]

Pro-lifers thought the legal case against abortion rights advocates was unassailable, yet supporters of abortion rights could claim one important precedent that had the potential to trump all of the other lower court decisions: *Griswold v. Connecticut* (1965). A year after the Supreme Court ruled in *Griswold* that laws against contraceptives violated the constitutional right to "privacy" in the "marriage relationship," the SHA claimed that the right to privacy should include the right to an abortion, a claim that was perhaps not surprising for an organization that had begun using rights-based language to advocate for abortion law repeal several years before anyone else. The SHA grounded its claim in the idea that the Constitution protected women from intrusive state control of their bodies. "Does the state have the right to force a woman to carry a pregnancy she doesn't want?" the SHA's newsletter asked in the spring of 1966. "Does the state own the woman's uterus?" These arguments—grounded partly in feminists' understanding of the Constitution and partly in their understanding of transcendent human rights—seemed radical in 1966, but within a few years, they were widespread. Women had a right to "jurisdiction over their own bodies" as a "minimal condition of human dignity," Jean Faust, a NOW board member, declared in 1969.[35] The pro-life movement had invoked principles of inalienable rights, constitutional law, and "human dignity" for years; now their opponents were doing so. In 1969,

the California State Supreme Court endorsed this line of argument in
*People v. Belous.*

*People v. Belous* concerned a doctor who had referred a woman to an
illegal abortionist in order to prevent her from endangering her life by
seeking an abortion in Mexico. The court declared that the phrase "necessary to preserve life"—the ground for a legal abortion—could mean many
things; if strictly interpreted, it could imply that abortions were valid only
if a pregnant woman would die without one, but if it were interpreted
more liberally, it could also justify an abortion that might avert a woman
from endangering her life. The law was too vague and thus invalid, the
court ruled.[36]

Because the law in question had already been replaced by the Therapeutic
Abortion Act of 1967, *Belous* had no direct effect. Nevertheless, observers
recognized it as a landmark ruling that would likely change the debate
over abortion laws. Most states at the time had laws that were similar to the
statute that was at issue in *Belous*, and while the California state supreme
court decision had no direct applicability in other states, everyone involved
in the abortion debate knew that it would only be a matter of time before
other state courts, or even the US Supreme Court, would consider the
argument posited in *Belous*. If the Supreme Court upheld *Belous*'s reasoning, state abortion laws across the nation could be invalidated on grounds
of vagueness. Other implications of the *Belous* ruling were even more
far-reaching. While *Belous* did not mention the Therapeutic Abortion Act,
legal analysts realized that since the court had ruled that the phrase "necessary to preserve life" was unconstitutionally vague, a clause allowing
abortion only if it were necessary to preserve a woman's "health," as the
Therapeutic Abortion Act stipulated, was even more vulnerable to a constitutional challenge for vagueness. "Health," after all, could mean almost
anything.

But for the pro-life movement, the most troubling aspect of *Belous* was
its reversal of a decades-old precedent of legal recognition of fetal rights,
and its replacement with the suggestion that abortion might be a woman's constitutional right. "The fundamental right of the woman to choose
whether to bear children" was a logical application of the "right to privacy"
that the US Supreme Court had recognized in *Griswold v. Connecticut* four
years earlier, the California court said. The state could infringe on this
right only if it demonstrated a "compelling interest" justifying such regulations, and only if the regulations were "narrowly drawn."[37] In essence,
*Belous* gave legal imprimatur to the argument that women's constitutional

right to privacy included a constitutional right to make abortion decisions without interference from the government. While the court did not say that this right was absolute and inalienable—-as some in the abortion rights movement believed—it did ground this right in constitutional law, the first time that a court had done so. After this decision, the language of constitutional rights became far more common in the abortion rights movement.

Pro-life lawyers in California had closely followed the *Belous* case, and for months they had privately expressed concern that the attorney general was not handling it very well. Nevertheless, they did their best to support the prosecution, with the Catholic Welfare Bureau and the state Right to Life League filing briefs in support of the state's position. When the attorney general lost the case, as they had feared he might, they prepared for an appeal to the US Supreme Court, where they hoped they could make a stronger case. Some pro-life legal experts in California, including John Noonan, worried that an appeal to the US Supreme Court might backfire, because pro-lifers could not be sure of victory, but other pro-life Catholic lawyers were more confident of a favorable ruling now that Warren Burger, rather than Earl Warren, was chief justice. In the end, the question was moot, because the Supreme Court declined to hear the appeal. Pro-lifers would be left with the *Belous* decision. As they recognized, the decision was a game-changer for them; it was a "major new challenge" that, as the National Right to Life Committee's December 1969 newsletter accurately predicted, would result in two new developments that would be difficult for the pro-life movement to fight against: it would make the courts a new battleground in the abortion debate, and it would also encourage the abortion law reform movement to shift its legislative effort from liberalization to repeal.[38] In short, the fight to protect the unborn would become a lot more difficult.

The consequences of the decision were even more disastrous for the right-to-life cause than pro-lifers had feared. Following the court's lead, hospital abortion committees in California began approving abortions for almost any pregnancy that might have the slightest negative impact on a woman's mental or physical health. The number of abortions rapidly increased. During the first year that the Therapeutic Abortion Act of 1967 was in effect, only 3,775 hospital abortions took place in California, because only a few pregnant women could qualify for a legal abortion if the law was strictly interpreted. After *Belous*, the number of legal abortions skyrocketed. In 1971, nearly 117,000 legal abortions were performed in the state.

The next year, the number reached 160,000. Governor Ronald Reagan, who had already begun to have second thoughts about the Therapeutic Abortion Act that he had signed into law, was dismayed that the court had stretched the interpretation of the law's health clause far beyond his original intention, and that under California's Medi-Cal program, taxpayers were expected to pick up the tab for some of these allegedly unjustified abortions. "When a fifteen-year-old girl can have, under Medicaid, at the taxpayers' expense, three abortions with the same psychiatrist each time simply giving a quick, off-the-cuff diagnosis that she has suicidal tendencies, this was not what I had in mind," Reagan told a representative of the National Right to Life Committee.[39]

Just as the National Right to Life Committee had predicted, abortion rights advocates interpreted *Belous* as a green light to introduce abortion law repeal bills in state legislatures. In March 1970, six months after the court ruling in *Belous*, Anthony Beilenson introduced such a bill in California, citing the court decision as a justification. He grounded his bill in the movement's newfound language of women's constitutional rights. "I think it is time that the legislature recognizes that every woman has a right *not* to bear children as well as to bear them, and that she has a right to privacy in matters relating to marriage, reproduction, sex and family life," Beilenson declared.[40]

The threat of a veto from Governor Reagan kept Beilenson's bill from becoming law, but the new language of inviolable rights that he and other abortion legalization advocates adopted made it nearly impossible for abortion rights activists to take seriously any claims on behalf of the fetus. Only a few years earlier, they had attempted to balance the interests of society, medicine, and pregnant women while still treating the fetus as worthy of at least some consideration. Early abortion liberalization laws gave the final decision to hospital abortion committees who, the laws assumed, could adjudicate among these competing interests. But if abortion was a women's rights issue, as many in the movement had come to believe, these rights could not be compromised.[41] The terms "pro-choice" and "right to choose" were not yet in use, but the concept behind them was becoming increasingly prevalent.

To support the argument that women had an absolute right to unrestricted abortion, activists began to argue that the fetus had almost no intrinsic value. "The early stages of an individual fetus," Garrett Hardin wrote in a *Redbook* magazine article on abortion in 1967, "are of very little worth." An embryo or fetus was not yet a person. "A set of blueprints is not a house; the DNA of a zygote is not a human being," he declared. Thus, in Hardin's view, "the drawbacks of a wanted abortion are . . . trifling."[42]

While other advocates of abortion rights generally avoided such blunt language, they did share the opinion that the fetus was not a person and had no inherent rights of its own. "No embryo or fetus can have the status of human life until it exists *in fact*, not just in possibility, as separate from the woman's body," the president of NOW's New York chapter, Ti-Grace Atkinson, declared in 1967. "An abortion is an act which interrupts the reproductive process. This act cannot take human life because there is no human life." Only a short time earlier, many abortion law reform advocates, including Alan Guttmacher, had been willing to concede that the fetus had some value and that abortion might be "killing," even if they believed that such "killing" was sometimes necessary to protect a woman's health or mental well-being. But by the early 1970s, when the abortion legalization movement had become an explicitly rights-based campaign, strident declarations of the fetus's non-personhood became de rigueur. If women had an absolute right to control their own reproductive systems for all nine months of pregnancy, the fetus could be accorded no rights at all. Such assertions were especially common among feminists, who saw any concessions to fetal rights as an attack on women's rights. "Legally, medically, philosophically, historically, economically, statistically, and morally a fetus is not regarded as a human being, a person, an individual," NOW's Abortion Task Force declared in 1971.[43]

A sizeable contingent of the population now scoffed at the pro-life claim that the fetus was a person—a claim that pro-lifers had long thought was self-evident. For most pro-lifers, each human life had value because it was a unique creation of God. Those who made this argument in secular terms similarly insisted that the intrinsic value of a fetus resided in its unique DNA, and that it was a dangerous precedent to begin defining the value of human life in terms of its capabilities or its perceived social value. But for many abortion rights advocates—even for some who were religious—what gave human life value was not its status as biological human life, but the degree to which it possessed the qualities of personhood, which they generally defined in terms of autonomy, mental capacity, and social value. Some abortion rights advocates stated this directly, as Ashley Montagu did when he claimed in 1967 that "the embryo, fetus, and newborn of the species does not really become functionally human until it has been humanized in the human socialization process." More commonly, activists refrained from defining the precise point at which personhood began, and instead pointed out the vast differences between an adult woman—whose rights must surely be protected—and a fetus (whose status as a human being was, in their view, questionable at best). They ridiculed pro-lifers for believing that "the cells undergoing meiosis" immediately after conception constituted a "human being, complete with soul ... despite the fact that one would not recognize it if one saw it on the head of a pin." Even a late-term fetus could not be a human being, some abortion rights advocates argued, because it lacked the bodily autonomy that was an essential quality of personhood. As Ti-Grace Atkinson said, "The denotative definitive characteristic of what it is to be a person (i.e., a human life) is existence as a single *separate* man, woman, or child."[44] By that definition, no fetus that was still in a woman's uterus could qualify.

This, pro-lifers believed, allowed people to decide which lives had value based solely on their size, appearance, or personal autonomy. In this utilitarian calculation, people who were completely dependent on others, in the way that a fetus was completely dependent on its mother, did not have the right to exist. This was exactly what pro-lifers such as Paul Harrington had predicted. The next step, they claimed, would be euthanasia—the killing of the defenseless elderly—and then infanticide.[45]

But advocates of abortion rights resented such claims. They were only trying to protect the lives of women, they argued. The pro-lifers, they charged, were religiously motivated and were unconstitutionally trying to impose their faith-based definition of human life on others. Employing a variation of the argument that Episcopal priest Lester Kinsolving and his liberal Protestant allies had been making since the mid-1960s, pro-choicers argued that since theologians, philosophers, and scientists could not reach a consensus on when human life begins, any attempt to codify that life begins at conception was invalid. As NARAL declared, "The moment when life begins is a theological argument that has no place in the legislatures and courts of a pluralistic society, founded on the concept of the separation of Church and State."[46] Each pregnant woman would have to decide the question for herself.

This struck pro-lifers as especially dangerous. The idea that "abortion is right for those who think it is right, and wrong for those who think it is wrong" would, if applied to "any other kind of act," seem absurd, Georgetown philosophy professor Germain Grisez argued. "If Hitler was quite sincere about his ideas for racial purification, that has not convinced the world that genocide was right for him."[47]

When Grisez began writing his book in 1967, he was already convinced that the abortion liberalization bills that several states had just passed were merely brief way stations on the road to "abortion on demand."[48] By 1970, when his book was published, Grisez's predictions were already beginning to come true.

## The Legalization of Elective Abortion in Hawaii

Hawaii was so distant that few people in the pro-life movement paid much attention to what was happening in its state legislature. An abortion rights movement coalesced with only limited opposition. The beleaguered Hawaiian pro-life movement consisted chiefly of a few Catholics who were not very politically influential, along with one activist— W. N. Bergin, a doctor in the city of Hilo who had been writing pro-life articles for Catholic medical journals for the previous four years and had corresponded with pro-life leaders from as far away as Boston. But Bergin had little influence in his own state. When the state legislature held its initial hearings on abortion legalization in early 1970, he was one of only three people who showed up to testify against the bill. The other two were a Catholic priest and a former president of the state Catholic Physicians' Guild. As one advocate of abortion rights wrote, explaining why her side had the advantage, "The key to the situation, of course, is that the Catholic hierarchy here simply does not have much influence on public opinion, and everyone knows this." Only half of Hawaii's citizens were Christians—a lower percentage than any other state in the Union—and even many of them were members of Protestant denominations whose ministers were lobbying for liberalization of the state's abortion law. Catholics constituted the largest religious group in the state, but because they were still a distinct minority, they faced a daunting task. What made it even more difficult was that some of the Catholics in the state legislature acted against the teachings of their Church and began leading the charge for a complete repeal of all abortion restrictions. No matter what the Church said, they believed, they could not impose their own moral beliefs about abortion on others.[49]

With Catholic pro-life forces in disarray, members of ZPG and other abortion rights supporters mobilized support from both of Honolulu's daily newspapers, many leading civic organizations (including Chambers of Commerce), and several Protestant denominations, as well as the Hawaii Council of Churches. Because most of the state's population was concentrated in a narrow geographic area around Honolulu, this was not difficult to do, and there was little that the Catholic Church could do to fight back, since it did not have the voting power to secure much influence in state politics. When hearings on the bill began, the pro-life cause already appeared doomed. The three pro-lifers squared off against a panel of Protestant clergy, medical professionals, and representatives from women's and family planning organizations, all of whom testified in support of either liberalization or full repeal. Hawaii's Republican Party had endorsed abortion law liberalization as early as 1968, and many Democrats were even more liberal on the question. Hawaii's leading proponent of abortion legalization, state senator Nadao Yoshinaga, was a fierce proponent of population control measures; later that year, he introduced a bill that, if it had passed, would have required every woman who had given birth to two children to be sterilized. Many of Yoshinaga's fellow legislators shared his concern about the societal costs of "unwanted" children.[50]

But the legislators' principal concern was that liberalized abortion laws, in the ten states that had adopted them during the previous three years, had not worked. It was time, the legislators thought, to find an approach that would. Many Republicans advocated liberalization of the state's abortion law, and the Democratic Party favored full repeal. It was unfair, they said, that wealthy women could fly to Japan for abortions, while the poor were forced to resort to unsanitary, illegal methods. Legalizing all abortions—but requiring that they be performed in hospitals by trained medical professionals—would eliminate the class-based inequities in current law and save the poor from the unscrupulous practices of illegal abortionists.[51]

A few pro-lifers did their best to persuade legislators that the fetus was a human being. Robert Pearson, a Maui building contractor, spent $7,000 to defeat the bill. But legislators dismissed the argument that the fetus was a human being as merely a religious opinion not grounded in science—despite the attempts of pro-lifers to appeal to the biological evidence of early fetal development. The law had always made a distinction between viable and nonviable fetuses, the legislators declared, and the new abortion law would as well. Fetuses that were viable would receive protection; those that were not viable would not.[52]

The day before the state senate vote, the Catholic Church in Hawaii realized the imminent threat it faced, and it mounted a last-ditch campaign to stop the bill. The bishop of Honolulu led 1,000 pro-life Catholics in a demonstration at the statehouse. It seemed to have little effect on the senate, which approved the abortion repeal bill by a vote of fifteen to nine, with the house then voting for the measure by a margin of thirty-one to twenty.[53]

Pro-life Catholics appealed to Governor John Burns, a Catholic, to veto the bill. Burns insisted that he was personally opposed to abortion and even called it "murder." He said that he was proud that his wife had chosen not to have an abortion when a pregnancy had endangered her health, though doctors had recommended it. But in spite of his reservations, he had already declared, before the bill was even out of the legislature, that abortion should be a matter of individual conscience. As a Catholic, he believed that he could not "in good conscience" sign the bill into law, but given the overwhelming public support for the bill, he did not believe that he had the right to impose his views on others by vetoing it. As an early practitioner of the politics of mere "personal opposition" to abortion, Burns allowed the bill to become law without his signature. Pro-lifers condemned the action. Paul Weyrich, a young conservative Catholic from Wisconsin who would later create the Heritage Foundation and become a nationally known New Right activist, blasted Burns in the pages of the conservative Catholic press for his "refusal to stand up and be counted" in the fight for life. "Like Pilate, you washed your hands of the matter, but death will still be the final result," he wrote.[54]

There were forty-six abortions in Honolulu during the first week after the law went into effect. Two months later, the total stood at 587. To protest the effects of the new law, Robert Pearson created a "cemetery for aborted children," a place with tombstones that marked the passing of each unnamed fetus in the first state to offer women unrestricted access to legalized abortion. During the next two years, he and his wife spent $20,000 building a home for women facing crisis pregnancies. He promised to pay all medical expenses incurred in childbirth if a woman chose not to have an abortion. By the summer of 1972, he had helped eighty women through their crisis pregnancies. It was a small number compared to the thousands of women in Hawaii who had abortions, but Pearson was happy that he was at least able to do something, no matter how limited, to rescue unborn children.[55]

Six weeks after Hawaii adopted its new law, the Alaska legislature passed a similar bill allowing elective abortion up to the point of viability, which at the time was considered twenty-six weeks. Alaska's Methodist governor vetoed the bill on human life grounds, saying that he opposed abortion as a matter of conscience, but the legislature overrode his veto by a vote of forty-one to seventeen. As in Hawaii, there was strong public support for the measure.[56]

## The Battle over Elective Abortion Legalization in New York

New York, where pro-lifers had been fighting abortion liberalization proposals since 1967, should have been a different story. Despite strong support among many state legislators and Governor Nelson Rockefeller for some form of abortion liberalization, Catholics had successfully beaten back a series of abortion liberalization proposals.[57] But in 1970, the stakes were higher, because the proposed law was not an ALI-style reform measure, but rather a bill to repeal almost all restrictions on abortion prior to twenty-four weeks' gestation—a proposal that would make New York's abortion policy the most liberal in the nation and likely turn the state into the destination of choice for women throughout the country who sought abortions.

The bishops were up against a united liberal Republican state government that was intent on removing restrictions on abortion in order to aid the medical profession, promote personal freedoms for women, and address the perceived problems of overpopulation and "unwanted" children. Three years earlier, Rockefeller and a large number of liberals in both parties had pushed abortion reform, but the Catholic Democratic Speaker of the assembly had prevented the bill from coming up for a vote. Now he was gone. The new Republican Speaker signaled his support for abortion legalization. Even more alarmingly, the Republican senate majority leader Earl Brydges, a Catholic from Niagara Falls who had long been on the Church's side in the fight against every abortion reform bill that had previously been introduced, announced that this time he would not block the measure. Swallowing his doubts, he not only allowed the legislation that the governor favored to be brought to a vote, he even helped craft it.[58]

The bill was the brainchild of Republican state representative Constance Cook, who had become a convert to the repeal movement after attending a NOW meeting. With approximately twenty or more New York women dying from illegal abortions each year, it was time to repeal all restrictions on abortion, "put the illegal abortionist out of business," and save women's lives, she said. Most of the state legislators who had once merely advocated an ALI-style liberalization bill quickly decided that Cook's full repeal measure was the right approach. Her bill attracted thirty-eight cosponsors.[59]

The Catholic response was surprisingly weak, because Catholics who opposed abortion did not believe that Cook's bill would become law. Three years earlier, in 1967, Catholics had mounted an all-out campaign to stop an abortion liberalization effort, and they had done the same the following year. In 1970, they did not put up the same fight. Although the state's bishops sent a letter to every state legislator declaring that Cook's bill abrogated the unborn child's "inalienable right to life and destiny," they made only a limited effort to mobilize their parishioners on the issue. Brydges's historic support for the Church's cause and his previous unwillingness to bring abortion bills to the floor had given the bishops the false impression that the senate was more staunchly opposed to abortion than it actually was, and they underestimated the effect that Brydges's unexpected acquiescence would have on the legislative body over which he presided. As late as March—nearly two months after Brydges's staff had drafted an abortion legalization bill for the senator to introduce—the New York diocesan paper *Catholic News* continued to describe Brydges as "an opponent of loosening the present safeguards on abortion in the state," a description that suggested that the Catholic press was badly out of touch with the realities in Albany. The reports on the abortion bill that appeared in *Catholic News* only one week before the senate vote on the measure gave no indication that the bishops thought the bill would pass or that they considered the matter an urgent priority. The *Catholic News* headline "Latest Abortion Bill Seen as No Different from Rest" hardly seemed calculated to alarm the faithful, so it was not surprising that state legislators reported receiving few letters protesting the bill. The bishops were also too preoccupied with the fight for state funding of parochial schools to devote their energy to fighting an abortion bill. The Church devoted far more effort to lobbying for the chance to get $20 million in state aid than to fighting abortion legalization, so several Catholic state senators felt free to break with the Church on abortion as long as they could still curry favor by supporting parochial school aid.[60]

Several Republicans and socially conservative Democrats—about two-thirds of whom were Catholic—tried to stop the bill's passage, but Brydges had overestimated the strength of this pro-life coalition. Brydges had likely supported abortion law repeal only because he thought that it was too radical to pass; by helping to draft a repeal bill, he thought he could stave off more modest liberalization proposals and preserve New York's restrictive abortion law while also appearing not to stand in the way of the Republican governor's effort to liberalize the law. But he had miscalculated. At the last minute, perceiving a wave of support for a bill that he had thought would be viewed as too extreme, he announced his opposition to the measure that he had helped to bring to the floor. Brydges's eleventh-hour statement came too late. The bill passed in the state senate by a vote of thirty-one to twenty-six. Eighteen of those twenty-six opposition votes came from Catholic senators. Four Catholics voted for the bill—a small number, to be sure, but one that was just high enough to secure the bill's passage.[61]

The vote shocked the bishops into action. They launched an all-out effort to stop the bill in the state assembly. On Easter Sunday, churches throughout the state read new pastoral letters against abortion. One bishop publicly prayed for the soul of a Catholic state representative who supported the bill. Pro-lifers descended on the statehouse to warn that if New York legalized elective abortion, euthanasia would not be far behind. Pro-life women in the state organized the first right-to-life demonstration ever to occur at the New York state capitol. Pro-life legislators also took up the gauntlet, accusing the proponents of abortion legalization of attempting to legalize "murder" and adopting the "basic philosophy of the Nazi tyranny." They argued that abortion legalization violated the commonly accepted liberal values that both they and abortion rights advocates shared. It was "inconsistent to seek legislation to destroy life," state representative Ferdinand Mondello declared, while at the same time supporting increased governmental spending on healthcare for the elderly and opposing the death penalty and the Vietnam War. The result of the pro-life lobbying was just as surprising as the earlier senate vote had been: the abortion bill, which had been expected to secure passage in the assembly, was defeated by three votes after eight hours of rancorous debate. Forty-nine of the sixty-two Catholics in the assembly, along with twenty-four state representatives who were not Catholics, voted against it.[62]

Undeterred, Constance Cook used a point of parliamentary procedure to bring the bill up for another vote the following week. The bishops escalated the pressure on those who had voted for the bill. They reminded them that it violated the UN's Declaration of the Rights of the Child. Diocesan papers printed the names of the Catholic legislators who had voted for abortion legalization and urged the faithful to send them letters of protest. Edward Golden told right-to-life advocates that they should "send a note of thanks" to all legislators who voted against the bill and a letter to all other legislators to "let them know how they feel." The campaign did succeed in convincing three legislators to switch their votes and oppose the bill, but several others unexpectedly switched to Cook's side. Cook reached the critical number of seventy-six affirmative votes when one Democrat representing a conservative Catholic district in the Finger Lakes region announced, with tears in his eyes, that he knew he was throwing away his political career by switching his vote from "no" to "yes," but he was willing to pay the price if his vote would end the inhumanity of restrictive abortion laws and save women's lives. He was correct about the political cost of his vote; less than two weeks later, the Cayuga County Democratic Party declined to nominate him for reelection, and his career in the state legislature was over.[63] Although there were many liberal Democrats in Manhattan who supported abortion reform, the issue was still the kiss of death for some Democratic politicians in socially conservative Catholic regions upstate.

The bill passed by a single tie-breaking vote cast by the Speaker. Over a wave of protest from the state's bishops, who warned that the measure would turn New York into a "bloody butchery unmatched by any place on Earth," Governor Rockefeller signed the bill into law within hours of its passage. Rockefeller's loyal lieutenant in the senate, Earl Brydges, broke out in sobs while reading the pro-life movement's "Diary of an Unborn Child" on the senate floor and reflecting on its final words: "Today my mother killed me." It was too late.[64]

Pro-life Catholics in New York believed that they had just seen the repudiation of the nation's founding values, and they feared that they had been "catapulted into an era of abortion reform that may well shake the foundations of civilized society," as the New York *Catholic News* phrased it. For years, Catholics had argued that the Declaration of Independence's promise of the "inalienable" right to life and the Fourteenth Amendment's guarantee that no life could be taken without "due process" had protected the lives of the unborn, and they had predicted that if those rights were ever taken away, no one's life would be safe. They therefore reacted in horror when what they had long warned against became law in New York. They believed that they were witnessing the transition from a constitutional order to a state with "Nazi" values, and they shuddered to think what would happen next. Bishop Edwin Broderick of Albany was especially pessimistic. Although he urged pro-lifers to pray that "society will rediscover its conscience and return protection to the unborn," he did not foresee much chance of that happening and instead predicted that things would soon get worse. "Let us . . . be prepared for the euthanasia, sterilization and compulsory abortion laws" to follow, he said. An editorial in the *Catholic News* issued a similar warning, adding infanticide to the list. "The Abortion Reform Law has torn down the structure which protects human life," the paper declared. "Once killing is used as a solution to social problems there is no end to Man's ingenuity in solving the problems of the future."[65]

Cardinal Terence Cooke urged New York Catholics to prepare for a strategy of conscientious resistance to the new abortion law and to commit themselves to "reverence and preserve unborn human life," even if the law did not. In a joint statement issued a few days before the law was scheduled to take effect, New York's bishops applauded hospitals, doctors, and nurses who refused to "participate in this grave evil of abortion"— reminding Catholics that those who did participate in an abortion would be subject to immediate excommunication—and asked hospitals that did offer abortions to respect the "conscience" of medical personnel who refused to assist. They were especially worried, they said, that the law permitting abortions would soon become coercive. "We are most concerned that the poor not be pressured into submitting to abortion for the sake of lower welfare costs," the bishops declared.[66]

Some pro-life Catholics in New York accused the bishops of merely issuing lamentations when stronger political action was required. New York pro-life Catholic Catherine Willis wrote a scathing critique of her state's bishops for the conservative Catholic lay newspaper *The Wanderer*, bemoaning the helpless position that she felt herself to be in. "It is difficult to describe one's feelings as a resident of New York City during those days before July 1," she wrote in November 1970, "... the growing awareness of the lack of any effective opposition whatsoever to the city administration's intentions; the gradual realization that one's own bishops were going to let it happen without opening their mouths; and the sickening knowledge that the passage of each twenty-four hours was bringing one day closer the killing of the children, atrocities in which one could not avoid being implicated oneself. It was like being a resident in Nazi Germany awaiting the announcement of the killing of the first Jew—had that event been announced in advance."[67]

Pro-life activists were especially angry that, as far as they could tell, the New York bishops had been too concerned about securing parochial school funding to make the fight against abortion a priority, leaving the fight against abortion to local pro-life organizations that did not have the resources to mount a successful lobbying effort. To some, this seemed to indicate a wider problem in the post-Vatican II American Catholic Church.

"Bishops, who should be providing unequivocal moral leadership, are easing their consciences allowing those in subordinate positions of influence
to hold the front lines of attack while they remain in the background, dealing with the opposition on other matters of greater interest to themselves,"
Bishop Thomas J. Riley of Cambridge, Massachusetts, complained in a
letter to one of his pro-life allies in June 1970. "Everything that has happened thus far seems to indicate that the bishops are reluctant to commit
themselves too deeply on the question of abortion."[68]

The bishops had actually done more than their critics assumed. They
had issued several pastoral letters condemning the abortion bill. They had
pressured individual Catholic legislators in the assembly to vote against
the measure when it came up for a vote the second time. They had encouraged the priests in their dioceses to preach homilies on abortion and to
make the pro-life message a central part of Easter Sunday services. But
to all appearances, they had been asleep at the wheel during the crucial
fight in the state senate, and for that inaction, some pro-lifers could never
forgive them.

Part of the problem, New York pro-lifers decided, was that they had
relied on the bishops to lobby for their cause instead of leading the campaign themselves. New York had several pro-life groups, but they were
primarily educational or letter-writing organizations that lacked political
influence. Edward Golden now recognized his mistake. "We realized we'd
been steamrollered," he said. "The people who had been conducting the
campaign in favor of abortion had done their work in the corridors of
the Legislature, and we hadn't." Golden decided that he and other pro-
lifers needed to "roll up our sleeves and really become political."[69] It might
already be too late for that strategy, it seemed.

New York quickly became the nation's leading abortion provider, just
as pro-life activists had feared. Because the state's new abortion law contained no residency requirement, any woman who could find a way to
travel to New York could easily obtain a legal hospital abortion. Indeed,
some abortion doctors in New York encouraged out-of-state women to
come to their facilities, with several conducting out-of-state advertising
campaigns. One abortion clinic operator in Niagara Falls offered a special
deal for women from the Midwest—a $400 package that covered not only
an abortion but also a roundtrip airline ticket from Detroit and lunch after
the operation was over. In the first fifteen months after New York legalized elective abortion, the state's doctors performed 200,000 abortions,
at least 60 percent of which were for nonresidents.[70] Pro-lifers might be

able to continue to maintain laws against abortion in many states, but with abortion services readily available in New York, such laws did little to deter women who wanted abortions from obtaining them. For all intents and purposes, the United States now had a policy of legal elective abortion for all but the poorest women.

Other defeats soon followed. Pro-lifers failed to prevent the legalization of elective abortion in Washington State, where voters approved a referendum to allow mostly unrestricted abortion up to the twentieth week of pregnancy. Catholics constituted only 13 percent of the state's population, so the pro-life movement faced a difficult battle. Although Voice for the Unborn, an organization headed by Seattle lawyer Kenneth Vanderhoef, put up billboards with pictures of plastic replicas of four-month-old fetuses and the slogan "Kill Resolution 20, Not Me," the effort had only limited effect. Voters approved the measure by a comfortable 100,000-vote margin out of nearly one million ballots cast. As was the case in New York, Catholics were dismayed. It was "shocking and frightening to realize that the majority of the citizens of Washington had voted in favor of killing in cold blood one segment of our society for the economic benefit and social convenience of another," the archbishop of Seattle declared.[71]

Pro-lifers were also caught off guard in Maryland. In the spring of 1970, when the Maryland General Assembly took up consideration of the most liberal abortion bill considered by any state—a measure removing all restrictions on abortion right up to the moment of birth—Catholic bishops issued no statements on the issue because, like their counterparts in New York, they were focused on a tuition aid bill for parochial schools, and they did not expect the abortion bill to pass. It was only after the Maryland House of Delegates passed the bill in April, a few days after New York adopted its abortion law, that the bishops were shocked into action. The Maryland Catholic Conference requested public hearings on the bill before the senate voted on it, and they lined up a list of pro-life speakers to testify against the measure. Pro-lifers crowded the galleries while carrying signs that said, "Kill the bill, not the baby!" Cardinal Patrick O'Boyle of Washington, DC, who had taken an active role in the campaign against abortion liberalization in 1968, sent a pastoral letter to all Catholic parishes urging Catholics to oppose the bill. These efforts were not sufficient, though, to prevent the state senate from passing the measure, which had the support of the *Washington Post*, the *Baltimore Sun*, the Maryland Council of Churches, several social welfare agencies, and, according to public opinion polls, a majority of Marylanders.[72]

A few liberals in the state legislature, such as Democratic state senator Margaret Schweinhaut, spoke out against the bill. Schweinhaut accused her colleagues of trying to save welfare costs by encouraging the poor to abort their unborn children. Pro-lifers applauded this line, but it did not affect the vote. Pro-life advocates then sent 25,000 letters to the governor's office to encourage him not to sign the bill, but proponents of the bill countered with an equal number of missives. Pro-lifers' chances of success initially appeared to be dim because the governor, Marvin Mandel, was a liberal Jewish Democrat who did not share Catholic views of fetal life. He stated that he did not oppose the abortion legalization bill on religious or ethical grounds, but a bill that allowed abortions in the eighth or ninth month of pregnancy and lacked a residency requirement was too much for him, and he ultimately decided to veto it.[73] It had been a close call for Maryland pro-lifers.

The midterm elections of 1970 brought other defeats for the pro-life movement. In Colorado, pro-lifers waged a spirited campaign against state senator Richard Lamm, the sponsor of Colorado's 1967 abortion liberalization bill and now a proponent of the legalization of elective abortion. They even distributed a flyer with a photo of a fetus in a glass jar in order to dramatize what Lamm's support for abortion rights really meant. But their efforts failed. Lamm lost some heavily Catholic districts that he had carried in previous elections, but he picked up new support from liberal Protestants who supported abortion legalization, and he succeeded in his reelection bid. Anthony Beilenson won reelection by a comfortable margin, carrying 71 percent of the vote. In Kansas, Bill Roy, a strong supporter of abortion rights who had helped to create Kansas's liberalized abortion law and had written a law journal article in favor of legalizing abortion, won a seat in Congress. And in New York, Constance Cook, the sponsor of the state's abortion legalization bill, kept her seat in the state assembly.[74]

The abortion rights movement had been so successful that 40 percent of Americans now wanted to repeal almost all restrictions on abortion, according to a 1970 Harris poll. Support for "legalizing abortion for almost any reason" was still low among Catholics—64 percent of whom expressed opposition to the idea—and much higher among Jews (71 percent in favor) than among Protestants (only 49 percent of whom were supportive, with 39 percent opposed). But the general trend was clear: support for the legalization of elective abortion was rapidly increasing among Americans across the board. Only four years earlier, in January 1966, a Gallup poll had shown that 73 percent of Protestants and 78 percent of Catholics had opposed legalizing abortion for cases in which "the family does not have enough money to support another child." Yet a Harris poll also showed that 41 percent of Americans continued to believe that abortion was "murder." The nation was now fully polarized, with 40 percent wanting to legalize almost all abortions and 41 percent believing that abortion killed human beings.[75]

At that point, some pro-lifers began looking to the US Supreme Court. Now that the California state supreme court had decided that restrictive abortion laws were unconstitutional, and now that "abortion on demand" was available in New York and Hawaii, only the US Supreme Court could provide a "definitive resolution of the problem" by ruling in favor of the "rights of the unborn child," California pro-life attorney J. J. Brandlin declared.[76] At the time, though, the Supreme Court did not have an abortion case on its docket, so the "definitive resolution" that Brandlin hoped for would have to wait.

# 6

## *A New Image*

IN THE SAME month that legislators in New York voted to legalize elective abortion, a Benedictine sociology professor at Saint John's University in Minnesota discovered a new strategy that would transform the pro-life movement. Having just obtained a medical film of a vacuum aspiration abortion procedure, he decided in April 1970 to show it to some Catholic college students in order to alert them to the full horrors of abortion. "A few students who were sympathetic to abortion were turned off completely, and some even walked out in disgust," the professor, Fr. Paul Marx, reported to the bishop of Duluth. "That kind of film is worth hours of lecturing and whole shelves of books."[1]

Only two months earlier, Marx had been in despair. "Charles, let's face it, we have lost the battle," he confided to his pro-life activist friend in California, Charles Carroll, in February 1970, the same month in which Hawaii became the first state to legalize elective abortion. Marx thought the argument against abortion was logically impeccable, but "we have lost the battle because, as St. Thomas Aquinas said in the 13th Century, most people live by their emotions, except that today they live by their emotions and TV."[2]

But then Marx discovered that the pro-life movement could use graphic images to make an emotional appeal that was at least as powerful as anything the abortion rights movement could offer. For the next two years, he and other pro-life activists would revitalize the right-to-life movement. The message would remain the same, but the medium and the messengers would be different. Instead of simply rehashing the philosophical and constitutional arguments against abortion legalization, the pro-life movement would use the power of fetal photography to convince the public that every abortion killed a human baby. Instead of relying on priests and philosophers, the pro-life movement would now look to Protestant spokespersons, liberal antiwar activists, college students, and, above all, women to convey its message.

## Graphic Images

For the previous decade, pro-lifers had generally eschewed graphic discussions of the abortion procedure. Pro-life literature of the 1960s had commonly described abortion as "murder" and had spoken of the fetus as a "child" who was "killed," but writers usually avoided any detailed descriptions of what an abortion actually entailed. Many Catholics were squeamish about engaging in a detailed discussion of a matter that violated their senses of modesty and propriety. In 1966, Cardinal McIntyre had written to a Los Angeles television station objecting to the extensive coverage that the station had devoted to abortion, a subject that he believed violated "good taste." "To our mind, the subject is not one for open discussion in the manner in which it has been indulged," he wrote. Similarly, the major pro-life books of the late 1960s, such as Charles Rice's *The Vanishing Right to Live* or Russell Shaw's *Abortion on Trial*, made no attempt to describe what actually happened under the abortionist's knife. The books contained no photographs either.[3]

Pro-lifers changed tactics in 1970. As they reacted in horror to the rapid legalization of elective abortion, pro-life advocates realized that they needed to escalate their rhetoric, so they decided to confront the public with the full horrors of the abortion procedure. Pro-lifers realized that most Americans had only a vague idea of what actually happened in an abortion, so their promotional materials began highlighting the gruesome aspects of the procedure. Catholic diocesan weeklies began publishing articles with titles such as "After about 10 to 12 Weeks, the Child Inside Is Cut into Pieces and Pulled or Scooped Out"; "Live, Aborted Babies Sold for Tests"; and "Today My Mother Killed Me: The Distressing Diary of an Aborted Child."[4]

In case any readers missed the point, the editor of the conservative Catholic newspaper *The Wanderer* prefaced one such graphic description with an exhortation to confront abortion rights advocates with a detailed discussion of the full brutality of the procedure. "The next time you encounter someone who discusses abortion as casually as a visit to the hairdresser or the bank, or if you are enduring the usual bleeding heart arguments by an abortion advocate, quote Dr. Dunn's graphic descriptions of abortion," he wrote. "Don't omit any of the details!"[5]

Pro-lifers took *The Wanderer's* advice to heart. Later that year, a California talk radio station that was sympathetic to the abortion rights cause gave a representative of a California pro-life group the opportunity to deliver a brief rebuttal to one of its editorials. The activist offered an emotionally laden description of the "cruel method by which this killing is accomplished." "Aborted babies die by being cut into pieces, suffocated or pickled alive," she told listeners.[6]

Pro-lifers had a lot of material to work with because in the early 1970s, abortion was a messy procedure. Abortions were often performed through dissection and curettage or, if they were later-term abortions, through the saline method or hysterotomy. With a D&C, as dissection and curettage was commonly called, the abortionist used a surgeon's knife to dismember the fetus in the uterus, and then extracted the pieces and reassembled them on the operating table. Abortionists had to make sure they fully extracted the entire fetus in order to prevent infection, so this method required physical confrontation with fetal remains. When a woman's uterus was injected with a saline solution, she would be induced to go into labor, and then the woman's body would eventually expel a fetus that had been destroyed by the salt solution. Women who experienced this type of abortion sometimes said in retrospect that they were horrified to see the blackened, dead fetus, with distinctively infant-like features, that emerged at the end of their abortion. Late-term abortions sometimes required a hysterotomy, which for some was the most troubling type of pregnancy termination. With this method, the woman would be put into labor and after a period of hours give birth to a premature infant with undeveloped lungs. The infant would usually take a few gasps and perhaps utter a short cry before turning blue and dying.[7] Nurses who were forced to assist with hysterotomies were often shocked by what they saw.

A survey conducted by *RN* magazine in early 1970 revealed that 77 percent of nurses—and 85 percent of those who specialized in obstetrics and gynecology—were opposed to "unrestricted abortion." In contrast to the rest of the population, where the strongest support for abortion legalization came from college students and recent college graduates, the youngest cohort of nurses was the group most strongly opposed to abortion, with 83 percent of nurses under the age of thirty stating that they opposed abortion law repeal. Most of these nurses were willing to permit abortion in cases of rape or for pregnancies that endangered a woman's health, but they had deep reservations about the procedure when it was not medically necessary.[8]

It was thus not surprising that some of the hospital nurses who were required to assist with abortions found the task repugnant. At a time when more than 97 percent of registered nurses were women—and 92 percent of doctors were men—conflicts arose between male physicians who believed that they were acting in women's best interests, and female nurses who abhorred the procedure. Some nurses categorically refused to participate in any abortions, while others concentrated their opposition on later-term abortions, such as second-trimester saline operations. "The fetus at this point is unmistakably a baby," Lois Mitchell, a registered nurse in Roslyn, Pennsylvania, told *RN* magazine in September 1970. "It looks unmistakably like the preemies next door. . . . It is terribly hard to escape the conclusion that when saline is injected a baby is killed. How can we who have dedicated our lives to preserving human life accept this responsibility?"[9]

When faced with the prospect of assisting with hysterotomies, a few decided to quit. "I couldn't possibly go on ignoring the live fetuses; or even putting the dead ones in buckets to be sent to the lab," one New York nurse said in the fall of 1970. Shortly before resigning, she was confronted with a fetus whose heart was still beating when it was delivered on the operating table. The doctor told her to leave it alone and let it die, but she refused, and instead carried it to the nursery in defiance of the doctor's orders. "I knew the fetus would probably die, but I had to give it a chance," she said. "I had to treat it as a human being."[10]

These live births distressed even some supporters of abortion rights, who wondered whether it might have been a bad idea for New York to allow unrestricted abortion as late as twenty-four weeks—less than four weeks before the age of viability. The fact that they looked like miniature, fully formed infants was disturbing to many of the nurses who were forced to dispose of their remains. In addition, it was difficult to avoid embarrassing situations in which a doctor's slight underestimation of gestational age could result in a live birth of a viable infant. During the first six months in which hospital abortions were allowed in New York, twenty-six of the state's 69,000 legal abortions resulted instead in live births. Twenty-five of those infants died within two days of birth, but one survived a saline abortion long enough to be put up for adoption.[11]

Pro-lifers noted that the line between abortion and infanticide was becoming blurred, just as they had predicted. Cardinal Terence Cooke inveighed against this injustice in a letter that was read during Sunday Mass at every church in the archdiocese. "Once this law was passed the abortionists lost no time in dealing their death-dealing trade," he wrote.

"Each day they grow wealthier from the killing of unborn children—some of whom can be heard to cry as they are dropped into the surgical trash can." Even some doctors who approved of abortion were appalled. "Live abortion," said the head of the legal department of the American Medical Association, was an "evil thing." He suggested that abortions should probably not be performed beyond twelve or fourteen weeks.[12]

In New York, 4,000 hysterotomies were performed between 1970 and 1972, and though this procedure accounted for only slightly more than 1 percent of all hospital abortions in the state—and though it would soon become even rarer, after doctors began using other late-term abortion techniques that contained less risk of a live birth—its shock value made it an ideal propaganda weapon for pro-life activists. "In 100 percent of the cases, the child is alive when it is removed from the womb," Cincinnati pro-life physician John C. "Jack" Willke reminded audiences. "After the umbilical cord is cut, the infant is tossed into a pail to die."[13]

Pro-lifers knew that if these descriptions were effective, photographs would be even more so. They began including prominent color photographs of live and aborted fetuses in their publications and public lectures. For twenty-five dollars, a pro-life organization could buy a set of ten slides from the Right to Life League of Southern California showing aborted fetuses that ranged in age from six to twenty-one weeks. Photographs of aborted fetuses that were eighteen weeks or older had a particularly strong emotional impact, because by that point, the fetuses looked like fully developed premature infants. The photographs showed them curled up, their lifeless bodies burned by saline solution. One photograph that appeared in multiple pro-life journals after it was taken by a Canadian pathologist in 1971 showed the bodies of several eighteen-to-twenty-four-week-old fetuses lying in a medical waste bucket. A California right-to-life organization reproduced this image on postcards that pro-lifers could mail to their state legislators who were considering abortion bills. "You can't tell somebody how bad it is," Gloria Klein, president of Michigan's Lifespan explained. "A picture is worth 1,000 words." She knew that some would object that the grisly photographs were in "poor taste," but she said that "the whole issue [of abortion] is in poor taste."[14]

Paul Marx and Jack Willke did perhaps more than any other pro-life activists to popularize the use of graphic images as a propaganda tool. Both men were Catholics, though both also resisted the charge that abortion was a "Catholic" issue. Marx was a liberal Democrat who had decided that his clerical office was such a hindrance in debating abortion rights advocates that whenever he gave a public lecture on the issue, he took off his collar, put on a tie, and insisted that people call him "Doctor Marx" instead of "Father." By focusing on science, not Church teaching, he thought he could change people's minds about abortion. Indeed, a scientific approach to sexuality was a passion for Marx, who traveled across the country giving sex education seminars at Catholic colleges. For years, he had pushed the Church to do more to promote knowledge of natural family planning (the rhythm method) among Catholic couples. For a brief period before *Humanae Vitae*, he had encouraged Catholic couples to use forbidden means of contraception if their consciences permitted it. Even after *Humanae Vitae*, he was reluctant to accept the pope's pronouncement on birth control. But a firm opposition to premarital sex, extramarital sex, homosexuality, "Playboyism," and abortion led him to take a more conservative stance on contraception by the end of the 1960s and eventually to make opposition to contraceptives a central part of his fight for the unborn.[15]

Willke came to the pro-life cause later than Marx did. They traveled in similar professional circles, since both men offered sex education to Catholic couples. But while Marx began to commit himself to pro-life work in 1968, Willke did not yet consider abortion an urgent political issue. Marx was convinced that Willke, who was in his early forties and seemed to have an unlimited supply of energy, would be useful to the cause. In the fall of 1970, he pointedly asked Willke what he was doing to stop abortion. Willke replied that he was too busy to become an activist. He had his own medical practice to worry about. His wife Barbara, a former nurse, was now busy serving as a full-time mother to their six children, ages five to nineteen. At the moment, other priorities seemed more pressing. "Family life means nothing if life itself isn't sacred," Marx responded.[16]

Willke was touched by the professor's rebuke. He and Barbara designed a four-hour workshop on the medical aspects of abortion and, at their own expense, mailed out 10,000 invitations to other medical professionals. Four hundred attended. That event launched the Willkes' pro-life speaking careers. They publicized their arguments through film strips and lectures. By 1972, they were speaking to a combined total of 70,000 people a year and giving 150 radio and television interviews.[17]

It was Jack Willke's use of images that proved especially effective. He illustrated his lectures with slides of fetal photographs—which he obtained from sympathetic doctors in the United States, Canada, and New Zealand—and then distributed the photographs for others to use.[18] He also made some of the first pro-life documentary films, an idea that he had gotten from Marx.

Both men realized the benefits of showing audiences taped footage of a vacuum aspiration procedure. By some standards, vacuum aspiration, which represented the latest development in abortion technology, offered the "cleanest" form of abortion. The procedure, which was usually reserved for fetuses that were younger than twelve weeks, was fast and efficient: the doctor simply dilated a woman's cervix, inserted a tube through it into the uterus, and then turned on the vacuum, which evacuated the contents of the uterus within seconds. The entire procedure took only a few minutes, and in most cases, a woman could go home the same day with no complications. The procedure left no fetal remains that would disturb patients or assisting nurses. For abortion doctors, the vacuum aspiration procedure was a godsend, so they produced educational films to train doctors how to do it. Willke, though, saw vacuum aspiration abortions as a ghastly example of a callous disregard for human life, and he thought that his audiences, if they knew what the procedure entailed, would view it in the same way. He purchased a British medical film on vacuum aspiration abortions and then edited it to highlight the parts of the procedure that were likely to have the greatest emotional impact. The image of the fetus being sucked into the tube and whisked away was particularly powerful.

Willke heightened the emotional impact of this footage by providing his own voiceover narration that calmly but firmly described the procedure. He consistently used the word "baby" rather than "fetus," and he highlighted the violent nature of the abortion process. "I would suggest the best narrative is a simple, clinical description of what is happening," he told Marx. "I would, however, use such terms as 'breaking up the baby into little pieces,' and explaining the difficulty of stretching a 'green' cervix, etc. . . . I then ask them to look closely and when they see white pieces coming through the suction tube, I comment that these are parts of the baby."[19]

The audience reaction was exactly what he had hoped for. "On two showings in Pittsburgh, one to a group of professional people . . . we had one teacher fainted dead away," Willke reported to Marx in December 1970. "On Duquesne campus the next morning, to a large student group, we lost a student nurse in the same fashion." To those who objected to graphic representations of abortion, Willke had a ready answer: the pro-life movement would win its argument only if it confronted the public with the full horror of what abortion really entailed.[20]

Some of the movement's most powerful photos of aborted fetuses came from the Rockville, Maryland, pro-life physician William Hogan. Hogan, whose brother Lawrence Hogan was a Republican representative in Congress who would later sponsor the first proposed Human Life Amendment, had used his medical credentials to gain access to abortions as they were taking place and photograph them. One of his photos depicted a hysterotomy abortion in its final stages—that is, two pairs of bloody, gloved hands holding a twenty-four-week-old fetus upside down in the air so that it could die from exposure. Another showed tiny dismembered feet, hands, and torsos from a D&C. When he showed color slides of these images to the members of the Maryland legislature as they were debating an abortion legalization bill in 1971, the audience gasped. Most Americans had never seen photographs of aborted fetuses before. "The presentation left some legislators and spectators squirming in their seats and shielding their eyes," the *Washington Post* reported. The bill's unexpected defeat in the Maryland House of Delegates may have been due to pro-lifers' intense lobbying efforts rather than to Hogan's images, but pro-lifers nevertheless believed that these pictures were a potent political weapon—undeniable proof of the violence of abortion and the humanity of the fetus.[21]

Groups affiliated with the NRLC turned some of the most horrific abortion pictures, such as the picture of aborted fetuses in a trash can, into postcards designed for mass mailings to state legislators. "Dear Elected Official," the back of this postcard stated, "Please tell me where you stand on the issue of abortion."[22]

Pro-lifers claimed that by distributing these shocking images, they were simply telling the truth about a subject that the news media refused to cover. "The great majority of you people who are reading this are finding out for the first time what abortion is all about," Missouri Citizens for Life declared in a letter accompanying its mass mailing of some of Willke's photographs. "Till now you have not been allowed to see what really goes on inside an abortion clinic. There are those who say that it is good to eliminate unborn children in the manner shown in the above pictures. How can it be wrong for us to show you exactly what they mean? We believe it is significant that the news media has never attempted to show you what an abortion does to an unborn child. Yet the news media is continually telling us that we need legalized abortion."[23]

The emotional impact of the images disturbed abortion rights advocates. "There should be no question about a woman's right to choose but when the issue is abortion, emotion comes to the fore," a Kansas City NOW chapter complained. "This is what the Right to Life groups count on! If they can inject enough emotionalism they stand an excellent chance of winning! Please don't allow yourself to be confused by the distortion of facts they employ," the NOW chapter implored. "When they begin passing out their full-color photographs of aborted fetuses, remember there is no way to tell an aborted fetus from a miscarried fetus and no way to tell if a fetus is malformed due to abortion or if it was developing in the womb with a malformation."[24] But no matter how much pro-choicers tried to downplay the pictures, they had a powerful shock value that was difficult to dismiss.

Abortion rights supporters mounted a counterattack, highlighting the horrific deaths of women who had resorted to illegal abortions. The symbol for that campaign became the coat hanger, an instrument, they said, that had been used to perform illegal abortions. When 1,500 abortion rights supporters held a demonstration outside St. Patrick's Cathedral in March 1970, they handed out red coat hangers to the crowd.[25] Shortly thereafter, line drawings of coat hangers began appearing in pro-choice promotional literature.

Pro-lifers quickly prepared a rebuttal. Although they admitted that women had resorted to a variety of dangerous home remedies to terminate their pregnancies, ranging from Lysol solutions to self-inflicted injuries, pro-lifers challenged pro-choice activists to come up with a single case in which a woman had died from a coat-hanger-induced abortion—or had even attempted to use a coat hanger as a tool for abortion. They doubted that this had ever happened, and when pro-choicers failed to provide evidence, they considered their case proved. In addition, they argued, proponents of legalized abortion greatly exaggerated when they claimed that 5,000 women per year died from illegal abortions. According to official government estimates, the number was less than 300.[26]

It was again Jack and Barbara Willke who took the lead in countering the pro-choicers' arguments. In 1971, they published *Handbook on Abortion*, which quickly became the pro-life movement's go-to guide. Within two years, it had sold 1.5 million copies. The book offered a detailed analysis of the horrors of abortion and relied on statistics to rebut pro-choice arguments. In keeping with the movement's current strategy, the book refrained from criticism of contraception or premarital sex, and instead focused on one central argument: that the fetus was a *"human* being." To support its case, the book reproduced an extensive array of photographs.[27]

Although the Willkes maintained an ambitious speaking agenda, their book reached a much broader audience than lectures ever could. Pro-lifers in Hawaii purchased 40,000 copies to give away. Other pro-lifers in various parts of the United States distributed the book en masse to Protestant churches that had not been active in the pro-life cause. In some churches, they set up tables outside the sanctuary and gave away free copies of the book. In other cases, they mailed copies to church leaders. The *Christian Standard*, a Church of Christ periodical, serialized the book. Other pro-lifers donated copies to their local libraries or brought the book into high school classes to use as a supplementary text. The book also became a model for pro-life speakers, who quickly incorporated the Willkes' arguments into their own lectures and borrowed some of their images and statistics.[28]

## Evangelicals and the Public Reaction against "Abortion on Demand"

The popularity of the Willkes' book among evangelical Protestants—a group that had largely eschewed the pro-life movement prior to 1970—was a sign of a widespread public backlash against abortion on demand. Prior to 1970, the pro-life movement had attracted few non-Catholics and, partly as a result, had largely been on the defensive. Public opinion polls showed that from the mid-1960s onward, approximately three-fourths of Americans accepted the idea that women in a few extreme situations should be given the legal right to terminate their pregnancies, especially if they did so at the recommendation of their doctors. But polls also showed that, even in the wake of its political successes in 1970, elective abortion did not command majority support. When the abortion rights campaign shifted its goal from liberalization to repeal, it gave the pro-life movement a sudden public relations advantage. Many people who had no objection to abortions that doctors deemed medically necessary nevertheless believed that allowing unrestricted abortion would encourage irresponsible behavior. Some of the pronouncements of the advocates of abortion law repeal seemed to support that idea. NOW's 1967 resolution calling for the repeal of all abortion restrictions stated that "NOW supports the furthering of the sexual revolution," an idea that alarmed many social conservatives.[29]

Pro-lifers had long warned that the abortion liberalization movement would soon lead to abortion on demand, but before the 1970s, proponents of abortion law liberalization had dismissed their concerns. After the legalization of elective abortion in New York, Hawaii, Alaska, and Washington, that was no longer possible.

The chaos in New York bolstered the pro-lifers' arguments. During the first three weeks in which elective abortion was legal in the state, three of the 2,000 women who obtained abortions from New York City hospitals died as a result of the procedure. Because an unusually high number of the initial abortions were late-term procedures, which were far more dangerous than first-trimester abortions, the rate of complications was much higher than abortion rights proponents had expected. With the state's hospitals performing more than 10,000 abortions every month by the end of the year, New York gave every indication that it was becoming the "abortion mill" that pro-lifers had warned about.[30] Across the nation, state legislators looked at the horrors coming out of New York—live births following botched abortion procedures, abortion-related deaths, the strain on the state's resources as a massive number of women arrived from out of state to obtain hospital abortions, and the seemingly endless churn of thousands of legal abortions every month—and became increasingly uneasy about liberalizing abortion laws in their own states. A few months earlier, many of these state legislators had been receptive to abortion liberalization proposals because of the dangers associated with illegal abortions. Now that was no longer their primary concern. Instead, they were mainly interested in making sure that their own states did not become like New York.

Seizing on this moment of public discomfort, pro-lifers regrouped and succeeded in blocking new proposals for abortion legalization in several states in the spring of 1971. In Wyoming, Indiana, and Illinois, they succeeded in getting abortion law repeal bills killed in committee. In Colorado and Montana, they defeated abortion law repeal bills on the House or Senate floor. One of their most striking successes occurred in Mississippi, where a state right-to-life organization orchestrated a letter-writing campaign that flooded state legislators' mailboxes with petitions against an abortion law repeal bill. When pro-lifers brought a coalition of hundreds of people, including not only Catholics but also Baptists and Jews, to speak against the abortion bill, the committee voted eleven to two to kill it. Altogether, at least twenty-five state legislatures took up consideration of permissive abortion legislation in the spring of 1971, and pro-lifers succeeded in defeating every one of those bills. For the previous four years, the pro-life movement had experienced several defeats in every legislative session, but now it enjoyed a banner year. James McHugh optimistically predicted to the *Washington Evening Star* that the tide might be turning in their favor.[31]

In the wake of the legalization of elective abortion, many people decided to join the pro-life cause for the first time, particularly in New York, now the nation's leading supplier of legal abortions. Prior to 1970, the state right-to-life organization that Edward Golden chaired was small and mostly ineffective; the Catholic Church in the state, rather than grassroots right-to-life organizations, was forced to take the lead in lobbying Albany when the legislature had debated abortion legalization. But immediately after New York passed its abortion law, Golden's Right to Life Committee began growing exponentially. By the spring of 1972, the committee had fifty county chapters and at least 200,000 members. Most of the new members were "politically inarticulate," Golden said. As a construction foreman and father of five, he could relate to these new recruits, and he taught the homemakers, factory workers, and dairy farmers who joined his organization how to lobby their state legislators by writing letters, making phone calls, and showing up to the state capitol in person. "They're home-bodies and they're effective," he said.[32]

For the first time, it appeared that the pro-life effort might have reached beyond Catholics. In a few states, particularly in the northern Midwest, Protestants were beginning to take the lead in pro-life organizing, and Orthodox Jewish organizations and Greek Orthodox Christians endorsed the pro-life cause. The president of the Church of Jesus Christ of Latter-day Saints also spoke out against abortion in the spring of 1970.[33] Prior to the 1970s, a handful of Protestants had enlisted in the pro-life campaign, but the Catholic Church had been almost alone in providing the movement with institutional support. Now that was beginning to change.

Perhaps the most important new source of support was evangelical Protestantism. By some estimates, evangelicals accounted for one-third of the American population. Their faith in the Bible as a guide to daily life and their emphasis on personal morality, especially in matters related to sex, might have made them natural allies of the pro-life cause. But before the legalization of elective abortion, evangelicals had given the pro-life movement little support. Most evangelicals still retained grave reservations about cooperating with Catholics, even after Vatican II, and many of them had no objection to legalizing abortion in cases of rape or medical necessity. Catholics, in turn, had made little effort to recruit evangelicals to their cause. The legalization of elective abortion roused some evangelicals to action. *Christianity Today*, the leading evangelical periodical, reversed its cautious endorsement of limited abortion law liberalization and began publishing strongly worded editorials against abortion, beginning with "The War on the Womb" in June 1970, shortly after Hawaii and New York legalized elective abortion. Such legislation seemed to ignore all fetal rights, which disturbed many evangelicals, who believed that a fetus had value even if they could not say for sure that life began at conception. The availability of abortion for any woman who wanted it would also encourage premarital or extramarital sex, they believed. "The connection between easy abortion and sexual promiscuity is obvious," Carl F. H. Henry declared in the spring of 1971.[34]

Henry, a Baptist, was one of the most revered evangelical theologians in the United States. He had edited *Christianity Today* for more than a decade, and he had written several books that had influenced evangelicals' views on politics and theology. In 1971, he began writing against abortion and published a strongly worded article against the procedure in *Eternity* magazine. Abortion, he declared, was "murder."[35]

Henry was not the only evangelical roused to action by the legalization of elective abortion. Others who had once been willing to permit abortion in extreme situations began rethinking that stance. In June 1971, Billy Graham's father-in-law L. Nelson Bell wrote that, as a physician, he had performed a few abortions that he thought were medically necessary, but he viewed "abortion on demand" as the "wanton destruction of life." "Not in years have I been as shaken as now, as I realize the widespread indifference to the implications of abortion on demand and the commercialization of this destruction of life," he wrote. Adoption, not abortion, was the answer for unwanted children.[36]

For a few evangelical converts to the pro-life cause, even Bell's stance, which still allowed for abortion in extreme situations, did not go far enough. In 1970, one group of pro-life evangelicals, calling themselves "Christians for Life," went so far as to picket a Billy Graham crusade because Graham, although opposed to abortion in most cases, was willing to permit it in cases of rape and incest, as well as when the mother's life was in danger. Graham had "hedged" on abortion, the group said.[37] Few evangelical pro-lifers felt that picketing a Graham crusade was necessary, but some of them were giving more thought to the Catholic position that life began at conception and that all abortions—or, at least, all abortions that were not necessary to save a woman's life—were tantamount to murder.

Evangelicals' shift on abortion even led some toward a surprising open-ness to alliances with Catholics. In May 1971, *Christianity Today*, which less than three years earlier had criticized Pope Paul VI's *Humanae Vitae* as "alien to biblical revelation," published an editorial urging evangelicals to join pro-life groups, and for those who were interested in doing so, it rec-ommended a publication by the New Jersey Right to Life Committee—a group that was still closely connected with the Catholic Church.[38]

Southern evangelicals likewise opposed elective abortion, but they were more reticent than northerners to join the pro-life campaign, partly because they thought that they could allow modest abortion law reform in their region without opening the door to abortion on demand. According to a 1970 *Baptist Viewpoint* poll, 80 percent of Southern Baptist pastors and Sunday school teachers opposed the legalization of elective abortion, but 71 percent believed that abortion should be legal in cases of rape and incest, and 70 percent favored allowing it when a woman's health was in danger—an opinion that accorded well with the modest abortion liberal-ization laws that several southern states adopted between 1967 and 1970. Still, despite Southern Baptists' unwillingness to embrace the right-to-life movement, the Southern Baptist Convention was sufficiently concerned about abortion on demand to pass a resolution in 1971 declaring that "soci-ety has a responsibility to affirm through the laws of the state a high view of the sanctity of human life, including fetal life." The resolution allowed for abortion in cases of "rape, incest, clear evidence of severe fetal defor-mity, and carefully ascertained evidence of the likelihood of damage to the emotional, mental, and physical health of the mother" (in essence, the reasons permitted by ALI-style abortion laws), but opposed those who advocated "making the decision a purely private matter between a woman and her doctor."[39]

A public opinion survey conducted at the end of 1972 indicated that the strongest opposition to abortion continued to come from churchgoing Catholics—83 percent of Catholics who attended church weekly or almost weekly opposed the legalization of abortion. But the survey also indicated that 63 percent of Protestant "fundamentalists"—a broad designation that the survey used to describe any evangelical who was not an "estab-lishment" Protestant—opposed abortion legalization. The figure rose to 75 percent among fundamentalists who attended church weekly. Even among establishment Protestants, 57 percent of weekly church attenders opposed abortion legalization, despite the official endorsements that their denominations often gave to abortion rights.[40] Catholics were able to capitalize on a growing discomfort with abortion among Protestants to show that the pro-life cause was not a sectarian campaign.

## *Women's Leadership*

Just as the pro-life movement was becoming more religiously diverse, it was also changing its image with regard to gender. Public opinion polls of the late 1960s showed that women were slightly more likely than men to oppose abortion, but the pro-life movement had not elected women to positions of leadership, instead relying almost exclusively on male doctors and lawyers—and sometimes Catholic priests or the occasional Protestant clergyman—to be their public face. The men in the movement had been slow to recognize that this was discrediting their cause in the eyes of feminists, but by the end of the 1960s, they were beginning to get the message. When Msgr. Paul Harrington failed to include even one female panelist at the pro-life educational symposium that he organized for the Archdiocese of Boston in 1969, pro-life advocate Mary Stine complained. Right-to-life forums with an all-male lineup of speakers had not been unusual, but Stine urged Harrington to reconsider this approach. "Wouldn't it be an improvement if these programs also included some women who have lived through tragic child-bearing situations?" she asked. "Women who alone must bear babies and care for them 24 hours a day, 365 days a year, must resent the implication that their thoughts on the subject of abortion are of such little importance. Most women will no longer meekly accept a group of men telling them what they must think and do." Women, Stine argued, could add a unique perspective to the abortion debate and persuade skeptical audiences toward the pro-life position in a way that male speakers could not. While male doctors might be qualified to explicate the biological evidence that showed human life began at conception, only women could provide "straightforward personal accounts" of their own experiences with pregnancy and childbearing. Such testimonies, she said, "might convince as many people of the wrong of abortion as even the most brilliant scholarly arguments."[41]

Harrington said that he had been unable to find qualified women willing to make the time and travel commitments to appear on his pro-life panels, but he acknowledged that women could contribute something to the pro-life movement's campaign that men could never provide, and that he should make a greater effort to include them in the future. "Women are more directly involved in the bearing and caring for children," he said, so "psychological insights can only come from a woman."[42]

Harrington was far from the only male pro-life advocate to realize belatedly, at the end of the 1960s, that pro-lifers could not make a fully persuasive argument against abortion legalization without giving prominent billing to female speakers. For years, right-to-life advocates had believed that doctors and lawyers (who, in the 1960s, were almost always men) were the best qualified to make the scientific and constitutional case for legal protection of fetal rights. In the early 1960s, this did not seem odd, because women were almost as rare among the abortion law reform movement's leadership. But when the campaign for abortion legalization became a women's rights cause, with women such as NARAL executive director Lee Gidding or ACLU attorney Harriet Pilpel taking leadership roles, pro-lifers realized that their failure to pay sufficient attention to the women in their movement had discredited their cause. "In these days of militant feminism, if you're going to speak against 'women's rights,' you had better have a woman saying it," the New Jersey Right to Life Committee's organizational handbook declared in December 1970.[43]

Finding women to speak out against abortion was not difficult, because women already made up the vast majority of the pro-life movement. For the previous five years, most of the letters that the movement had sent to state legislators had come from women. Women had convened several of the first pro-life meetings. Most of the volunteer pro-life lobbyists who had knocked on legislators' doors in state capitols or phoned their offices had been women. Women had performed almost all of the secretarial work for pro-life organizations. There were millions of pro-life women in the United States, and there were thousands who had signed up for pro-life work. Socially conservative, married, devout Catholic women in their thirties and forties had been the backbone of the pro-life movement from its inception.[44] Once pro-lifers had to confront feminist arguments, they decided that they should allow women to hold positions of power in the movement.

Women were already seizing the reins on their own. In 1968, for instance, two Catholic women in Georgia—a state where there was no organized right-to-life movement and where Catholic priests had almost no political influence—created a group to lobby the legislature against an abortion law reform bill and castigated Catholic clergy for failing to mount a more concerted opposition. Their efforts failed to stop the bill, but they demonstrated the desire of women to take matters into their own hands in the absence of male leadership. On Long Island, Ellen McCormack helped organize other local pro-life women into a lobbying group, and in March 1970, they wrote letters to every state senator in New York urging them to vote against a bill to legalize abortion.[45] Some of the male leaders in the right-to-life movement paid little attention to these efforts and instead concentrated on cultivating the professional image that they believed a lineup of male doctors and lawyers conveyed. But women's efforts to gain control of the pro-life movement and reshape it to reflect their concerns soon became too pronounced for any male leader to ignore.

In the spring of 1970, at the same time that the Pennsylvania Catholic Conference was organizing the state's first major pro-life group, Pennsylvanians for Human Life, a Pittsburgh Catholic mother named Mary Winter convened a group of twelve women in her living room to launch an alternative group called Women Concerned for the Unborn Child (WCUC). Under Winter's leadership, WCUC posited a distinctly feminine—though staunchly anti-feminist—form of pro-life activism that soon came to characterize much of the larger movement. Presaging Phyllis Schlafly's STOP-ERA campaign of a few years later, Winter and other pro-life women argued that women's maternal nature made them uniquely suited to argue against the destructive forces of feminism and defend women's true interests, which were integrally related to motherhood.

Winter was a former fourth grade teacher and Duquesne University graduate who was the wife of an optometrist and the mother of six children—a number that would soon rise to seven. Later press reports described her as "soft-spoken" and "unpretentious," with a desire to "lead a simple life as a wife and mother of a large family." When an abortion rights organization came to her area, she decided that something had to be done to stop it. She was "shocked" that many of the leaders of the abortion rights movement were women, because it had never occurred to her that a woman would want to kill her unborn children. "The anti-life mentality is so foreign to the feminine mentality which, I believe, is biologically, instinctively geared toward the protection and nurturing of the young and the helpless," she said.[46] She decided that women needed to counter the feminist voices that dominated the media.

Although Winter's approach differed slightly from the strategy that Catholic male pro-life leaders such as James McHugh had adopted, male pro-lifers welcomed her activism. The NRLC invited Winter to serve as vice president, and Pennsylvanians for Human Life joined WCUC in some of its campaigns. Within two years, 2,500 women had joined Winter's organization; within four, its membership had increased to more than 7,000.[47]

When the Pennsylvania legislature considered an abortion legalization bill in 1972, Winter was on hand to offer a woman's perspective on the issue, in contrast to the lineup of doctors, lawyers, and clergymen who had dominated the pro-life testimony at previous legislative hearings. Like other pro-lifers, Winter appealed to the humanity of the fetus and its need for legal protection, but then she introduced a theme that most men in the pro-life movement had ignored—social obligations to pregnant women. Legalizing abortion, she argued, would allow society to evade its responsibility to care for pregnant women who were in need. Women would be pressured to have abortions that they did not want, and they would be left to suffer the scars while the rest of a male-dominated society continued to ignore their real needs. "Deserted, depressed and penalized, she is thus under pressure to destroy her own unborn child to return herself to everyone's favor," Winter said. "When she is offered abortion as the only answer, she then submits to a degrading procedure that is mentally and physically hazardous—but society is satisfied, her family breathes a sigh of relief, the baby's father has been spared responsibility and the physician smiles as he rings up another sale."[48]

Winter and the other women in the pro-life movement introduced an idea that would become a staple of pro-life ideology for decades to come—the idea of women as victims of money-grubbing, exploitive doctors. As Winter argued, when women made the decision to have an abortion, they were often confused and scared. Pro-lifers did not blame them for their choices. Instead, they expressed their outrage at abortionists, for whom they had no sympathy. Abortion doctors were callous and greedy, they argued, and they deserved to be punished for their crimes. But the women who used their services did not. Pro-choice feminists frequently argued that pro-lifers would punish women who obtained abortions, but pro-lifers insisted that they wanted to do no such thing. In the minds of pro-lifers, the women who obtained abortions were rarely free agents, so they deserved compassion, not condemnation. In the 1960s, few of the male pro-life leaders had said very much about the women who obtained abortions, and what little they had said had been pointedly critical, but as women became leading spokespersons for the movement, they changed that. Male pro-lifers quickly adopted this rhetoric as well.[49]

Winter also took on pro-choice feminists directly by arguing that if they truly supported women's rights, they would not want to legalize abortion. She supported the feminists' campaign for "an end to discrimination based upon sex," but she could not see how legalizing abortion—a goal that more men than women supported and that *Playboy* founder Hugh Hefner promoted—would accomplish that. Legalizing abortion would only enrich male abortion doctors and allow men to escape the consequences of their sexual exploitation of women, while leaving women to suffer the emotional consequences that resulted from terminating an unborn child's life. "I find it simply incredible when I see the new feminists and male population control technocrats and other women exploiters like the Playboy Foundation use each other to foster their own ends," Winter said. "Women who lead the abortion-feminist movement are willing to tolerate and work with the sexploitative men for the money and power the men provide to promote abortion." This too became a staple argument of the pro-life movement. As Winter said, abortion was the "ultimate exploitation of women."[50]

Above all, Winter promoted a feminism of difference that had little in common with the second-wave feminism then in vogue. Instead, it bore a distinct resemblance to nineteenth- and early twentieth-century feminism, which celebrated gender differences and sought to protect women's rights as mothers and guardians of the home. "One of the reasons women are so special is precisely *because* we can conceive and that we *are* equipped physically and psychologically to nurture and protect new life," Winter said. "However, the new feminists consider that ability a definite liability, some even call it a curse, thereby denying the unique value of feminine biology and psychology."[51]

Embracing the feminism of difference, pro-life women argued that because women were the only ones who could experience pregnancy, they had a unique insight into the value of unborn life. Pro-choice feminists had made a similar argument in favor of abortion rights—male legislators had no right to tell women what to do with their bodies. Pro-life women, in turn, argued that men had no right to foist legalized abortion—which would soon become coerced abortion for some women, they suspected—on women who, as a group, were still more strongly opposed to abortion than men were. When the Maryland state legislature took up consideration of an abortion legalization bill in 1970, pro-life Democratic state senator Margaret Schweinhaut told her colleagues that, as a woman, she had a unique claim to authority in speaking out against abortion legalization. "It is curious to me that you gentlemen can speak so freely about something you know so little about," she said. "We are dealing here with human life."[52]

Just as Winter denounced second-wave feminism while calling herself a "pro-life feminist," several women in the pro-life movement likewise embraced the feminist label, but defined the term differently than pro-choice feminists did. "In my feminist view, every abortion represents an abandonment of women and children," declared Sidney Callahan, one of the leading self-identified pro-life feminists in the early 1970s. Callahan was a liberal Catholic who opposed capital punishment and war, and who viewed the fight against abortion as another social justice campaign for the rights of women as well as fetuses. Like Winter, she viewed women who obtained abortions as victims of men: boyfriends, abortion doctors, and a patriarchal society that gave women few resources to exercise their feminine prerogatives as mothers. The legalization of abortion gave men an excuse to treat women as sexual objects, pro-life feminists argued. As Juli Loesch memorably phrased it a decade later, "The idea is that a man can use a woman, vacuum her out, and she's ready to be used again. . . . It's like a rent-a-car or something."[53]

For most of the pro-life feminists, the key to equality for women was not sexual liberation, but rather a defense against sexual exploitation. In this regard, the pro-life feminists were much more similar to early twentieth-century first-wave feminists such as Florence Kelley and Jane Addams than they were to second-wave feminists such as Pauli Murray or Gloria Steinem. Some of the American feminists of the late nineteenth century had spoken out against birth control, abortion, prostitution, and male sexual licentiousness on the grounds that all of these practices made it easy for men to exploit women. They had coupled their demands for women's equality in the political sphere with calls for the legal protection of women. The self-identified feminists in the pro-life movement did the same. They supported equal pay legislation and women's rights in the workplace, but they also favored anti-abortion legislation that, in their view, would recognize biologically based gender differences and protect vulnerable women from being pressured into giving up their right to be mothers. "Full feminine humanity includes distinctly feminine functions," Callahan wrote. "Women need not identify with male sexuality, male aggression, and wombless male lifestyles in order to win social equality."[54]

The pro-life feminists accused other feminists of refusing to listen to them. Most second-wave feminists were wary of the pro-life women's emphasis on biological gender differences, and because they believed that sexual equality and reproductive freedom, rather than freedom from sexual exploitation, were the keys to women's liberation, they had little sympathy with pro-lifers' argument that abortion harmed women. When Pat Goltz began speaking out against abortion in 1971 at the meetings of the Columbus, Ohio, chapter of NOW, where she was a member, she quickly found herself ostracized, and in 1974, she was formally expelled. By then, Goltz had already teamed up with Catherine Callaghan, another member of the Columbus NOW chapter, to form Feminists for Life to unite women who opposed abortion while simultaneously supporting other feminist goals. Goltz, for instance, supported the Equal Rights Amendment (ERA), and argued that pro-choice feminists' advocacy of abortion rights had made it more difficult to win support for the amendment in pro-life state legislatures. While the majority of the hundreds of thousands of women who joined the pro-life movement in the early 1970s did not self-identify as feminists, enough did so to make Feminists for Life a viable organization. When Goltz was invited to present a workshop on pro-life feminism at the National Right to Life Committee's 1974 annual meeting in Washington, DC, it was a sign of mainstream pro-life leaders' eagerness to make common cause with the feminists in their movement.[55]

Numerous pro-life women who did not identify with the feminist movement also organized their own local right-to-life groups in the early 1970s. Although Fr. McHugh had directed bishops across the nation to organize state right-to-life chapters in 1968, many states lacked one even in the early 1970s. Pro-life women who realized the urgency of fighting abortion legalization bills realized that if they wanted a local lobbying organization to represent their cause, they would have to start their own. They invited women from their neighborhoods and churches to help them fight abortion bills. A few of the women who did this, such as Carolyn Gerster, who cofounded Arizona Right to Life in 1971, were Protestants who had no reason to wait for the Catholic Church to act. They simply wanted organizations to prevent the legalization of abortion in their states, so they created local lobbying groups that, in some cases, quickly grew to include thousands of members. In Michigan, for instance, Gloria Klein, a Presbyterian full-time homemaker in a Detroit suburb and mother of three young girls, organized People Taking Action against Abortion in the fall of 1970. Klein's organization, which later changed its name to Lifespan, began as a group of ten people meeting in her living room, but by 1974, it had 15,000 members.[56]

Regardless of whether or not they identified themselves as feminists, the women who became pro-life activists often viewed abortion in somewhat different terms than their male counterparts did. They were particularly likely to favor material assistance to women who were facing crisis pregnancies in addition to laws to ban abortion. In 1968, Louise Summerhill, a devout Catholic fifty-two-year-old mother of seven in Toronto, created Birthright, an organization that provided telephone counseling to women who were contemplating abortion and offered them material resources and a place to stay for the duration of their pregnancies. If she gave women the support they needed to carry their pregnancies to term, they might be deterred from resorting to abortion, she thought. This also was a rights issue. "It is the right of every pregnant woman to give birth, and the right of every child to be born," was Birthright's charter slogan.[57]

When Summerhill launched Birthright, she had only a single-room office and had to rely on a $400 gift from Catholic clergy in order to purchase her first phone line and answering machine, but by relying on volunteer help from other women, she was able to spread her message rapidly. Birthright quickly became popular in the United States, especially after several states legalized elective abortion in 1970. Many state right-to-life committees launched affiliated Birthright chapters, with twenty-four-hour hotlines operated by homemakers and other women who volunteered their time. The National Right to Life Committee invited Summerhill to give a report on Birthright at its national convention in the summer of 1970. By 1973, Birthright had more than one hundred chapters in the United States distributed across thirty-six states.[58]

The organization billed itself as "nonsectarian" and included several Protestants on its executive board, but like other pro-life organizations, the bulk of its support came from Catholics, and it benefited from the endorsement of the Church hierarchy. The Archdiocese of Boston, for instance, designated December 30, 1973, as "Birthright Sunday," with all of the priests in the archdiocese required to read a letter promoting Birthright during Sunday Mass. And when New York opened its first Birthright chapter, exactly one year after the state had legalized elective abortion, the organization operated under Church direction, and the press release announcing its opening came from New York's archbishop. Birthright was particularly strong in major metropolitan areas of the North, where Catholic churches were most numerous and abortion services were also most readily available.[59]

Because Birthright viewed social welfare for pregnant women as the best way to reduce the abortion rate, it attracted many female volunteers whose political sympathies resided with the left. For instance, the head of the New Brunswick, New Jersey, Birthright office, Anne McCracken, the mother of two preschool-aged children and a former Peace Corps volunteer and schoolteacher, was attracted to anti-abortion activism because it appeared to her to be a logical extension of her protests against the Vietnam War. "Suddenly I realized, here I am protesting wars and killing while 25,000 babies were aborted in New York, 30 miles away in three months," she said. "What a death rate."[60]

Birthright's first international convention was keynoted by Eunice Kennedy Shriver, who, as President John F. Kennedy's younger sister and the wife of the liberal Democratic politician Sargent Shriver, was known for her progressive politics and her advocacy for the disabled, as well as for her pro-life work. Adoption, not abortion, was the answer to unwanted pregnancies, Shriver said. She proposed creating a registry of one million couples who wanted to adopt so that Birthright could send a clear message to women facing crisis pregnancies that there were hundreds of thousands of loving families who would be willing to give them the help they needed to carry their pregnancies to term and provide for their children once they were born.[61]

Shriver's advocacy of progressive political solutions to reduce the incidence of abortion reflected a larger, comprehensive liberal political agenda that was quickly coming to characterize much of the pro-life movement. Now that the movement had gained a new image, it was ready to adopt a new form of politics. Many pro-lifers had long been sympathetic to political liberalism, but in the early 1970s, they would make a new effort to graft their advocacy of rights for the unborn onto a larger, socially conscious, liberal political agenda that would include antiwar activism, poverty relief, and racial justice, along with programs to help unborn children and their mothers.

# 7

# *Progressive Politics*

"THE SOLUTION TO the woman's problems is neither to offer her abortion, nor merely to prohibit it, but rather to demonstrate that there are humane alternatives," a brochure produced by Minnesota Citizens Concerned for Life (MCCL) proclaimed in 1971. "This means that we must provide counseling, medical care, financial assistance, homes for unwed mothers, adoption agencies and effective welfare programs."[1]

The solutions that MCCL promoted as "socially progressive" captured the attention of pro-lifers throughout the nation. Instead of merely trying to prohibit abortion, they began to think about ways in which they could create a culture that valued human life so much that abortion would be unthinkable. Their goal of promoting a comprehensive ethic of life and social justice led them to embrace other human rights causes, such as antiwar activism and poverty relief. Their movement began to attract traditionally liberal constituencies, such as college students, liberal Protestants, socially conscious women, and even a few African Americans. The early 1970s was still a promising time for rights-based political liberalism, even if a Republican was in the White House and a grassroots conservative movement was rapidly mobilizing. In this heady time of antiwar protests and demands for racial justice and poverty relief, the pro-life movement found common cause with political progressives. Nowhere was that more evident than in Minnesota, the home state of Hubert Humphrey and Walter Mondale and also the leading liberal state pro-life organization of the early 1970s.

## *The Victory of Liberal Pro-Lifers in Minnesota*

The Minnesota pro-life movement had shown few signs of promise when it began in the 1960s. A small, beleaguered, and almost exclusively Catholic effort, it faced seemingly insurmountable challenges in its fight against a liberal Protestant push for abortion law reform. The push for liberalized abortion laws had begun early in Minnesota, and by 1967, it had gained so much ground that one of the state's Catholic clerics suggested that it might be time for right-to-lifers to support the least liberal abortion legalization measure they could find in order to stave off the threat of a more radical bill. The state's nine Catholic bishops quickly distanced themselves from this suggestion and urged Catholics to maintain a staunch pro-life stance, and they issued a joint statement defending the value of fetal life. Their efforts succeeded at first, but everyone knew that the abortion rights lobby would return in the next legislative session. With the Minnesota House Subcommittee on Abortion Laws now endorsing abortion law liberalization, the cause seemed to have strong political support.[2]

MCCL began as a small, grassroots effort to forestall the abortion legalization that many were predicting. Initially, it consisted of twenty-five pro-lifers who gathered at the home of Catholic housewife Alice Hartle in June 1968 in order to form a new lobbying group. Hartle fit the typical profile of a pro-life activist at the time: she was a devout Catholic, married to a physician, and the mother of nine children. In addition to her faith and her ethical convictions, Hartle had another reason for opposing abortion: she had had rubella during one of her pregnancies and as a result, her daughter Mary had been born with a heart condition and a visual impairment. Yet Mary had grown up to be an intelligent young woman (she later became an outspoken pro-life advocate). It was unthinkable to Hartle that her state legislators were considering a bill that would allow women with rubella to terminate the lives of their unborn children on the grounds that they might be born with handicaps.[3]

Most of the other twenty-five members of the fledgling group that met in Hartle's living room also fit the usual profile. Most were Catholic. One was a theology professor at St. Paul Seminary. Another was a nun. Several others were physicians.[4]

But one couple did not fit the stereotype. Fred and Marjory Mecklenburg were self-described liberal Methodists in their early thirties. Not only did they belong to a Protestant denomination that was playing a leading role in the push for reproductive rights, but Fred was a member of Planned Parenthood, and Marjory was not even sure of her position on abortion. Both Mecklenburgs were strong advocates of contraception because of their belief in women's rights and concern about overpopulation. Despite their unusual background, the other members at the meeting decided that they might be the answer to their prayers. Fred, a gynecologist, was strongly opposed to abortion, and Marjory quickly came around. Their youthful energy was appealing to a small organization that included several older members. Fred's profession gave him good connections, and he had already established a reputation among his colleagues as an opponent of abortion. Best of all, the Mecklenburgs offered living proof that the pro-life cause was not just for Catholics. As women's rights advocates, political liberals, Methodists, and advocates of contraception, they would be immune from all of the charges that abortion rights advocates commonly leveled at Catholics. Accordingly, MCCL elected Fred Mecklenburg as its first president.[5]

Marjory did not sit on the sidelines for long. After examining the "facts and logic" on both sides of the abortion controversy, she concluded that her liberal, feminist values led inexorably to a pro-life stance. The abortion rights movement, she believed, offered a false solution for the problems women faced. The availability of legal abortion would encourage men to pressure the women they had impregnated to destroy the unborn children they were carrying, thus producing "medical and psychological risks for the woman which are not insignificant." Legalized abortion would contribute to the sexual commodification of women, she believed—the "final victory of the Playboy philosophy." Legalizing abortion would not address the "underlying social and economic pressures" that led women facing crisis pregnancies to feel compelled to abort. She therefore threw herself wholeheartedly into the pro-life cause, believing that she had a duty not only to stop abortion from being legalized but also to work toward the improved social conditions that she believed would reduce the "pressures" that women faced to terminate their pregnancies. Her drive and organizational skills quickly became legendary within the movement. Within four years, she would become president of MCCL, and her work on behalf of the pro-life cause would eclipse her husband's.[6]

The Mecklenburgs quickly recruited other young liberals to MCCL. The organization's officers included Thomas and Darla St. Martin, an Episcopalian couple in their mid-thirties who linked their opposition to abortion to a broader commitment to social justice and women's rights, and Anna Lawler, a medical technologist who was approximately the same age as the St. Martins and equally liberal in her politics. The organization's state coordinator, Joe Lampe, was even younger; when he joined the organization, he was still a computer science student at the University of Minnesota, but he soon decided to drop out of college in order to devote up to seventy hours a week to his pro-life work. Although several of the people who had gathered in Alice Hartle's living room in 1968 had come from an older generation, by 1971, nearly all of the organization's leaders were under forty, and most were liberal Protestants. MCCL also attracted the interest of liberal Protestant pastors; several ministers from the Episcopal and American Lutheran Churches joined the organization. MCCL made a special effort to appeal to liberal Protestants by bringing in the pro-life Methodist theologian Paul Ramsey to speak, by encouraging each local chapter to appoint someone to reach out to area churches, and by doing everything that it could to root its pro-life arguments in medical science rather than Catholic natural law theology.[7]

MCCL adopted a politically progressive ethos that appealed to many liberal Protestants. From its inception, MCCL coupled its denunciations of abortion with a call for material assistance to pregnant women. Its charter document pledged "to promote and encourage assistance in the care and rearing of children with birth defects" and "promote enlightened care and assistance to mother and child in difficult, unwanted and illegitimate pregnancies."[8] MCCL's ultimate goal was to create a society in which women did not feel the need to resort to abortions, but in the short term, the organization focused on the more immediate task of stopping abortion liberalization bills in the state legislature. It was a difficult challenge.

Most people expected the Minnesota legislature to pass an ALI-style liberalization law in the spring of 1969. Public opinion was in its favor. But MCCL mobilized its forces, bringing in an ecumenical coalition of doctors, women, and Protestant ministers to testify against the bill. Charles Carroll traveled from California to make a guest appearance on a Minneapolis television program. Yet MCCL's efforts seemed insufficient until it received a stroke of luck. During the legislative hearings, members of the Radical Women's Caucus, which thought the bill did not go far enough, disrupted the committee hearings. The protest may have done what the Mecklenburgs could not: convince legislators that the abortion rights movement was divided and alienate potential supporters. In the end, the abortion liberalization measure was defeated in committee by a vote of nineteen to thirteen, a pleasant surprise for MCCL.[9]

The Mecklenburgs realized that they had to be better prepared for the next legislative session. Both political parties in Minnesota had endorsed abortion legalization, and all of the state's major newspapers supported it. A liberal abortion measure was almost certain to pass when the legislature reconvened in early 1971, NARAL leaders predicted. MCCL would have to do what no pro-life organization had yet tried: change the legislature. The organization embarked on a systematic voter mobilization effort aimed at electing pro-life candidates. In 1970, MCCL surveyed candidates for the state legislature to determine their views on abortion, and then compiled a voter guide for MCCL members, encouraging them to elect pro-life candidates—a group that included a twenty-eight-year-old Catholic priest running on a strongly pro-life platform.[10]

The effort produced a more strongly pro-life legislature, but the Mecklenburgs took no chances that it would remain that way. They flooded the state legislators' mailboxes with pro-life materials. When the legislature took up consideration of an abortion liberalization bill in 1971, MCCL brought "busloads of people" to testify against the measure, overwhelming the capacity of the room where the legislative hearings were held. The measure was easily defeated in committee.[11]

By that point, MCCL had become the leading state pro-life organization in the Midwest. By the beginning of 1971, it had established eighty chapters throughout the state. Its monthly newsletter had a circulation of 21,500. It had launched a state chapter of Birthright in order to provide practical help to Minnesota women who were facing crisis pregnancies. Most importantly, with eight lobbyists on its staff, it had become a formidable political force. When it held a dinner for lawmakers in January 1971, one hundred state legislators attended.[12]

## A Politically Progressive, Youth-Oriented Pro-Life Movement

MCCL's success with a liberal, youth-oriented approach reflected a broader trend in the pro-life movement. Yet in its appeal to young progressives, the pro-life movement had to confront a dilemma: What stance would the movement take on other issues of human life, such as war, capital punishment, and poverty? These were not abstract issues but urgent matters of current debate. The nation was polarized over the Vietnam War. Courts were in the midst of debating the death penalty. Great Society poverty relief was still on voters' minds. The pro-life movement had previously attracted people who were united in their opposition to abortion, but who disagreed over other matters of life and death.

The American Catholic Church itself was divided. For most of the twentieth century, the Church had identified with political liberals on questions of social welfare, while also giving strong support to America's wars.

This stance did not seem odd to most people, because since the beginning of the Cold War, liberalism on domestic questions had commonly been paired with aggressive foreign policies. As leaders of a strongly anticommunist Church, Catholic bishops in the United States had cheered on the efforts of both Democrats and Republicans to stop the threat of communism and totalitarianism abroad. But by the late 1960s, many liberal politicians were beginning to denounce the war in Vietnam and to question the nation's Cold War foreign policy. Left-leaning students, joined by a few academics, writers, civil rights activists, and mainline Protestant ministers, were even more critical. Many American Catholics welcomed this shift toward a liberalism based on human rights—a direction in which the global Catholic Church, under the leadership of Pope John XXIII, had already been moving. Vatican II had proclaimed the universal, inalienable principle of human dignity, while Pope John XXIII's encyclical *Pacem in Terris* (1963) had provided a ringing affirmation of human rights, racial equality, and the need for global disarmament.[13]

Moved by these proclamations, some priests joined their liberal Protestant clerical counterparts in speaking out against the Vietnam War, the death penalty, and racial discrimination. Daniel and Philip Berrigan, brothers and priests, led other Catholics in an invasion of a draft board office in Catonsville, Maryland, in 1968. They poured blood on draft files to demonstrate their opposition to the Vietnam War. While most priests did not participate in such radical protests, many spoke out against the war in other ways or organized local efforts to combat poverty or defend human dignity. Some of the more conservative bishops, such as Cardinal James McIntyre, at first tried to silence the outspoken liberal clergy in their dioceses, but by the late 1960s, a number of bishops were joining their priests' calls for social justice and the protection of human life. In California, Thomas McGucken, the archbishop of San Francisco who had spent decades working on behalf of civil rights causes, took a stand against capital punishment by urging Governor Edmund G. Brown in 1966 to commute the sentences of all of the state's death row prisoners to life in prison. The following year, Fulton Sheen, whose long-running popular television show had made him one of the nation's best-known bishops, called for the withdrawal of all American troops from Vietnam.[14]

Yet many members of the Church hierarchy remained nervous about the political radicalism of some of the liberal clergy. Cardinal Francis Spellman spoke out in support of the Vietnam War, Alabama bishop Thomas Toolen tried (unsuccessfully) to stop priests and nuns from participating in the civil rights march in Selma in 1965, and the Jesuit superiors in New York disciplined Daniel Berrigan for his antiwar protests. Some high-ranking clergy continued to defend capital punishment well into the 1970s. The nation's 59,000 priests and 260 bishops represented the full range of political opinion on most issues.[15]

The laity was even more divided. The nation's faithful Catholics included liberal antiwar Democrats such as Senator Eugene McCarthy, radicals such as the "Catonsville Nine," leftist labor organizers such as Cesar Chavez, pacifists such as Dorothy Day, and conservative Republicans such as William F. Buckley Jr. and Phyllis Schlafly. While the lay editor of the liberal Catholic periodical *Commonweal* championed a progressive line, lauding bishops who spoke out against racial injustice and the Vietnam War, the staunchly conservative lay-run Catholic paper *The Wanderer* took the opposite position, criticizing bishops such as Sheen and praising those who continued to champion the fight against communism. On the whole, the American Catholic clergy were becoming increasingly willing to support some of the political causes of the left, but there were still plenty of conservatives, among both the clergy and the laity, who complained about the leftward drift of the Church's leaders.[16]

The pro-life movement drew its support from across the spectrum of both Catholic and Protestant political opinion. Daniel Berrigan and Phyllis Schlafly both opposed abortion, even if they could agree on almost nothing else. *The Wanderer* and *Commonweal* disagreed vehemently about the Vietnam War, but both published anti-abortion articles. Many of the mainline Protestant converts to the pro-life cause in the late 1960s, such as Richard John Neuhaus, denounced the Vietnam War and positioned themselves on the political left.[17] Yet by the beginning of the 1970s, the pro-life cause was also gaining increasing support from evangelicals, most of whom were more politically conservative than either Catholics or mainline Protestants and were not at all inclined to join antiwar protests.[18] Politics for the right-to-life coalition had been much simpler a decade earlier, but the Vietnam War had brought just as much division to both the Catholic Church and the right-to-life movement as it had to the country, and now pro-life activists had to decide how to respond.

At first, the National Right to Life Committee (NRLC) tried to maintain unity in the movement by narrowly focusing on abortion, with euthanasia and infanticide—two other issues on which everyone in the movement could agree—receiving occasional mention as well. This strategy seemed necessary, because even the organization's executive leadership was divided over politics. James McHugh was a liberal who included some antiwar references in one of his pro-life communiques, but the NRLC's executive director Juan Ryan was a much more hawkish conservative with a naval background, a membership in the National Rifle Association, and a record of voting Republican. McHugh's support for some of the most liberal members of his Church bothered Ryan at times, but the two men were close friends and reached a tacit agreement to keep the peace by saying little to each other about politics outside of abortion.[19]

Yet for many new recruits, it seemed hypocritical to decry abortion while saying nothing about other imminent threats to human life. Many pro-lifers were genuinely disturbed by the American government's disregard for human life in warfare, and they wanted the movement to speak out against all attacks on human life, whether those attacks were directed against an unborn baby in the womb, a convicted criminal in an electric chair, or a civilian in a Vietnamese village.

These concerns prompted a change in pro-life rhetoric. Opponents of abortion had often framed their cause as a human rights campaign and had argued that abortion was part of a much broader societal disrespect for human persons. But they had drawn a distinction between murder (including abortion) and legitimate killing in order to defend the country or carry out justice. By the end of the 1960s, that distinction did not seem quite so clear-cut to some pro-lifers. As some in the Church questioned the Vietnam War and the execution of convicted criminals, a number of people in the right-to-life movement did the same, and by the late 1960s and early 1970s, many pro-lifers were adamant opponents of both war and capital punishment. Norman St. John-Stevas, a British right-to-life activist (and member of Parliament) whose *The Right to Life* (1963) was the first book-length defense of the pro-life position, declared in 1972 that he was opposed to capital punishment and the Vietnam War, because he believed that it was the only "fully logical position" for a pro-lifer to take. Georgetown philosophy professor Germain Grisez likewise declared in 1970 that he was opposed to nuclear deterrence and capital punishment, as well as abortion. While he accepted the Catholic idea that there could be just wars, he argued that the Vietnam War, which "poses many problems from an ethical point of view," was not one of them.[20]

Charles Carroll likewise declared his opposition to the Vietnam War, racism, and the death penalty. "I marched with Martin Luther King in Selma," he reminded his fellow pro-lifers at a rally in Washington, DC, in 1972. "I marched with Cesar Chavez in Delano. I have opposed capital punishment." For Carroll, the fight against abortion was simply a part of his larger commitment to defending the value of human life.[21]

Yet other pro-lifers balked. Many American Catholic bishops tacitly supported the Vietnam War, at least in its early years, because of their strong opposition to communism. Even the few who spoke out against it were not necessarily consistent pacifists. The Catholic Church had supported "just war" theory since the time of St. Augustine; it was not a pacifist church, despite the presence of a handful of conscientious objectors in its ranks. Nor was it even officially opposed to capital punishment. While several pro-lifers insisted that capital punishment was wrong, a number of prominent pro-life Catholics, such as Charles Rice, insisted that the death penalty, when given for the crime of murder, was actually a way to signify respect for the value of human life, because it punished someone who had taken a life. Several pro-lifers distinguished between "innocent" human life that must be preserved and "guilty" human life that did not deserve such protection.[22]

An outspoken, growing minority of young, left-leaning pro-lifers rejected the arguments of the movement's conservatives. They saw a connection between the antiwar movement and the pro-life movement, and they wanted to link the two. They tried to reframe the pro-life cause as a campaign against all violence, starting with abortion but extending to war, capital punishment, and all other forms of injustice. "While our sons are dying in Vietnam, it doesn't make much sense to promote violence in our own society by relaxing our abortion law," Anna Lawler and Angela Wozniak, legislative chairs of MCCL, argued in 1971.[23]

Questions about the war were especially likely to come from college students, a group that pro-lifers needed but who were least likely to support their cause. A Harris poll taken in 1970 indicated that 46 percent of Americans under thirty supported the removal of all restrictions on abortion, while only 30 percent of those over fifty did. Polls that specifically tested for the views of the college-aged population showed an even starker divide. In 1972, for instance, 76 percent of eighteen- to twenty-year-olds in Michigan favored legalizing elective abortion, compared with only 38 percent of those over sixty. There was also an educational divide. Fifty-three percent of those with only a high school education opposed the legalization of elective abortion, compared to only 37 percent of the college-educated.[24] College students were the strongest base of support for the abortion rights movement, but the pro-life movement needed younger people to remain viable.

Pro-lifers could take comfort in the fact that a small minority of committed Catholic students remained opposed to abortion. Catholic bishops received letters from anxious nursing majors who wondered how they should respond, as faithful Catholics, if they were called upon to assist in an abortion, or who asked for pro-life materials to support their "convictions" on the subject.[25] Because these students represented some of the most conscientious, devout members of their generation, they were highly likely to couple their opposition to abortion with a championship of the Church's standard of sexual ethics, including opposition to premarital sex. Yet they were not political conservatives. They opposed the Vietnam War and often took liberal positions on issues of poverty relief and civil rights. If they joined a political organization to fight against abortion, they wanted to make sure that the organization accorded with their values.

It was not surprising, therefore, that when pro-life organizations tried to recruit on college campuses, the students had one question for them: What about the war? In September 1970, Fr. Gerald Lytle, who had been trying to recruit new members for Pennsylvanians for Human Life (PHL) on some of the state's campuses, told a meeting of the Human Life Task Force of the Diocese of Harrisburg that unless PHL took a "stronger stand ... against the war," it was unlikely to recruit many students. But most of the other clergy at the meeting believed that anything that distracted from the fight against liberalized abortion laws was likely to weaken the organization. They decided to send the Catholic students some of the pope's condemnations of the war in Vietnam—thus assuring them that the Church did take the morally correct position on the issue, even if evidence for that was not always found in the statements of American bishops—and then encourage those who were interested in connecting the antiwar cause with the pro-life movement to do so in their own organizations.[26] Groups that wanted to link the pro-life cause with other "life" issues would be welcomed, but the Church's primary channel of pro-life work, the NRLC, would maintain a narrow focus.

Several campus pro-life organizations of the early 1970s embraced a much broader range of social justice causes, including opposition to the war. Save Our Unwanted Life (SOUL), which two twenty-one-year-old female students at the University of Minnesota formed in 1971, argued that "the most 'liberal' cause is protecting other people's lives," beginning with the unborn. "If you are against killing in Vietnam, you should be against abortion," Sue Bastyr, one of SOUL's cofounders, argued. The other cofounder, Maureen Clements, argued that the pro-life message was also an environmentally sensitive one. "The womb is the first ecological environment," she argued. "Abortion pollutes the womb."[27]

Under the guidance of Thomas Hilgers, a young graduate fellow in obstetrics at the Mayo Clinic, SOUL championed the "philosophy of involvement" as an alternative to abortion. Sounding very much like an advocate for the New Left, or at least like a veteran of the Robert Kennedy or Eugene McCarthy presidential campaigns, Hilgers defined the "philosophy of involvement" as "the *desire* to give oneself unreservedly to another human being who is in need of that help and second, and most important, the implementation of that desire through an *actual commitment*." Abortion was the cheap, irresponsible, and violent solution to problems that required human investment. He encouraged couples to adopt the "unwanted" minority and handicapped babies that were too often the victims of abortion. He advocated the establishment of "birth insurance," which would offer benefits to couples who unexpectedly gave birth to disabled children requiring expensive care. And he encouraged a broad attack on the forces of economic injustice. The War on Poverty, he said, should be "something more than just a backyard skirmish." If pro-lifers wanted to deter women from having abortions, they would need to fight the forces that made it difficult for an impoverished single woman to raise a child. "It's not so much that the woman rejects the child as that society rejects the pregnant woman," SOUL member Edythe Thompson explained.[28]

SOUL's two cofounders practiced what they preached by volunteering for Birthright. Their message quickly caught on; by May 1971, SOUL had 200 student members registered at several campuses throughout Minnesota, including Catholic colleges such as Saint John's, as well as state universities. Several of the students who joined the organization were not religious at all—in fact, two of the eight founding members described themselves as atheists or agnostics—and many had not thought much about the implications of abortion until the leaders of SOUL made the case that the pro-life cause was a natural outgrowth of the antiwar movement. A few of the members had been vocal advocates of abortion rights before SOUL's arguments convinced them to switch sides. Some had had abortions themselves and had come to regret it. Others had had religious upbringings and characterized themselves as "Jesus people." But few were conservatives. "We consider ourselves an extremely liberal group," Sue Bastyr told a reporter.[29]

For most of 1971, the pro-life student groups that formed at college campuses throughout the nation were independent entities, but that fall, four members of SOUL—two women and two men—embarked on a tour of college campuses in the Midwest to locate fellow students who shared their commitment to being "pro-life, pro-love and pro-peace." They initially found some allies in a student pro-life group at Cleveland State University in Ohio and eventually recruited enough campus advocates of the pro-life cause to hold a "Thanksgiving for Life" conference in Illinois in November 1971, soliciting a telegram of greeting from Eunice Kennedy Shriver for the occasion. It was at that conference that seventy pro-life students from twenty-six states formed the National Youth Pro-Life Coalition (NYPLC). The parallels with the NRLC were striking, since both organizations were formed as national coalitions of state organizations. But unlike the NRLC, the NYPLC was completely independent of direction from the Catholic Church (though many of its members were Catholic) and did not hesitate to take liberal stands on the controversial political issues that the NRLC had eschewed. The founders of the NYPLC declared that their cause was a civil rights movement for the unborn, and they expected to borrow the successful techniques that the civil rights movement had pioneered a decade earlier.[30]

Although the NYPLC was considerably more liberal than the NRLC, it had the full support of the older generation of NRLC leaders, who viewed it as an effective way to recruit young people to the cause. A few weeks before SOUL's "Thanksgiving for Life" conference, NRLC executive director Michael Taylor sent out a mass appeal to state NRLC chapter leaders, encouraging them to finance travel to the conference for any SOUL members who did not have the money to get there on their own.[31] While SOUL's image might have been radical, its left-leaning political stances were fully in keeping with Catholic doctrine. Indeed, some NRLC members who had only given hints of their antiwar beliefs may have secretly appreciated that the students were preaching a message that the NRLC could not officially proclaim.

The members of the NYPLC tried to engage in the type of direct political activism that was popular among politically engaged students in other organizations. Some of them traveled to Wisconsin to "confront" the Democratic presidential candidates shortly before that state's primary and force them to "publicly declare their position on abortion." After shadowing the candidates in their "pro-life bus" and tracking each candidate down for a comment on the issue, they were disappointed to discover that all of the candidates were "tragically uninformed about the war on the unborn in America" and that none "offered positive alternatives to stressful pregnancies."[32]

In September 1972, the NYPLC organized a march on Washington. The rally featured a musical performance by the pro-life rock band Gladstone, speeches at the Lincoln Memorial, and a moment for participants to throw copies of their birth certificates into a "large recycling barrel" to protest the "erroneous role of birth [instead of conception] as the beginning of human life." The featured speakers—including the young antiwar Lutheran minister Richard John Neuhaus, who had served as a McGovern delegate at the Democratic National Convention the previous month—were chosen for their appeal to a pro-life crowd that embraced the politics of the left. "The anti-abortion forces are not instruments of political and social conservatism," Neuhaus declared. "Rather they are related to the protest against the Indochina war, the militarization of American life, and the social crimes perpetrated against the poor."[33]

In a show of rebellion against materialism, the students celebrated their lack of resources and expressed pride in organizing the march on a shoestring budget. The advertisements for the event, which were handwritten mimeographs, encouraged marchers to bring sleeping bags so that they could sleep on the floor of Catholic University's gymnasium. "The NYPLC is run by young people who have no money," the flyers proclaimed. "This rally is being financed in the red." By contrast, they said, the abortion industry represented heartless capitalism, sacrificing the interests of women and children for money. Abortion "is a multi-million dollar business, one that demeans the whole concept of what it means to be a doctor," Thomas Hilgers said. "A profession that has been directly responsible for the destruction of over one million human lives in the United States in the last three years is a profession whose ethical standards must be deeply questioned by all members of society."[34]

Unfortunately for the students, the rally failed to meet expectations. The NYPLC had reserved 2,000 camping spots in addition to the floor space at the Catholic University gym, but the march attracted only 500 people.[35] After spending a year and a half organizing a student pro-life movement, Sue Bastyr discovered that she had fewer allies among her peers than she had thought. Left-leaning students would continue to play a role in the pro-life movement for several years, but they would be marginalized.

Yet the students' interest in linking the pro-life cause with the causes of the left was reflected in some of the rhetoric of the mainstream right-to-life movement. By 1972, some of the highest-ranking members of the American Catholic clergy had decided that the pro-life and the antiwar causes could not be separated. In the spring of 1972, Thomas Gumbleton, auxiliary bishop of Detroit, attempted to persuade the National Conference of Catholic Bishops to endorse the antiwar cause as a natural extension of the Church's campaign against abortion. The bishops did not issue the official declaration that Gumbleton wanted, but his own archbishop, Cardinal John Dearden, did. "We cannot be selective in our love for life," Dearden declared in September 1972. "The very same reasons call on us to protect it wherever and however it is threatened, whether through the suffocation of poverty or in villages ravaged by napalm or unborn life in a mother's womb."[36]

Dearden was not alone in this view. When the bishops of the United States agreed to designate a week in October 1972 as "Respect Life Week," they encouraged priests to couple their condemnations of abortion with calls for poverty relief, peace, and respect for the lives of the elderly. Some individual bishops added a condemnation of the Vietnam War to that list. "From the abortionist to the advocate of euthanasia, from the dropping of bombs on the innocent, to the starving of millions for political reasons, from the degredation [sic] of the migrant worker, to racial injustices of every sort, from poisoning of our youth with drugs, to the neglect of the elderly and handicapped, life is being attacked," the bishop of Madison, Wisconsin, declared in an official letter to his diocese in observance of "Respect Life Week" in 1972. "We must stop these attacks. Human life must be defended, it must be reverenced, it must be preserved in all its stages from conception to death."[37]

This line of argument appealed to some prominent liberal politicians, especially Catholic ones, and it offered them a way to embrace the pro-life cause without betraying their liberal principles, an option that had not been as evident a few years earlier. In 1967, Senator Robert Kennedy had signaled the link between liberalism and abortion rights when he defied his Church's stance and endorsed a proposed liberalization of New York's abortion law. But the right-to-life movement's successful effort to link its cause to a larger liberal human rights agenda that included opposition to the Vietnam War allowed the movement to regain some of the liberal support that it had lost in the late 1960s. In 1971, Kennedy's younger brother Ted, a senator from Massachusetts who was now, as his family's torchbearer, one of the best-known liberals in Washington, endorsed the right-to-life cause in language that closely echoed the new liberal pro-life rhetoric that his sister Eunice Kennedy Shriver had helped to promote, drawing connections between the protection of the unborn and a broader ethic of social justice. "Wanted or unwanted, I believe that human life, even at its earliest stages, has certain rights which must be recognized—the right to be born, the right to love, the right to grow old," he declared. "When history looks back to this era it should recognize this generation as one which cared about human beings enough to halt the practice of war, to provide a decent living for every family, and to fulfill its responsibility to its children from the very moment of conception."[38]

## Recruiting African Americans

Some pro-lifers also began to connect their movement to the cause of civil rights for African Americans. In 1972, immediately after elective abortion was legalized in Washington, DC, Patrick Cardinal O'Boyle, who had a long history of supporting civil rights and who had delivered the invocation at the March on Washington, declared that in a city that was 71 percent African American, "no one can ignore the implications of genocide." Immediately, the city's press denounced the statement, but James McHugh defended it. Forced sterilization programs, which Catholics had opposed, were still a very recent memory, so it was not difficult for many pro-lifers to imagine state social workers pressuring impoverished single African American women to terminate their pregnancies.[39]

By 1972, white pro-lifers throughout the nation—even in the Deep South—were linking their movement to the cause of African American civil rights and accusing their opponents of promoting racism, eugenics, and even genocide. "Abortion does concern the poor and especially black citizens," the Louisiana Right to Life Association declared in 1972. "Abortion is advocated as a way of reducing the number of illegitimate children and reducing the welfare rolls. Who do you think abortionists have in mind?"[40]

African Americans were the demographic group most likely to oppose abortion—in fact, opposition to abortion was higher among African American Protestants than it was even among white Catholics. But pro-life organizations had little connection to black institutions—particularly black churches—and they were far too Catholic and too white to appeal to most African American Protestants.[41]

In spite of these obstacles, a handful of African American professionals in a few states, including Michigan, Minnesota, and Massachusetts, did join pro-life organizations and take leadership positions, beginning in the early 1970s. White pro-life organizations welcomed their contributions as proof of the diversity of their movement. Several of these African Americans were more politically liberal than their white counterparts in the movement, but their concern for unborn human life was the same, and they were even more likely than whites to view legal abortion as a eugenic tool on a par with forced sterilization. Erma Craven, for instance, the chair of the Minneapolis Committee on Human Rights and a member of MCCL, was a county social worker who argued that abortion legalization was often the product of racism, especially in the South. Mississippi, which in 1966 had legalized abortion in cases of rape, had preceded Colorado and California in liberalizing its abortion law, and North Carolina, which had voted down an equal employment opportunity bill in the same year in which it adopted a liberalized abortion policy, was not far behind. Craven used these examples as evidence that the South was waging war on the "unborn Negro."[42]

Many African Americans agreed. The Black Panther Party initially opposed both abortion and birth control, believing that both amounted to eugenic efforts to suppress the black population. During the 1970s, some of the leading African American civil rights activists were pro-lifers. Jesse Jackson, for instance, contributed an article on abortion to the *National Right to Life News* in 1977 that linked the abortion cause to larger concerns about poverty and social justice. Abortion rights advocates' denial of fetal personhood was analogous to the refusal of many whites to recognize the personhood of African Americans in the nineteenth century, he said, and the promotion of abortion as a solution to overpopulation was evidence of a callous indifference to the real needs of the poor. "Politicians argue for abortion largely because they do not want to spend the necessary money to feed, clothe, and educate more people," Jackson declared.[43]

Some white members of the NRLC were delighted to trumpet Jackson's support for their cause, and Americans United for Life considered inviting him to serve as a board member of the organization. But the African American pro-life activist who had the greatest appeal for them was Mildred Jefferson, a Boston surgeon who, in 1951, had become the first black woman to graduate from Harvard Medical School.[44]

Jefferson was a celebrity within the pro-life movement from the moment she joined the cause in 1970. She was forty-four years old at the time, but could have easily passed for someone fifteen or twenty years younger. Invariably pictured with perfectly styled hair, an erect posture, and a disarming smile, Jefferson was a telegenic personality. She was also intelligent, a skilled debater, and the "greatest orator of our movement," one NRLC officer declared. For a movement eager to shed its image as the preserve of older white male Catholic clerics, Jefferson was the ideal representative. A black Methodist woman, she was everything that the Catholic bishops were not. And with her Harvard Medical School degree and her teaching position at the Boston University School of Medicine, she also had impeccable medical credentials. As soon as she engaged in her first televised debate with abortion rights advocates in Massachusetts in 1970, Catholic pro-life advocates took notice and decided to recruit her for more public relations events. "As the representative of Cardinal Cushing and all the Catholic Bishops of Massachusetts on the abortion issue, I wish to extend to you my congratulations and best wishes on your very fine presentation," Msgr. Paul Harrington wrote to her in June 1970. "I hope that I may be able to call on you for your helpful assistance and cooperation."[45]

In spite of her public visibility, Jefferson was an enigma to many—a fierce guardian of her own privacy. Though she gave many public speeches on behalf of the movement, they contained no snippets of autobiography. In her interactions with the press, she was notoriously tight-lipped about her own feelings or life experiences. She refused to tell journalists her age or to discuss her religious beliefs with anyone except to say that she believed in God and was a Methodist. She was not a regular churchgoer, yet she retained her membership in a mainline Protestant denomination that was officially pro-choice. Though she rarely gave interviewers any insight into her personal biography—other than to state her medical credentials—those who did the requisite research discovered that she had been born into a minister's family in a small town in east Texas in 1926 and had earned her B.A. at Texas College before fleeing the segregated South for Boston. She was not a family person; she had grown up as an only child, she had no children of her own, and her only marriage would end in divorce.[46] Yet these nuggets of biographical information seemed to offer little clue as to why a professional woman in a liberal northeastern city, with no religious reasons for opposing abortion, would choose to devote herself to a movement that was filled with people who had little in common with her.

Jefferson insisted that she was convinced of abortion's evils because of the medical evidence. But occasionally her personal writings suggested something broader. Jefferson had said nothing about abortion during the late 1960s, when liberalization bills were being discussed. But when the

American Medical Association (AMA) voted to rescind its policy against abortion and when four states legalized elective abortion, she felt that she had to act. The AMA's vote represented an attack on the integrity of the profession. Doctors, she said years later, were given "an almost unlimited license to kill." "I became a physician in the tradition represented by the Hippocratic Oath," she declared, a tradition that "obliged the society not to ask the doctor to kill." The legal availability of elective abortion threatened the long-term survival of minority groups, and it also encouraged the patterns of irresponsibility that she believed threatened contemporary society. "Abortion on demand," she wrote in 1970 during her first months of activism, was the "most destructive proposition" of "the credo: License without Responsibility."[47]

Before Jefferson joined the pro-life campaign, the relatively few black activists in the movement were liberal Democrats who were strong supporters of an expanded social welfare state. Jefferson, by contrast, was a conservative who supported Richard Nixon and eventually joined the Republican Party. For her, the ethic of personal responsibility was paramount, and it was a central reason that she opposed abortion. Like several other black conservatives, she was convinced that her own self-determination had allowed her to break into a male-dominated white enclave, and she assumed that others with similar talent could do the same. "I have never been enslaved, so I do not need to be liberated," she said. Feminism "is a concept for which I have no philosophical nor intellectual appreciation." Above all, she detested a victim mentality, saying that people were often "enslaved by their own attitudes." When pressed, she could name instances of direct discrimination that she had faced because of her race or gender, including a denial of career opportunities at Boston University Hospital. But such slights, she said, were "the price of the game." She could have sued, she said, but she chose not to. "Sure, it was unfair," she admitted. "But life is not necessarily fair."[48] Jefferson's conservative philosophy of personal responsibility probably would not have received a favorable hearing in SOUL or the NYPLC, and it was not even an argument that James McHugh generally made, but many in the NRLC welcomed it.

Jefferson was bothered by the lack of convincing spokespersons in the pro-life movement. "Physicians and other non-religious voices had to speak out to balance the discussion," she declared. In order to bring this balance to the movement, she joined Massachusetts Citizens for Life (MCFL) and immediately threw herself into the cause by engaging in debates with pro-choice opponents in the state. By 1973, she was president of the Value of Life Committee, vice president of MCFL—which by then was a 50,000-member organization—and vice-chair of the NRLC's board of directors.[49] Two years later, she would be elected president of the NRLC.

Jefferson quickly became one of the most sought-after speakers at national pro-life events. She gave her audiences a barrage of medical evidence: The fertilized egg was genetically different from the sperm or the ovum and thus represented new life that must be protected. Abortion was dangerous for women; it resulted in uterine scar tissue and increased the risk of sterilization. Jefferson believed that medical facts, rather than religious rhetoric or natural law arguments, should convince people to oppose abortion. Like other African American pro-life activists, Jefferson argued that abortion was "a class war against the poor and genocide against blacks," but her critique of abortion was far broader than that.[50] On scientific, medical, and philosophical grounds, Jefferson believed that pro-life activists had the better arguments, and she was eager to take those arguments to the public through legislative testimony and televised debates. By 1972, the public face of the pro-life movement was still mostly white—Jefferson remained an exception—but increasingly Protestant and female.

## Near Victory

When the NRLC convened in Philadelphia in June 1972 for its third annual convention, its program reflected the new progressive politics and religious diversity of the movement. The conference program still set aside time for Catholic Mass on Sunday morning, but it also gave the many Protestants who attended the option of going to an ecumenical prayer service at a Methodist Church. The program included a lecture by the Unitarian Harvard Divinity School professor George Huntston Williams titled "Abortion: An Ecumenical Issue." Marjory Mecklenburg was on hand to give a presentation on "Positive Alternatives to Abortion: Legislative Programs," at which she promoted social welfare programs for women in the name of pro-life advocacy. Sidney Callahan gave a talk entitled "The Feminist Movement: A Pro-Life Approach." Perhaps most surprisingly, the NRLC allowed Fred Mecklenburg to share a platform on population issues with Randy Engel and James McHugh.[51] The two Catholics were likely uncomfortable with Mecklenburg's membership in Planned Parenthood and his promotion of birth control—a stance that would especially have rankled Engel, who championed her Church's conservative position on the issue—but the inclusion of both a woman and a Protestant birth control advocate on the panel along with a Catholic cleric was a sign of how far the NRLC had come in its effort to project a diverse, progressive, and ecumenical image.

That image was producing a political turnaround. Only a few weeks before the NRLC convention, pro-lifers in New York succeeded in doing what most observers on both sides of the abortion debate had thought impossible: they convinced the state legislature to repeal the state's permissive abortion law.

This stunning victory for pro-lifers in New York was the result of a two-year effort that began as soon as the state legalized abortion. Although many pro-lifers were in despair at that moment, Edward Golden refused to give up hope. Realizing that the bill had passed by a razor-thin margin, he resolved to win the votes to repeal it. Under his guidance, New York right-to-lifers successfully targeted some of the bill's legislative supporters for defeat in 1970 and then lobbied the incoming legislators. During the 1971–72 legislative session, Golden brought busloads and carloads of pro-life grassroots activists to the state capitol every day.

He also recruited a few Orthodox Jews and Protestants to the cause. Golden estimated that in 1971, the New York Right to Life Committee had membership that was still 95 percent Catholic; by 1972, that figure was down to 85 percent. The organization was also much larger. With its 200,000 or more members (one estimate put the figure at 300,000), New York Right to Life was possibly the most powerful pro-life organization in the country.[52]

New York pro-life organizations benefited from widespread discontent with the state's abortion policy. By 1972, even some of the original advocates of legalization felt that the law had gone too far and had produced unintended consequences. The high number of abortions performed on out-of-state women, which strained the capacities of New York hospitals and contributed to the state's reputation as an abortion mill, bothered some people. Even more troubling were the occasional reports of botched late-term abortions.

State senator James Donovan realized that he had the votes for repeal, which would mean a return to a ban on abortion in all cases except when it was necessary to save a woman's life. His biggest obstacle, though, remained Nelson Rockefeller. Rockefeller had been a proponent of abortion rights for years, but because he sensed the public's unease with unrestricted abortion and legislators' growing support for repeal, he offered a compromise. He would agree to a measure that would limit abortion to the first sixteen weeks of pregnancy, he said—a proposal that he later raised to eighteen weeks after consulting with physicians—rather than allowing abortions up to twenty-four weeks, as the law currently did.[53]

But Donovan was convinced that he could get much more, and pro-lifers escalated the pressure on lawmakers to pass his repeal bill. Cardinal Terence Cooke proclaimed April 16, 1972, as "Human Life Sunday" and encouraged priests to deliver homilies against abortion. The Knights of Columbus organized an interfaith march that drew 10,000 pro-life protestors to Central Park. Six hundred demonstrators descended on the capitol in Albany carrying signs that said "Give Life a Chance" and "Live and Let Live." This time, women took the lead in lobbying legislators, and an Orthodox Jewish rabbi spoke at the pro-life rally in Central Park. The pro-lifers' signs featured fetal photographs and referenced the images that had become an essential part of the movement's message. "Babies Want to See the World, Not the Inside of a Garbage Can," one of the signs proclaimed.[54]

The lobbying behind the scenes may have been even more effective. Under Golden's leadership, the New York Right to Life Committee spent $10,000 on mailings to mobilize its members to action. Golden encouraged them to make a special effort to talk to freshman legislators who might still be undecided.[55]

The hearings were even more emotional than they had been two years earlier. At those initial hearings, some pro-life legislators had issued dire warnings about the horrors that might ensue if abortion were legalized, but now, pro-life politicians were able to confront their fellow legislators with graphic evidence of those horrors. Donovan distributed packets of fetal photographs to every member of the senate, accompanied by the caption "What the unborn would like every legislator to know." One assembly representative punctuated his speech by holding up an aborted fetus preserved in a glass jar. Another gave a graphic description of a D&C procedure. "Can we tear a child apart limb from limb because of an accident of fate that he has not been born?" he asked.[56]

After six hours of debate in the assembly and another seven hours in the senate—a record for that legislative season—pro-lifers won a victory in both houses. The assembly passed the repeal bill by a vote of seventy-nine to sixty-eight; the senate likewise adopted it by a vote of thirty to twenty-seven. As expected, the governor vetoed the measure. But partisans on both sides of the debate expected that Rockefeller might join President Nixon's Cabinet the next year, and if that happened, the governorship would then pass to Lieutenant Governor Malcolm Wilson, a strongly pro-life Catholic. Even if Rockefeller remained governor, pro-lifers in New York were poised to elect a veto-proof supermajority in the legislature. Several legislators who had voted in favor of abortion legalization in 1970 had switched their votes in 1972. The tide was turning in their favor.[57]

The pro-life movement's near victory in New York alarmed pro-choice activists. To lose in New York would be a severe blow to the campaign for abortion legalization, because New York was the nation's leading supplier of abortions. It was also the birthplace of some of the first abortion rights organizations and the home of Betty Friedan, Alan Guttmacher, and other pro-choice luminaries. It had important strategic and symbolic significance. In reaction to pro-lifers' unexpected success, NARAL hired a new political consultant to focus entirely on New York, and it set up a new political action organization devoted solely to defeating right-to-life candidates in the state. But NARAL's executive director was still worried. "Retaining the law in the next session of the legislature will be even more difficult than in this one," she confided to an ally.[58]

Pro-lifers, on the other hand, found reason for optimism, not only in New York but across the nation. "The New York vote ... tells Right to Life organizations that, with sufficient effort and planning, citizen groups can realistically hope to effect a roll-back of easy abortion laws," Michael Taylor wrote. "The road to repeal is not easy, but with perseverance, dedication and planning, there is reason for hope."[59]

Until 1972, pro-lifers had been on the defensive, trying desperately to stop abortion legalization measures wherever they appeared, but not always succeeding. Now, after building a massive nationwide grassroots coalition, and after defeating abortion legalization proposals in states across the nation, pro-lifers had gained the confidence they needed to go on the offensive. They would repeal the abortion legalization proposals that had already passed. They would tighten existing abortion laws. They would then enact their progressive political vision by passing legislation extending prenatal care and health insurance for pregnant women. They would educate the public about the horrors of abortion and create a culture of life throughout the land.

Pro-lifers really believed that their side could prevail. The battle would be difficult, but they saw signs that victory might at last be in sight.

Walter Trinkaus and Elizabeth Goodwin, cofounders of one of the nation's first pro-life organizations, the Right to Life League (founded in December 1966). As an attorney and leader in the California right-to-life movement in the 1960s, Trinkaus formulated some of the movement's earliest constitutional arguments. Goodwin's efforts helped women gain a greater leadership role in the movement. (Right to Life League of Southern California)

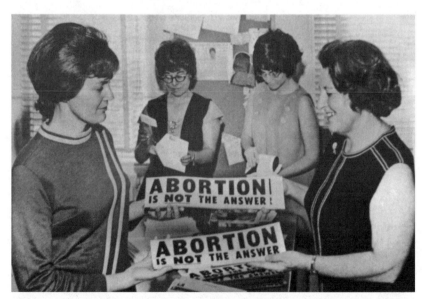

Right to Life League volunteers in southern California stuffing envelopes with brochures and bumper stickers for a mass mailing, 1971. Although the Right to Life League did not succeed in stopping abortion law liberalization in California, it provided a model of grassroots organizing and inspired pro-life mobilization in other states. (Right to Life League of Southern California)

Randy Engel (seated, center, in leopard-print blouse) with Pennsylvania pro-lifers affiliated with Women Concerned for the Unborn Child, September 1973. Engel was the pro-life movement's leading defender against the arguments of population control advocates and a nationally known spokesperson for the pro-life cause. She was also an opponent of contraception and a strong critic of Fr. James McHugh's efforts to distance the pro-life movement from the campaign against birth control. (Diocese of Pittsburgh Archives and Records Center)

Fr. Paul Marx lecturing on abortion, 1971. In the early 1970s, Fr. Marx was a liberal Democrat and opponent of the Vietnam War, but his opposition to abortion prompted him to begin voting Republican. (Saint John's University Archives)

Dr. John C. "Jack" Willke and Barbara Willke, with Rep. Lawrence Hogan
(R-MD), April 1974. The Willkes, authors of the bestselling *Handbook on Abortion*
(1971), became national leaders in the pro-life movement partly because of their
innovative use of fetal photographs. In 1973, Hogan introduced the Human Life
Amendment in Congress. (Photo courtesy of Dr. J. C. Willke)

Mary Winter (left) with Pat Bennett at a Pittsburgh pro-life center, August 1973. Winter, the founder of Women Concerned for the Unborn Child, recruited thousands of women to the movement and reframed the pro-life cause as a campaign for women's interests. (Diocese of Pittsburgh Archives and Records Center)

Mary Winter in a "Lifemobile," as Celeste Oesterle (of Pennsylvania Foundation for Life) looks on, May 1976. As the slogans on the "Lifemobile" suggest, most pro-lifers of the 1960s and 1970s believed that they were defending a fundamental American right grounded in the Declaration of Independence and the Constitution. (Diocese of Pittsburgh Archives and Records Center)

Louise Summerhill, the Canadian grandmother who founded Birthright in 1968 at the age of 52. With its slogan "It is the right of every pregnant woman to give birth, and the right of every child to be born," Birthright became the pro-life movement's leading provider of abortion alternatives and material assistance for women facing crisis pregnancies. (Birthright International)

Marjory Mecklenburg (far left) with three other leaders in the National Right to Life Committee (NRLC) during the early 1970s: Judy Fink (Pennsylvania), Mildred Jefferson (Massachusetts), and Robert Greene (Kentucky). As a leader in Minnesota Citizens Concerned for Life (MCCL), the NRLC, and American Citizens Concerned for Life (ACCL), Mecklenburg pushed the pro-life movement to reach out to Protestants and adopt a more politically progressive stance. (Minnesota Citizens Concerned for Life)

Joe Lampe, state coordinator of Minnesota Citizens Concerned for Life (MCCL), at MCCL's office in 1972. As one of the nation's leading pro-life organizations, MCCL encouraged a liberal brand of pro-life politics that advocated for state-funded care for pregnant women in addition to anti-abortion legislation. (Minnesota Citizens Concerned for Life)

Edward Golden speaking at the March for Life in Washington, DC, on the first anniversary of *Roe v. Wade*, January 22, 1974. Golden founded the New York Right to Life Committee in 1965; it had more than 200,000 members by the summer of 1972. (Photo courtesy of the family of Edward J. Golden)

A New York pro-life protest, July 1973. The New York Right to Life Committee nearly succeeded in overturning New York's liberal abortion law in 1972, but *Roe v. Wade* stopped the organization from further attempts to outlaw abortion in the state. Here, the demonstrators use some of the movement's iconic fetal photographs to persuade the public of the humanity of the unborn child. (Photo by Keystone-France/Gamma Keystone via Getty Images)

Mildred Jefferson speaking on behalf of the pro-life cause in Minnesota, accompanied by two MCCL leaders, Ruby Kubista and Leo LaLonde. (Minnesota Citizens Concerned for Life)

Pro-life march in Pittsburgh organized by Pennsylvanians for Human Life and Women Concerned for the Unborn Child, 1973. Protests against *Roe v. Wade* occurred in numerous cities across the country throughout 1973, culminating in a national March for Life in January 1974 that brought more than 5,000 pro-lifers to the Washington Mall on the first anniversary of *Roe v. Wade*. (Diocese of Pittsburgh Archives and Records Center)

Pro-lifers in Norfolk, Virginia, protest the opening of Norfolk's first abortion clinic, October 1973. As abortion clinics opened in cities throughout the country in the months following *Roe v. Wade*, they became sites of pro-life protests. At the time of this protest, the Virginia state legislature refused to comply with *Roe*'s requirement to legalize abortion, but that did not stop abortion clinics from opening in the state. The slogan "Adoption, not abortion" reflected a widely shared determination among pro-lifers of the early 1970s to provide positive alternatives to abortion. (*The Virginian-Pilot*)

Dr. Fred Mecklenburg with Fr. William Hunt (a Minneapolis priest affiliated with American Citizens Concerned for Life [ACCL]) and Eunice Kennedy Shriver, February 1975. Mecklenburg, Shriver, and ACCL were committed to a politically progressive vision for the pro-life movement—a vision that the movement largely abandoned after the late 1970s. Shriver, whose husband Sargent failed to retain the pro-life movement's support when he ran for president in 1976, was at the center of the controversy. (Minnesota Citizens Concerned for Life)

Ellen McCormack (left) with Mary Winter (center) and Donna Grab (from People Concerned for the Unborn Child), March 1976. McCormack's campaign for the 1976 Democratic presidential nomination gave the pro-life cause a few delegates at the Democratic National Convention, but it could not stop the party from affirming *Roe v. Wade*. (Diocese of Pittsburgh Archives and Records Center)

A pro-life Reagan delegate at the 1976 Republican National Convention. Ronald Reagan's endorsement of the pro-life cause in 1976 brought pro-lifers into the Republican Party, prompting the GOP to officially endorse a pro-life constitutional amendment. (Religion News Service)

Mildred Jefferson meeting with Ronald Reagan and pro-life congressional Republicans at the White House, January 22, 1981. Pro-lifers gave Reagan strong support in 1980 because of his endorsement of the Human Life Amendment. (Ronald Reagan Library)

A pro-life demonstration in West Los Angeles on the tenth anniversary of *Roe v. Wade*, January 22, 1983. When pro-lifers lost their campaign in the Senate for a constitutional amendment in the early 1980s, they escalated their protests and attempted to change the Supreme Court in order to overturn *Roe*. (*The Tidings* Archive, Los Angeles)

A pro-life demonstration in front of the Supreme Court at the March for Life in Washington, DC, January 22, 2013. Many of the hundreds of thousands of pro-lifers who participated in the March for Life on the fortieth anniversary of *Roe v. Wade* were high school or college students under the age of thirty—a self-proclaimed "pro-life generation." In the background, pro-choice counter-demonstrators protest the pro-life message—a sign of the nation's continued polarization over abortion. (Photo by Mandel Ngan/AFP/Getty Images)

## 8

# *National Battle*

THE PRO-LIFE MOVEMENT'S euphoria was short-lived. As soon as pro-lifers found a way to win in state legislatures, advocates of abortion rights brought their campaign to the nation's polling booths and courtrooms. They introduced ballot initiatives to legalize abortion, and they made abortion an issue in the presidential election of 1972. Pro-lifers faced even greater challenges in the nation's courtrooms. Judicial opinion, which had long been on their side, was beginning to turn against them. And public opinion surveys indicated that, for the first time, a majority of Americans supported the legalization of elective abortion. Pro-lifers were being challenged on several fronts.

## *The Cultural Forces Arrayed against the Pro-Life Movement*

Despite pro-lifers' successes in the legislative arena, cultural shifts were rapidly undermining their public support. Americans' attitudes toward sexual behavior were undergoing a sea change. In the summer of 1972, as pro-lifers concluded their second year of sweeping legislative victories, movie theaters across the nation were showing an explicitly pornographic film (*Deep Throat*) for the first time, newsstands were starting to augment their stacks of *Playboy* magazines with more explicit fare from *Penthouse* and similar periodicals, and some of the earliest national gay liberation groups were publicly defending the rights of homosexuals, often using the confrontational tactics of direct-action politics. The sexual revolution was perhaps most evident on college campuses, where surveys indicated that unmarried college women were more likely than ever to be having sex.

In 1958, for instance, one study of Midwestern college women had shown that only 21 percent had engaged in premarital sex, but a follow-up study in 1968 showed that 34 percent had. As behavior changed, so did values. While only 17 percent of Midwestern college women had approved of premarital sexual intercourse in 1958, 38 percent did so in 1968. National surveys showed similar results. By 1975, according to a Gallup poll, 85 percent of college seniors thought that there was nothing "wrong" with "sexual relations before marriage."[1]

This revolution in sexual attitudes and behavior led to an increased demand for abortion among unmarried women, who accounted for two-thirds of all abortions by the early 1970s and whose pregnancies were now more likely to end in termination than in live births. One study of female college students in Virginia and North Dakota found that the students who approved of premarital sexual activity were also the ones most likely to say that they would have an abortion if they became pregnant. While the sexual revolution was certainly not the only factor—or even the primary factor—in college students' increasing support for the repeal of abortion restrictions, it was not surprising that as premarital sex gained greater support on college campuses, so did abortion rights. Eighty-three percent of first-year college students in 1970 supported legalizing abortion.[2]

The new cultural trends of the time were reflected in the nation's entertainment. *The Andy Griffith Show* had been replaced by far grittier and racier fare such as *M\*A\*S\*H, All in the Family*, and *Maude*. At the beginning of the previous decade, a movie production code had sharply restricted cinematic depictions of nudity and sexual intimacy, but now, filmmakers filled the screen with such subjects, not only in overtly pornographic films, but even in ostensibly more general-interest movies such as *Carnal Knowledge* and *A Clockwork Orange*. Americans of the early 1970s were confronted with images of sexually liberated single women who directly challenged the traditional sexual mores that had once undergirded the nation's anti-abortion laws.[3]

The sudden increase in environmental consciousness, as demonstrated in the celebration of the first Earth Day in 1970 and the creation of the Environmental Protection Agency that same year, also may have hurt the pro-life movement, since it made the population control movement's arguments seem more persuasive. Zero Population Growth's (ZPG) membership grew from 700 in September 1969 to 30,000 by the end of 1970. Millions of couples began planning for smaller families. Polls showed that most Americans now wanted to have only two children, whereas only a few years earlier, they had preferred three.[4]

The pro-life movement also faced a growing challenge from feminists. Four years earlier, women's rights had not been a major concern for most politicians, but the rapid cultural and political victories of the National Organization for Women (NOW) and its allies had transformed the nation's political debate almost overnight. In March 1972, the Senate passed the Equal Rights Amendment (ERA) by a vote of eighty-four to eight, sending it to the states for ratification. Hawaii ratified the amendment within an hour; twenty-nine other states would do so within the next year. A movement that few people had taken seriously only four years earlier now seemed unstoppable. At the Republican National Convention of 1972, several female delegates and campaign strategists pledged to support the ERA, as did the party platform and its presidential candidate, Richard Nixon. Among Democrats, the feminist influence was even more pronounced. Women's rights advocates such as Gloria Steinem and Bella Abzug showed up to the Democratic National Convention in force and convinced the party not only to endorse the ERA—which surprised no one—but also to support fourteen other proposals for women's rights, including maternity health benefits and antidiscrimination measures for women in the workforce. Since NOW had been campaigning for abortion legalization since 1967 and had succeeded in branding the issue as a feminist cause, the newfound political influence of women's rights activists did not bode well for the pro-life movement. Although a few pro-lifers embraced the feminist label and publicly supported the ERA, prominent feminists such as Steinem and Betty Friedan insisted that reproductive rights were a nonnegotiable part of the feminist agenda. Some feminist delegates at both conventions pushed for an official endorsement of abortion rights in their party platforms in 1972.[5]

The Catholic pro-life movement had been forged in the New Deal era, when political liberalism had been based primarily on a concern for economic security, and when most government policies had attempted to uphold the ideal of the two-parent nuclear family headed by a male breadwinner. Most Catholic supporters of the right to life had been comfortable with this form of economic liberalism, which closely paralleled the social vision of the Catholic Church. But now, feminists and their allies were challenging that long-held liberal consensus, creating a new rights-based liberalism that was more individualistic and that no longer had as its primary goal the economic security of the male-headed household.[6] Both parties showed signs of embracing this new rights-based liberalism—and with it, an endorsement of abortion rights—which meant that the pro-life movement, which had long branded itself as a liberal cause, would face new challenges.

Indeed, the pro-life movement was rapidly losing public support. An August 1972 Gallup poll showed that 64 percent of Americans believed that "the decision to have an abortion should be left solely to the woman and her doctor"—a shift of twenty-four points since the end of 1969.[7] Even as pro-lifers won political battles, they lost ground in the larger culture. The sexual revolution, environmentalism, and feminism were all chipping away at support for the pro-life cause.

Yet most pro-lifers chose not to confront these forces directly. They were especially wary of attacking environmentalism or appearing to oppose women's rights, since these were causes that appealed to many pro-lifers, especially those on the political left. Pro-lifers continued to think of themselves as human rights activists, not social conservatives, and they did not preach a message of chauvinism or sexual prudery—even if, privately, the major pro-life leaders remained strongly traditional on sexual issues, with several refusing to accept contraception. Thus, while some individual pro-lifers opposed the ERA, the pro-life literature of the early 1970s generally avoided any direct discussion of the issue, and a number of pro-life leaders publicly favored the amendment. Similarly, the most widely distributed pro-life book of the early 1970s, Jack and Barbara Willke's *Handbook on Abortion*, listed "the polluting of our planet" as a social problem that needed to be addressed, along with racial discrimination and "the billions being spent on bombs instead of people."[8] Although most pro-lifers had little sympathy for the population control policies that ZPG advocated, even on this issue, a few of the more liberal Protestant right-to-life advocates were willing to find common ground in promoting contraception. Sexual promiscuity and pornography did not find any support among pro-lifers, but rather than launch an assault on the sexual revolution, they preferred to focus on the issue of fetal rights. By continuing to frame their cause strictly in rights-based terms, pro-lifers won victories in spite of the cultural forces arrayed against them, and they continued to gain support from rights-conscious liberals who sympathized with the feminist or environmentalist movements.

## Abortion Policy in the Nixon Administration and the Presidential Election of 1972

While many pro-lifers were liberal Democrats, they also knew that if they were to gain national victories, they needed to win the support of the Nixon administration. During his first term, Nixon had remained neutral on abortion, while simultaneously allowing population control and abortion rights advocates in the administration to loosen existing abortion restrictions. Because the nation's polarization over abortion did not divide neatly along party lines, Nixon thought that it would only hurt Republicans to discuss the issue openly. After all, how could a party whose congressional representatives included some of the nation's strongest abortion rights advocates, such as Senator Robert Packwood, as well as leading opponents of abortion, such as Representatives John Schmitz and Lawrence Hogan, reach a consensus? "Just say it's a State matter," Nixon advised congressional candidates during the midterm elections of 1970. To do otherwise, he thought, would be detrimental to the party.[9]

Yet, regardless of his reticence to say very much about the issue publicly, Nixon's administration furthered reproductive rights. In July 1969, Nixon gave an address to Congress on the "problems of population growth." By the end of the century, he warned, the United States might have 300 million people and the world might have 7 billion. To find ways to reduce the growth rate, he appointed a presidential commission on population growth, chaired by John D. Rockefeller III, who had long advocated legalizing elective abortion and who gave money to support the cause. Nixon also signed into law legislation establishing a National Center for Family Planning Services and an Office of Population Affairs within the Department of Health, Education, and Welfare. Those who could not afford to buy contraceptives should receive them free of charge through government social programs, he said. In August 1970, the Department of Defense issued a mandate requiring all military bases to provide abortions for members of the military and their families, regardless of state and local laws. A Catholic lawyer in Houston sued to try to stop a Texas Air Force base from providing abortions in violation of state law, but a federal judge rejected his claim.[10]

But just as it appeared that the president was being pushed into the abortion rights camp, pro-lifers decided to mount their own lobbying efforts. They could not let the president hide behind a stated position of neutrality and "states' rights" as long as his administration was furthering the cause of abortion legalization. "Where, Mr. President, are the rights of the unborn child being secured in the recent Department of Defense promulgation?" Joseph Stanton, president of Massachusetts's Value of Life Committee, wrote in November 1970. He warned the president that the Department of Defense directive was a violation of the Fourteenth Amendment's due process clause. Nixon therefore had a constitutional duty to stop this policy immediately. Nixon ignored Stanton's demands. A few months later, in March 1971, the president's standing among pro-lifers plummeted further when his population commission issued an interim report that signaled its willingness to loosen restrictions on abortion. James McHugh declared that "since the Commission was originally called for by President Nixon, and its members were chosen by him, it seems imperative that citizens write to Mr. Nixon expressing their serious concern about the course that the Commission is taking."[11]

Nixon did change course, though the impetus for this came not from the National Right to Life Committee (NRLC), but from Catholic Democratic senator Edmund Muskie. Muskie, the frontrunner for the Democratic presidential nomination, did not intend to move the Nixon administration to the right on the issue when he expressed his opposition to the legalization of elective abortion in a television interview with journalist David Frost in April 1971. He merely intended to clarify his position and pick up votes for his campaign. But his words had an unanticipated effect. "I'm concerned about diluting in any way the sanctity of human life," Muskie said in response to Frost's question on abortion. He justified his stance using common pro-life arguments. "If it becomes all right to take a life in that stage, then how easy will it be to slip into the next step?" he asked. "Should people in old age who are senile—does it then become legitimate to take their lives?"[12]

The Nixon campaign team knew they needed Catholic votes to secure the president's reelection. Muskie's statement worried them greatly. Nixon decided not to give any ground. A few days later, he declared that he also believed in the "sanctity of life" and opposed "abortion on demand." Echoing the arguments of the right-to-life movement, Nixon declared that "the unborn have rights also, recognized in law, recognized even in principles expounded by the United Nations." He then put these words into action by reversing the Defense Department's policy.[13]

Pro-lifers were delighted, and they began quoting Nixon's statement in their promotional literature. The NRLC offered the president an official commendation and encouraged pro-lifers to send letters of thanks to the White House. "President Nixon has been forthright and courageous in stating his opposition to abortion on demand," McHugh declared.[14]

Some of Nixon's advisers—particularly Pat Buchanan and Charles Colson—told the president that a conservative stance on abortion might help him increase his share of the vote among conservative Catholics. Nixon seemed eager to follow their advice, not only for political reasons, but also because much of the support for abortion law repeal came from a culturally liberal, feminist left that he personally despised. In April 1972, he told White House aide H. R. Haldeman in a private White House conversation that abortion, along with marijuana use, was an issue that he wanted to "hit . . . hard" in the upcoming presidential campaign. The next month, when Rockefeller's commission recommended the legalization of elective abortion as a way to reduce population growth, Nixon immediately repudiated the suggestion.[15] He was quickly becoming a president that the pro-life movement could support.

Not content to rest their hopes on a single party, pro-lifers then turned their attention to the Democrats. After Muskie dropped out of the race, pro-lifers were left without a reliably pro-life candidate. The two remaining frontrunners for the nomination—Senators George McGovern and Hubert Humphrey—had hinted that they were in favor of legalizing elective abortion. Pro-lifers knew that both candidates were facing strong pressure from abortion rights supporters within their party, but they hoped to counteract that pressure with a show of strength from their own side. Humphrey seemed like the better target. In June 1971, the Minnesota senator told the NRLC that he was opposed to abortion, but in October, he backtracked, telling the press that abortion should be a matter "between the woman and her doctor." Pro-lifers responded to Humphrey's shift with a barrage of letters. Humphrey again vacillated and promised to release a statement clarifying his position. But he never did. "What of the Senator's claims and promises?" Michael Taylor asked members of the NRLC in May 1972.[16]

Rather than write off Humphrey as unreliable, pro-lifers used a backlash against McGovern's position on abortion—which was more liberal than Humphrey's—to push both candidates to the right. McGovern had begun his race for the nomination with a reputation for supporting abortion rights, and his campaign attracted a lot of support from prominent pro-choice feminists, such as the actress Shirley MacLaine. In May 1972, in the midst of McGovern's fight for the nomination, the *Congressional*

*Record* reported that he said he favored the "reform of abortion laws" to allow decisions about abortion to be made "by the woman involved in consultation with her physician." Conservative Catholics responded with a wave of protest. The Archdiocese of Omaha ran a half-page newspaper advertisement attacking him.[17]

At this point, Humphrey sensed that the abortion issue might be a way to peel off a few Catholic votes from McGovern in the upcoming Nebraska primary. He went on the attack. The tactic seemed to work, because Humphrey's poll numbers in Nebraska surged. McGovern sensed danger. He had expected Nebraska, which bordered his home state of South Dakota, to be an easy victory, but now he found himself fighting for his political life. In response to Humphrey's attacks, he scheduled a half-hour broadcast on four issues of concern to Catholics, devoting the most time to abortion. The broadcast showed him telling a Catholic nun that he believed abortion should remain an issue for states to decide without interference from the federal government, and that he favored some restrictions on abortion. McGovern survived the Nebraska primary, but the experience made him cautious about abortion. Because of his campaign's belief that their candidate could not win if either he or the Democratic Party endorsed abortion rights, his aides worked hard to keep abortion out of the party platform later that summer. There was now a prevailing assumption among many Democrats that an abortion rights endorsement would "cost Senator McGovern several million votes."[18]

This was exactly what pro-lifers had hoped to accomplish when they attacked McGovern for his record on abortion. "It is important that the state and national platforms of the parties do not favor the relaxation of state abortion laws," Michael Taylor instructed NRLC members in May 1972. "Pressure on the major candidates in the primaries is one way of helping to insure that this does not happen."[19]

Some of McGovern's pro-choice feminist supporters were aghast. They insisted that abortion would not be a losing issue for the candidate, and they were dismayed that he had retreated from his original position simply because of pro-life activism. "The idea that abortion is so extremely controversial has gained credence because of the mistaken feelings of people that all Catholics are opposed to it as a result of noisy demonstrations by the well-financed but relatively small Right-to-Life groups who have been carrying fetuses around in lab bottles," McGovern delegate Carol Greitzer protested. "Actually, all the polls show that the majority of Americans are in favor of liberalized abortion laws and that the figures for Catholics are not far behind."[20]

Some of McGovern's pro-choice feminist delegates felt that the candidate had betrayed their cause, and they came to the Democratic National Convention in Miami determined to introduce a platform statement endorsing abortion rights, regardless of their candidate's wishes. Due to party rule changes that enhanced women's influence at the convention and a cultural shift that encouraged party leaders to pay more attention to rights-conscious movements, feminists now exercised an unprecedented degree of power within the party, and some of them wanted to use that power to make sure that the Democratic presidential candidate did not compromise on an issue that they believed was essential to their cause. McGovern realized his dependency on his feminist supporters, but his experience in Nebraska was still fresh in his mind. When the Women's Caucus brought an abortion rights party platform plank to a floor vote, McGovern's campaign managers headed off a firestorm by privately convincing some of the pro-choice delegates to sacrifice their own preferences for the sake of the candidate and vote against the measure, even while continuing to proclaim that delegates were free to "vote their conscience" on the issue. Pro-lifers, who were worried about the efforts of the Women's Caucus, also did everything that they could to maintain their pressure on McGovern. Michael Taylor urged pro-lifers to contact Democratic Party delegates and remind them that the McGovern campaign team did not want the party platform to mention abortion. In the end, the pro-choice platform plank was defeated by a vote of 1,570 to 1,103, with even Shirley MacLaine voting against it for the sake of her favored candidate. Some pro-lifers, though, continued to mistrust McGovern. Taylor complained that pro-lifers were given less speaking time than pro-choice delegates were, and that the McGovern campaign had shown no interest at all in pro-lifers' point of view. "The McGovern opposition to abortion in the platform was based on simple political expediency," he wrote.[21]

McGovern continued his efforts to convince pro-lifers—and particularly pro-life Catholics—that he was not their enemy. In recognition of the power that pro-life Catholics still exercised in the party, he selected a Catholic advocate of the right-to-life cause, Thomas Eagleton, as his running mate. When Eagleton was forced to resign from the campaign a few weeks later, McGovern replaced him with another Catholic who was even more well known in pro-life circles—Sargent Shriver. Shriver's wife, Eunice Kennedy Shriver, had been a supporter of the pro-life cause for several years and as recently as July, she had written a pro-life article for the Catholic periodical *Our Sunday Visitor.* Regardless of McGovern's personal views on abortion, he entered the fall campaign season determined to put the issue behind him and win the pro-life Catholic vote. His campaign team included the former social action director for the Archdiocese of San Antonio, Matthew Ahmann, who handled the campaign's outreach to devout Catholics and assured them that McGovern shared their "deep concern for life." Ahmann prodded McGovern to speak in Catholic churches during "Respect Life" week and frame his position on abortion in a way that would avoid alienating pro-lifers.[22]

Pro-lifers appeared to have done the unthinkable: they had overcome the strong feminist lobbying power in the Democratic Party and had forced McGovern, an abortion rights supporter, to backtrack on his position. Yet they remained suspicious of McGovern. A few pro-lifers publicly supported him, but most found his official stance of neutrality on abortion unsatisfying. They wanted a president who would work for the pro-life cause. "I do not believe that an option for murder should be left up to the individual state laws," one pro-life woman from Louisville, Kentucky, told Sargent Shriver. Even some pro-life members of the antiwar left who agreed with McGovern's position on Vietnam found that his stance on abortion made it impossible for them to support his candidacy. "We need to be against all wars, including the war on the unborn," Fr. Paul Marx wrote. For that reason, he said, "I most likely will be voting for Nixon, something I never dreamt I would do."[23]

The Nixon campaign team encouraged the president to make a concerted effort to solicit the votes of the pro-life Catholics who were defecting from McGovern. Pat Buchanan recommended that the White House produce a flyer contrasting the candidates' positions on abortion and distribute it at the National Right to Life Convention in June, and then "attempt to have the flyer included in at least one mailing by every right-to-life group in the United States."[24] Charles Colson likewise urged the president's campaign team to portray McGovern as a supporter of abortion, regardless of his claims to the contrary. Republicans distorted a (then-anonymous) Democratic senator's characterization of McGovern to brand him as a supporter of "acid, amnesty, and abortion."[25]

Nixon found it easier to attack McGovern's positions than to embrace the pro-life cause himself, and he never went quite as far as Colson and Buchanan wanted in positioning himself as a pro-life candidate. Nevertheless, in a sign of how much he valued the votes of pro-life Catholics, he did take the unusual step of sending a letter to Cardinal Terence Cooke to endorse pro-lifers' efforts to repeal New York's permissive abortion law. "Your decision ... to act in the public forum as defenders of the right to life of the unborn, is truly a noble endeavor," Nixon wrote. "In this calling, you and they have my admiration, sympathy and support." When Governor Nelson Rockefeller, who was the New York state chair of Nixon's reelection campaign, expressed his dismay that the president had taken the unprecedented step of interfering in a state debate over abortion and had positioned himself against a Republican governor on this issue, the White House issued the implausible excuse that the letter was simply a statement of the president's personal views and was not intended for publication.[26] Nixon said no more about abortion for the rest of the campaign, but he had already said enough to win the support of pro-lifers.

Buoyed by Nixon's encouraging statement, some right-to-life activists thought they had a chance of adding a pro-life clause to the Republican Party platform. Michael Taylor encouraged NRLC members to lobby platform committee members. The effort did not succeed, partly because the Nixon campaign team included a number of pro-choice Republicans who thought the president had already ceded too much to the pro-lifers. Rita Hauser, the vice-chair of the Committee to Re-elect the President, was pro-choice, and she encouraged the president to move to the left on abortion or at least temper his pro-life commitments. A few other Republican women, such as Jill Ruckelshaus, wife of the director of the Environmental Protection Agency, attempted to get the Republican Party to endorse abortion rights.[27] In this political environment, pro-lifers could do little more than keep the party neutral. Although that was less than they wanted, Nixon's previously expressed support for their cause went a long way toward mollifying them.

Many pro-lifers realized that the victory that they had won was more symbolic than substantive, since Nixon's conversion to the pro-life cause seemed less than heartfelt, and McGovern's sudden desire to court the pro-life Catholic vote appeared to be nothing more than a political calculation. In the end, both candidates insisted that abortion was an issue best left to the states, which meant that, in the assessment of the *Catholic Star Herald*, "neither Nixon nor McGovern will be of much help in the fight for the rights of the unborn."[28] Nevertheless, pro-lifers had won a political victory by preventing either candidate from endorsing abortion rights, and they had forced each of them to make significant concessions. Both Nixon and McGovern entered the general election with more conservative positions on abortion than they had held only a few months earlier.

## Referenda Victories in Michigan and North Dakota

Abortion rights advocates reacted to pro-lifers' success by changing their strategy. After suffering dozens of defeats in state legislatures in 1971 and 1972, they decided to take the issue directly to voters. A voter referendum had succeeded in legalizing elective abortion in Washington State in 1970, and abortion rights proponents expected that the strategy would work elsewhere. They chose Michigan and North Dakota—two states whose legislatures had refused to legalize abortion—as their major targets. In November 1972, voters in Michigan would have the option to legalize abortion for any reason during the first twenty weeks of pregnancy (a measure very similar to the Washington referendum), while North Dakotans would vote on whether to adopt an ALI-style reform law.

Abortion rights advocates had failed to get a bill passed in the Michigan legislature and had experienced no success in state courts, but when they decided to try for a state referendum, they were easily able to collect the 300,000 signatures required to put a measure on the ballot. Members of the Michigan Catholic Conference appealed to the courts to stop the referendum, but their efforts failed. By September, it looked like the pro-lifers' cause was doomed; a public opinion poll showed that Michigan voters supported Proposal B by 57 to 37 percent.[29]

The stakes in the referendum fight were high, not only because Proposal B would reverse the pro-life movement's two-year streak of victories, but because it would be only the second time that voters themselves—rather than a state legislature—had approved abortion legalization. It would confirm pro-choice activists' argument that public opinion was on their side.

Despite the odds against them and the dire predictions of the polls, pro-lifers had one key organizational advantage. Unlike in New York or Washington, where the pro-life cause had been concentrated mainly in the Catholic Church and had been ineffective as a result, Michigan pro-lifers had followed the Minnesota model of grassroots, ecumenical organizing. A young Presbyterian mother, Gloria Klein, headed the state's leading right-to-life group, and she was joined in the pro-life effort by several other prominent leaders in the state, including the Presbyterian gynecologist Richard Jaynes, who at one point had successfully sued for legal guardianship of the state's unborn fetuses.[30]

Fully mindful of what was at stake, Jaynes launched an all-out campaign through his new organization, Voice of the Unborn, which coordinated efforts among the more than two dozen right-to-life groups in the state. By the beginning of November, Voice of the Unborn had more than 10,000 members, with a group of leaders drawn from the ranks of the state's most prominent right-to-life activists, including Klein, who served on the executive committee. Because Jaynes was a Protestant, his organization was uniquely suited to reach the state's Missouri Synod Lutherans, Baptists, Presbyterians, and Christian Reformed Church members, but he also worked closely with the Michigan Catholic Conference. The vice president of his organization was a graduate of Aquinas College, and the executive director of the Michigan Catholic Conference sat on the organization's board. Voice of the Unborn relied on appeals in Catholic churches to raise some of the $200,000 it spent on the campaign.[31]

The Michigan Catholic Conference also took a leading role in the pro-life effort by encouraging priests to devote two Sundays—October 1 and 8—to preaching on abortion, and it mailed pro-life information kits, which had been put together by a local advertising agency, to Catholic churches throughout the state. The Catholic Church distributed more than one million copies of a four-page pamphlet featuring color photographs of fetal development. Every parish in the state received a twelve-minute slide presentation on the same subject. Individual Catholics, acting outside of official Church auspices, also did what they could to defeat Proposal B. One insurance salesman, a father of nine, raised funds from fellow Catholics to put up more than fifty pro-life billboards in the state, including a series of four giant billboards on a Detroit section of Interstate 75 that featured a picture of Jesus and the message "Stop Abortion Now. Thou Shalt Not Kill. Don't Take a Life That I Have Given. Vote No in November."[32]

But mobilizing Catholics and pro-life Protestants would not be sufficient to defeat Proposal B, Jaynes realized. He had to find a way to change the minds of people who had already expressed support for the measure. His crucial breakthrough came in September, when a survey commissioned by Voice of the Unborn discovered that more than 50 percent of Proposal B supporters did not realize that the referendum would legalize abortion up to the twentieth week of pregnancy. Publicizing this might be a way to reduce support for the measure. Voice of the Unborn embarked on a campaign focusing on images of eighteen- and nineteen-week-old fetuses, and asked voters whether they really wanted to permit their destruction. Many did not. By the end of October, only 43 percent of Protestants and only 26 percent of Catholics still said that they supported Proposal B. At the beginning of September, Protestants had favored the measure by a 60 to

34 percent margin. The referendum's proponents realized that they were in trouble. Most press reports attributed the shift to the power of the fetal images and voters' discomfort with second-trimester abortions. Abortion rights advocates insisted that while most abortions would no doubt occur in the early months of pregnancy, allowing abortion up to the twentieth week was necessary to allow women to abort if an amniocentesis, which could not be performed until the second trimester, revealed fetal deformities. While such arguments had worked in the mid-1960s, they no longer had the same persuasive power when weighed against photographs of second-trimester fetuses, with all of their well-developed, infant-like features clearly visible. In addition, Voice of the Unborn appealed to the liberal and humanitarian sentiments of many Michigan voters. "Michigan was the first state in America to outlaw the death penalty for criminals," a Voice of the Unborn advertisement reminded voters. "Proposal B would legalize the death penalty for thousands of unborn babies. Keep Michigan from permitting the slaughter of the innocents."[33]

Voice of the Unborn's willingness to link the pro-life cause with opposition to capital punishment may have stemmed in part from the political ideology of its director, state representative Rosetta Ferguson, an African American Democrat from Detroit. Although Jaynes remained in charge of Voice of the Unborn's general operations, Ferguson directed many of the campaign's logistics, and it was under her direction that the organization mailed out 250,000 flyers to African Americans that explicitly linked abortion to concerns of race. As a strong civil rights advocate, Ferguson was ideally situated for this role. She was chair of the House Civil Rights Committee and had authored a bill to require Michigan's social studies textbooks to include coverage of black history, which she considered one of her proudest legislative accomplishments. Having been born twelve miles from Jackson, Mississippi, and having grown up in the Deep South during the Depression, Ferguson was acutely aware of poverty and racial discrimination, and she feared the consequences of legalized abortion for women who were black and poor. Abortion legalization was "black genocide," she said—a white racist effort to convince impoverished, African American single mothers to kill their unborn children. To bolster her case, she reminded voters that the previous year, the Tennessee legislature had considered a bill to deny welfare benefits to women who had more than one "illegitimate child" unless they agreed to be medically sterilized. Her flyers also reminded African Americans that Senator Barry Goldwater—against whom African Americans had voted overwhelmingly in the 1964 presidential election—supported legalization. And in one of the earliest examples of an argument that would soon become commonplace, Ferguson compared abortion legalization to the Supreme Court's *Dred Scott* decision of 1857. Just as the *Dred Scott* decision had denied the personhood of African Americans, so Proposal B attempted to deny the personhood of the fetus. African Americans must never agree to this social injustice, Ferguson argued. She took comfort in a recent Harris poll that showed that most did not. "It is the black community—not the Catholic community—that today shows least support for permissive abortion," her flyers declared.[34]

Proposal B was defeated by a 61 to 39 percent margin. Pro-lifers had pulled off "one of the most startling and successful campaigns in Michigan political history," the *Detroit Press* declared. Partisans on both sides of the debate agreed that descriptions and images of late-term abortions had turned the tide.[35]

North Dakota's voter initiative was spearheaded by a doctor at Minot Air Force Base and had the support of some physicians in the state. Compared to New York's abortion law or the proposed referendum in Michigan, it was a moderately conservative measure that might have been expected to pass in a state where Catholics comprised less than 20 percent of the population. North Dakota's largest denomination, the American Lutheran Church, had officially endorsed abortion rights. Yet pro-life Catholics managed to convince 78 percent of the state's voters to cast their ballots against the abortion referendum—a margin of victory that far exceeded their expectations.[36]

They won by using the state's Catholic Conference and local parishes to organize right-to-life chapters, and then entrusting their leadership to prominent Protestant doctors or lawyers whenever possible. The vast majority of members of pro-life organizations in North Dakota were Catholic, but the president of the North Dakota Right to Life Association, Al Fortman, was a Lutheran doctor who worked assiduously to create pro-life alliances between Catholics and mainline Protestants. Fortman was genuinely ecumenical. He enjoyed an excellent relationship with several of the state's Catholic bishops and forged ties with some of the state's Protestant ministers by linking the pro-life issue to other social justice causes, such as opposition to the Vietnam War, that interested mainline Protestant clergy. By the end of the summer, Fortman's organization had 30,000 members, a newsletter that reached 150,000 readers, and a campaign war chest of $100,000—an impressive feat in a state whose population barely exceeded 600,000.[37]

Fortman, along with several of his Protestant colleagues in the North Dakota Right to Life Association, had been sympathetic to some therapeutic abortion reform laws in the late 1960s, but after unrestricted first- and second-trimester abortions became legal in New York and several other states, he changed his mind. The argument that his organization made in the weeks leading up to the vote on the abortion referendum reflected what had happened in New York. The so-called therapeutic abortion reform that voters had been asked to approve, they claimed, was in reality an "abortion on demand" bill whose vague "health" clause would soon turn the state into an "abortion mill."[38] If the pro-life movement could win even in a heavily mainline Protestant state such as North Dakota, it could win anywhere, pro-lifers reasoned. An ecumenical coalition, the use of graphic images, and the fear of abortion on demand could convince a majority of voters—including many who did not identify with the right-to-life cause—to vote against legalizing abortion.

Emboldened by their victories, pro-lifers prepared to go on the offensive. They had to do something to curb abortion in New York. Immediately after the election, one member of Voice of the Unborn reminded his fellow pro-lifers that doctors and abortion referral agencies had sent "40 thousand babies from Michigan to their deaths in New York" during the previous two years, and that the victory in the fight against Proposal B had done nothing to stop that. It was time to make abortion referrals a felony offense and also time to create counseling programs and adoption agencies to address the needs of women facing crisis pregnancies. Pro-lifers in North Dakota came to a similar conclusion. They could deter women from leaving the state for abortions elsewhere only if they offered them the resources they needed to carry a crisis pregnancy to term. In the next legislative term, the North Dakota Right to Life Association promised, it would introduce legislation to create a list of "life rights," which would include state-funded daycare centers for the poor and public healthcare.[39]

## The Battle in the Courts

Pro-lifers had to remain vigilant because state and federal court decisions threatened to strip them of their victories. For years, courts had been their key allies. Courts had recognized fetal rights in the 1930s and 1940s and reaffirmed the value of fetal life in the 1960s. Although pro-lifers suffered a rare legal setback in 1969 when the California state supreme court ruled against a restrictive abortion law in *People v. Belous*, favorable rulings from other state courts mitigated *Belous's* damage and restored pro-lifers' confidence. In *Babbitz v. McCann* (1970), a US district court in Wisconsin ruled against a physician who claimed that Wisconsin's abortion law, which allowed abortion only to save a woman's life, was a violation of the Fourteenth Amendment. In issuing this ruling, the court specifically took issue with *Belous*, suggesting that the case had been wrongly decided. State and federal courts in Iowa, Louisiana, Massachusetts, Minnesota, Missouri, and Vermont also gave the pro-life movement favorable decisions during the summer and fall of 1970, leading the NRLC to take heart at this "trend away from any judicial approval of unrestricted abortions." The next year brought another victory when the Michigan state supreme court ruled in a wrongful prenatal death case that the fetus was a "person" with an existence separate from the mother, and that "the phenomenon of birth is not the beginning of life; it is merely a change in the form of life."[40]

The NRLC also claimed victory in the first US Supreme Court decision on abortion, *United States v. Vuitch* (1971), which reversed a lower court ruling that had invalidated the District of Columbia's restrictive abortion law on grounds of vagueness. While this ruling did not directly reverse *Belous*, it did seem to go against the California court's principal argument, and it gave lower courts reason to pause before citing *Belous*. Furthermore, by refusing to declare that anyone had a constitutional right to abortion, *Vuitch* gave the pro-life movement reason to hope that perhaps the Court would rule in their favor when it considered the constitutionality of anti-abortion laws.[41]

But *Vuitch* was followed by a string of lower court decisions striking down state restrictions on abortion. In 1972, state supreme courts in Vermont and Florida, as well as the previously friendly high court of New Jersey, struck down restrictive abortion laws. In November, California's state supreme court struck down most of the restrictions on abortion in California's Therapeutic Abortion Act, thus effectively legalizing elective abortion in the state. Federal courts also struck down some or all of Connecticut and Wisconsin's restrictions on abortion. These defeats were especially galling because pro-lifers had won every one of their state legislative campaigns in 1971 and 1972. Yet the courts threatened to deprive them of these victories. In Michigan, for instance, abortion rights supporters who had lost in the legislature and in a referendum announced that they would take their fight to the state supreme court.[42]

Some pro-lifers suggested that the best way to prevent defeats in the courts would be to pass a constitutional amendment protecting the unborn, but NRLC executive secretary Michael Taylor rejected the idea. Pro-lifers were on a legislative winning streak, and the NRLC did not want to lose momentum by waging a quixotic fight for an unnecessary constitutional amendment. Besides, Taylor pointed out, the wording of such an amendment might divide allies in the movement. Officially, the Catholic Church opposed abortion in any circumstances. But most pro-lifers accepted the necessity of abortion to preserve a mother's life, and several Protestant pro-life activists thought that abortion was justifiable in cases of rape. Up to this point, the NRLC had complied with James McHugh's directive to find common cause with anyone who opposed abortion on demand and abortion law liberalization. In Taylor's view, that had been a highly successful strategy. Haggling over the wording of a constitutional amendment might destroy this unity.[43]

Pro-life congressional representatives Lawrence Hogan (R-MD) and John Schmitz (R-CA) worried that the NRLC was blind to the threat of an unfavorable Supreme Court decision. If the Supreme Court ruled in favor of abortion rights, it would wipe away all of their hard-won legislative victories. Conservative Republicans like Schmitz had long decried the decisions of the Warren Court, and even though the Court was now led by Nixon appointee Warren Burger, their suspicions of judicial overreach remained. Only a constitutional amendment, Schmitz believed, could protect the pro-life cause from the Supreme Court's "judicial tyranny." In the summer of 1972, Schmitz introduced the first Human Life Amendment proposal in Congress. "An individual, from the moment that he is conceived, shall not be deprived of life, liberty, or property, without due process of law," Schmitz's amendment stated.[44]

Yet Schmitz encountered opposition from within the movement. Most pro-lifers were not conservative Republicans, and they did not share Hogan and Schmitz's fear of the Supreme Court. Instead, they saw the Court's judicial activism on behalf of minority rights as a hopeful sign that it might be willing to issue a sweeping decision affirming the constitutional rights of the unborn, just as it had issued several such decisions on behalf of African Americans and women. Pro-life lawyers had long claimed that the Fourteenth Amendment already protected unborn children; by proposing a constitutional amendment, Schmitz implied that it did not. If pro-lifers conceded this point, their legal strategy would be doomed. For that reason, the NRLC encouraged pro-lifers to oppose

Schmitz's amendment. In October 1972, Michael Taylor suggested that because of recent conservative appointments to the Supreme Court, the pro-life movement had reason to hope that the upcoming ruling in *Roe v. Wade* would bring "a halt to the liberalization of abortion laws." A declaration from the Supreme Court that abortion was not a constitutional right—or even that fetal life was constitutionally protected under the Fourteenth Amendment, as pro-lifers argued—could give them their ultimate victory over the abortion rights movement.[45]

## *Roe v. Wade*

By the time that Michael Taylor sent out his communique, pro-life lawyers had been preparing legal arguments in *Roe* and its companion case *Doe v. Bolton* for more than a year. When the Supreme Court heard initial oral arguments in 1971, pro-life advocates submitted several *amici curiae* briefs outlining their standard constitutional arguments on fetal rights, and they thought that they had a good chance of persuading the Court to give them a favorable verdict. As Fr. Paul Marx remarked in a private letter in May 1971, "It would be difficult to imagine that the United States Supreme Court would declare it a personal civil right of every woman to abort."[46]

In both cases, the attorneys for the plaintiffs sought a sweeping declaration that a woman's constitutional right to privacy gave her a right to an abortion, and that all anti-abortion laws, as well as the ALI-style therapeutic abortion statutes, were unconstitutional. In the spring of 1970, when the cases were filed, this was still a bold claim, though it was rapidly winning public support. The Texas and Georgia district courts that initially heard these cases ruled in favor of the plaintiffs, which bolstered their confidence when the cases reached the Supreme Court in the fall of 1971.

Lawyers for the states of both Georgia and Texas argued that abortion restrictions were appropriate because the state had a legitimate interest in protecting "fetal life." This was the argument that the pro-life movement had been making for years, but the attorneys—particularly the attorney for the state of Texas—struggled to articulate it during oral arguments and failed to present a coherent defense of restrictive abortion laws. The lawyer representing the state of Texas could not explain why women in his state were not prosecuted for self-abortion if the primary purpose of the restrictive abortion statute was to protect fetal life, nor could he explain why his state's law contained no exception for rape. The defense lawyer for the state of Georgia, a young assistant attorney general named Dorothy

Beasley, delivered a stronger performance, beginning with her opening statement that the central issue in the case was "the value which is to be placed on fetal life." But she struggled to explain why, if preservation of fetal life was so important, her state allowed abortion in cases of rape, fetal deformities, and instances when pregnancy endangered a woman's health, while prohibiting abortion more generally.[47]

Indeed, the attorneys seemed more interested in addressing other legal arguments—such as whether the plaintiffs had standing to sue—than in addressing the fundamental issues of fetal life. At one point, the Texas state attorney even drifted into a bit of personal philosophizing that indicated he was as unsure about the beginning of human personhood as most Americans outside of the pro-life movement were—a concession that surely did not help his case. "There are unanswerable questions in this field," he said, when asked if he was prepared to argue that the fetus deserved legal protection even at "one hour" after "impregnation." "When does the soul come into the unborn—if a person believes in a soul?" he asked. "I don't know."[48]

Pro-life lawyers had complained before about the poor quality of state attorneys' attempts to defend restrictive abortion statutes.[49] This time, they decided that they would take matters into their own hands. In 1971, they sent the Court their own *amici curiae* briefs to make the arguments that the state attorneys were unprepared to deliver.

Charles Rice, a Notre Dame law professor who had been producing pro-life materials for years, filed a brief on behalf of the new pro-life organization Americans United for Life (AUL) reiterating the pro-life movement's longstanding Fourteenth Amendment argument. Rice cited several decades' worth of tort cases in which lower courts had awarded damages to plaintiffs who had lost an unborn child in an accident. In some of those cases, judges had explicitly recognized the personhood of the fetus.[50]

A group of lawyers led by Dennis Horan, also affiliated with AUL, filed another brief consisting of several pages of fetal photographs and other medical evidence to persuade the Court that medical science supported the pro-life movement's claim that fetuses were human persons with constitutional rights. More than 200 pro-life doctors, including most of the leading medical professionals in the movement—Mildred Jefferson, Fred Mecklenburg, Joseph Stanton, and others—signed their names to the brief.[51]

Ellen McCormack's Long Island-based organization, Women for the Unborn, which now had 2,000 members, submitted a brief arguing that

"permissive abortion constitutes an infringement on the rights and interests of women as well as of unborn children," because abortion did not
solve women's problems or make them happier. The laws against abortion deterred women from making a choice that would likely ruin their
lives, and women would suffer if that safeguard were taken away. "Most
women seeking to take the life of their unborn baby, like most people seeking to take their own life, desire to be stopped by someone," Women for
the Unborn claimed.[52] This argument posited a view of gender that might
have appealed to the Supreme Court of the early twentieth century, but it
seemed distinctly out of step with the opinions of a Court that had just
affirmed the equality of men and women under the law in cases such as
*Reed v. Reed* (1971). Perhaps for that reason, the justices did not refer to its
arguments.

Juan Ryan and other attorneys in the NRLC hoped their brief would
have a greater effect. In sixty-one pages, they attempted to dismantle every
abortion rights argument that they thought would appeal to the justices.
They offered detailed arguments against the claims that legalized abortion would help the poor or that anti-abortion laws discriminated against
women or inappropriately interfered with the work of doctors. They sought
to demonstrate that the abortion statutes at issue in *Roe* and *Doe* were not
"unconstitutionally vague." Most importantly, they offered a detailed list of
cases in which lower courts had affirmed the value of fetal life, a view, they
said, that was rooted not only in traditional constitutional interpretation
but also in the English common law tradition. The NRLC lawyers argued
that if the fetus had inalienable rights under the Constitution, the "right
to privacy" that the justices had asserted in *Griswold* could not be used to
deprive the fetus of those rights, which meant that the right to privacy did
not apply to abortion. The original purpose of the late nineteenth-century
anti-abortion Texas statute that was at issue in *Roe* was to protect the life of
the fetus, the lawyers argued. That purpose was just as valid in the 1970s
as it had been in the 1880s, and the Supreme Court would therefore be
wrong to strike down the law.[53]

The Court initially seemed to indicate that it had only limited interest
in listening to arguments from either side. Chief Justice Warren Burger
arranged for the Court to begin hearing oral arguments in the cases
before the two newest justices, Lewis Powell and William Rehnquist,
had been sworn in, which would have made them ineligible to vote in
the decisions—a move that seemed highly unusual if the chief justice
had wanted a historic, path-breaking decision. Furthermore, he allowed

only the perfunctory one hour for oral arguments in each case; whenever the Court issued a major ruling, observers noted, it usually allocated far more time than that. Thus, the *American Medical News* concluded that there was "little likelihood" that the Court would overturn the Georgia and Texas abortion statutes. The lawyers for the plaintiffs in the two cases glumly admitted as much. The Court would probably dismiss the plaintiffs' claims in *Roe* on procedural grounds, Sarah Weddington told NARAL president Lee Gidding in August 1971, and abortion rights advocates would be denied the landmark decision that they sought.[54]

The Supreme Court surprised observers by refraining from issuing a ruling, and instead decided to rehear the cases in the fall of 1972, after all of the Court's new justices had been seated. By that time, the pro-life movement was stronger, both numerically and politically, than it had been a year earlier. Yet in the courts, the abortion rights movement had won some important victories. A majority of the lower courts that had tested the constitutionality of restrictive abortion statutes had ruled in favor of abortion rights, invalidating restrictive abortion rights statutes. The "right to privacy," which lay at the heart of the *Roe* and *Doe* plaintiffs' claims, had received an important reiteration earlier in the year when the Supreme Court ruled, in the birth control case *Eisenstadt v. Baird* (1972), that unmarried people were entitled to the same privacy as married people. *Griswold* had located the right to reproductive privacy in the institution of marriage, but *Eisenstadt* placed that right where the pro-choice movement wanted it: with the individual. "If the right of privacy means anything, it is the right of the individual, married or single, to be free from unwarranted governmental intrusion into matters so fundamentally affecting a person as the decision whether to bear or beget a child," the Court declared. Weddington quoted this line when she argued her case again before the Supreme Court, because it seemed to support everything that she had been arguing. If a woman had the constitutional right to make reproductive decisions without the interference of the state, surely the state could not legitimately prohibit her from having an abortion.[55]

Pro-lifers continued to argue that there was one compelling question that *Eisenstadt* had not addressed, one that made all the difference in the world. That question was the personhood of the fetus. If the Fifth and Fourteenth Amendments encompassed fetal life, a woman's right to reproductive privacy could not extend to actions that would terminate the life of a fetus. During the second round of oral arguments in October 1972, Justice Byron White pressed Weddington on this essential question.

"Is it critical to your case that the fetus not be a person under the due process clause?" he asked. "Would you lose your case if the fetus was a person?" The lawyers for the states of Texas and Georgia had wanted to discuss other issues, but for pro-life activists, the personhood of the fetus was the only relevant question. White was persuaded by this line of reasoning, and he wanted to see how Weddington would respond to it.

Weddington tried to dodge the question, so White pressed her on it again. This time, she hedged, conceding only that if the fetus was a person, there would have to be a "balancing of interests" between the fetus and the mother, not a negation of the right to an abortion altogether. But she quickly returned to her main argument: the question was irrelevant, because the fetus was clearly not a person under the terms of the Fourteenth Amendment or any other section of the Constitution, including the due process clause of the Fifth Amendment. At most, a fetus had only "statutory rights"—that is, rights conveyed upon it by the legislative statutes of individual states. Women, by contrast, had a full *constitutional* right to an abortion grounded in the right to privacy, specified by *Griswold* as one of the Ninth Amendment's implied rights. "It seems to me that you do not balance constitutional rights of one person against mere statutory rights of another," she told the Court.[56]

The justices were not satisfied with that argument. Harry Blackmun questioned Weddington again on the issue of fetal personhood, as did Potter Stewart. They wanted her to concede that if the fetus was a person with constitutional rights, a woman could not have a constitutional right to unrestricted abortion. "If it were established that an unborn fetus is a person, with the protection of the Fourteenth Amendment, you would have an almost impossible case here, would you not?" Stewart asked. This time, Weddington reluctantly acknowledged the force of the argument. "I would have a very difficult case," she conceded.[57]

This was what pro-lifers wanted to hear. It finally seemed, in the second round of oral arguments, that at least some of the justices saw the logic of the pro-lifers' position. So did the attorney for the defense. In the re-argument, his arguments focused almost entirely on medical testimony about the fetus, combined with the case history detailing how lower court judges had recognized the value of fetal life. Once again, he stumbled badly when cross-examined by the justices. But at least he focused his argument on the critical issue of fetal personhood.[58]

The justices' questions indicated that *Roe* would turn on two central issues. The first was whether a woman's constitutional right to privacy gave her the right to an abortion under the "penumbra" of the Ninth Amendment. The second was whether fetal life was constitutionally protected under the terms of either the Fifth or Fourteenth Amendment. The case was thus a contest between two competing constitutional rights. If one of the rights were granted, it would nullify the other.

Justice Harry Blackmun recognized this, which was why the majority opinion that he wrote in *Roe* not only presented an argument explaining why the constitutional right to privacy gave women a right to an abortion, but also included a systematic refutation of each of the arguments in favor of fetal rights. Theologians and philosophers disagreed on when human life began, Blackmun argued, so pro-lifers' use of medical testimony to argue for the personhood of the fetus was not persuasive. Although courts had often awarded damage claims for injuries *in utero*, these precedents were insufficient to confirm pro-lifers' claim that fetuses had legal rights, because the law had always treated birth as the point at which human life began. Furthermore, the Fourteenth Amendment applied only to persons "born in the United States," a qualification that clearly did not apply to the unborn.[59]

By arguing that the fetus did not have any constitutional rights, Blackmun undercut the central argument of the pro-life movement, but he was not yet ready to concede that fetal life had no value or that the state had no right to protect it under any circumstances. At some point during pregnancy, he believed, the state might have a "compelling interest" in protecting fetal life. He was not sure, though, where that point was. He personally favored drawing the line at the end of the first trimester, a line that he admitted was "arbitrary." Thurgood Marshall and Lewis Powell advocated drawing the line at viability, arguing that if only first-trimester abortions were permitted, some women who needed an abortion might not be able to obtain one, since the first twelve weeks of pregnancy offered a very narrow time frame for performing abortions. After spending several days discussing the issue with his colleagues, Blackmun produced an awkward compromise in the opinion that he wrote for the Court. Women had an unrestricted right to an abortion during the first trimester, he declared. During the second trimester, up to the point of viability, the state could implement restrictions on abortion, but only for the purposes of protecting a woman's health, not for the purpose of preserving fetal life. After viability, states had the option, though not the requirement, to ban abortion entirely, as long as they made exceptions for cases in which abortion was needed to protect a woman's life or health.[60]

On January 22, 1973, the court ruled, seven to two, in favor of the plaintiffs. Blackmun thought that his ruling offered concessions to all sides, and he tried to present it as a compromise that should not alarm anyone. "It should be stressed that the Court does not today hold that the Constitution compels abortion on demand," he said. "It does not today pronounce that a pregnant woman has an absolute right to an abortion. It does, for the first trimester of pregnancy, cast the abortion decision and the responsibility for it upon the attending physician."[61]

Regardless of Blackmun's attempt to strike a measured tone, the decision that he wrote was sweeping in its outcome; it required the legislatures of forty-six of the nation's fifty states to rewrite their abortion laws and make them as liberal as New York's, and it delivered a firm victory to the abortion rights cause that pro-lifers refused to accept. For the previous year and a half, while *Roe* was being litigated, pro-life lawyers had made a concerted effort to convince the Supreme Court to accept their interpretation of the Constitution. Some of them had hoped that the Court would give them the definitive constitutional victory that they had been seeking. What they received instead was a systematic dismissal of their arguments. Blackmun had "contravene[d] the law of God," ignored the scientific evidence in favor of fetal life, and misinterpreted the Constitution, they said. "It is hard to think of any decision in the 200 years of our history which has had more disastrous implications for our stability as a civilized society," Cardinal John Krol declared as soon as the decision was announced.[62]

Blackmun had little notion of the firestorm he had just ignited. Within days, his mailbox was flooded with missives from angry pro-lifers. Some compared him to Herod and Hitler, while others pleaded with him to reconsider the case. Many predicted the imminent legalization of euthanasia, a development that pro-lifers had long warned about. Blackmun was taken aback by the uproar. "The mail has been voluminous and much of it critical and some of it abusive," he complained to a friend on January 31, a week after delivering the majority opinion in *Roe*. "I suspect, however, that the furor will die down before too long. At least I hope so."[63]

NARAL president Lee Gidding similarly dismissed the pro-lifers' apocalyptic laments as the words of "fanatics." "Before you know it this will be past history and abortion will be just another medical procedure," she confidently predicted. "People will forget about this whole thing."[64]

Gidding and Blackmun could not have been more wrong. Pro-lifers saw *Roe* not as a moment to surrender their arms, but rather as the beginning of a new phase of their campaign—a phase that would be far more grueling and much more challenging than any that had preceded it. "It may take a quarter of a century," Fr. James McHugh said, shortly after *Roe* was issued. "It may take fifty years. But I feel confident that it will happen." *Roe*, he asserted, "will be reversed."[65]

## 9

# *After* Roe

ON JANUARY 11, 1973, members of the North Dakota Right to Life Association braved the frigid temperatures in Bismarck to convene their first annual convention. Having won a sweeping victory at the ballot box only two months earlier, they were optimistic about the future and were ready to move on to the second phase of pro-life activism—campaigning for social welfare legislation that would give women facing crisis pregnancies the help they needed to carry their pregnancies to term. The conference program included sessions on "Health Insurance for Unwed Mothers," "Subsidized Adoption," and "Day Care Centers."[1] It was not enough to keep abortion illegal, they thought; they needed to create a compassionate society in which abortion would seem unnecessary and unthinkable.

But that new phase never came. Less than two weeks after the North Dakota Right to Life Convention met, the Supreme Court issued its decision in *Roe v. Wade*. A right-to-life movement that had just begun to think about expanding its goals and moving on to new campaigns suddenly had to focus all of its energy on one central task—overturning *Roe*. It was a task that would transform the movement and ultimately lead pro-lifers to make alliances with politicians who had very different goals from the ones that the right-to-lifers in Bismarck had promoted.

## *The Pro-Life Reaction to* Roe

*Roe v. Wade* fell like a bombshell on the pro-life community. During the previous two years, pro-lifers had won victories in dozens of state legislatures, but in one moment, the Supreme Court eviscerated all of them. Even worse, the ruling explicitly deprived the fetus of personhood and

constitutional protection. For years, pro-lifers had compared the legalization of abortion to the policies of Nazi Germany, and they had warned of
a coming holocaust for the unborn. It seemed to them that the moment
had now arrived, and they feared for their nation. "The horrible truth is,
the Court's decision put our nation officially in favor of *killing by law*,"
*National Review* writer J. P. McFadden declared. It was "morally indistinguishable from Hitler's genocide."[2]

The Court's denial of personhood to the fetus reminded pro-lifers
of *Dred Scott v. Sandford* (1857), in which the Court deprived African
American slaves of the same right. "As it did in 1857, our country shall
surely suffer and suffer terribly for this decision," Lena Hohenadel,
co-chair of the Lancaster County Chapter of Pennsylvanians for Human
Life predicted. In order to symbolize the connection, 30,000 pro-lifers
gathered in November 1973 at the St. Louis courthouse where Dred Scott's
case had been tried, and listened to Mildred Jefferson, the most prominent African American in the movement, give a fiery denunciation of *Roe*.
"We are determined that the Supreme Court decision on abortion shall
not stand," she said. Politicians "pandering for abortion shall find our
judgments harsh," she declared. "We will consider they are bargaining in
blood and will not vote for them."[3]

Other pro-lifers invoked the Vietnam War. "It is ironic, and profoundly
tragic, that a nation which has just concluded a prolonged and unbeliev-
ably destructive war in Southeast Asia should now turn to the large scale
destruction of its unborn children," Minnesota Citizens Concerned for
Life declared. It called *Roe* "a declaration of war against the unborn—a
declaration which, unless reversed or overturned, will mean 500,000 to
1,000,000 fetal deaths per year in the United States.... With the possible
exception of atomic weapons, no instrument of modern warfare can rival
the destructiveness of the abortionist's arsenal."[4]

American Catholic bishops told the faithful that they must refuse to
comply with the decision. "We have no choice but to urge that the Court's
judgment be opposed and rejected," the National Conference of Catholic
Bishops declared on January 24, 1973. "Doctors, nurses and health care
personnel" must "stand fast in refusing to provide abortion on request,
and in refusing to accept easily available abortion as justifiable medical
care."[5]

Pro-life Catholics' willingness to defy the Supreme Court en masse was
unprecedented, but so was the Supreme Court ruling. In Catholics' view,
the nation's highest judicial institution had directly defied the Declaration

of Independence and the law of God, and they were shocked. Catholics who had come of age in the mid-twentieth century had grown up in an era when the American Catholic Church had identified its goals with those of the nation. Baby Boomer Catholics grew up hating communism, loving baseball, and cheering when John F. Kennedy, one of their own, was elected president. They had seen close ties among Church teachings, New Deal liberalism, and the Democratic Party. The Supreme Court's decision called all of this into question. It appeared that the law of the state was now diametrically opposed to the law of God, and that the Supreme Court, the institution many liberals of the 1960s and 1970s looked to as a guarantor of civil rights, might be an enemy of the most fundamental human right of all—the right to life. Fr. James McNulty told the national convention of the Knights of Columbus that "the comfortable meld of Catholic and American has been disastrously upset."[6]

But it was not only Catholics whose faith in the nation was shaken. Some pro-life evangelicals also felt the same way. *Christianity Today* declared in an editorial on *Roe* that "Christians should accustom themselves to the thought that the American state no longer supports, in any meaningful sense, the laws of God, and prepare themselves spiritually for the prospect that it may one day formally repudiate them and turn against those who seek to live by them."[7]

The public remained deeply divided. A 1973 National Opinion Research Center survey showed that 51 percent of Americans opposed the legalization of elective abortion, while only 46 percent supported it. A Gallup poll taken the following March showed that Americans were nearly evenly divided over *Roe*, with 47 percent supporting the decision and 44 percent opposed. Most of those who opposed *Roe* believed that abortion was wrong because it killed human beings. In January 1973, 50 percent of American women—and 36 percent of American men—believed that human life began at conception, according to a Gallup survey. Two years later, when Gallup asked respondents to state at what point the fetus became a person, 51 percent of American women—and 33 percent of American men—chose conception.[8] Collectively, these opinion polls indicated that the Court had legalized a procedure that approximately half the public opposed and that four out of ten Americans believed was murder.

Outraged by the Supreme Court's disregard for unborn human life, thousands of new recruits—most of whom were women—joined pro-life organizations. By May 1973, Michigan Citizens for Life (formerly Voice of the Unborn) had increased its membership to more than 50,000, up from 10,000 only six months earlier. Three years later, the organization had 200,000 members, 75 percent of whom were women. By contrast, the National Organization for Women (NOW) had only 30,000 members nationwide in 1973.[9]

## The Reaction of State Legislatures

*Roe* created a crisis for state legislatures, which had become increasingly pro-life in the early 1970s. Many state legislators decided to defy the ruling. In fact, *Roe* galvanized pro-life sentiment even in states that had been pioneers in passing ALI-style therapeutic abortion laws only a few years earlier. Elective abortion was too much for even some of the proponents of limited therapeutic abortion laws to accept.

The new outrage against abortion was especially evident in the South, where people had previously been hesitant to embrace the pro-life cause. Indeed, in the late 1960s, the nation's Bible Belt had been the one region of the country most receptive to abortion law liberalization. North Carolina liberalized its abortion law in 1967 with little fanfare or controversy, as did Georgia in 1968. In the late 1960s, the abortion laws in Alabama (which allowed for abortion in cases when a pregnancy endangered a woman's health) and Mississippi (which permitted abortion in cases of rape) were more liberal than the laws in New York or any of the New England states. Because mainstream evangelicals generally did not see a problem with abortion in cases of medical necessity, southern legislatures had encountered little opposition when they liberalized their laws. By the end of 1970, five southern states had adopted ALI-style therapeutic abortion laws, with two others (Alabama and Mississippi) maintaining abortion statutes that, while falling short of the ALI guidelines, were nevertheless more liberal than the policies of most other states.[10]

But no state in the South legalized elective abortion before *Roe*, and large numbers of Southern Baptists and other evangelical Protestants opposed the idea. When a Mississippi state legislator introduced a bill in the spring of 1971 to legalize elective abortion up to the twenty-fourth week of pregnancy (as in New York), the bill was routed in committee, eleven to two.[11] It was thus hardly a surprise when some southern state legislatures decided to resist *Roe*'s mandates.

In Alabama, the state right-to-life organization supported a bill that would have allowed first-trimester abortions only if the "pregnant woman's attending physician" determined that an "abortion was necessary"—a measure that the bill's sponsor believed "would keep people from coming in here in truck-loads for abortions." The state house of representatives passed the bill over NARAL's opposition, but in the end, Alabama decided to maintain an even more restrictive abortion policy by keeping its original, pre-1973 law banning most abortions, even though it conflicted with the Supreme Court's guidelines. A federal court struck down Alabama's law in 1975, but the state still kept it on the books, even though it was not rigidly enforced.[12]

Other southern states that had adopted ALI-style abortion bills also refused to comply with *Roe*. As late as December 1973, Arkansas was still refusing to allow abortion in any cases except those in which a pregnancy endangered a woman's life or health, and Arkansas women who wanted an abortion had to travel to Dallas or Kansas City to get one. In Virginia, the General Assembly chose not to amend the state's abortion statute, and instead passed a resolution urging the Supreme Court to reconsider its abortion ruling. South Carolina did not revise its abortion statute until the state supreme court struck down its law, and even when it did pass a revised measure, the new law subjected first-trimester abortions to a doctor's "professional medical judgment," a vague clause that was probably unenforceable but nevertheless gave deference to the prevailing view that there should be some restrictions on a woman's freedom of access to abortion. Some of the lawmakers who crafted the South Carolina bill admitted that they were trying to create the most restrictive bill that the Supreme Court would allow.[13]

The delays drastically limited abortions, at least for a few months. "In the South as a whole, almost no public hospitals are complying with the Court decision," abortion rights activist Lawrence Lader complained to the associate director of the American Civil Liberties Union in April 1973. Statistics supported his claim. In 1973, fewer than 10 percent of the nation's legal abortions occurred in the South.[14]

Several states in the Midwest and Great Plains also resisted the Court's ruling. Although Kansas had adopted a liberalized abortion law in 1969, the national backlash against abortion on demand in the early 1970s had bolstered pro-life sentiment in the state. Only a few days before the Court issued its decision in *Roe*, the Kansas Senate took up consideration of a bill to make abortion a felony. With pro-life sentiment running strong, Martha Evans, a member of Topeka Right to Life, advised the state legislature to defy the Supreme Court. "This is not the time to be puppets of the court," she declared. "Just as the Supreme Court erred in the *Dred Scott*

decision, it has erred in this decision." The senate took her advice, rejecting a bill to bring the state's abortion policy into compliance with *Roe*.[15]

North Dakota also refused to pass an abortion law, in essence defying someone to challenge the state to comply with *Roe*. That challenge
came in November 1974 when a district court struck down North Dakota's
longstanding anti-abortion law. Yet even after that court challenge, North
Dakota's hospitals refused to offer abortions, so North Dakota women who
wished to terminate their pregnancies often had to travel to neighboring
states—usually to Rapid City, South Dakota, or Minneapolis, Minnesota,
both several hours away.[16]

Some of the strongest opposition to abortion came from the heavily
Catholic states of New England. In Massachusetts, the American Civil
Liberties Union estimated that it could muster no more than thirty
pro-choice votes in the 280-seat legislature. Instead of passing a bill to
comply with *Roe*, the legislature passed a bill drafted by Massachusetts
Citizens for Life that included such restrictions as a ban on abortions after
the twentieth week of pregnancy. Only a pocket veto by the governor—a
Unitarian and Republican moderate in the Rockefeller mold—prevented
the bill from becoming law and facing a court challenge.[17]

Rhode Island, the nation's most heavily Catholic state, reacted to *Roe* by
passing a bill declaring that human life began at conception and was therefore entitled to legal protections. A district court immediately declared it
unconstitutional. The Rhode Island legislature then passed another bill
prohibiting abortion of viable fetuses except in cases when it was necessary to save a woman's life. The legislator who proposed that bill conceded
that it was not ideal, but he recognized that in the aftermath of *Roe*, it was
the best he could do. "If we can save some, it's better than not saving any,"
he said. Yet even this bill did not pass court scrutiny. Two years after *Roe*,
Rhode Island still had no abortion law.[18]

Rhode Island's citizens engaged in public demonstrations in support of
the pro-life cause. The Providence police chief suggested that Providence's
1973 Columbus Day parade—an important celebration in one of the country's most heavily Italian-American cities—be turned into a "March for
Life," a suggestion to which the Catholic Church immediately agreed. The
Knights of Columbus organized the event, which began with a special
Mass for life celebrated by the bishop of Providence. The governor of the
state—like most of his constituents, a Catholic Democrat—proclaimed the
entire week "Respect Life Week." Yet in the end, the citizens and the state
government were powerless to prevent the federal judiciary from bringing

legalized abortion to Rhode Island. Planned Parenthood of Rhode Island opened the first abortion clinic in the state in 1975.[19]

Rhode Island's campaign of noncompliance, though unsuccessful, inspired pro-lifers elsewhere. While Rhode Island's law was still being litigated, the Catholic Diocese of Wheeling, West Virginia, cited it as evidence that West Virginia did not have to pass legislation that complied with *Roe*. Indiana legislators adopted a law that gave citizenship to fetuses. In Utah, where public sentiment generally reflected the Church of Jesus Christ of Latter-day Saints' prohibition on abortions except in cases of medical necessity, the state government adopted a law giving doctors the right to deny women abortions at any stage of pregnancy. A federal court struck it down.[20]

In the end, courts prevented state legislatures from stopping abortions. In Virginia, the state attorney general declared that despite the General Assembly's refusal to pass a bill complying with *Roe*, women in the state had a constitutional right to abortion. Half of the state's hospitals began offering abortion services within a year of *Roe*, even while the state's anti-abortion law remained on the books. And when hospitals failed to meet the demand for abortion services, abortion clinics moved in to pick up the slack.[21]

Before *Roe*, abortion clinics had been almost unknown. Even in New York, the vast majority of abortions had been performed in hospitals, because tight regulations had made it difficult for clinics to operate. Because *Roe* did not permit any restrictions on abortion during the first trimester, abortion clinics began opening in every area of the country, even in states where there was still strong public resistance to abortion. Atlanta, for instance, had seven abortion clinics by December 1973. Abortion clinics were also operating in thirty-one other states by that point, and by the beginning of 1974, these clinics were providing more than half of all abortions in the United States. Pro-lifers denounced the clinics as "abortion mills" or "abortuaries," and they began picketing them, but there was nothing that they could do to stop them. Only two states (North Dakota and Louisiana) managed to prevent any abortions from being performed in 1973, and only three others (Mississippi, Utah, and West Virginia) succeeded in limiting the procedure to those deemed medically necessary. The next year, abortion clinics entered even these last holdouts. In Louisiana, the state government in Baton Rouge resorted to every legal tactic it could muster to prevent abortion clinics from operating in the state, but after the state lost a court battle over the issue, a clinic opened in

New Orleans in July 1974. In North Dakota, there were 150 legal abortions in 1974, followed by 890 in 1975—many of them performed by an ob-gyn in Jamestown who offered a service that other doctors and hospitals in this pro-life stronghold refused to provide. Eventually, a women's health clinic in Fargo, staffed with doctors flown in from Minnesota, further thwarted attempts to keep abortion out of the state. If pro-lifers were unable to prevent the availability of legal abortion services, they were equally powerless to stop the trends that were making abortion more affordable and accessible. By March 1973, most insurance policies that covered maternity care also paid for abortions. At the same time, the Internal Revenue Service announced that abortions were tax-deductible as medical expenses.[22]

The number of legal abortions continued to increase. There were nearly 750,000 legal abortions performed in the United States in 1973. In 1975, the number exceeded one million. In 1980, it was over 1.5 million. By that point, there was nearly one abortion for every two live births in the United States.[23]

## The Quest for a Human Life Amendment

Pro-lifers now knew that their only hope was a constitutional amendment guaranteeing the right to life from the moment of conception. Just as the civil rights movement sought constitutional protection for the rights of African Americans—and just as the feminist movement was currently engaged in a struggle for a constitutional amendment to guarantee gender equality in the United States—so too did the pro-life movement, which considered itself a civil rights movement for the unborn, make a constitutional amendment to protect the unborn its primary goal. Before 1973, pro-lifers considered a Human Life Amendment (HLA) superfluous; it was far better, they believed, to use existing case law to convince the courts that the Constitution *already* protected the unborn. When *Roe* decisively rejected this argument, pro-lifers turned to the amendment process.

Constitutional amendments were a popular political strategy for special interest groups on both the right and the left in the early 1970s. During the previous decade alone, three constitutional amendments had been passed and ratified, and a fourth—the Equal Rights Amendment—had been approved by both houses of Congress and seemed to be well on its way to ratification. Other constitutional amendment proposals, such as a school prayer amendment, were also being seriously considered in

Congress. The backlash against *Roe* in state legislatures and among the public gave pro-lifers hope that they too could obtain an amendment.

Pro-lifers believed that a constitutional amendment would be a decisive victory for the unborn that would likely never be reversed. It would put a complete end to legal abortion in the United States and, more importantly, it would ensure that the unborn had constitutional rights that no one could abrogate. In addition, as Charles Rice noted, an amendment that defined the right to life as inviolate from the moment of conception would stop the "growing drive toward euthanasia of the retarded, the aged and the sick," which pro-lifers had long predicted would follow the legalization of abortion. The HLA would make it clear that "life is the gift of God and not of the State," and would ensure that the Supreme Court would never again have the power to deny a class of persons the right to life.[24]

Only a week after *Roe*, Representative Lawrence Hogan (R-MD) officially introduced an HLA for congressional consideration. "Neither the United States nor any State shall deprive any human being, from the moment of conception, of life without due process of law," Hogan's amendment proposal read.[25]

The proposal received an immediate endorsement from freshman senator Jesse Helms (R-NC), who introduced an identical proposal in the Senate. A Southern Baptist from North Carolina, Helms came from a religious group and region that were only beginning to mobilize against abortion. Indeed, his home state had been one of the first three states to adopt a liberalized abortion law (in 1967), and it had done so without significant opposition. By 1973, though, many Southern Baptists were beginning to move to the right on abortion, and Helms was at the forefront of this group. Two years earlier, he had produced a television commentary linking abortion with moral permissiveness and also warning, as many pro-life Catholics did, that legalized abortion would soon lead to legalized euthanasia.[26] In connecting the legalization of elective abortion with sexual promiscuity and juvenile delinquency, Helms echoed sentiments that other Southern Baptists held, but his sponsorship of the HLA placed him ahead of even some of the most conservative pastors in his denomination in proclaiming that life began at conception.

Not all pro-lifers agreed with the wording of the amendment. In an alternative proposal, Senator James Buckley (Conservative-NY) introduced an amendment to define the word "person" in the Fifth and Fourteenth Amendments as inclusive of unborn life at "every stage of their biological development." Unlike Hogan's amendment, his amendment contained an explicit exception for abortions that were necessary to save the life of the mother—though some pro-life lawyers claimed that the Hogan amendment would not prevent state laws from including that exception. Buckley was a Catholic whose brother William F. Buckley Jr. was one of the best-known conservative intellectuals in America, but his amendment proposal received endorsements from some political liberals and Protestants, including Senators Mark Hatfield (R-OR) and Harold Hughes (D-IA), two evangelicals who had earned reputations as political progressives because of their opposition to the Vietnam War and their championing of social welfare programs.[27]

Regardless of whether they favored the Hogan or Buckley version, pro-life organizations, including the National Right to Life Committee NRLC, immediately made passage of the HLA their top priority. In western Massachusetts, Gilbert Durand organized the Committee of Ten Million in order to gather 10 million letters in support of the proposed amendment. After mailing promotional literature to 18,000 Catholic priests and 14,000 pro-life activists across the nation, he succeeded in gathering 2.5 million letters by the first anniversary of Roe v. Wade; six months later, he acquired the full 10 million to present to Congress. Pro-lifers also took their cause to state legislatures and received official endorsements of their constitutional amendment proposals. By April 1973, sixteen state legislatures had passed resolutions asking Congress to approve a version of the HLA.[28]

Pro-lifers had little success in convincing members of Congress to take the Hogan or Buckley proposals seriously. The unfolding Watergate scandal, the nation's energy crisis, and the country's economic problems seemed far more pressing, especially since abortion was a political hot potato that most members of Congress did not want to touch. According to a 1976 Gallup poll, only 45 percent of Americans supported a constitutional amendment to "prohibit abortions except when the pregnant woman's life is in danger"—which meant that even though a substantial minority of voters favored the idea, the HLA never had a realistic chance of passage.[29]

The only anti-abortion constitutional amendment proposal that may have had a realistic chance was an amendment to restore the pre-Roe status quo by giving states the right to decide their own abortion policies. This amendment, which Representative G. William Whitehurst (R-VA) introduced, had the endorsement of Republican House minority leader Gerald Ford, and it appealed to many Republicans and conservative southern

Democrats who believed that the Court had overreached in *Roe*. Some pro-choice activists feared that it could win majority support in Congress. But while this may have been the pro-life movement's best hope, pro-life leaders rejected it as an unacceptable compromise. Pro-lifers did not want to merely turn back the clock; they wanted to end the practice of legal abortion in the United States once and for all. In July 1973, the NRLC adopted a resolution condemning the states' rights amendment and declaring that the only amendment that would be acceptable was one "which applies to all human beings, including their unborn offspring from fertilization and at every stage of their biological development thereafter." "A mandatory Human Life Amendment offers the only vehicle for restoring legal protection for all human life," the NRLC declared.[30]

With Congress disinclined to support their cause, pro-lifers made it a priority to elect HLA supporters in the 1974 midterm elections. They agreed that the effort would be nonpartisan and single-issue; the only question that mattered was whether a candidate supported the HLA. In the months leading up to the elections, the NRLC and its fifty state affiliates polled all candidates for Congress to find out their views on one issue—a "mandatory human life amendment." Some state NRLC affiliates distributed the same survey to state legislative candidates.[31]

Nearly all national pro-life leaders endorsed this strategy, regardless of their political views. Even though several of the leading sponsors of the HLA were archconservatives like Jesse Helms and James Buckley, the president of the National Youth Pro-Life Coalition, Thomas Mooney, who was a twenty-eight-year-old self-described "left-liberal" who had volunteered for George McGovern's presidential campaign, supported the idea of single-issue voting. He shuddered to think that this strategy might eventually force him to support Buckley's reelection, and he remained hopeful that he could find a sufficient number of pro-life liberal candidates so that he would not have to endorse conservative Republicans. Nevertheless, when pressed on the question, he, like almost all other pro-life leaders, declared that abortion was such an important issue that it trumped all others. In a survey from the mid-1970s, approximately 12 percent of Americans echoed those sentiments, saying that they would vote for a pro-life candidate even if they disagreed with that person on most other issues. (Fifteen percent of Americans took the opposite position, saying that they would vote for pro-choice candidates whenever possible).[32]

By defining "pro-life" as being in support of the HLA, the NRLC and other pro-life organizations effectively redefined the movement and alienated some liberal supporters. Although the pro-life movement was still thoroughly bipartisan in the mid-1970s, with large numbers of both Republicans and Democrats in the movement, pro-life liberal Democratic politicians were more likely than pro-life Republicans to oppose the HLA and to emphasize solutions that reduced the abortion rate, rather than simply making abortion illegal.

Some of these pro-life liberals, such as Eunice Kennedy Shriver, opposed the HLA because they viewed it as a futile distraction. "I really would like to see it pass, but frankly, I don't think it has a chance," Shriver said. In her view, it made no sense to pursue such a "divisive" goal when there were more realistic ways to reduce the abortion rate, such as offering material assistance to women who were facing crisis pregnancies. Instead of campaigning for the HLA, Shriver lobbied for legislation that she thought would have an immediate effect on the abortion rate, such as the National School-Age Mother and Child Health Act, a bill to create teen crisis pregnancy and infant care centers throughout the nation. "The best way to fight abortion is really to offer alternatives to abortion," she declared in 1975. "No matter what the law says you still have the problem of people wanting not to have a baby. And what can you do about that? What kind of alternatives can you offer?"[33]

Shriver's desire to pursue legislative solutions that reduced the abortion rate rather than prohibit the procedure became a major dividing line between liberal and conservative pro-lifers. Most pro-life activists, following the lead of the NRLC, focused mainly on banning abortion. In their view, any political strategy that was concerned only with reducing the abortion rate would not address the fundamental question of whether unborn human life would be legally protected. But for liberal pro-lifers like Shriver, this monolithic focus on a long-shot constitutional amendment was misguided, because it ignored the ways in which pro-lifers could save unborn lives in the short term. Shriver's approach appealed to several pro-life activists in the liberal states of the northern Midwest. Foremost among these activists was Marjory Mecklenburg, a friend of Shriver and a longtime advocate of linking the pro-life cause to a larger social justice agenda.

In 1974, Mecklenburg saw her chance to break with the NRLC's strategy. After chafing under the NRLC's conservative Catholic leadership for several months, she resigned from the board of directors and then started a new organization, American Citizens Concerned for Life (ACCL). As a national organization of state affiliates with a Washington lobbying office on K Street, ACCL was a rival to the NRLC. But it was also a different type of organization, modeled along the lines of Minnesota Citizens Concerned for Life. It represented Mecklenburg's liberal Protestant values by combining opposition to abortion with promotion of contraception and support for social legislation that would help women facing crisis pregnancies. ACCL, Mecklenburg told the progressive Lutheran pro-life pastor Richard John Neuhaus in 1974, was an "organization concerned with finding solutions to social problems, not just banning abortion." "Abortion will not be rejected by society as a legitimate practice until other solutions are found to deal with the real problems many pregnant women and families face," Mecklenburg declared.[34]

The early ACCL board read like a "who's who" of progressive pro-lifers whose politics were too liberal for the NRLC. Senator Mark Hatfield's name headed the list, but Mecklenburg also invited Methodist theologian Paul Ramsey, the Unitarian Harvard Divinity School professor George Huntston Williams, and the left-leaning Catholic feminist Sidney Callahan to join. But ACCL was not a uniformly liberal organization. Mecklenburg continued to reach out to both Republican and Democratic politicians, and she made it her goal to "prize diversity" within ACCL. There would be no litmus tests beyond opposition to abortion.[35]

Because of her new emphasis on preventing abortion rather than merely prohibiting it, Mecklenburg, in contrast to most other pro-life leaders, was sometimes willing to support political candidates who did not favor the HLA, provided that they supported legislation designed to reduce the abortion rate. ACCL devoted much of its resources to lobbying for legislation to benefit pregnant women, such as the Pregnancy Disability Act, which Mecklenburg argued would give working women an incentive to carry their pregnancies to term because they would not have to worry about losing their jobs and facing financial hardships as a result of their decision to have a baby.[36]

If Mecklenburg's vision had come to dominate the pro-life movement, perhaps pro-lifers would have allied with the political left. But ACCL never became a dominant voice among pro-lifers; although it attracted the support of some liberal Protestants and progressive Catholics, it remained much smaller than the NRLC. In 1976, it had a mailing list of only 17,000, while the NRLC had one million members organized in 2,800 chapters throughout the nation. By 1983, when the NRLC had 26,000 members in Minnesota alone—and hundreds of thousands more nationwide—ACCL's national membership was down to only 7,000. Like the NRLC, ACCL quickly accrued a large debt, but unlike its much larger rival, it foundered under the weight of its obligations.[37] For most pro-lifers, the HLA was paramount.

The nation's leading Catholic prelates sided with the NLRC. At the annual meeting of the nation's bishops in November 1973, they voted to create a separate political advocacy organization, the Committee for a Human Life Amendment, to lobby for the HLA from its Washington headquarters and mobilize voters on behalf of candidates who supported the amendment. In its first year of operation, 145 of the nation's 169 dioceses sent contributions to the committee, resulting in a total budget of $361,000, which the new organization used to lobby Congress and conduct a national voter survey. Their greatest task, the leaders of the committee believed, was to convince their fellow Catholics that they should vote only for candidates who were committed to the HLA. To disseminate that message, they set up "human life councils" in individual parishes, and relied on parish volunteers to go door to door to speak to fellow Catholics.[38]

In 1974, four cardinals took the unprecedented step of testifying on Capitol Hill during congressional debates on the HLA. Their visit was evidence of the importance that the Church placed on the HLA; never before had such high-ranking prelates lobbied in person for a piece of legislation. "Every week, since the Supreme Court's decisions of January 22, 1973, there have been as many deaths from abortion as there were deaths at Nagasaki as a result of the atomic bomb," Cardinal John Krol, archbishop of Philadelphia, told the Senate Judiciary Committee. The solution was a constitutional amendment protecting all "innocent human life."[39]

A few Catholics on the left worried that the bishops were making a mistake by privileging the constitutional amendment strategy over other solutions, such as social welfare legislation. If pro-life activists placed all of their emphasis on the HLA, "the anti-abortion cause will become the political tool of the right wing, of those who would resolve complex political problems with instant constitutional amendments," *Commonweal* warned in 1974. Some liberal Catholics also feared that the bishops' insistence that any amendment would have to protect all unborn human lives without exception would derail efforts for a more realistic compromise, such as a states' rights constitutional amendment. In their testimony before the Senate Judiciary Committee, the cardinals had even expressed concern about Senator James Buckley's version of the HLA, because it allowed for abortion when a woman's life was in danger. Such a purist stance, some pro-lifers believed, would alienate potential allies and head off more pragmatic approaches. "The Human Life Amendment's most dangerous opponents are its rigoristic Catholic supporters," *America* magazine stated shortly after the cardinals' testimony on Capitol Hill. "Unwillingness to compromise could mean a total defeat instead of a partial victory."[40]

Despite the political risks, the National Conference of Catholic Bishops (NCCB) pressed ahead with its campaign for the HLA. The NCCB had been slow to react to the threat of abortion legalization in the late 1960s. After *Roe v. Wade*, the bishops felt they had to make up for lost time. In 1975, the NCCB issued a "Pastoral Plan for Pro-Life Activities," which included, among other things, a plan of action to pass the HLA. While it focused primarily on the issue of abortion, it grounded that issue in the larger context of other threats to human life, such as euthanasia, that the pro-life movement had been concerned about for years. It also devoted a lengthy section to aid for women facing crisis pregnancies and called for "continued efforts to remove the social stigma that is visited on the woman who is pregnant out of wedlock and on her child" in order to reduce the abortion rate. But in spite of this endorsement of the social action that liberal pro-lifers favored, the document concluded that ultimately, pro-life success depended on passage of the HLA—which most liberal politicians did not support. A "comprehensive pro-life legislative program must . . . include . . . passage of a constitutional amendment providing protection for the unborn child to the maximum degree possible," the Pastoral Plan declared. The document directed every bishop to appoint a diocesan pro-life director and every state Catholic conference to form a state pro-life committee. Most controversially, the document called for the formation of committees in every congressional district for the specific purpose of lobbying Congress on behalf of the HLA. While the bishops stipulated that those congressional committees should be independent of the Church, they also said that the chairs of these committees could serve as liaisons to the diocesan pro-life committees, suggesting that there would be a close working relationship between the bishops and the lobbyists for the HLA.[41]

## The Split between Pro-Lifers and the Democratic Party

The bishops' decision to treat abortion as the nation's most important political issue—and to frame that issue primarily in terms of passage of the HLA—brought them squarely into conflict with the Democratic Party, to which Catholics had maintained close ties for decades. Many Democrats, especially those who were Catholic, expressed their personal opposition to abortion. Some Catholic Democrats in Congress, such as Representative Jim Oberstar (D-MN) and Senator Thomas Eagleton (D-MO), were even willing to champion the HLA.[42] But because of the increasingly strong influence of the feminist movement, it would have been political suicide for a Democratic presidential candidate to endorse a constitutional amendment that would have banned abortion nationwide. One by one, the nation's leading Catholic Democrats—including those who had recently supported the pro-life movement—expressed their opposition to the HLA and thus fell from grace in the eyes of the pro-life movement.

Perhaps nowhere was the rupture between the Democratic Party and the pro-life movement more evident than in the career of the nation's highest-profile Catholic Democratic politician, Ted Kennedy. The Kennedy family had long enjoyed a special mystique among American Catholics. In 1960, 80 percent of American Catholic voters had cast their ballots for Ted's older brother Jack, who became the nation's first Catholic president. Though Ted's own failures to live up to Catholic doctrine in his personal life were legendary, for much of his early career, he attempted to follow the principles of his faith when casting votes in the Senate. His signature issue, national healthcare, reflected a longstanding priority of the American Catholic Church, as did his concern for social justice for the poor. On the issue of abortion, he took a pro-life stance long after his brother Robert broke with Catholic teaching to endorse abortion law liberalization, and in the early 1970s, NOW leaders considered him an opponent because of his belief that the law must protect all humans "from the very moment of conception."[43]

Kennedy maintained his opposition to abortion for a short time after *Roe v. Wade*, but in 1975, the year that the bishops issued their Pastoral Plan, he broke with the Church on the issue. As a member of the Senate Judiciary Committee, he voted against all proposed versions of the HLA, while simultaneously defeating attempts in the Senate to cut off Medicaid funds for abortions. At a time when the American Catholic Church was beginning to make the HLA its primary political priority, Kennedy's abandonment of his previous pro-life convictions seemed particularly grievous. Boston's archbishop, Cardinal Humberto Medeiros, scheduled a forty-five-minute conversation with the senator in September 1975 in an attempt to bring him back to pro-life orthodoxy. It did not work. Kennedy, according to the cardinal's report, expressed confusion about when human life really began. In public, Kennedy continued to express personal opposition to abortion, but voted against any attempts to restrict it. He defended his actions by appealing to ACCL's approach, which emphasized prevention of abortion more than constitutional prohibition of it. "I share the view of the American Citizens Concerned for Life, Inc., which holds that 'women must not be faced by circumstances to seek an abortion because of the lack of an acceptable alternative and an implied national policy against life,' " Kennedy told his critics.[44]

NRLC leaders were not assuaged. Mildred Jefferson spent the fall of 1975 traveling across her home state of Massachusetts to speak out against Kennedy. Although Marjory Mecklenburg continued to ally with Kennedy in promoting legislation that would benefit women facing crisis pregnancies, Kennedy's actions on this front meant nothing to pro-lifers within the NRLC.[45]

It came as no surprise when leading Senate Democrats helped to kill the HLA. After delaying a vote on the amendment proposals for two years, Senator Birch Bayh (D-IN), the chair of the Senate subcommittee on constitutional amendments, brought all six anti-abortion constitutional amendment proposals to a committee vote in September 1975 and helped to defeat all of them. Comparing the proposed HLA to Prohibition, he said that the Eighteenth Amendment's lack of success in stopping Americans from drinking should make anyone wary of believing that a constitutional prohibition on abortion would stop women from terminating their pregnancies. Because Bayh was a contender for the 1976 Democratic presidential nomination and one of the party's leading authorities on constitutional amendments, his opposition to the HLA signaled the direction that the party would take. Given Senate Democrats' increasingly united opposition to the HLA and Republicans' lack of enthusiasm for it, it was impossible to imagine the Senate passing an HLA anytime in the foreseeable future. The only anti-abortion amendment proposal that came close to passage in committee was a states' rights amendment that failed on a tie vote. The Buckley amendment failed by five to two. Pro-lifers were disappointed but undaunted. James McHugh promised that the temporary defeat would only "serve as a springboard for a new and more determined effort."[46]

Yet pro-lifers realized that, in a future push for the HLA, they might not find much support from Democrats, especially those with presidential ambitions. That was true even of Sargent Shriver, the husband of Eunice Kennedy Shriver. That Shriver would betray their cause by failing to endorse the HLA was especially galling to some pro-lifers, because in 1975, when Shriver began preparing his bid for the Democratic Party's presidential nomination, many pro-lifers had considered his pro-life credentials impeccable. He was a devout Catholic whose personal opposition to abortion ran deep, and his wife had been a national leader in the fight against legalized abortion since the earliest days of the pro-life movement. Convinced that Shriver was the candidate whose policies were most likely to stop abortion in America, Marjory Mecklenburg, a longtime friend of both Shrivers, joined the campaign's advisory committee and began contributing to it financially. Other liberal pro-life activists were similarly enthusiastic. Pro-life lawyer David Louisell volunteered for the campaign. Pro-life Methodist theologian Paul Ramsey joined Mecklenburg on Shriver's advisory committee. Shriver, California pro-life law professor John Noonan wrote in November 1975, "may be the best person" to "get the issue [of abortion] into presidential politics." Noonan's support was conditional, however; he expected Shriver to make pro-life policies a central part of his campaign. Shriver's personal beliefs about abortion were well known, but those beliefs meant little to Noonan and his fellow pro-life activists if Shriver was not prepared to translate them into substantive policies. "We must continue to insist that no one can take seriously a statement that a candidate is personally opposed to abortion but politically impotent to help in its prevention," Noonan said.[47]

Shriver quickly antagonized many of his pro-life potential supporters in the fall of 1975 when he declared on *Meet the Press* that although he was "not personally in favor of abortion," he "agree[d]" with the Supreme Court's ruling in *Roe v. Wade* and did not support any efforts to overturn the decision. Aiding pregnant women, he said, rather than passing an HLA, was the best way to reduce the abortion rate. Pro-lifers who had supported Shriver were dismayed. "He'd be much better off if he'd just get up there and say, 'I think abortion is murder and you better know it,'" one former adviser from his 1972 vice-presidential campaign told the press in December 1975.[48]

Shriver thought that his promotion of positive alternatives to abortion, such as the "life support centers" for pregnant women that his wife was championing, would gain him credibility with pro-life activists. "The truth is, that I've done more over the last ten years on this issue than anyone else in or out of public life in America," a frustrated Shriver exclaimed after pro-lifers began to desert his campaign in droves.[49] His claim was exaggerated, but he did have a point; he and Eunice had hosted a national conference on abortion in 1968, several years before some of the NRLC's national officers of the mid-1970s—including the organization's president, Mildred Jefferson—had joined the right-to-life movement. That ought to count for something, he thought.

For a few pro-lifers on the left, such as Marjory Mecklenburg, it did. But even Mecklenburg believed that Shriver needed to couple his promotion of alternatives to abortion with an endorsement of the HLA and a clear statement of opposition to *Roe v. Wade*. Shortly after joining Shriver's campaign, Mecklenburg had asked him for "some assurance . . . that his abortion position will be one which will call for the overturn of the *Roe v. Wade* decision." The ACCL newsletter urged pro-lifers in the fall of 1975 to write to Shriver encouraging him to link his support for abortion alternatives with an endorsement of the HLA.[50]

Shriver could not understand why the pro-life movement wanted this, and he refused to give it. "An amendment is not the best way to help people," he said. Even a states' rights amendment would take ten years to be ratified, he argued, and after it was enacted, the nation's largest states, including New York and California, would undoubtedly still allow abortions. The HLA was even more unrealistic; it was impossible to imagine it ever getting out of Congress. On this issue, Shriver and his wife were in agreement. "No one—not even if the Lord came down himself—could get through a constitutional amendment to override the Supreme Court decision in favor of allowing abortion," Eunice told the *Ladies Home Journal* in early 1976.[51]

But pro-lifers believed that the president could use the moral authority of his office to move an amendment through Congress, and when Shriver showed no signs of wanting to do that, they repudiated his candidacy. By February 1976, even Mecklenburg was becoming frustrated. Although she continued to support Shriver until he dropped out of the race, she conceded in February that he was losing the pro-life vote. "At this time he doesn't stand out in any way as more pro-life than other presidential candidates," she told her fellow advisers on Shriver's campaign committee.[52]

If pro-lifers were disappointed with Shriver, they were outraged at Birch Bayh, widely considered one of the early frontrunners for the nomination. Because pro-lifers blamed Bayh for the defeat of the HLA in the Senate committee he chaired, they made it a point to picket his campaign speeches, sometimes employing such dramatic props as surgical gowns stained red. When he spoke at the University of Notre Dame, 400 pro-lifers held a prayer vigil in protest.[53]

Another contender, Georgia governor Jimmy Carter, seemed untrustworthy on the issue. He expressed his personal opposition to abortion, yet refused to endorse the HLA. Worse, he had written a foreword to a book that endorsed abortion rights, which, in the view of many pro-lifers, made his professions of personal opposition to abortion seem implausible. They wondered if his waffling on the issue during the campaign was a strategy of deliberate deceit in order to attempt to make his position seem acceptable to all sides. Shortly before the Iowa caucuses, Carter told the Des Moines diocesan paper that he favored a "national statute" to restrict abortion, a move that may have led some Iowa pro-life Catholics to think that he might favor the HLA—which he did not. Some pro-lifers thought that misimpression may have contributed to Carter's victory in Iowa, which was critical to the success of his bid for his party's nomination. Pro-lifers felt duped, and Carter's opponents felt cheated.[54]

Some of the Democratic candidates whom pro-lifers targeted for defeat were puzzled at the vehement opposition they received from the right-to-life movement, because they considered themselves opponents of abortion. Of the various candidates for the Democratic presidential nomination, only Representative Morris Udall and Governor Milton Shapp were ardent supporters of a woman's right to choose; the rest had strong reservations about abortion, and some opposed federal funding for the procedure. Shriver's personal opposition to abortion was well known, and Carter was opposed to Medicaid funding for abortion. Even Bayh, who was the chief target of pro-lifers' wrath, believed in using the power of the state to curb abortion rates. In 1975, he had sponsored an "Alternatives to Abortion" package of legislation that, if enacted, would have provided federally funded life support centers to offer nutritional, health, and educational help to pregnant teenagers so that they would have "a real alternative to abortion," and would have also required private health insurance maternity policies to cover unmarried women. Such legislation closely echoed the proposals that Marjory Mecklenburg and other liberal pro-lifers had been making for years, yet it did nothing to improve Bayh's standing among people who were angry with him for helping to defeat the HLA. To most pro-life activists, statements of personal opposition to abortion were worse than useless, while legislation designed to reduce abortion rates ultimately failed to address the legal status of human life. They thought that candidates who professed personal opposition to abortion while simultaneously opposing the HLA were merely trying to win their votes through lip service, and they resented this cynical approach. George Wallace, the only serious contender for the Democratic presidential nomination who endorsed the HLA, highlighted his pro-life platform in his appeals to Cuban-American Catholics in Florida, but some political observers viewed his newfound interest in reaching out to Catholics as yet another sign of his Machiavellianism.[55] He received little support from the national pro-life movement.

In the absence of a viable Democratic presidential contender who would champion their cause, pro-lifers decided to run one of their own. Ellen McCormack, a pro-life leader, devout Catholic, and fulltime homemaker from Long Island, New York, had never run for political office before, but she nevertheless entered the Democratic Party presidential primaries with the backing of the right-to-life movement. Pro-life leaders knew that she would never win the nomination, but they hoped that her presidential campaign would force people to pay attention to abortion. Under the terms of a new campaign finance law that went into effect in 1975, any presidential primary candidate who raised at least $5,000 in small contributions from individuals in at least twenty different states was eligible for matching federal funds. Right-to-life activists realized that by qualifying for these matching grants, they could run graphic television advertisements on behalf of their cause for only half the amount they would normally be required to spend. At the same time, stations that might not normally air pro-life advertisements would be compelled to accept McCormack's ads if they were running advertisements for other political candidates. Pro-life activists were firmly convinced that television advertising worked, because public opinion polls taken during their campaign against the Michigan abortion referendum in 1972 had revealed the effect that images of twenty-week-old fetuses had on public opinion. If they could show enough people what really happened in an abortion, they were convinced they could win the debate and pass the HLA.[56]

Pro-lifers had been thinking for several years about launching a third-party, single-issue campaign for president in order to attract public attention. In November 1973, Dennis Horan, a member of the NRLC's legal advisory committee, suggested that if a pro-life candidate ran for president on a third-party ticket in 1976, that person might receive three or four million votes and would get free airtime on television that could be used for pro-life commercials. With neither the Republican nor Democratic Parties showing much interest in the pro-life cause, pro-lifers thought they had little to lose by boycotting the two-party system and throwing their support to a third-party candidate. Pro-lifers, in fact, tried such a strategy on a local scale in 1974, when New York right-to-life activist Barbara Keating ran on a third-party ticket to challenge pro-choice liberal Republican senator Jacob

Javits. She raised enough money for only two television commercials, but she nevertheless received 16 percent of the vote, enough to ensure that the newly formed Right to Life Party would remain on the New York state ballot in the next election cycle. Even more importantly, New York pro-lifers thought, referrals to Birthright increased in the immediate aftermath of Keating's television commercials.[57] Apparently, the images had a direct effect on viewers. How much more could be accomplished with a national presidential candidacy that right-to-life activists throughout the country would support?

McCormack was the leader of the Long Island pro-life group Women for the Unborn and had been writing pro-life articles since the early 1970s. She had helped Keating design her television commercials in 1974.[58] She therefore thought that she knew what she needed to do to gain publicity for the pro-life cause.

McCormack raised more than $500,000 in small contributions from individuals, which allowed her to become the first female presidential candidate in US history to qualify for matching federal campaign financing and Secret Service protection. She then used that money to air a television commercial featuring Mildred Jefferson showing images of the feet of a ten-week-old fetus and describing what happened during an abortion.[59] By most standards, the campaign commercials were unusual. They said nothing about McCormack's record or about any other candidate in the presidential race. Instead, they focused entirely on the abortion issue. But that was their intent; McCormack was running the commercials not to win the presidential nomination but instead to increase public support for the HLA.

Nevertheless, in the course of her campaign for president, McCormack was forced to occasionally speak out on other issues, a process that revealed her political ideology for what it was—that of a socially conservative Democrat. Unlike Republican presidential aspirant Ronald Reagan, she supported détente with the Soviet Union, and unlike the New Right—but like many right-to-life activists—she favored federally funded childcare for poor women. Yet she spoke out against the feminist movement and expressed her opposition to busing policies designed to achieve racial integration in public schools. Repeatedly, she insisted that she was running on behalf of the common person, as well as the unborn child, though she also admitted that her campaign was "basically a one-issue candidacy." She was a stay-at-home mother of four who had never attended college but had instead gotten married after graduating from parochial school. She described herself as a "housewife from Merrick." Her husband was a New York City police officer. Her family was devoutly Catholic. As a registered Democrat, McCormack, in a previous era, might have voted for pro-union Democratic politicians, though she also enthusiastically supported Conservative Party senator James Buckley because of his support for what she called "Catholic values." In the current election climate, she felt that no presidential candidate represented those values. "I don't see anyone on any ticket I could vote for," she said. "If the right to life issue is at the bottom of their priorities, I cannot support them."[60]

For many pro-lifers, McCormack's candidacy was also their last chance to turn the Democratic Party around. "The Democratic Party has ignored us completely," Mildred Jefferson lamented in February 1976. "They don't understand the issue. We have to win some delegates so that when we get into their convention, we can talk with them."[61] McCormack's delegates, pro-lifers hoped, could force the Democratic Party to adopt a pro-life platform plank—or, at the very least, block the pro-choice platform plank that many feminists within the Democratic Party were promoting.

Despite McCormack's lack of political experience, her candidacy attracted sizeable support from pro-life voters. Her best showing came in Vermont, where she received 9 percent of the vote, but she also did well in South Dakota (8 percent) and Rhode Island (4 percent), as well as a handful of other states with strong pro-life movements. In Boston, she received only eight fewer votes than Bayh. The Catholic Church was crucial to her (limited) success. In Covington, Kentucky, the local bishop sent a letter to parishioners encouraging them to consider a candidate's stance on abortion, and 30 percent of Democratic primary voters in Covington then cast their ballots for McCormack.[62]

McCormack's delegates came to the convention determined to win an endorsement for the pro-life position, but they faced difficult odds. Few observers expected that the platform committee would pledge support for the HLA; the best that pro-lifers could hope for was to keep any mention of abortion out of the platform or perhaps secure an endorsement for social welfare legislation to help women facing crisis pregnancies. Marjory Mecklenburg wrote to the Democratic platform committee asking the party to approve such measures. The party's "historic concern for the underprivileged and disenfranchised," she argued, should make the party amenable to pro-life Democrats' concerns for the unborn child.[63]

While most of the members of the platform committee were unwilling to follow Mecklenburg's suggestions, they were keenly aware of the damage that the abortion issue had done to George McGovern's candidacy in 1972, and they wanted to avoid a similar controversy in 1976. Polls showed that both parties were nearly evenly split on the abortion issue. Forty-eight percent of Democrats in March 1976 favored a constitutional amendment prohibiting abortion, while 44 percent opposed it. The figures were almost identical for Republicans, at 48 percent in favor and 47 percent opposed.[64] Any stance that the Democratic Party took on the issue could polarize the electorate and lose votes.

Several pro-life Democrats, including former Speaker of the House John McCormack (no relation to Ellen), sent the platform committee statements in support of protecting the unborn child's right to life. After graphically describing a late-term abortion procedure, McCormack called right-to-life activists "modern abolitionists." Given its historic concern for social justice, McCormack argued, the party needed to come to the aid of the "innocent and defenseless unborn."[65]

While McCormack was a senior statesman in the party, his views carried limited weight. Democrats were committed to women's equality, and the party's increasingly vocal pro-choice wing viewed abortion rights as essential to that commitment. Nearly all of the contenders for the Democratic presidential nomination opposed the HLA, as did most of the prominent liberals in the party who were not running for president; it was therefore unthinkable that the party would endorse it. Nor would pro-choice delegates allow their party to remain silent on the subject, especially after their disappointment with McGovern's decision to duck the issue in 1972. At a time when the Catholic Church and pro-life activists were pressuring Congress for an HLA, pro-choice Democrats wanted to officially endorse *Roe v. Wade* and a woman's right to choose.

The platform committee proposed a compromise: The party platform would officially acknowledge the diversity of views among Democrats on the issue, but the party would also oppose an HLA on pragmatic grounds. It would appeal to the authority of the Supreme Court, thus indirectly endorsing *Roe v. Wade* without directly declaring that women had a constitutional right to an abortion. "We fully recognize the religious and ethical nature of the concerns which many Americans have on the subject of abortion," the platform stated. "We feel, however, that it is undesirable to attempt to amend the U.S. Constitution to overturn the Supreme Court decision in this area." In adopting this wording, the party rejected proposed wording from the California state Democratic Party endorsing the "right to individual control over the use and functions of one's body," and it likewise repudiated Mecklenburg's call for an endorsement of policies to reduce the abortion rate. Delegates from several heavily Catholic states voted against the measure, but it still passed by a large margin. The party thought that it was steering a centrist, moderate course, as did its nominee Jimmy Carter. Both soon found themselves in trouble with pro-lifers.[66]

Shortly before the convention, Mecklenburg warned the party that if it adopted a platform plank stating that it was "undesirable to amend the Constitution" to protect unborn life, pro-lifers would be angry, no matter how carefully the party tried to avoid a direct endorsement of abortion rights. It would be better, Mecklenburg argued, "to delete from the platform all pro and con statements on the legal status of abortion" than to adopt a compromise. "Apparently you do not realize that the proposed plank adopts the legal position advocated by those groups favoring abortion and will alienate millions of Americans from the Democratic Party," she told the platform committee.[67]

Mecklenburg correctly gauged the sentiments of pro-life activists. To protest the new platform, 10,000 pro-lifers led by Ellen McCormack gathered in New York just outside the convention hall to denounce the party for repudiating the HLA. The rally against abortion dwarfed all other protest rallies at the convention. Only 700 gay rights activists, for instance, gathered in New York to protest the party's refusal to endorse civil rights for homosexuals.[68]

The protest was only the harbinger of a nationwide pro-life reaction against the Democrats. The party's platform was "morally offensive in the extreme," Joseph Bernardin, archbishop of Cincinnati and president of the NCCB, declared. Pro-life leaders vowed never to support Carter. "It was Jimmy Carter and his representatives who forced the Democratic Party to go on record as endorsing abortion," Fran Watson, chair of McCormack's presidential campaign, declared. "Not even George McGovern went that far." Mildred Jefferson was equally fierce. "As abortion became a millstone around McGovern's neck in the 1972 campaign, it will be a chain around Carter's ankles in 1976," she declared.[69] Even if the final split between the Democratic Party and the pro-life movement was not yet fully evident in 1976, the platform fight prompted pro-lifers to look for new allies among conservative Republicans, a political group that had thus far given their cause only limited support.

## The Pro-Lifers' Conversion
## to the Republican Party

The Republican Party was far from an obvious home for pro-lifers in the mid-1970s. A number of prominent Republican senators—including liberals such as Edward Brooke and Lowell Weicker, moderates such as Robert Packwood and Howard Baker, and conservatives such as Barry Goldwater and John Tower—were pro-choice, and even some of the Republican Party leaders who objected to *Roe v. Wade*, such as President Gerald Ford, supported a states' rights amendment rather than the HLA. Aside from the New Right freshman senator Jesse Helms, pro-lifers found little support for the HLA even among the most conservative Republican senators. And outside of Congress, Republican support for the HLA was almost as scarce. Ford's vice president—Nelson Rockefeller, the man largely responsible for the most liberal state abortion law ever enacted— was one of the GOP's strongest champions of abortion rights. The chair of the Republican National Committee was a pro-choice women's rights advocate. And First Lady Betty Ford was a strong supporter of abortion rights who had declared on national television that *Roe* was a "great, great decision." In response, Nellie Gray, organizer of the annual March for Life in Washington, DC, announced in November 1975 that pro-lifers would hold monthly pickets outside the White House for an entire year, right up until Election Day, to protest the first lady's comments and the adminis- tration's support for legal abortion. "Betty, we don't want the right to kill," one of their signs proclaimed.[70]

Yet pro-life leaders endorsed Ford en masse less than a year later. This would have been inexplicable except for one thing: the Ford campaign's shift to the right on the abortion issue in response to a primary challenge by Ronald Reagan. Reagan had not begun his political career as a strong opponent of abortion rights. He started off on the wrong side of right-to- lifers when, as governor of California, he signed an abortion liberalization bill in 1967. Yet, even then, pro-lifers sensed that Reagan could be won over. He was hardly enthusiastic about abortion law liberalization, and before signing the bill, he had insisted that the clause allowing abortions for fetal deformities be deleted. When Elizabeth Goodwin of the Right to Life League met with him shortly before the bill reached his desk, she reported that he expressed sympathy for her position. The next year, when California state senator Anthony Beilenson introduced another abortion liberalization measure, Reagan opposed it. From then on, he used his position as governor to block any attempts at further liberalization.[71] Thus, when Reagan decided to challenge Ford for the Republican Party nomination in 1976, pro-lifers viewed him as a potential friend.

Reagan exceeded their expectations. In October 1975—a month before he officially announced his candidacy—he agreed to an exclusive interview with *National Right to Life News* editor Alice Hartle and pledged his support for the "aims" of the Human Life Amendment. He still believed in the right of a woman to have an abortion if a pregnancy threatened her life, but he was opposed to abortion for any other reason. "The interrupting of pregnancy is the taking of a human life," he declared.[72]

Reagan's willingness to endorse at least the concept of the HLA—even if he did not yet commit himself to a specific version of the amendment—stemmed partly from his belief that the Supreme Court had overreached in *Roe*. "The Supreme Court decision," he complained several years later, "overruled the historic role of the states in legislating in areas concerning abortion and took away virtually every protection previously accorded the unborn." This was a common complaint among conservative Republicans. Some who were unwilling to support the HLA still favored the sort of "states' rights" amendment that Ford did. Reagan's support for the HLA was also closely tied to his opposition to federal funding for abortion, another position that appealed to many conservatives, including some who were pro-choice. Barry Goldwater, for instance, who believed in a woman's right to choose on libertarian grounds, saw no need, as a fiscal conservative, for the government to fund it. Neither did George H. W. Bush, a strong supporter of family planning who opposed the HLA but approved of Republican attempts to prohibit federal funding for abortion.[73] Thus, even though the Republican Party as a whole had not previously been inclined to give the HLA much support, there were elements within the party's broader political principles—especially those of the party's right wing—that could be channeled toward opposition to abortion rights. Reagan took this opposition even further than most Republicans did at the time by endorsing the HLA. Regardless of whether Reagan's support for the amendment was a sincere conviction, a calculated move to attract pro-life support in a difficult primary race against an incumbent president, or simply a spur-of-the-moment decision with long-term political consequences that he did not fully anticipate at the time, it had a momentous effect on the pro-life movement's relationship to the Republican Party. Coinciding as it did with the simultaneous pro-life Catholic reaction against the Democratic Party, Reagan's endorsement changed the partisan equation on abortion and offered an incentive for the Republican Party to shift course.

Reagan's alliance with the pro-life movement pressured Ford to take a stronger stance against abortion rights. On the eve of the Republican National Convention in August, Ford was still trying to fend off Reagan's challenge, win over conservative Republican delegates, and find a way to shore up his sagging campaign as he headed into the general election. Shifting to the right on the abortion issue would mollify cultural conservatives in the Reagan camp, win over a few Catholic Democrats, and perhaps even help Ford among evangelical Protestants, White House advisors such as James Reichley argued. In response to this advice, Senator Bob Dole (R-KS), an abortion opponent who was vying to be Ford's running mate, met with Reagan delegates and members of Ellen McCormack's campaign team (an unusual move since McCormack was running as a Democrat) to find out what sort of platform statement on abortion they might be willing to accept. He then gave the task of co-writing the abortion platform plank to Senator Jesse Helms, a staunch Reagan supporter and one of the party's strongest champions of the HLA. The result was a platform statement that was diametrically opposed to the Democrats' endorsement of *Roe*. "We protest the Supreme Court's intrusion into the family structure through its denial of the parents' obligation and right to guide their minor children," the platform stated. "The Republican Party favors a continuance of the public dialogue on abortion and supports the efforts of those who seek enactment of a constitutional amendment to restore protection of the right to life for unborn children." Republicans debated among themselves whether this platform statement endorsed the HLA or merely a "states' rights" amendment (Ford preferred the latter interpretation), but regardless of the precise meaning of the "constitutional amendment" that the party now officially supported, it was clear that, unlike the Democratic Party, the GOP did not support *Roe v. Wade*.[74]

Twenty-eight Republican feminists signed a minority report asking the party not to adopt this platform plank, but most pro-choice Republicans were willing to accept it in the interest of party unity. The Republican Women's Task Force, which in other circumstances might have challenged the statement, decided not to object, since it feared that a fight over abortion might prompt angry social conservatives to rescind the party's endorsement of the Equal Rights Amendment. Thus, although many leading Republicans continued to endorse abortion rights, the party was now officially, in the words of Mildred Jefferson and other pro-life leaders, the "Party of Life."[75]

Although President Ford was not an enthusiastic champion of the pro-life cause, pro-life leaders supported his campaign because of the platform. Mildred Jefferson said that she hoped to mobilize twenty-five million pro-life Americans to "enter the ballot box on Nov. 2 with some consideration of the abortion issue in mind," which, she said, "will give Ford a clear edge." In some states, such as New Jersey, right-to-life chapters formally endorsed the president—a legally dubious move for tax-exempt organizations. Marjory Mecklenburg, who had been working with the Democrats, switched to the Republican side and began working for the political affairs division of the Ford campaign, where she used her position to send out campaign letters to pro-life leaders and pastors.[76]

After Ford lost the election, pro-lifers quickly forgot about him, since they never had much confidence in his pro-life sympathies anyway. But they did not forget Reagan or the GOP platform. During the next four years, the NRLC and other pro-life organizations continued to cultivate the ties that they had begun developing with the conservative wing of the Republican Party. Their strong desire to elect members of Congress who supported the HLA led them into close association with a new group of political players who were even more conservative than Reagan—the New Right grassroots activists who were trying to reshape Congress.

In the late 1970s, pro-lifers launched several political action committees—or PACs as they were often called—in order to raise money for congressional candidates who had pledged to support the HLA. These PACs had close ties to New Right political activists, because it was the New Right (a populist conservative movement of the 1970s that promoted tax cuts and reductions in social welfare spending) that had the fundraising expertise, the organizational experience with PACs, and the desire to help pro-lifers reshape Congress along conservative lines. The first of these groups, the National Pro-Life PAC, was organized in Illinois in the spring of 1977 under the direction of a Dominican priest, Fr. Charles Fiore, who wanted to avoid another debacle like the election of 1976, which, in the end, had left pro-lifers with no major victories. Pro-lifers needed to find a way to change the composition of Congress and avoid electing another pro-choice Democrat like Jimmy Carter to the White House. To accomplish that goal, Fiore recruited the field director for the American Conservative Union, Peter Gemma, to serve as the executive director of a PAC that would raise money for candidates who pledged to support the HLA.

As a single-issue organization, the National Pro-Life PAC was willing to support both liberals and conservatives, but as Gemma readily conceded, there were far more conservatives than liberals who were willing to vote for the HLA. The organization's first national political action conference, held in the spring of 1979, featured a lineup of Republican New Right stars, including Jesse Helms and Paul Weyrich. Fiore was unapologetic about this close cooperation with the right, because he insisted that he had no compunction about working with liberal Democrats—as long as they endorsed the HLA. He applauded the work of Democrats for Life, a group that had formed in 1976 in order to lobby for a reversal in the Democratic Party's endorsement of abortion rights. "It is important that pro-life be truly a two-party system," he wrote, when urging pro-life Democrats to assist in "returning their party to respect for life." At the same time, though, he declared that in his view, the Democratic Party had "lost its soul . . . to the radical feminist advocates who would 'choose' to kill unborn babies," and he held out only limited hope for a reversal in the party's position. He was thus compelled to work with the Republicans.[77]

The Life Amendment Political Action Committee (LAPAC) was even more closely identified with the New Right than the National Pro-Life PAC was. Founded by the conservative Catholic couple Paul and Judie Brown in 1977, LAPAC worked closely with New Right activist Paul Weyrich, who gave LAPAC office space in his Committee for the Survival of a Free Congress. Weyrich was interested in electing congressional candidates who were conservative on a broad range of fiscal and social issues, while the Browns cared only about abortion and insisted that they would begin endorsing liberal candidates as soon as liberals endorsed the HLA. Despite this theoretical difference in approach, Weyrich recognized that if pro-lifers made the HLA a political litmus test, they would by necessity be voting for conservative candidates most of the time, and he thus viewed them as potential recruits for the New Right coalition. "Whether they want to or not, right-to-lifers find they have to work with New Right activists, simply because no one else cares about protecting the unborn," Weyrich declared.[78]

The pro-life PACs demonstrated their political muscle in the midterm elections of 1978 when they worked alongside New Right operatives to elect several freshman conservative Republicans to the House and Senate. The surprise victory of Roger Jepsen in a Senate race in Iowa was the best demonstration of the pro-life movement's newfound voting power. A former lieutenant governor who had been out of office for several years,

Jepsen seemed ill-equipped to challenge incumbent Democratic senator Dick Clark. But both the National Pro-Life PAC and LAPAC supported Jepsen's campaign. Even more importantly, he received the support of local pro-life groups. On the Sunday before the election, Iowa pro-lifers combed the parking lots of Catholic churches, handing out 300,000 pamphlets highlighting Clark's pro-choice voting record. The result was a massive shift in the Catholic vote that propelled Jepsen to victory.[79]

After the success of the pro-life PACs in 1978, the NRLC decided to form its own PAC. This was in some ways hardly a surprise, because although the NRLC was officially separate from both the National Pro-Life PAC and LAPAC, there were close connections among the members of these organizations. NRLC president Mildred Jefferson chaired LAPAC's advisory board. The NRLC's decision to launch its own PAC committed the organization to a more overt—and ultimately more partisan—role. "The movement has turned a corner and . . . we are now firmly ensconced in the political arena," Carolyn Gerster, who succeeded Jefferson as NRLC president in 1978, acknowledged. The NRLC's PAC also committed itself to raising money for congressional candidates who supported the HLA. And like the other pro-life PACs, it worked closely with the New Right.[80]

The HLA remained the movement's focus despite the incremental victories it was winning in other areas. In 1976, for instance, Representative Henry Hyde (R-IL) succeeded in passing a legislative amendment that ended most federal funding for abortion, reducing the number of federally funded abortions by 99 percent. This unexpected political victory instantly made Hyde, a freshman congressman, one of the movement's most celebrated allies in Congress, and it earned him a keynote speaking slot at the 1976 NRLC convention. It also set in motion a wave of new state restrictions on abortion funding, which may have contributed to a reduction in abortion rates. By 1978, only sixteen states plus the District of Columbia provided funding for elective abortion, which meant that in most states, women who wanted abortions would either have to pay for the procedure themselves or do without. The Hyde Amendment also helped cement the nascent alliance between the pro-life movement and the GOP, because it offered a way for fiscally conservative pro-choice Republicans to find common ground with pro-lifers. As Barry Goldwater told voters in 1980, "I want to make it perfectly clear that a woman can have an abortion if it's in the interest of herself and her child, but I don't want the federal government paying for it." Republicans continued to be divided over abortion, but by the end of the 1970s, much of the party's conservative wing could at least unite around the belief that taxpayer dollars should not fund the procedure.[81] For many pro-lifers, including some liberal Democrats in the movement, this counted for a lot, because they believed that cutting off federal funding for abortion would save unborn lives and because they did not want their tax dollars paying for a procedure that they believed was murder. Yet as much as they might applaud the Hyde Amendment, pro-lifers knew that it was no substitute for their ultimate goal. As they entered the 1980 election season, they renewed their efforts to elect pro-HLA candidates.

By 1980, pro-life activists were already moving into the Republican Party, but the increasing number of evangelicals in the pro-life movement accelerated this trend. Public opinion surveys showed that by the beginning of the 1980s, evangelicals were even more likely than Catholics to say that *Roe v. Wade* was wrongly decided. Although the nation's major pro-life organizations remained heavily Catholic (70 percent of the NRLC's members were Catholic in 1980), the increasing salience of the pro-life issue among evangelicals meant that much of the political impetus for abortion restrictions would now come from evangelical Protestants. This was welcome news to most Catholic pro-life activists, who had long been trying to prove that their cause was not sectarian. At first, they had tried to ally with mainline Protestants and Jews, but by the end of the 1970s, many of their allies were coming from evangelical churches. The alliance seemed to make sense. Even if evangelicals and Catholics differed sharply on Christian doctrine, they found common ground on many moral issues. Evangelical converts to the pro-life cause also shared the fervent religiosity of their devout Catholic colleagues. In 1980, 90 percent of the NRLC's members, regardless of faith tradition, reported that they attended religious services at least once a week, and 87 percent said that religion was either "extremely" or "very" important to them.[82]

Yet if evangelicals and Catholics shared a common religious fervor, their approaches to politics differed. Many of the Catholics in the movement had long been social justice-oriented Democrats, and in the early 1970s, many of their liberal Protestant allies, such as Marjory Mecklenburg, had attempted to link the movement with the political causes of the left. For many Catholic and liberal Protestant pro-lifers, saving unborn babies was a human rights issue, just as providing help to unwed mothers was. Pro-life evangelicals saw the issue differently. Most of them were political conservatives who linked abortion with other issues of sexual morality. For them, pro-life activism was part of a broader campaign to restore Christian morality in America.

Francis Schaeffer, a popular evangelical writer who may have done more than any other person to mobilize evangelicals on behalf of the pro-life cause, framed the abortion issue as part of a broader narrative of national moral decline. *How Should We Then Live?*, a documentary film and book that Schaeffer released in 1976, presented the Supreme Court's decision in *Roe v. Wade* as the culmination of a long drift away from moral absolutes in public law and culture, particularly with regard to sexual ethics. Schaeffer elaborated on this analysis in his next major film project, *Whatever Happened to the Human Race?* (1979), a four-hour documentary on abortion that ended with an appeal to the audience to work for the restoration of a Christian legal and cultural framework that would protect human life.[83]

Evangelicals of the late 1970s were already campaigning against secularization on a variety of fronts. They were fighting gay rights, pornography, sex education, and the ERA, and they were speaking out against the Supreme Court's rulings on school prayer and Bible reading. They were championing candidates who assured voters that they were "born again" or who promised to restore moral order. But the abortion issue gave them an even more powerful symbol of the dangers of secularization. Secularism, they now argued, led not only to the loss of societal sexual mores or gender confusion, but also to a culture of death. In the early 1980s, abortion quickly became the signature issue of the new Christian Right.

For many Americans, Jerry Falwell, a Virginia Baptist megachurch pastor and televangelist, was the public face of the new Christian Right, and it was Falwell's public activism that helped to cement the alliance between pro-life activism, campaigns against secularism, and the promotion of a conservative Republican agenda. Falwell, who was strongly influenced by Schaeffer, saw the fight against abortion as part of a larger campaign against "secular humanism" and sexual licentiousness. In 1978, he preached a series of televised sermons that gave equal time to denunciations of abortion, homosexuality, and pornography. When he created the Moral Majority in 1979, he made the campaign against abortion a top priority, but also framed it as part of a larger fight against feminism, gay rights, and even communism. It was this last cause that prompted Falwell to oppose calls for a nuclear freeze, a stance that put him at odds with the antinuclear position of the NCCB and many Catholic pro-life activists.[84]

An increasing number of evangelical denominations also joined the pro-life campaign. In 1980, the Southern Baptist Convention, the nation's largest Protestant denomination, rescinded the moderate endorsement of liberalized abortion laws that it had adopted nine years earlier and called for an HLA. At the same time, the convention also passed resolutions against gay rights, pornography, and the teaching of evolution in public schools. Several other major evangelical denominations—including the Presbyterian Church in America, the Christian and Missionary Alliance Church, and the Assemblies of God—also passed pro-life resolutions in the late 1970s and early 1980s, sometimes coupling them with broader condemnations of secularization and sexual immorality.[85]

For evangelicals who were concerned about the moral direction of their country, pro-life activism promised a way to reclaim their nation from a culturally liberal federal government that had demonstrated its defiance of Christian principles in *Roe v. Wade*. In 1973, when *Roe* was issued, many evangelicals had found the decision only moderately alarming, but by the end of the 1970s, after the gay rights movement, the rising divorce rate, and the explosion of pornography had placed abortion in a larger cultural context of moral decline, they found *Roe* far more disturbing. Their quest for political allies led them to side with Republican politicians.[86]

Most evangelical pro-lifers did not join the NRLC or other pro-life groups, but instead used their own organizations, such as the Moral Majority, to lobby against abortion. Pro-life organizations such as the NRLC, in turn, decided not to adopt the Moral Majority's larger cultural agenda, but to instead remain narrowly focused on protecting unborn human life. Nevertheless, the fact that most evangelicals saw a connection between abortion, gay rights, feminism, and sexual licentiousness would affect the future direction of the movement.

Most pro-life activists already shared evangelicals' concerns about sexual licentiousness, but after distancing themselves from the Catholic Church's historic opposition to contraception, they had focused strictly on fetal rights. After 1980, pro-lifers would increasingly argue that to fight abortion, they had to challenge the broader sexually licentious culture. According to a survey of pro-life activists taken in June 1980, 87 percent of NRLC members believed that premarital sex was "always or almost always wrong," 96 percent believed the same about homosexuality, and 80 percent thought that divorce should be more difficult to obtain. As the pro-life movement was shifting to the right on sexual issues, the Democratic Party was shifting to the left. In 1980, the party platform added the term "sexual orientation" to its official list of groups that must be protected from discrimination.[87] In the emerging culture wars, pro-lifers were likely to be much more sympathetic to the rhetoric of the new Religious Right than to the platform of the Democratic Party.

Pro-lifers' widespread opposition to the ERA also put them at odds with both the Democratic Party and the feminist movement. Feminists of the 1970s made ratification of the ERA their primary goal, and they convinced Democratic leaders to make it a top priority as well. In fact, this was such an important issue for Democrats that, in 1980, the party refused to fund the campaign of any candidate who opposed the amendment. The pro-life movement had shown hardly any interest in the ERA when Congress held hearings on it at the beginning of the 1970s, and even after Phyllis Schlafly's STOP-ERA campaign began mobilizing conservative women across the country in opposition to the amendment, pro-lifers were divided on the issue, and the national pro-life organizations stayed out of the fight. But Schlafly's claim that the amendment could be used to mandate legalized abortion on the grounds of gender equality convinced many pro-lifers to reconsider their stance and begin speaking out against the ERA. Some pro-lifers advocated a modified ERA, with an addendum protecting the unborn, but since this was never a real political option, they were forced to reject the amendment entirely. A poll of NRLC members in 1980 showed that only 9 percent supported the ERA at a time when more than 50 percent of the American population favored it. Pro-lifers did not view their antipathy to the ERA as a sign of antifeminism; indeed, they thought of themselves as gender egalitarians in some areas. Throughout the late 1970s, the top leadership posts at the NRLC were filled by women, and women comprised the majority of pro-life activists. Sixty-three percent of NRLC members in 1980 were women, and many of them shared the feminist movement's beliefs about the need for equal opportunity for women in the workplace. Seventy-one percent of NRLC members believed that "women should have an equal role with men in running business, industry, and government." Ninety percent said that they would support a female candidate for president.[88] Yet their widespread opposition to the feminist movement's favorite cause pushed them into the antifeminist camp and exacerbated the tensions between their movement and the Democratic Party.

When Ronald Reagan spoke out against both abortion rights and the ERA, he received more enthusiastic pro-life support than any previous political candidate. Pro-lifers had endorsed Reagan during his presidential campaign of 1976, but they became more fervent supporters in 1980, largely because Reagan made an early, concerted effort to reach out to the movement's leaders. In July 1979, he sent Henry Hyde a letter reiterating his support for the HLA and condemning *Roe v. Wade*. Hyde immediately sent copies of Reagan's letter to pro-life leaders throughout the nation, which was exactly what the Reagan campaign had intended. Reagan's "forthright support for a Human Life Amendment," Hyde told pro-lifers, indicated that "he has the kind of pro-life spirit we need in the White House." "The cause of life itself," he wrote, "has been handed a most significant opportunity to make a major advance on the national scene." Hyde urged pro-lifers to do whatever they could to help Reagan win the nomination.[89]

The letter prompted an outpouring of support for Reagan from the pro-life community. Because no other presidential candidate from either the Democratic or Republican Party had yet endorsed the HLA, Reagan's early support for the pro-life movement's signature issue assured him of strong support from pro-life activists as he headed into the primaries. Peter Gemma enthusiastically endorsed Reagan, as did the NRLC's PAC. By January, Reagan had commitments of support from the state right-to-life organizations in New Hampshire, Vermont, New Jersey, and several other eastern states. The Iowa Pro-Life Political Action Council endorsed Reagan shortly before the state caucuses.[90]

The Reagan campaign team also capitalized on the annual March for Life in Washington by dispatching Senator Richard Schweiker to read a message of support from Reagan. Although the march was nonpartisan, thousands of marchers wore buttons that said "Vote Pro-Life," which to them meant a refusal to support any candidate who did not endorse the HLA. As the marchers proceeded past the White House, they chanted "Jimmy Carter, stop the slaughter." Shortly after the march, Reagan sent March for Life Director Nellie Gray a letter of support and, at her request, a promise in writing that he would support the Helms-Dornan Human Life Amendment, the specific version of the HLA that Gray favored. The next day, Gray sent her pro-life mailing list a letter endorsing Reagan for president. Although she had been a Democrat whose own politics were far from conservative, Reagan's support for the HLA won her over.[91]

While many pro-lifers liked Reagan, the NRLC under the leadership of Carolyn Gerster and Jack Willke was especially dedicated to supporting him. In June 1980, Willke and Gerster requested a meeting with Reagan and followed it with an enthusiastic report of their confidence in him. When they read Reagan's brief statement of support to the annual meeting of the NRLC, they were met with wild applause. Willke then spent the next five months campaigning for Reagan among pro-lifers. "I probably spent almost as much time in his campaign office in Arlington as I did in our office," he later recalled.[92]

Pro-lifers realized that Reagan's nomination might give them an opening to transform the Republican Party into the party of life. Four years earlier, the GOP had approved a platform plank endorsing an anti-abortion constitutional amendment, but only a few Republican politicians had taken that plank seriously. Pro-lifers believed it was imperative to keep the GOP officially committed to the HLA. To accomplish that task, the NRLC launched the Pro-Life Impact Committee, headed by Marlene Elwell of Michigan Right to Life. Elwell, a Catholic, had been active in the Michigan pro-life movement since the fight against Proposal B in 1972, and because the Republican National Convention was scheduled to be held in Detroit, it seemed to make sense to put a Michigan pro-life leader in charge of lobbying the convention delegates. At the time, Elwell was still a registered Democrat whose politics leaned to the left. She had marched with Martin Luther King Jr. and Cesar Chavez.[93] But now, she viewed the pro-life cause as the most important social justice issue, and if Reagan was the only major-party presidential candidate who would champion it, she was willing to work with him.

Elwell wasted no time in organizing a lobbying group. From the moment in early April when she was appointed to lead the Pro-Life Impact Committee until the convention in July, she did everything she could to lobby the Republican delegates for her cause. With an initial operating budget of only $5,000, her resources were limited, but because she worked with a small staff and relied mostly on volunteer labor, she was able to use her meager funds to maximum effect. She gathered together fifty pro-life activists—one for each state—and instructed each of them to contact all of the Republican delegates in their designated states to urge them to support the HLA in the party platform. The NRLC gave Elwell some additional help by mailing a copy of Jack and Barbara Willke's *Handbook on Abortion* to each of the 1,994 Republican delegates. The Pro-Life Impact Committee drafted an anti-abortion platform plank for the delegates and encouraged them to pass it. Forty pro-life volunteers came to the convention to distribute pro-life armbands, buttons, and signs to delegates who sympathized with their cause and to encourage them to keep their commitment to the pro-life platform plank. Elwell reported that because the media's attention was focused on the platform committee's debate over the ERA, few noticed what she was doing for the pro-life cause; this worked to her advantage. The pro-lifers also benefited from the support of Christian Right organizations such as the Moral Majority, which sent representatives to the Republican convention and increased the pressure on the party to adopt a pro-life platform plank. In the end, Elwell was able to get everything she wanted from the platform committee, which approved the pro-life plank she had created, pledging support for an HLA and the restriction of federal funding of abortion. "We are all overjoyed with the unity of purpose expressed by the Republican platform and the commitment of Governor Reagan on the issue of abortion," a press release from the NRL-PAC exulted after the platform committee approved the pro-life statement by a vote of seventy-five to eighteen.[94]

It was a watershed moment in GOP history. Four years earlier, when the party had hastily approved an anti-abortion platform statement that most GOP leaders outside the pro-life movement ignored or honored only with lip service, few observers thought it marked a permanent shift in the party's direction. But in 1980, when the party easily beat back a challenge to the platform and insisted that the party honor Reagan's wishes by pledging itself to the passage of an HLA, some pro-choice Republicans realized that they had lost control of the party to the pro-life movement. RNC chairwoman Mary Dent Crisp resigned from the Republican National Committee and joined John Anderson's campaign because of her opposition to Reagan's pro-life views. Polls showed that the majority of Republicans were still pro-choice and that they were more likely than Democrats to favor keeping abortion legal. The highest-ranking Republican in the Senate, Howard Baker, supported abortion rights. Many of the party's most respected members remained committed to a woman's right to choose. But those forces were on their way out. With Reagan's blessing, pro-lifers were now the ones poised to set the party's direction, and they relished the opportunity to do so. When George Bush, who had previously expressed his opposition to the HLA, accepted Reagan's invitation to become his running mate, pro-lifers forced him to pledge his support for the entire Republican platform, including its call for a constitutional amendment to protect the unborn.[95] From then on, it would be impossible for any Republican presidential or vice presidential candidate to do otherwise.

When the Democratic Party adopted a platform reiterating its support for *Roe v. Wade* and calling for federal funding of abortions for the poor, it signaled the growing divide between the parties. With one party officially endorsing *Roe v. Wade* and the other officially pledged to its reversal through an HLA, pro-lifers felt that they had no choice but to link their movement's fortunes with those of the GOP.

# *Epilogue*

ON THE FORTIETH anniversary of *Roe v. Wade* in January 2013, perhaps as many as half a million people—more than twice the number that had participated in the iconic March on Washington in 1963—braved the winter temperatures in Washington, DC, to join the March for Life and protest against abortion outside the Supreme Court building. Thirty-nine years earlier, the first March for Life had drawn a crowd that barely exceeded 5,000. Now, nearly half a century after Elizabeth Goodwin, Walter Trinkaus, James McHugh, and other Catholic opponents of abortion had organized the country's first right-to-life groups, the issue of abortion was even more polarizing than it had been in the early 1970s.[1]

In the 1970s, neither side in the abortion debate had expected that the fortieth anniversary of *Roe* would be greeted with a large protest. Pro-choice activists had predicted that within a few years, the polarization over abortion would be forgotten and the vast majority of Americans would accept the Supreme Court's decision. Pro-life activists, on the other hand, had hoped that they would soon pass the Human Life Amendment (HLA), overturning *Roe* and protecting all human life from the moment of conception. The fact that neither side got what it wished for was a testimony to both the success and failure of the pro-life movement.

The pro-life movement had succeeded in restricting abortion and making Americans uncomfortable with the procedure. Forty-eight percent of Americans considered themselves "pro-life" in 2013, while only 45 percent considered themselves "pro-choice." Twenty percent wanted to make abortion illegal in all circumstances, and an additional 38 percent wanted abortion to be legal only in "a few circumstances." While public opinion on a few other hot-button social issues, such as same-sex marriage, had rapidly shifted to the left, pro-lifers had moved both social attitudes and national policy to the right. By 2013, the abortion rate was lower than it had been at any point since the early 1970s. Fewer than 1,800 abortion providers were still in business, while 2,500 pro-life crisis pregnancy centers across the nation were offering women alternatives to abortion and convincing thousands of women each year to carry their pregnancies to term. In several states, abortion services were now confined to only a single facility, as abortion regulations in some of the more strongly pro-life states made it increasingly difficult for abortion providers to operate. Pro-lifers had also gained a foothold in the Republican Party; 59 percent of Republicans in 2013 wanted to make nearly all abortions illegal.[2]

Perhaps the most encouraging sign for the movement was the large number of young people who were committed to the pro-life cause. Forty years earlier, college students had been the most avid supporters of legalizing abortion. But a majority of the demonstrators at the 2013 March for Life were high school and college students, with many carrying signs proclaiming "I Am the Pro-Life Generation." Public opinion polls confirmed what the march suggested: Americans under thirty were indeed more strongly opposed to abortion than their parents were, a phenomenon that would have been unimaginable to abortion rights supporters in the early 1970s.[3] From the perspective of many pro-choice activists, it looked like the pro-lifers were winning.[4] Yet the failure of pro-life activists to pass "Personhood Amendments" (ballot referenda to protect human life from the moment of conception) in even the most strongly pro-life states and their inability to overturn *Roe v. Wade* showed that they had not yet convinced a majority of Americans that all unborn life was worthy of legal protection.

The simultaneous success and failure of the pro-life movement was a result of the movement's defiance of conventional political categories and its concomitant embrace and rejection of late twentieth-century American liberal values. Even in the midst of its apparent political success, its ultimate goal remained elusive.

## *Pro-Lifers' Alliance with the GOP after 1980*

Pro-lifers' disappointment with the Republican Party began almost immediately after Ronald Reagan's election in 1980. The pro-lifers who voted for Reagan expected that his election would give them the catalyst they needed to pass the Human Life Amendment (which both Reagan and the Republican Party platform had endorsed), but that proved not to be the case. In fact, none of the proposed versions of the HLA even made it out of committee in the Senate. Although the Republicans had a majority in the Senate in the early 1980s, that did not mean that the Senate was inclined to pass pro-life legislation, since the Republican Party still had many pro-choice members, including Senate majority leader Howard Baker. Many pro-lifers realized that the best they could hope for was a states' rights amendment rescinding *Roe*. This proposed constitutional amendment, authored by Senator Orrin Hatch (R-UT), divided the pro-life movement. In the mid-1970s, most pro-life leaders, as well as the nation's Catholic bishops, had opposed states' rights amendment proposals as inadequate, since they would do nothing to provide constitutional protection for the unborn. By the early 1980s, however, a number of pro-lifers who had once opposed such amendments decided that the Hatch amendment was the best they could get. In a divided vote, the National Right to Life Committee (NRLC), under the leadership of Jack Willke, endorsed the Hatch amendment, but a number of other prominent pro-lifers, including Nellie Gray, Judie Brown, and Robert Byrn, publicly spoke out against it. When it reached the Senate floor in June 1983, the Hatch amendment received only forty-nine votes, eighteen short of the two-thirds majority required for passage.[5]

The Hatch amendment was the only anti-abortion constitutional amendment proposal to receive a vote from the full Senate, and when it failed, pro-lifers turned their attention to the Supreme Court. In March 1984, Americans United for Life Legal Defense Fund held a conference titled "Reversing *Roe v. Wade* through the Courts," and other pro-life organizations, including the NRLC, also made this cause a top priority.[6] Pro-lifers of the late 1980s remained committed to the Human Life Amendment, but they now thought that a Supreme Court decision overturning *Roe* would be an important first step.

This new strategy required pro-life activists to develop even closer alliances with Republicans than they had before, because only Republican presidents seemed likely to appoint justices willing to overturn *Roe*. After several Democratic senators who had campaigned as pro-life candidates voted against the confirmation of one of the NRLC's favorite Supreme Court judicial nominees, Judge Robert Bork, in the fall of 1987, the NRLC decided that its new judicial strategy would succeed only if Republicans controlled the Senate. "A Democratic Senate majority means a Judiciary Committee directed by pro-abortion Joe Biden," the *National Right to Life News* warned its readers in 1988. The NRLC worked hard to turn out the pro-life vote for George H. W. Bush that year, and it campaigned for dozens of pro-life congressional candidates, most of whom were Republicans. In return, pro-lifers got a Court that seemed more favorable to their position. After the appointment of several conservative justices by Presidents Reagan and Bush, the leaders of the NRLC expected that they would see *Roe* reversed within only a few months. They were therefore dismayed when the Supreme Court reaffirmed *Roe* in *Planned Parenthood v. Casey* (1992), with three recent Republican appointees—Sandra Day O'Connor, Anthony Kennedy, and David Souter—joining in an opinion that upheld a woman's right to an abortion.[7]

Two decades later, pro-lifers were no closer to their goal. There were still only four justices on the Supreme Court who would likely vote to reverse *Roe*. But pro-lifers were not deterred; instead, they became even more strongly committed to the Republican Party, continuing their quest for an elusive fifth vote on the Court.

As the nation's abortion debate turned into a fight over the Supreme Court, the parties' polarization over the issue became more pronounced, and politicians who had once felt free to disagree with their party on abortion no longer did so. During the 1980s, Democrats Jesse Jackson (who had once written for *National Right to Life News*), Dick Gephardt (who had cosponsored a version of the HLA in the 1970s), and Al Gore (who had once said that abortion was "arguably the taking of a human life" and who had had a pro-life voting record in Congress) changed their positions. At the same time, George H. W. Bush, who had opposed the HLA when he competed in the Republican presidential primaries in 1980, reinvented himself as a pro-life candidate, which allowed him to win the support of the NRLC when he ran for president again in 1988.[8]

In the lower house of Congress, which had no role in the confirmation of Supreme Court justices, the abortion debate was less partisan, and a number of Democrats, especially those representing heavily Catholic districts in the North or socially conservative districts in the South or Midwest, continued to cast reliably pro-life votes. As late as 1992, more than one-third of the Democrats in the House of Representatives met the NRLC's strict standards for being pro-life candidates. But the number of pro-life Democrats in Congress continued to decline in the 1990s, and by the time that Jim Oberstar, one of the last of the liberal Democratic pro-life stalwarts in the House of Representatives, was defeated for reelection in 2010, they had become a rarity. They became even scarcer after the NRLC made opposition to

President Barack Obama's healthcare plan a political litmus test on the grounds that some of the contraceptives covered by Obamacare were "abortifacients." As a result, there were only three Democrats in the House who earned 100 percent ratings from the NRLC in 2014. In the Senate, there were none.[9]

## The Pro-Life Movement's Alienation from the Democratic Party

Many pro-lifers were reluctant to leave the party of Franklin Roosevelt, but a larger cultural shift in both the party and the nation made it impossible for them to remain loyal Democrats. Until the 1960s, both parties had championed the male-headed, two-parent family as a social ideal, and that idea had undergirded Catholics' loyalty to the Democratic Party. For three decades following the creation of the New Deal, most liberal Democrats had grounded their calls for social welfare programs and economic uplift in the principle of helping the male-headed household—a concept that closely accorded with the Catholic Church's teaching that the family unit was the foundation of society. But in the late 1960s and 1970s, liberal Democrats exchanged this family-centered ideal for a new rights-based ethic grounded in individual autonomy and social equality, thus alienating many theologically conservative Catholics, including the pro-lifers who viewed the defense of fetal rights as a liberal campaign and who had hoped to ally with Democrats.[10]

Catholics of the 1960s and 1970s certainly believed in individual rights; even some of the most doctrinally conservative clerics, such as Cardinal Patrick O'Boyle, were outspoken supporters of the civil rights movement, and the entire pro-life movement was grounded in the language of the inalienable, individual rights of the fetus. In fact, Catholics of the mid-twentieth century thought that their Church's natural law theology provided the ultimate framework for universal human rights. But to conservative Catholics, these rights were always accompanied by responsibilities and were rooted not in the autonomous self but in a human dignity that was ultimately derived from a divine Creator and safeguarded by the family and the Church. When American liberals of the 1960s attempted to divorce their rights advocacy from transcendent theological claims, Catholics balked. When the Democratic Party decided that the rights of women to bodily autonomy and gender equality superseded the fetus's right to life, pro-lifers were outraged.[11]

At first, pro-lifers tried to meet liberals on their own ground by defending the rights of the fetus in language that seemed indistinguishable from the constitutional rights claims that women, gays, and African Americans were making, while eschewing references to the larger ethic of sexual responsibility and the family-centered ideal that might have branded their campaign as a throwback to an earlier era. Yet in the end, despite their appropriation of the language of rights-based liberalism, their campaign failed to win the support of liberals who realized that fetal rights were incompatible with the values of bodily autonomy and gender equality.

Once autonomy and equality became liberal Democrats' primary concerns, it was only a matter of time before many devout Catholic pro-lifers who had long been loyal Democrats faced a stark choice. Would they swallow their reservations about the Democratic Party's position on abortion in order to further other goals? Or would they abandon their other political convictions and work with the Republicans? Pro-lifers who chose to work with pro-choice Democrats despite their differences over abortion usually argued that liberal social welfare policies and universal health insurance programs would do more than conservative regulations to reduce the abortion rate, which was an argument that pro-life liberals such as Sargent and Eunice Shriver had advanced in the mid-1970s and that continued to win the support of some liberal evangelicals and antiwar Catholics in the 1980s. As many of these politically liberal pro-lifers realized, conservative Republicans were less likely than Democrats to embrace the comprehensive ethic of social responsibility that the American Catholic Church and many leaders of the pro-life movement had long favored. By joining with the Republicans, pro-lifers might find allies who wanted to make abortion illegal, but in turn, they would have to accept a militaristic foreign policy and an individualistic approach to economic questions that were at odds with Catholic social teaching.[12] For some pro-lifers on the political left, that compromise was unacceptable, which is why a number of them campaigned for liberal Democratic candidates and continued, for at least a short time, to champion the causes of the left.[13]

Yet this stance was never popular with leaders of the NRLC or with most pro-life activists, because few were willing to abandon their movement's longstanding commitment to securing legal protection for the unborn. If the pro-life cause was a matter of constitutional rights, as they claimed, legal protection was non-negotiable. Thus, for the NRLC, there was never any thought of endorsing candidates who promised to reduce the abortion rate but refused to support the Human Life Amendment or other legal restrictions on abortion. And even some of the pro-life liberals who were willing to accept this idea winced at the thought of endorsing politicians who not only championed a pro-choice stance but staunchly defended the right of women to obtain late-term abortion procedures that pro-lifers considered especially heinous. When President Bill Clinton vetoed the Partial-Birth Abortion Ban Act in 1996, *Sojourners* magazine, a liberal evangelical journal that was usually a reliable ally of the political left, called the action "obscene and stupid."[14]

While most pro-life activists decided that they could not countenance the national Democratic Party's stance on abortion, many were nevertheless happy to work with individual Democratic politicians who embraced the pro-life label and were willing to endorse the HLA. This was an especially popular strategy for pro-life liberals in the mid-1980s, when they still thought they had a chance to regain influence in the party. Democrats for Life refused to endorse the Democrats' presidential tickets (since those always featured pro-choice candidates), but nevertheless worked for pro-life Democratic candidates at the local level and attempted to elect pro-life delegates to the Democratic National Conventions. Yet the chilly reception that these conventions gave to Democratic politicians who refused to toe the party line on abortion rights only served to confirm pro-lifers' growing suspicions of the party. When the organizers of the 1992 Democratic National Convention refused to give Pennsylvania's Catholic Democratic governor Bob Casey a speaking slot to present a defense of his pro-life views, the snub confirmed many pro-lifers' belief that the Democratic Party wanted nothing to do with their cause. NRLC president Wanda Franz charged that the Democratic leadership was determined to "ignore and suppress" the views of pro-life Democratic members of Congress.[15]

In response, Casey embarked in 1992 on a national speaking campaign in order to reverse the party's direction on abortion. Blaming its "abortion on demand position" for a long series of presidential election defeats, he said that it was time for the party to move "back to the mainstream" and recapture the votes of pro-lifers. At the very least, he said, the party should replace its pro-choice platform with a statement that extended "tolerance" to the party's pro-life minority. But ideally, he said, the party should adopt a platform recognizing that the pro-life position was fully in keeping with liberal values. "The powerless and the voiceless have been our natural constituency," Casey declared. "Let us add to this list the most powerless and voiceless member of the human family: the unborn child." *National Right to Life News* gave Casey's crusade prominent coverage throughout the 1992 election season, perhaps because it closely echoed the views of the original NRLC leaders. Yet when Casey's campaign failed, the NRLC interpreted it as a sign that the Democratic Party was now a lost cause. Casey declared that "there is a litmus test for presidential candidates" in the Democratic Party and that "if you're pro-life, you don't qualify," and NRLC PAC director Carol Long concurred. While insisting that the NRLC was still officially bipartisan, she added, "But the truth is that in most states, the Republican Party far more often than the Democratic Party offers candidates who are pro-life."[16]

Pro-life liberals of the 1980s who had hoped to find left-leaning politicians willing to champion their agendas of opposition to nuclear arms buildup and the death penalty (as well as abortion) were similarly disappointed. Many pro-lifers had been promoting an alliance between peace activism and the pro-life cause since the beginning of the 1970s, but the nation's Catholic bishops gave this idea new life in the 1983 pastoral document "The Challenge of Peace." Those who wanted to "end the scourge of war" needed to "begin by defending life at its most defenseless, the life of the unborn," the bishops declared. The bishops' strong opposition to President Reagan's policy of nuclear arms buildup, as well as their outspoken antipathy to capital punishment, gave some pro-lifers hope that the Catholic Church and the liberal wing of the Democratic Party could be allies in defense of a "consistent ethic of life" (or, as Cardinal Joseph Bernardin phrased it, a "seamless garment" of life) if only the Democrats would embrace the Catholic Church's stance on abortion. In hopes that they could find a coterie of politicians willing to do this, the left-leaning Catholic pro-life activist Juli Loesch joined with a small group of liberal evangelicals, including Michigan Democratic state senator Stephen Monsma and antipoverty activist Ronald Sider, to form JustLife PAC, which raised money in the late 1980s for candidates willing to sign on to all parts of Bernardin's "seamless garment"—opposition to abortion, the death penalty, and nuclear arms buildup. But by 1992, JustLife was finding fewer Democratic congressional candidates to endorse and was also encountering difficulties attracting funds for what seemed to be a quixotic effort. It folded in 1993. While vestiges of the liberal pro-life movement survived, the million-member NRLC, which was many times larger than any of its liberal organizational rivals, continued to strengthen its ties to conservative Republican politicians.[17]

The nation's Catholic bishops were initially reluctant to follow the lead of the pro-life movement in treating abortion as a litmus-test issue.

Indeed, on most political issues other than abortion, the bishops in the early 1980s were much closer to the Democrats than to conservative Republicans, and they were at first not inclined to let the abortion issue push them into the Republican camp. From the moment that President Reagan took office, they lobbed attacks at his administration, first for his threats against social welfare programs and then because of his nuclear arms buildup and his missile defense program. The bishops' 1983 pastoral letter "The Challenge of Peace" decried abortion, but only in the context of a much longer condemnation of the nuclear arms race.[18]

Yet when Democrats in 1984 decided to strengthen their party's official endorsement of abortion rights, and when the party's presidential nominee Walter Mondale selected pro-choice Catholic congresswoman Geraldine Ferraro as his running mate, some Catholic clerics decided that they could not remain silent. Abortion, New York archbishop John O'Connor declared in a televised address in June 1984, was a "matter of life or death," so he did not see "how a Catholic in good conscience can vote for a candidate who explicitly supports abortion." While O'Connor and other Catholic bishops continued to insist that they were not making a partisan endorsement, the Church hierarchy's increasing willingness to treat abortion as a uniquely heinous issue—an "unspeakable crime," as Vatican II had declared—encouraged many theologically conservative, pro-life Catholics to make the issue their primary criterion in voting, especially after Pope John Paul II highlighted its importance in his 1995 encyclical *Evangelium Vitae*. When pro-choice Catholic senator John Kerry ran for president as the Democratic nominee in 2004, some bishops chose to deny him communion solely because of his stance on abortion, an action that the US Conference of Catholic Bishops (USCCB) officially endorsed. Although Cardinal Joseph Ratzinger sent a memo to American bishops that summer stating that Catholics might be allowed to vote for a pro-choice candidate if there were "proportionate reasons" for doing so, some bishops said that they could not imagine that, in practice, those reasons would ever exist. "How can any citizen vote for a politician who is pro-abortion?" Oklahoma City archbishop Eusebius Beltran asked in a pastoral letter in 2008. "There is no other issue more important. All other issues are moot if the right to life is not respected and protected."[19]

Even in the midst of their increasing willingness to make opposition to abortion their highest political priority, the nation's bishops continued to speak about the importance of hunger relief and call for a political agenda based on "the needs of the poor and vulnerable not the contributions of the rich and powerful," as the USCCB's pastoral letter "Faithful Citizenship" declared in 2004. The bishops' political agenda of 2004, in other words, bore a distinct resemblance to President Franklin Roosevelt's rhetoric of seventy years earlier, with the Church's pro-life stance on abortion heading the list of ways that the bishops believed politicians could protect the "poor and vulnerable." But unfortunately for the bishops, the New Deal liberalism of the 1930s had long since disappeared, giving way instead to a polarization between a pro-choice, rights-based liberalism of the Democratic Party and a pro-business, hawkish neo-conservatism of the Republicans, neither of which met with the bishops' approval. Few politicians were willing to couple an anti-abortion stance with restrictions on handguns and assault weapons, opposition to the death penalty and "preemptive" war, and support for global poverty relief programs, a liberal immigration policy, a "living wage," and environmental initiatives—all of which were also part of the bishops' political proposal. "A Catholic moral framework does not easily fit the ideologies of 'right' or 'left,' nor the platforms of any party," the bishops declared. As a result, "some Catholics may feel politically homeless, sensing that no political party and too few candidates share a concern for life and dignity." Yet in the end, those who went to the polls had to make a choice, and for those who shared the bishops' belief in the primacy of protecting the unborn, voting for candidates who pledged to implement restrictions on abortion seemed to be the only viable option, even if most of those candidates showed little interest in the rest of the Church's political priorities.[20] Any support that these single-issue Catholic voters gave to Republican candidates was a grudging concession to the political realities that *Roe v. Wade* had created; it by no means signaled a heartfelt commitment to the GOP platform.

Occasionally, even some of the pro-lifers who had become Republican partisans raised a cry of protest when the party moved too aggressively against some of the maternal aid programs that their movement had long supported. When a newly elected Republican Congress attempted in early 1995 to pass legislation that would have denied additional AFDC benefits to single mothers who had more children, the NRLC lobbied against the proposal, claiming that this anti-child policy would drive women receiving public assistance to have abortions. Most of the time, though, the NRLC and other pro-lifers turned a blind eye to such policies. Their attempts to assist women facing crisis pregnancies were now carried out almost exclusively in the private realm. They largely abandoned their cause of government-provided maternal health insurance, which had

conservative evangelicals of the late 1970s created the Religious Right and recast the pro-life cause as a conservative issue. Baptist televangelist Jerry Falwell's Moral Majority made abortion one of its top political priorities, but in contrast to the Catholic bishops, Falwell connected the issue to a bevy of other politically conservative causes—such as campaigns to restore prayer in schools, stop the advances of the gay rights movement, and even defend against the spread of international communism through nuclear arms buildup. Some pro-life Catholics were wary of the evangelicals' newfound interest in their cause, and at first most chose to continue working through their own organizations, such as the NRLC, rather than the Moral Majority or other Religious Right organizations. It was not until the late 1980s, when Randall Terry's Operation Rescue brought Catholics and Protestants together for a national campaign of pro-life civil disobedience, that a sizeable number of Catholics and evangelicals began working alongside each other in the same pro-life organizations. Yet even before that moment, a few conservative Catholics such as STOP-ERA founder Phyllis Schlafly, New Right activist Paul Weyrich, and Weyrich's associate Connie Marshner infused the pro-life movement with a socially conservative agenda that linked opposition to abortion to a more comprehensive "pro-family" campaign that included a defense of private Christian schools and opposition to gay rights, feminism, and "secular humanism." All of these conservative activists worked closely with both the Republican Party and with the emerging Religious Right; Weyrich, in fact, had helped to create the new Christian Right by recruiting Falwell for conservative political activism and assisting him in organizing the Moral Majority.[23]

Abortion was one of Weyrich's central concerns, and in the late 1970s and early 1980s, he provided office space to several pro-life organizations, including Fr. Paul Marx's Human Life International. But unlike the pro-life activists (such as Marx) who had been political liberals, he saw the battle to overturn *Roe v. Wade* as an inseparable part of a larger conservative fight. The New Right activists saw pro-life activism as part a campaign to defend traditional moral values that a liberal secular state had attacked. It seemed obvious to New Right activists that even if many of the pro-lifers of the late 1970s were still liberal Democrats, they would join the New Right as soon as they realized that their campaign to protect the unborn was really a conservative cause. As the Catholic New Right fundraiser Richard Viguerie said, "The abortion issue is the door through which many people come into conservative politics, but they don't stop there. Their convictions against abortion are like the first in a series of falling dominoes. Then we lead them to a concern about sexual ethics and standards among young people. This leads to opposition to secular humanism, then particularly in the schools with a purportedly decadent morality we point out that secular humanism is identified as both the godfather and the royal road to socialism and communism—which points the way to minimally regulated free enterprise at home and to aggressive foreign and military policy to counter the Communist threat of Russia and its many surrogates."[24]

Not all pro-lifers followed this path; the Catholic bishops, for instance, remained conspicuously absent from the Reagan coalition, and they strongly protested the New Right activists' assertion that pro-life activism should lead people to favor an "aggressive foreign and military policy." But after the early 1980s, antiwar liberals were a minority in the pro-life movement, and with Reagan in the White House and the Democratic Party firmly pro-choice, they were an ineffective minority at that; only the conservative activists had the political influence to get anti-abortion legislation passed. As Weyrich told pro-lifers who remained skeptical about joining the conservative movement, they really had no choice.[25]

The New Right's approach to fighting abortion—which quickly became the Christian Right's approach—was to make the pro-life cause part of a much broader campaign to restore conservative social values. Abortion and sexual immorality were twin problems that had a single remedy, Falwell argued. The answer to both was to mobilize a large coalition of millions of "pro-family" conservatives in defense of traditional morality. "If we had not gone to sleep for the last thirty years, there could never have been a climate that would have allowed the existence of a Supreme Court that could legalize murder on demand," Falwell declared in a 1980 sermon. "There could not have been legislation to allow pornography as it exists today.... There would not be all of this homosexual explosion today. The problem is that we have been silent too long."[26]

By arguing that abortion had been legalized primarily because conservative Christians had left the public square and the nation's sexual morals had declined, Falwell and other Christian Right activists changed the pro-life movement's traditional narrative. Before the mid-1970s, pro-lifers had almost invariably argued that abortion's legalization was a product of the nation's lack of respect for the "sanctity of human life." Whether the pro-lifers were liberals like Senator Mark Hatfield or conservatives like law professor Charles Rice, they had agreed that the nation's acceptance of legal abortion stemmed from its broader disrespect for human life in all of its forms. By casting their campaign as a quest to protect the lives of a defenseless minority, pro-lifers of the 1960s and 1970s made their movement a liberal cause, so that even the conservatives in the movement grounded their arguments primarily in the language of universal human rights.[27] They believed that their most natural allies could be found in the antiwar or civil rights movements.

But by the end of the 1970s, it became apparent that a political coalition that was forged around other "life issues" was unlikely to have much effect on abortion law. The peace activists and opponents of capital punishment and nuclear arms buildup had mostly won their campaigns, at least temporarily. Skepticism about the nation's involvement in foreign wars was now widespread, and the Strategic Arms Limitation Treaty had brought a temporary hiatus to the nuclear arms race. The death penalty was almost obsolete; there were only two executions in the United States in 1979 and none in 1980. And yet, even as it seemed that Americans placed a higher value than ever on the lives of convicts, soldiers, foreign civilians, and minorities, the number of legal abortions continued to rise, reaching more than 1.5 million a year by 1980.[28] What had happened? Why, in a climate of growing concern for the value of human life, had pro-lifers failed to convince a majority of Americans of the value of fetal lives?

The Christian Right gave pro-lifers a new narrative for their movement: abortion legalization may have been the result of a widespread disrespect not for human life but for "Judeo-Christian" moral values, especially in the area of sexual ethics. Pro-lifers could win their campaign, the Christian Right activists suggested, by turning back the tide of the sexual revolution and helping conservative Christians recapture political institutions that had become too secularized or culturally liberal. While most Catholics remained wary of at least some parts of the Christian Right's agenda, the idea that there was a connection between sexual licentiousness and abortion, and that fighting abortion would require confronting a much larger sexual revolution, appealed to many theologically conservative Catholics because it accorded well with traditional Catholic teaching on the subject. The classic papal encyclicals on contraception, *Casti Connubii* (1930) and *Humanae Vitae* (1968), had linked abortion with contraception and other sexual sins, and prior to the late 1960s, Catholics who spoke out in favor of the right to life for the unborn frequently denounced contraception as a related evil. Fr. James McHugh and other right-to-life activists of the late 1960s had made a concerted effort to dissociate the pro-life movement from its traditional connection to Catholic campaigns against birth control and to frame the issue solely as a human rights cause, not as a campaign for sexual morality. But a few years after *Roe v. Wade*, many pro-lifers who had once accepted McHugh's strategy began to wonder if they had made a mistake. Evidence of an alarming sea change in sexual values could be seen almost everywhere. By the late 1970s, the national divorce rate was 50 percent, half of all Americans said that there was nothing wrong with premarital sex, and X-rated movie theaters were doing a brisk business.[29] The conservative political turn in America after 1980 did little to abate the continued liberalization of American attitudes toward sexuality; the number of cohabiting unmarried couples continued to increase, as did the out-of-wedlock pregnancy rate.

Pro-lifers found plausible statistical evidence to support their claim that the demand for abortion was partly a product of the sexual revolution, which had separated sex from marriage. Women who became pregnant out of wedlock were far more likely than married women to terminate their pregnancies. By the beginning of the twenty-first century, 83 percent of the nation's 1.3 million abortions per year were obtained by unmarried women. Even though out-of-wedlock pregnancy no longer carried the same stigma that it had in an earlier era, many women who became pregnant outside of marriage felt far less equipped than their married counterparts to deal with unintended pregnancies, especially if they were poor and had other children already (a situation that applied to more than half of all women who obtained abortions) or if they were pursuing educational or career goals that they thought would be interrupted by an ill-timed pregnancy.[30]

Pro-lifers had long been divided in their response to this correlation. In the early 1970s, many pro-lifers, both Catholic and Protestant, had tried to reduce the abortion rate among unmarried women by offering these women the resources they needed to carry their pregnancies to term and by advocating for national welfare and health insurance programs to reduce poverty, which they believed contributed to abortion. Some mainline Protestant pro-lifers, including Fred and Marjory Mecklenburg, had advocated distributing contraceptives as a way to reduce demand for abortions, an approach that had widespread support from family planning advocates outside of the pro-life movement. Advocates of family planning argued that if they could ensure access to affordable birth control for all women of childbearing age, abortion rates would decrease. But Catholics who had long viewed abortion as the product of a "contraceptive mentality" were loath to sign up for a birth control campaign. At first, they settled for silence on the issue; the NRLC refused to either endorse or condemn contraception.[31]

As evangelical Protestants began joining the pro-life movement in greater numbers, it became even more difficult for pro-life organizations such as the NRLC to take a stand against contraception, because at the time, most evangelicals—like the vast majority of mainline Protestants—saw nothing wrong with birth control. But by the end of the twentieth century, an increasing number of pro-lifers were beginning to realize that they could not talk about abortion without also talking about sex. The social conservatism of most evangelicals made them eager to link the pro-life cause with a broader conservative attack on sex outside of marriage, and the traditional sexual views of many of the Catholics who remained active members of the movement made them receptive to this shift as well. Faced with a choice between the possibility of gaining potentially modest reductions in the abortion rate by promoting contraception or attacking what they saw as the root cause of abortions, many of them chose the latter course, even though it set them at odds with prevailing cultural trends.[32]

Thus, throughout the 1980s and 1990s, Catholic pro-lifers who had once described their movement as a human rights campaign associated with the political left began repositioning their cause as a campaign for conservative sexual values, while many of the evangelicals in the move-ment followed suit by moving closer to the Catholic position on contra-ception. Juli Loesch, the left-leaning, feminist, Catholic pro-life activist who had once been associated primarily with anti-nuclear politics, dis-tanced herself from leftist political activism and began denouncing the sexual revolution in articles such as "Unmarried Couples Shouldn't Live Together." Judie Brown's organization American Life Lobby became more vocal in speaking out against "sexual permissiveness." In the early 1990s, a host of pro-life organizations, ranging from Lutherans for Life to Fr. Paul Marx's Human Life International, began issuing promotional literature attacking the "homosexual agenda." "I think it is generally agreed that the widespread acceptance of abortion is a direct fruit of the sexual revolution," one contributor to the American Life Lobby's maga-zine declared in 1989.[33]

Many pro-lifers became strong advocates of natural family planning (NFP), a method of fertility control that the Catholic Church endorsed because it did not involve the use of forbidden contraceptives. Two of the leading members of the politically leftist National Youth Pro-Life Coalition—Save Our Unwanted Life (SOUL) cofounder Sue Bastyr and the physician Thomas Hilgers—married each other and then devoted much of their professional careers to promoting NFP. Fr. Marx, another former peace activist, also made NFP one of his primary causes during the last few decades of his life because, he said, "Once you have contraception, legal abortion often follows eventually." Protestants had once been skeptical about this argument, but by the beginning of the twenty-first century, a few evangelicals in the movement began echoing these statements. Some evangelicals who did not maintain an absolutist opposition to all contraceptives nevertheless joined with Catholics to oppose abortifacients, a category that, in their view, included some of the most popular forms of birth control, such as the pill and the intrauterine device (IUD). Evangelical pro-lifers were especially vocal in speaking out against sexual promiscuity, and some conservative Catholics joined them in this effort. On college campuses, students who joined pro-life organizations often signed up for newly created chastity organizations as well, since, in their minds, there was a close correlation between sexual abstinence before marriage, saving unborn lives, and—in most cases—conservative religious faith.[34]

## *The Dilemmas of Making the Pro-Life Campaign a Culturally Conservative Cause*

In the late twentieth and early twenty-first centuries, many pro-lifers thus returned to the sexually conservative message of the Catholic doctors and clerics who had spoken out against abortion in the 1930s and 1940s—a message that pro-lifers had largely abandoned in favor of human rights talk during the late 1960s and early 1970s, but that seemed strangely relevant once again. Yet it was doubtful that this return to an anti-contraceptive, sexually conservative message made the movement more politically successful. In the New Deal era, when several states still had laws prohibiting the sale of contraceptives and when homosexuality was still treated as a mental illness or a crime, the sexual conservatism of abortion opponents had not necessarily been a political liability. But after the sexual revolution of the late twentieth century, it was. In a nation in which more than 90 percent of unmarried people would have sex outside of marriage at some point in their lives, and in which more than 99 percent of sexually active women of childbearing age used contraceptives, opposing either seemed to be a losing proposition.[35] Could a pro-life movement that linked itself to the cause of chastity succeed in winning the support of a majority of the population? On the other hand, if pro-lifers refused to confront the sexual revolution directly, could they succeed in changing the public's attitude on abortion? Could they really expect to eliminate abortion and protect unborn lives as long as tens of millions of unmarried American adults were having sex with every intention of avoiding pregnancy even if their contraceptives failed?

Pro-lifers faced a difficult choice: they could either address the root causes of abortion by fighting against the sexual revolution, placing themselves well outside the cultural mainstream, or they could attempt to create a larger, more viable political coalition by framing their campaign for the unborn solely as a human rights cause. In actuality, pro-lifers never abandoned either approach, because in their view, the fight against abortion remained both a campaign for human rights *and* a battle against the sexual revolution. As a result, it remained an uneasy fit for both political parties. Because the sexual revolution was deeply entrenched in American culture, the fight against a "contraceptive mentality" was not a battle that could be won through politics. Yet until pro-lifers changed Americans' attitude toward sexual behavior, there was little chance that they could pass a constitutional amendment protecting the unborn.

A similar dilemma confronted the movement on questions of gender and women's rights, an area where pro-lifers again tried to position themselves as progressives even while retaining a traditionalist mindset. Pro-lifers of the early 1970s thought that they were advancing women's health and well-being by advocating government programs to assist women facing crisis pregnancies and by forming organizations to help women receive the healthcare and material assistance they needed. Pro-lifers expanded their programs to help unmarried, impoverished mothers in the 1980s. They continued to treat women who obtained abortions as victims rather than perpetrators, as evidenced by the creation of new organizations such as Rachel's Vineyard, founded by Catholic psychologist Theresa Burke in 1986 to help women who had had abortions find emotional healing. Many such women joined the pro-life cause, and the pro-life movement made a few high-profile converts among early advocates of the right to choose. In the late twentieth century, both the "Jane Roe" (Norma McCorvey) of *Roe v. Wade* and the "Mary Doe" (Sandra Cano) of *Doe v. Bolton* became pro-life activists. Organizations such as Feminists for Life continued to frame the pro-life cause as a women's rights campaign and claimed the mantle of late nineteenth-century feminists such as Susan B. Anthony, who, they believed, had opposed abortion.[36]

Yet pro-lifers' claims put them squarely at odds with the mainstream feminist movement, which argued that women could not achieve true liberation and equality without gaining the right to control their own bodies. The conflict between these views stemmed partly from a difference of opinion over the nature of unplanned pregnancy. Many pro-choice feminists viewed unwanted pregnancy as an obstacle to a woman's ability to pursue her own dreams. Even worse, an unwanted pregnancy was an unsolicited intrusion on a woman's body, and since many pro-choicers equated human freedom with bodily autonomy and free choice, some argued that pro-lifers' attempt to force women to carry their unwanted pregnancies to term was an assault on women that was akin to rape. "Rape denies us bodily integrity; so does restricting abortion," sociologist Wendy Simonds wrote.[37]

Many pro-lifers, by contrast, viewed unplanned pregnancies as unexpected gifts. Thus, when Arizona Right to Life president Margot Sheahan's teenage daughter became pregnant out of wedlock in the late 1970s, she viewed the unintended pregnancy as a blessing, even though she disapproved of sex outside of marriage and encouraged premarital chastity. Her response was not to encourage her daughter to abort, but instead to form the organization Unwed Parents Anonymous to assist others in dealing with both the stigma and the challenges of such potentially disruptive pregnancies. In the late twentieth century, several rape victims who had become pregnant as a result of sexual assaults became advocates for the pro-life cause, claiming that having an abortion would have only compounded the emotional trauma they faced, and that the children whom they had conceived in such tragic circumstances gave them joy in the midst of the pain they were experiencing. In the twenty-first century, one pro-life attorney who had been conceived in rape—Rebecca Kiesling—became a sought-after speaker at pro-life events, where she used her personal story to argue that no matter how evil the circumstances of a conception might be, each newly created human life had value and should never be aborted. For pro-lifers, no pregnancy—even one that was the result of a sexual assault—was ever a curse.[38]

Because they viewed pregnancy and motherhood in radically different terms than pro-choice feminists did, pro-lifers did not see the conflict between their own pro-life campaign and gender egalitarianism. Instead, they thought that women's rights would be respected only when their roles as life-givers and mothers were fully honored. Just as pro-choicers such as Simonds viewed restrictions on abortion as an assault on women's "bodily integrity," so many pro-life women who viewed motherhood as a biological gift argued that abortion was an attack on women's bodies and their own identities as women. "As a woman, a capacity to become pregnant is part of who I am," Jennifer Bryson, a member of the Witherspoon Institute, a conservative think tank in Princeton, New Jersey, wrote in 2014. "Abortion is an act of violence against a woman's body. A woman's body is by design capable of pregnancy; only a physical invasion of force, whether material or chemical, can interrupt an existing pregnancy in a woman."[39]

Would women's rights be advanced if women pursued personal autonomy and the right to choose, while viewing unwanted pregnancies as misfortunes to be avoided at all costs, or would they instead be advanced if women embraced their biological capacity to become mothers as a gift that could not be separated from their identity as women? The debate about abortion was a conflict over gender, even though most pro-lifers of the late 1960s and early 1970s had been slow to recognize this fact. It was not a conflict of men against women, as some pro-choicers believed; instead, it was a debate between two different groups of women. Although the debate over abortion had begun in the early twentieth century as a conversation among male doctors and lawyers, it became in the early 1970s a women's debate, with women comprising the majority of both pro-life and pro-choice activists.[40] Both groups of women believed that their own positions advanced women's well-being, but because of their sharply contrasting views on pregnancy, the two sides had radically different notions of what liberation for women entailed.

Pro-lifers' decision in the late 1960s to sidestep these larger issues and focus on the claim of fetal rights ultimately proved insufficient to resolve this larger clash of values. The debate was not just about what constitutes a human person or the point at which human life begins, but about sexuality, pregnancy, personal autonomy, and gender roles. In the 1930s, the conflict between Catholic and secular physicians over abortion had pitted a defense of fetal rights against the claim that women's lives would be saved if abortion were legalized. A similar conflict of rights confronted the pro-life movement in the early twenty-first century, as defenders of fetal rights clashed with those who grounded their arguments for abortion rights in appeals to the rights of personal privacy, bodily autonomy, gender equality, and sexual freedom. Without confronting the larger cultural shifts that had led to the separation of sex from marriage and procreation, and the concomitant belief that unplanned pregnancies were an obstacle to women's liberation, the pro-life movement was unable to forge a consensus in support of the full protection of human life from the moment of conception. The best pro-lifers could do was to increase Americans' discomfort with abortion and make the procedure a little more difficult to obtain.

## Large Setbacks and Incremental Gains

When pro-lifers realized in the late 1980s that they would not receive the Human Life Amendment that they had expected the Reagan administration to give them, some became angry and decided to embrace a strategy of direct action. "The pro-life movement is limping," John Cavanaugh-O'Keefe, an advocate of nonviolent sit-ins at abortion clinics, wrote in 1984. "Legislation may shape the future, but children are dying now."[41]

Cavanaugh-O'Keefe was not alone in either his frustration or his proposed solution. In the late 1980s, many pro-life activists followed his lead in turning to a form of nonviolent civil disobedience that was consciously styled on the techniques of the civil rights movement. If the pro-life movement was a "civil rights movement for the unborn," many younger pro-lifers thought, why should they not use the direct action techniques of their civil rights forebears? At the very least, they thought that even if blocking the door to an abortion clinic did not lead to the reversal of *Roe v. Wade*, it "prevented a child from being killed." Between 1987 and the early 1990s, Randall Terry's Operation Rescue convinced tens of thousands of evangelical and Catholic pro-lifers to break the law by blocking abortion clinic entrances in mass acts of nonviolent civil disobedience that would often lead to jail time. Forty thousand Operation Rescue volunteers had been arrested by 1991.[42]

For a handful of radical activists, nonviolent civil disobedience gave way to violence, which the NRLC strongly condemned. Jack Willke tried to keep his associates in the NRLC from participating in any lawbreaking, even if it was nonviolent, and he strongly opposed all violence against property or people, even if pro-lifers argued that it was necessary to save the unborn. He pleaded with the lawbreakers and arsonists in the movement to change their tactics. But these protestations meant nothing to a small contingent of anti-abortion radicals who appealed to the Christian theologian Dietrich Bonhoeffer's (unsuccessful) attempt to assassinate Adolf Hitler as a model for their own actions. If abortion killed human beings, and if it really was a "holocaust," as opponents of abortion had been saying for decades, violence that saved unborn lives and prevented

God's judgment on a disobedient nation was justified, the small, radical organization Army of God argued. Inspired by such rhetoric, protestors firebombed or otherwise damaged more than two hundred abortion clinics in the late twentieth century, and during the 1990s, they murdered seven abortion providers and associated clinic personnel, with another abortion doctor killed in 2009. Most of the assassins bore little resemblance to the faithful Catholics who had launched the pro-life movement in the mid-twentieth century. Although at least one (James Kopp) was a zealous adherent of the Catholic faith who was deeply disturbed by abortion, most of the others were subscribers to a radical Protestant theology that was influenced by Old Testament stories of prophetic violence. One of the murderers was an ultraconservative Presbyterian minister who advocated the imposition of Old Testament law on the United States and who was defrocked by his denomination for his violent pronouncements. A few of the others were schizophrenic. Most were firm believers in the Army of God's frequently repeated biblical exhortation, "Whoso sheddeth man's blood, by man shall his blood be shed." Yet even if these practitioners of violence were hardly representative of the hundreds of thousands of members of the NRLC or the millions of other Americans who opposed abortion, they nevertheless tarnished the image of the pro-life movement—with 61 percent of Americans in 1995 believing that the pro-life movement encouraged violence.[43]

Pro-choicers charged that the pro-life movement's apocalyptic rhetoric had instigated the killings, even if most pro-lifers professed an abhorrence of violence. After pro-lifers had spent half a century saying that legalized abortion was analogous to Hitler's genocidal destruction of Jews and that it was the murder of unborn children, was it any wonder, pro-choicers asked, when a few people in the movement decided to pick up a gun or a homemade firebomb to stop what they believed was child-killing?[44] Yet many pro-lifers, including the leaders of the NRLC and the Catholic and Protestant activists who had joined the movement in the 1960s and early 1970s, saw the matter differently. In their view, the violence was a repudiation of the pro-life movement's historic defense of all human life. The violence of abortion could never be stopped by anti-abortion violence, they thought. In the end, the peaceful tactics of the NRLC, the nation's largest pro-life organization, eventually came to characterize the movement once again, and more militant anti-abortion organizations shrank or faded away entirely—especially after legislation and court decisions offered greater protection to abortion clinics, making it difficult for some of the more militant pro-life organizations to engage in the type of disruptive protests that had been common in the late 1980s and early 1990s.[45]

After the violence lessened and the sit-ins ceased, the debate over abortion moved out of the streets and back into the halls of Congress and state legislatures, where pro-lifers began to win incremental victories, largely because their alliances with conservative Republicans finally started to pay dividends. Their most spectacular success was the passage of the Partial Birth Abortion Ban Act in 2003, which was the first time that the federal government had prohibited any abortion procedure. When the Supreme Court upheld that law as constitutional in *Gonzales v. Carhart* (2007), pro-lifers realized that the nation's high court might allow them to make further inroads against *Roe*. In the 1970s and 1980s, many state legislatures had passed parental notification laws and restrictions on abortion funding, both of which the Supreme Court upheld as constitutional, but when state legislatures had attempted to go further, as Louisiana had in 1991 by passing a ban on most forms of abortion, the courts had stopped them. The Supreme Court's willingness to uphold a ban on a specific type of late-term abortion in 2007 emboldened state legislatures to impose new limits on abortion. In the second decade of the twenty-first century, several states instituted a new round of abortion restrictions, including mandatory ultrasounds and waiting periods, new safety guidelines for clinics, and a reduction in the upper gestational age limit for second-trimester abortions from twenty-four weeks to twenty. As a result, the number of abortion clinics in the United States continued to decline, as did the total number of abortions. By 2011, the total number of abortions in the United States was at its lowest level since 1975. One in five pregnancies still ended in abortion, but as new abortion regulations caused the number of abortion clinics to continue to decrease sharply—with more than fifty closing in 2013 alone—abortion was much more difficult to obtain than it once had been, and it seemed that the pro-lifers' strategy of incremental legislative changes was working. Despite their failure to overturn *Roe* through a Supreme Court decision or a constitutional amendment, pro-lifers had done the next best thing: they had turned the country back to a situation that was remarkably similar to the one that had existed immediately before *Roe v. Wade*. By the time of *Roe*'s fortieth anniversary, nearly one-third of the nation's legal abortions occurred in either California or New York, with abortion services much more limited (and state funding for abortions nearly nonexistent) in some of the more socially conservative areas of the country.[46]

But turning the clock back to the early 1970s was never the pro-life movement's goal; its real aim was to enshrine respect for unborn human life in the nation's legal code. On that score, the movement did not fare nearly as well. At the same time that the movement was succeeding in instituting new legal restrictions on abortion in many midwestern and southern states, it failed to stop embryonic stem cell research or the abortion-inducing drug RU-486, which the Food and Drug Administration approved in 2000 for use in the United States. In vitro fertilization (IVF), a process that pro-lifers of the late 1970s had opposed because it often involved the destruction of embryonic human life, proved so popular even among conservative Christian couples that the pro-life movement largely gave up trying to fight it. Pro-lifers found that Americans' strong discomfort with late-term abortion—a discomfort that pro-lifers had done much to stimulate by distributing photographs of second- and third-trimester fetuses—did not necessarily lead them to value human life during its first few days or weeks of existence. This meant that pro-lifers' ultimate goal—constitutional protection of fetuses from the moment of conception—remained just as elusive as it had in the 1970s. When voters in Mississippi, one of America's most strongly anti-abortion states, considered a state referendum in 2011 to protect unborn human life from the moment of conception, they rejected the measure because of their fear that the amendment would restrict popular fertility treatments and ban some forms of birth control, such as IUDs.[47] Even for some of the most staunchly pro-life voters in conservative states in the Deep South and Midwest, it was one thing to ban abortion, but another to allow concern for newly fertilized eggs to prevent medical research, restrict IVF, and prohibit some of the most popular forms of contraception. When faced with the choice to protect all human life from the point of conception or maintain the legal availability of their favorite contraceptives and fertility treatments, some socially conservative voters realized that they were not quite as consistently pro-life as they claimed to be.

Pro-lifers thus greeted Roe's fortieth anniversary with a mix of hope and frustration, because the incremental gains they had won from their alliance with the Republicans had fallen far short of what they had anticipated in 1980. In spite of the restrictions on abortion that the movement was able to secure, some pro-lifers who still sympathized with the political left wondered whether it would have been better for their movement to focus on reducing the abortion rate—which, they argued, Democratic anti-poverty and healthcare policies would likely do—rather than focusing solely on prohibiting abortion by law. Women who obtained abortions were disproportionately poor and nonwhite; more than 40 percent were below the poverty line. The number-one way to reduce the abortion rate, Richard Doerflinger, the deputy director of the USCCB's Secretariat for Pro-Life Activities, declared in February 2013, was to "fight poverty."[48]

While this political prescription sounded like a call to work with liberal Democrats again, it was not. Doerflinger went on to say that any program designed to fight abortion would have to also "end publicly funded abortions," encourage sexual abstinence among teens, and "uphold strong marriages."[49] Such an approach to social welfare relied on a set of assumptions about gender and sexuality that American liberals abandoned at the end of the 1960s and that seemed strikingly anachronistic to most Democrats in the early twenty-first century.

The pro-life movement was thus left to continue soldiering on in the Republican Party—a party that gave scant attention to poverty reduction, social welfare provisions, or the other causes that had interested pro-life leaders of an earlier generation, but which at least endorsed their goal of overturning *Roe v. Wade* and protecting human life in constitutional law from the moment of conception. Republicans had given little support to the pro-life cause before *Roe*. In many ways, it was *Roe* itself that had produced this uneasy alliance and prompted both sides to enter into a marriage of convenience that at times was fraught with tension. During the forty years after *Roe*, several Republican presidential candidates had attempted to distance themselves from the pro-life movement, only to be forced to renew their support for the cause. Pro-lifers, in turn, had sometimes registered their anger at Republicans, but had always returned to the fold when they realized how little the Democrats would offer them.[50] And over time, a strange thing happened. As the other moral regulatory causes that the Christian Right championed—causes such as school prayer or opposition to pornography or gay rights—eventually lost public support and, in a few cases, faded away entirely, the pro-life cause remained the one moral issue that was capable of attracting a younger generation to the Republican Party. It did so because unlike any of the other campaigns for moral regulation, it was a human rights cause that the millennial generation, which had grown up in an era of rights consciousness, could easily understand and claim as its own. The pro-lifers' alliance with the GOP and the Christian Right had never been able to obscure the fact that the movement was, at its heart, a human rights campaign for the unborn, which meant that it could still appeal to those who were reluctant to embrace some of the other tenets of conservatism. Indeed, although the movement's roots in the language of liberal rights-consciousness had made it an awkward fit for the Republican Party in the late twentieth century, it may, in the end, have been the movement's saving grace, allowing it to live on for another generation.

The thousands of young demonstrators waving signs at the March for Life that said "I Am the Pro-Life Generation" were probably not sufficient to reverse the larger cultural shifts that had led to abortion legalization. But they were a sign that the movement was not going to lose its fervor anytime soon. They were a sign that the future political prospects for the movement might be better than some had once expected. They might have even been an indication that *Roe v. Wade* would not last forever. Whether they were a harbinger that abortion legalization itself was in jeopardy or that the nation would make a commitment to protecting fetal life was not so clear. But at the very least, the pro-life movement remains a major political and cultural force in American life, and the value of unborn human life that concerned physicians championed in the 1930s has found a new generation of defenders.

# *Notes*

### A NOTE ON TERMINOLOGY

1. *The Associated Press Stylebook*, 39th ed. (New York: Basic Books, 2004), emphasis in original.

2. Even some opponents of abortion have made the claim that people who oppose gun control or support capital punishment and nuclear arms buildup are not consistently "pro-life." See, e.g., Ronald J. Sider, *Completely Pro-Life: Building a Consistent Stance* (Downers Grove, IL: InterVarsity Press, 1987), 11–13.

3. For more on the origins of rights-based language in the campaign for abortion legalization, see Mary Ziegler, "The Framing of a Right to Choose: *Roe v. Wade* and the Changing Debate on Abortion Law," *Law and History Review* 27 (2009): 281–330.

### INTRODUCTION

1. For an explanation of this book's use of the term "pro-life," see "A Note on Terminology."

2. Robert D. McFadden, "Lobbying on Abortion Increases at Capitol," *New York Times*, May 8, 1972; "Thousands Here Urge Repeal of Abortion Statute," *New York Times*, April 17, 1972.

3. The Lutheran minister was Richard John Neuhaus, who converted to Catholicism years later.

4. These sixteen states were Colorado (1967), California (1967), North Carolina (1967), Georgia (1968), Maryland (1968), Kansas (1969), Delaware (1969), Arkansas (1969), New Mexico (1969), Oregon (1969), South Carolina (1970), Virginia (1970), Hawaii (1970), New York (1970), Alaska (1970), and Washington (1970); Mary C. Segers and Timothy A. Byrnes, "Introduction: Abortion Politics in American States," in *Abortion Politics in American States*, ed. Segers and

Byrnes (New York: M. E. Sharpe, 1995), 3; Kristin Luker, *Abortion and the Politics of Motherhood* (Berkeley: University of California Press, 1984), 272.

5. Michael Taylor, direct mail on behalf of National Right to Life Committee (NRLC), February 12, 1971, folder: "National Right to Life Committee, 1970–1972," box 5, North Dakota Right to Life Association Records (NDRLA), State Historical Society of North Dakota, Bismarck; Michael Taylor, direct mail on behalf of NRLC, May 7, 1971, folder: "Legislation, Various States', 1964–1971," box 4, NDRLA; William E. Farrell, "Governor Vetoes Abortion Repeal as Not Justified," *New York Times*, May 14, 1972.

6. Two exceptions to the trend of largely ignoring the abortion issue in histories of postwar conservatism are Robert O. Self's *All in the Family: The Realignment of American Democracy since the 1960s* (New York: Hill and Wang, 2012); and David T. Courtwright's *No Right Turn: Conservative Politics in a Liberal America* (Cambridge, MA: Harvard University Press, 2010). Courtwright's book, like most analyses of the issue, discusses abortion politics mainly in the context of *Roe* and post-*Roe* Supreme Court decisions. Self's monograph includes more detail about the pre-*Roe* history of the pro-life movement, but examines the subject only in the context of the political and cultural debate over women's rights and gender equality. For other historical studies that see the pro-life movement as a product of gender politics, see Luker, *Abortion and the Politics of Motherhood*; and Rickie Solinger, *Pregnancy and Power: A Short History of Reproductive Politics in America* (New York: New York University Press, 2005). For a study that views the pro-life movement as a right-wing religious movement, see Dallas A. Blanchard, *The Anti-Abortion Movement and the Rise of the Religious Right: From Polite to Fiery Protest* (New York: Twayne, 1994). For the theory that the pro-life movement emerged as a backlash against *Roe v. Wade*, see Kerry N. Jacoby, *Souls, Bodies, Spirits: The Drive to Abolish Abortion since 1973* (Westport, CT: Praeger, 1998). For a thoughtful critique of this view, see Linda Greenhouse and Reva B. Siegel, "Before (and after) *Roe v. Wade*: New Questions about Backlash," *Yale Law Journal* 120 (2011): 2028–2087. For an informative, detailed history of the debate over abortion from the 1960s through the 1990s, see David J. Garrow, *Liberty and Sexuality: The Right to Privacy and the Making of Roe v. Wade*, 2nd ed. (Berkeley: University of California Press, 1998). Few other historians have traced the history of the pro-life movement, although many have written about abortion. Histories of the abortion rights movement and *Roe v. Wade* include Garrow, *Liberty and Sexuality*; and N. E. H. Hull and Peter Charles Hoffer, Roe v. Wade: *The Abortion Rights Controversy in American History*, 2nd ed. (Lawrence: University of Kansas Press, 2010). For examples of journalistic and sociological studies of the pro-life movement in recent years, see James Risen and Judy L. Thomas, *Wrath of Angels: The American Abortion War* (New York: Basic Books, 1998); and Ziad Munson, *The Making of Pro-Life Activists: How Social Movement Mobilization Works* (Chicago: University of

Chicago Press, 2008). For a history of American attitudes toward fetal life and abortion, see Sara Dubow, *Ourselves Unborn: A History of the Fetus in Modern America* (New York: Oxford University Press, 2011).

7. Rickie Solinger, *Reproductive Politics: What Everyone Needs to Know* (New York: Oxford University Press, 2013), 15.

8. Linda Gordon, *The Moral Property of Women: A History of Birth Control Politics in America*, 4th ed. (Urbana: University of Illinois Press, 2002), 300.

9. I am not the only historian to question the prevailing historical consensus that the pro-life movement emerged as a conservative backlash against women's rights. Mary Ziegler's *After* Roe: *The Lost History of the Abortion Debate* (Cambridge, MA: Harvard University Press, 2015) shares this skepticism. With several other academic studies of pro-life activism during the 1970s and 1980s scheduled to be released within the next few years, we may be on the verge of seeing a much broader challenge to this long-held misunderstanding of the pro-life movement's ideological origins. Yet as of now, histories of late twentieth-century American politics continue to portray the pro-life movement as a conservative, anti-feminist movement. Self's *All in the Family* is a leading example of a recent historical portrayal of the pro-life movement as a product of conservative backlash.

10. "Catholics to Fight Birth Control Aid," *New York Times*, June 10, 1937; Walter R. Trinkaus, "Legal Objections to Pending Bill Authorizing Abortions, A.B. No. 2310," presented on behalf of California Conference of Catholic Hospitals, July 20, 1964, folder 14, box 513, Anthony C. Beilenson Papers, University of California, Los Angeles.

11. "Two 'U' Students Push 'Liberal' Drive against Abortion," *Minneapolis Star*, October 2, 1971; Rosetta Ferguson, Voice of the Unborn, "Is Abortion Black Genocide?" (1972); and "Have You Considered?" Voice of the Unborn flyer (1972), folder 3, box 1, Lifespan, Inc., Records, Bentley Historical Library, Ann Arbor, MI. For a discussion of why rights-based language appealed to both liberals and conservatives in the United States after the 1960s, see Daniel T. Rodgers, *Age of Fracture* (Cambridge, MA: Harvard University Press, 2011).

12. James R. Sikes, "Kennedy Predicts Abortion Reform," *New York Times*, February 18, 1967; Homer Bigart, "Kennedy Defends View on Abortion," *New York Times*, February 23, 1967; Segers and Byrnes, "Introduction: Abortion Politics in American States," 3; "Legal Abortion: Who, Why, and Where," *Time*, September 27, 1971.

13. Lee Gidding to George W. Kellogg, May 18, 1972, folder: "CA, 1972," carton 2, MC 313, NARAL Records, 1968–1976, Schlesinger Library, Harvard University; Michael Taylor, direct mail on behalf of the National Right to Life Committee, "New York State Repeal Drive," May 19, 1972, folder: "Abortion in New York (1 of 3)," box 23, Rev. Paul V. Harrington Papers, Archives of the Archdiocese of Boston.

14. For an early articulation of the pro-choice movement's defense of "choice," see Robert DiVeroli, "Abortion Stand: A Freedom Plea," *San Diego Evening Tribune*, April 16, 1975.

15. Mary Winter, "Abortion—The Abandonment of Women and Children," testimony given to the Shapps Abortion Commission Hearings, Pennsylvania, 1972, single folder in Mary Winter Papers, Schlesinger Library, Harvard University.

16. For a detailed study of American Catholics' views of the meaning of freedom, as well as their longstanding belief in government policies to aid families, see McGreevy, *Catholicism and American Freedom*.

17. Stuart Auerbach, "Kennedy Backs Abortion Aid," *Washington Post*, April 11, 1975; Democratic Party Platform of 1976, http://www.presidency.ucsb.edu/ws/?pid=29606; Robert E. Burns, "Dr. Jefferson and the Politicians," *Wanderer*, December 4, 1975; James M. Perry, "Shriver Falls Victim to His Own Church," *National Observer* (Washington, DC), January 31, 1976; Dexter Duggan, "Still Waiting for Shriver," *National Right to Life News*, December 1975, 8.

CHAPTER 1

1. "Physicians Split on Birth Control," *New York Times*, June 11, 1937.

2. James C. Mohr, *Abortion in America: The Origins and Evolution of National Policy, 1800–1900* (New York: Oxford University Press, 1978), esp. 147–170; Sara Dubow, *Ourselves Unborn: A History of the Fetus in Modern America* (New York: Oxford University Press, 2011), 13–20; Simone M. Caron, *Who Chooses? American Reproductive History since 1930* (Gainesville: University Press of Florida, 2008), 26–28. Mohr's study emphasizes the role that physicians' interest in bolstering the credibility of their own profession played in their campaign against abortion, while also citing other factors such as the physicians' interest in improving the birthrate among native-born Protestants, discouraging illicit sex, preserving traditional gender roles, and protecting the life of the fetus. Other studies emphasize additional factors such as the physicians' interest in marginalizing midwives, who commonly performed abortions (Leslie J. Reagan, *When Abortion Was a Crime: Women, Medicine, and Law in the United States, 1867–1973* (Berkeley: University of California Press, 1997), 90–91). While all of these concerns may have been factors in the physicians' campaign, their own statements about their motivations continually emphasized their interest in saving fetal life. For an examination of nineteenth-century physicians' concerns about fetal life, see Frederick N. Dyer, *The Physicians' Crusade against Abortion*, 2nd ed. (Sagamore Beach, MA: Science History Publications, 2005).

3. Reagan, *When Abortion was a Crime*, 84–85; Frederick J. Taussig, *The Prevention and Treatment of Abortion* (St. Louis, MO: C. V. Mosby, 1910), 79.

4. John T. Noonan Jr., "An Almost Absolute Value in History," in *The Morality of Abortion: Legal and Historical Perspectives*, ed. John T. Noonan Jr. (Cambridge,

MA: Harvard University Press, 1970), 7–46; John Connery, *Abortion: The Development of the Roman Catholic Perspective* (Chicago: Loyola University Press, 1977), 304–307; David Albert Jones, *The Soul of the Embryo: An Enquiry into the Status of the Human Embryo in the Christian Tradition* (London: Continuum, 2004); Timothy A. Byrnes and Mary C. Segers, eds., *The Catholic Church and the Politics of Abortion: The View from the States* (Boulder, CO: Westview Press, 1992), 2–3; Hector Treub et al., *The Right to Life of the Unborn Child: A Controversy* (New York: Joseph F. Wagner, 1903).

5. For this self-defense argument from Protestants, see Frank J. Curran, "Religious Implications," in *Abortion in America: Medical, Psychiatric, Legal, Anthropological, and Religious Considerations*, ed. Harold Rosen, 2nd ed. (Boston: Beacon Press, 1967), 156. For an early twentieth-century debate on whether abortion was permissible in cases when it would save a woman's life, see Treub et al., *The Right to Life of the Unborn Child*.

6. Reagan, *When Abortion Was a Crime*, 113–117. For an example of press coverage of abortion in the early twentieth century, see "Illegal Abortion Case Is Continued," *Washington Post*, February 9, 1929.

7. Dyer, *The Physicians' Campaign against Abortion*, 121–130; Allan Carlson, *Godly Seed: American Evangelicals Confront Birth Control, 1873–1973* (New Brunswick, NJ: Transaction, 2012), 24–25, 124.

8. Carlson, *Godly Seed*, 21–35, 87.

9. Lambeth Conference, Resolution 15, "The Life and Witness of the Christian Community—Marriage and Sex" (1930), http://www.lambethconference.org/resolutions/1930/1930-15.cfm; Caron, *Who Chooses?*, 89; Tom Davis, *Sacred Work: Planned Parenthood and Its Clergy Alliances* (New Brunswick, NJ: Rutgers University Press, 2005), 42–43; Kerry N. Jacoby, *Souls, Bodies, Spirits: The Drive to Abolish Abortion since 1973* (Westport, CT: Praeger, 1998), 39.

10. Caron, *Who Chooses?*, 122; Gerald Kelly, "Catholic Teaching on Contraception and Sterilization," *Linacre Quarterly* 21 (August 1954): 72.

11. Johanna Schoen, *Choice and Coercion: Birth Control, Sterilization, and Abortion in Public Health and Welfare* (Chapel Hill: University of North Carolina Press, 2005); Dorothy Roberts, *Killing the Black Body: Race, Reproduction, and the Meaning of Liberty* (New York: Vintage Books, 1997); Margaret Sanger, "Sterilization (A Modern Medical Program for Health and Human Welfare)," June 5, 1951, https://www.nyu.edu/projects/sanger/webedition/app/documents/show.php?sangerDoc=239501.xml; Lutz Kaelber, "Eugenics: Compulsory Sterilization in 50 American States," http://www.uvm.edu/~lkaelber/eugenics/.

12. "Cheapening Human Life," *America*, January 5, 1924, 283.

13. Leslie Woodcock Tentler, *Catholics and Contraception: An American History* (Ithaca, NY: Cornell University Press, 2004), 133–134. Although the Catholic Church permitted couples to attempt to prevent conception by engaging in periodic abstinence from sexual intercourse during a woman's peak fertility period

(a birth control method known as "natural family planning" or the "rhythm method"), church doctrine prohibited the use of contraceptives (which some Catholics called "artificial birth control"). Following common contemporary usage, I often use the term "birth control" in this book as a synonym for contraceptives, even though some opponents of contraception have insisted that they oppose only "artificial" birth control, not "natural" forms of birth control such as "natural family planning." In saying that the Catholic Church opposed birth control in the twentieth century, I mean that the church opposed all forms of contraceptives and sterilization—not that it invariably prohibited all methods of limiting fertility.

14. Tentler, *Catholics and Contraception*, 170.

15. For a history of Catholic natural law philosophy, see Alasdair MacIntyre, *God, Philosophy, Universities: A Selective History of the Catholic Philosophical Tradition* (Lanham, MD: Rowman and Littlefield, 2009). For the Protestant theologian Reinhold Niebuhr's objections to natural law theology, see Robin W. Lovin, *Reinhold Niebuhr and Christian Realism* (New York: Cambridge University Press, 1995), 108.

16. "Cheapening Human Life," 283; Edward J. Heffron, LTE, *New York Times*, February 27, 1942.

17. Margaret Sanger, "Birth Control or Abortion?" *Birth Control Review* (December 1918): 3–4, http://www.nyu.edu/projects/sanger/webedition/app/documents/show.php?sangerDoc = 232534.xml; Wilfrid Parsons, "A Crisis in Birth Control," *America*, May 4, 1935, 80.

18. Pius XI, *Casti Connubii* (1930), http://w2.vatican.va/content/pius-xi/en/encyclicals/documents/hf_p-xi_enc_31121930_casti-connubii.html, sect. 63–64.

19. Lambeth Conference, Resolution 16, "The Life and Witness of the Christian Community—Marriage and Sex" (1930), http://www.lambethconference.org/resolutions/1930/1930-16.cfm; Sanger, "Birth Control or Abortion?," 3–4.

20. For evidence of the lack of a consistent Protestant theological position on abortion in the early 1950s, see Curran, "Religious Implications," 153–161.

21. Tentler, *Catholics and Contraception*, 67–68, 86, 100, 189–190.

22. Catholic Medical Association, "History," http://cathmed.org/about/history/; "The Federation of Catholic Physicians' Guilds," *Linacre Quarterly* 21 (February 1954): 21; "In the Memory of Man," *Linacre Quarterly* 24 (May 1957): 39–42; Ignatius Cox, "Looking Forward," *Linacre Quarterly* 24 (May 1957): 44.

23. "Plan World Fight on Birth Control," *New York Times*, May 25, 1931; Gerald Kelly, "Doctors Ask These Questions," *Linacre Quarterly* 22 (November 1955): 138.

24. "Catholics to Fight Birth Control Aid," *New York Times*, June 10, 1937.

25. John T. McGreevy, *Catholicism and American Freedom: A History* (New York: W. W. Norton, 2003), 150–154.

26. Schoen, *Choice and Coercion*, 25–74; McGreevy, *Catholicism and American Freedom*, 142–144, 151–153; Tentler, *Catholics and Contraception*, 40–42.

27. Frederick J. Taussig, *Abortion: Spontaneous and Induced, Medical and Social Aspects* (St. Louis, MO: C. V. Mosby, 1936), 26; Reagan, *When Abortion Was a Crime*, 134–135, 305, n. 13.

28. Taussig, *Abortion*, 401.

29. "Dr. W. J. Robinson, Urologist, Is Dead," *New York Times*, January 7, 1936; William J. Robinson, *If I Were God: A Freethinker's Faith* (New York: Free Thought Association, 1930); William J. Robinson et al., *Sex Morality: Past, Present and Future* (New York: Critic and Guide, 1912), 17–39; William J. Robinson, *Sex, Love and Morality* (New York: Eugenics Publishing Co., 1928), 131–135; William J. Robinson, *The Law against Abortion: Its Perniciousness Demonstrated and Its Repeal Demanded* (New York: Eugenics Publishing Co., 1933). For more information on Robinson's campaign for birth control, see Linda Gordon, *The Moral Property of Women: A History of Birth Control Politics in America*, 3rd ed. (Urbana: University of Illinois Press, 2002), 115–117; Reagan, *When Abortion Was a Crime*, 139.

30. Robinson, *Sex, Love and Morality*, 45, 116–117; Robinson, *The Law against Abortion*, 13, 23, 37–38, 45, 68–69, 117.

31. Robinson, *Sex, Love and Morality*, 11, 13–16, 52; Robinson, *The Law against Abortion*, 23.

32. For one of the many contemporary examples of the continued saliency of this argument for the pro-choice movement, see NARAL Pro-Choice America, "The Safety of Legal Abortion and the Hazards of Illegal Abortion," http://www.prochoiceamerica.org/media/fact-sheets/abortion-distorting-science-safety-legal-abortion.pdf.

33. A. J. Rongy, *Abortion: Legal or Illegal?* (New York: Vanguard Press, 1933); Reagan, *When Abortion Was a Crime*, 132–134; "Huge Profit Laid to Abortion Ring," *New York Times*, October 16, 1941.

34. Rongy, *Abortion*, 85–98.

35. "Dr. W. J. Robinson, Urologist, Is Dead"; "Funeral Services Today for Dr. A. J. Rongy; Died at Mt. Sinai Hospital at the Age of 71," *Jewish Telegraphic Agency*, October 12, 1949, http://www.jta.org/1949/10/12/archive/funeral-services-today-for-dr-a-j-rongy-died-at-mt-sinai-hospital-at-age-of-71; Reagan, *When Abortion Was a Crime*, 139, 142.

36. Taussig, *The Prevention and Treatment of Abortion*, 61, 79–81.

37. Taussig, *Abortion*, 26, 422.

38. Taussig, *Abortion*, 317–321, 422.

39. Taussig, *Abortion*, 29–30, 396–397, 400–401, 446, 451–452.

40. "Liberal Policies Urged on Doctors," *New York Times*, January 28, 1936.

41. For an example of a repetition of Taussig's statistics decades after they had become outdated, see Jerome M. Krummer, "A Psychiatrist Views Our Abortion Enigma," in *The Case for Legalized Abortion Now*, ed. Alan F. Guttmacher (Berkeley, CA: Diablo Press, 1967), 115. By the mid-1960s, the annual number

of reported abortion-related deaths was only 200, according to statistics compiled by the Guttmacher Institute ("Lessons from Before Roe: Will Past Be Prologue?" *The Guttmacher Report on Public Policy*, March 2003, http://www. guttmacher.org/pubs/tgr/06/1/gr060108.html).

42. "Physicians Split on Birth Control."

43. "Catholic Physicians Meet," *New York Times*, June 11, 1942.

44. Fred Rosner, *Biomedical Ethics and Jewish Law* (Hoboken, NJ: Ktav Publishing House, 2001), 175–185.

45. H. Close Hesseltine et al., "Limitation of Human Reproduction: Therapeutic Abortion," *American Journal of Obstetrics and Gynecology* 39 (April 1940): 550–551; William E. Studdiford, Response to Samuel A. Cosgrove and Patricia A. Carter, "A Consideration of Therapeutic Abortion," *American Journal of Obstetrics and Gynecology* 48 (September 1944): 311; George H. Ryder, Response to Walter T. Dannreuther, "Therapeutic Abortion in a General Hospital," *American Journal of Obstetrics and Gynecology* 52 (July 1946): 64.

46. Lambeth Conference, Resolution 16, "The Life and Witness of the Christian Community—Marriage and Sex" (1930), http://www.lambethconference.org/ resolutions/1930/1930-16.cfm; "Episcopal Bishops Favor Information on Birth Control," *New York Times*, October 21, 1934; Bob Jones Sr., "Editor's Page," *Bob Jones Magazine*, January 1930, 1; John R. Rice, *The Home: Courtship, Marriage, and Children* (Wheaton, IL: Sword of the Lord, 1945), 156; Curran, "Religious Implications," 153–174. For a brief overview of fundamentalist opposition to abortion prior to 1950, see Matthew Avery Sutton, *American Apocalypse: A History of Modern Evangelicalism* (Cambridge, MA: Harvard University Press, 2014), 145–147.

47. Glanville Williams, *The Sanctity of Life and the Criminal Law* (New York: Knopf, 1957), 236–247.

48. Dagmar Herzog, *Sexuality in Europe: A Twentieth-Century History* (New York: Cambridge University Press, 2011), 75–77.

49. "The Abortion Racket: What Should Be Done?" *Newsweek*, August 15, 1960; Alan F. Guttmacher to Keizo Tahara, December 28, 1966, folder 23: "Correspondence—Abortion—S, 1961–1969," box 1, Alan Frank Guttmacher Papers, Countway Library of Medicine, Harvard University; Alan F. Guttmacher to Leo J. Holmsten, November 18, 1968, folder 12: "Correspondence—Abortion—H, 1964–1969," box 1, Guttmacher Papers; Lawrence Lader, "The Scandal of Abortion—Laws," *New York Times*, April 25, 1965; "Suggests Doctors Relax 'Hypocrisy,'" *New York Times*, January 31, 1942.

50. David Dempsey, "Dr. Guttmacher Is the Evangelist of Birth Control," *New York Times*, February 9, 1969.

51. Alan F. Guttmacher to Garrett Harden, December 30, 1963, folder 12: "Correspondence—Abortion—H, 1964–1969," box 1, Guttmacher Papers; Alicia Armstrong, "Updated Abortion Laws Asked," *Milwaukee Journal*, May 5, 1961.

52. Joseph B. Schuyler to Alan F. Guttmacher, 24 April 1961, folder 23: "Correspondence—Abortion—S, 1961–1969," box 1, Guttmacher Papers.

53. J. Gerard Mears, "In Fear and in Secret They Do Damnable Deeds," *America*, May 2, 1942, 96.

54. Reagan, *When Abortion Was a Crime*, 116–131; Mohr, *Abortion in America*, 230–245.

55. Samuel A. Cosgrove and Patricia A. Carter, "A Consideration of Therapeutic Abortion," *American Journal of Obstetrics and Gynecology* 48 (September 1944): 299–314; Obituary for Patricia Ann Carter, *Charleston (SC) Post and Courier*, February 22, 2004.

56. Reagan, *When Abortion Was a Crime*, 174; Albert E. Catherwood, Response to H. Close Hesseltine et al., "Limitation of Human Reproduction: Therapeutic Abortion," *American Journal of Obstetrics and Gynecology* 39 (April 1940): 561, and Hesseltine's response, 561.

57. Howard Hammond, "Therapeutic Abortion: Ten Years' Experience with Hospital Committee Control," *American Journal of Obstetrics and Gynecology* 89 (June 1964): 350; "Dilemma Is Seen in Abortion Law," *New York Times*, July 28, 1959; "The Abortion Racket."

58. Roy J. Heffernan and William A. Lynch, "What Is the Status of Therapeutic Abortion in Modern Obstetrics?," *American Journal of Obstetrics and Gynecology* 66 (August 1953): 335; Lawrence Lader, *Abortion* (Indianapolis: Bobbs-Merrill, 1966), 24–28.

59. Heffernan and Lynch, "What Is the Status of Therapeutic Abortion in Modern Obstetrics?," 335.

60. H. Close Hesseltine, F. L. Adair, and M. W. Boynton, "Limitation of Human Reproduction: Therapeutic Abortion," *American Journal of Obstetrics and Gynecology* 39 (April 1940): 552.

61. Hesseltine et al., "Limitation of Human Reproduction," 552; Jane Eliot Sewell, "Cesarean Section—A Brief History," 1993, NIH, US National Library of Medicine, http://www.nlm.nih.gov/exhibition/cesarean/index.html; Charles Leavitt Sullivan and Elmore M. Campbell, "One Thousand Cesarean Sections in the Modern Era of Obstetrics," *Linacre Quarterly* 22 (November 1955): 117.

62. Sullivan and Campbell, "One Thousand Cesarean Sections in the Modern Era of Obstetrics," 117. For a late nineteenth-century discussion of the medical aspects of craniotomy and the ethical issues involved in choosing between maternal and fetal life, see Thomas Radford, *Observations on the Caesarian Section, Craniotomy, and on Other Obstetric Operations*, 2nd ed. (London: J. & A. Churchill, 1880), 51–67.

63. Rachel Benson Gold, "Lessons from Before *Roe*: Will Past Be Prologue?," *Guttmacher Report on Public Policy*, March 2003, http://www.guttmacher.org/pubs/tgr/06/1/gr060108.html.

64. Christopher Tietze, "Therapeutic Abortions in New York City, 1943–1947," *American Journal of Obstetrics and Gynecology* 60 (July 1950): 147; Harold

M. Schmeck Jr., "Abortions Found Easier to Obtain," *New York Times*, June 22, 1965; Alan F. Guttmacher to Clay H. Johnson, October 5, 1961, folder 14, box 1, Guttmacher Papers.

65. T. Raber Taylor, "A Lawyer Reviews Plan for Legalized Abortions," *Linacre Quarterly* 26 (November 1959): 138.

66. Curran, "Religious Implications," 154–160.

67. "Catholics Draft Human-Rights Aim," *New York Times*, February 2, 1947; McGreevy, *Catholicism and American Freedom*, 258; "Catholics Propose U.N. Rights Draft," *New York Times*, March 26, 1950; Pius XII, "Marriage and the Moral Law," Address to the Italian Association of Catholic Midwives, Rome, November 26, 1951, http://www.catholicpamphlets.net/pamphlets/MARRIAGE%20AND%20THE%20MORAL%20LAW.pdf.

68. Lee Gidding to Balfour Brickner, March 21, 1972, folder: "MA, 1972," box 3, MC 313, NARAL Records, 1968–1976, Schlesinger Library, Harvard University.

69. This line of argument appeared in numerous Catholic and pro-life publications of the 1960s and early 1970s. For an example of its systematic exposition, see Charles E. Rice, *The Vanishing Right to Live: An Appeal for a Renewed Reverence for Life* (Garden City, NY: Doubleday, 1969).

CHAPTER 2

1. Transcript of Planned Parenthood conference on abortion, New York, 1955, in *Abortion in the United States*, ed. Mary Steichen Calderone (New York: Hoeber-Harper, 1958), 176, 179; Paul H. Gebhard et al., *Pregnancy, Birth, and Abortion* (New York: Harper, 1958); Anthony Lewis, "Legal Abortions Proposed in Code," *New York Times*, May 22, 1959.

2. T. Raber Taylor, "A Lawyer Reviews Plan for Legalized Abortions," *Linacre Quarterly* 26 (November 1959): 137; Gerald Kelly, "Medico-Moral Notes," *Linacre Quarterly* 22 (May 1955): 56; United Nations, Declaration of the Rights of the Child, December 10, 1959, http://www.unicef.org/malaysia/1959-Declaration-of-the-Rights-of-the-Child.pdf.

3. Taylor, "A Lawyer Reviews Plan for Legalized Abortions," 140; Joseph T. Tinnelly, "Abortion and Penal Law," *Catholic Lawyer* 5 (Summer 1959): 190; William B. Ball to Paul V. Harrington, May 28, 1966, folder: "Abortion, 1965–1967," box 1, Rev. Paul V. Harrington Papers, Archives of the Archdiocese of Boston.

4. Timothy A. Byrnes and Mary C. Segers, eds., *The Catholic Church and the Politics of Abortion: The View from the States* (Boulder, CO: Westview Press, 1992), 5.

5. Sagar C. Jain and Steven Hughes, "California Abortion Act 1967: A Study in Legislative Process" (Chapel Hill: Carolina Population Center, 1969), 17–19.

6. David J. Garrow, *Liberty and Sexuality: The Right to Privacy and the Making of Roe v. Wade*, 2nd ed. (Berkeley: University of California Press, 1998), 281–282; "Leader Elected by Presbyterians," *Los Angeles Times*, May 26, 1962.

7. "Mother, Rebuffed in Arizona, May Seek Abortion Elsewhere," *New York Times*, August 1, 1962; Marian Faux, Roe v. Wade: *The Untold Story of the Landmark Supreme Court Decision That Made Abortion Legal*, 2nd ed. (New York: Cooper Square Press, 2001), 42–51.

8. Robert Finkbine, "Husband Tells Reasons for Seeking Operation," *Los Angeles Times*, August 5, 1962; "Mental Tests Completed in Finkbine Case," *Los Angeles Times*, August 10, 1962; Sherri Finkbine, "The Lesser of Two Evils," Address to the Conference on Abortion and Human Rights, January 9, 1966, folder: "Conference on Abortion, Jan. 9, 1966," box 1, MC 289, Society for Humane Abortion Records, Schlesinger Library, Harvard University; Lawrence Lader, *Abortion* (Indianapolis: Bobbs-Merrill, 1966), 13.

9. George Gallup, "Public Gives Its Views on Finkbine Case," *Los Angeles Times*, September 20, 1962.

10. Finkbine, "The Lesser of Two Evils"; W. N. Bergin, draft of article for *Hawaii Medical Journal*, July 26, 1966, folder: "Abortion and Contraception (1 of 19)," box 20, Harrington Papers.

11. UPI, "Mrs. Finkbine Abortion Hit by Vatican Radio," *Los Angeles Times*, August 20, 1962.

12. "'Baby Case' Pair Head for Sweden," *Los Angeles Times*, August 3, 1962; NC, "Couple's Offer to Adopt Baby to Prevent Abortion Declined," *Catholic Bulletin* (St. Paul, MN), August 3, 1962, 1.

13. Finkbine, "Husband Tells Reasons for Seeking Operation"; Joseph J. Alvin, LTE, *Los Angeles Times*, August 11, 1962.

14. NC, "Acquittal in Infant Slaying Hit," *Catholic Bulletin* (St. Paul, MN), November 16, 1962, 8; Norman St. John-Stevas, *The Right to Life* (New York: Holt, Rinehart and Winston, 1963, 1964), 6–17; Germain Grisez, *Abortion: The Myths, the Realities, and the Arguments* (New York: Corpus Books, 1970), 91–92, 239.

15. St. John-Stevas, *The Right to Life*, 16.

16. Garrett Hardin, "Semantic Aspects of Abortion," *Etc.: A Review of General Semantics* 24 (September 1967): 266.

17. "'Liberal' Abortion Bill Proposed," *Catholic Bulletin* (St. Paul, MN), October 19, 1962, 2.

18. Taylor, "A Lawyer Reviews Plan for Legalized Abortions," 140; Richard T. Doherty, "Unborn's Life a Right," *Catholic Bulletin* (St. Paul, MN), October 26, 1962, 4.

19. Jain and Hughes, "California Abortion Act, 1967," 19.

20. Timothy Manning to Nicholas P. Connolly, December 6, 1962, folder: "Abortion, 1962–1965," Archives of the Archdiocese of Los Angeles; William R. Burke, Memo to Roman Catholic Bishops of California, Report on A.B. 2614, Therapeutic Abortion Hearings, San Diego, CA, December 17–18, 1962, folder: "Abortion, 1962–1965," Archives of the Archdiocese of Los Angeles; Martha S. Robinson, "Walter Trinkaus, Friend and Colleague," *Loyola of Los Angeles Law Review* 29 (June 1996): 1385–1386.

21. Report of Staff of Committee on Criminal Procedure, California State Assembly, on Therapeutic Abortion, n.d. [late 1963 or early 1964], folder 9, box 509, Anthony C. Beilenson Papers, University of California, Los Angeles; Walter R. Trinkaus, "Legal Objections to Pending Bill Authorizing Abortions, A.B. No. 2310," Presented on behalf of California Conference of Catholic Hospitals, July 20, 1964, folder 14, box 513, Beilenson Papers.

22. *Smith v. Brennan*, 157 A.2d 497, New Jersey Supreme Court (1960), http://law. justia.com/cases/new-jersey/supreme-court/1960/31-n-j-353-0.html; *Raleigh Fitkin—Paul Morgan Memorial Hospital v. Anderson*, 201 A.2d 537, New Jersey Supreme Court (1964), https://www.courtlistener.com/nj/b7CE/raleigh-fitkin-p aul-morgan-mem-hosp-v-anderson/; Walter Trinkaus's statement in debate with Anthony Beilenson at University of California, Los Angeles, November 17, 1965, UCLA Communications Studies Digital Archive.

23. Statement on Kansas Senate Bill 343 by representatives of the lay organizations of the four dioceses of Kansas [1963], reprinted in National Catholic Welfare Conference's Family Life Bureau, "Abortion and the Right to Life," n.d., folder: "Abortion Legislation and Litigation (1 of 7)," box 23, Harrington Papers; J. J. Brandlin to E. E. Epstein, September 4, 1964, folder 8, box 510, Beilenson Papers; Right to Life League, Press Release [spring 1967], folder 16, box 511, Beilenson Papers.

24. Zad Leavy, LTE, *Los Angeles Daily Journal*, June 23, 1965.

25. Jain and Hughes, "California Abortion Act, 1967," 20.

26. "The Newsmakers," *California News Reporter*, May 15, 1967; Lou Cannon, "California's Abortion Law: A Road Not Taken," *Real Clear Politics*, April 4, 2013, http://www.realclearpolitics.com/articles/2013/04/04/californias_abor tion_law_a_road_not_taken_117773.html.

27. For an early example of Catholic use of the Hippocratic oath to advance the right-to-life cause, see T. Raber Taylor, "Annotations on The Oath of Hippocrates and The Geneva Version of The Hippocratic Oath," *Linacre Quarterly* 23 (May 1956): 35.

28. RNS, "Abortion Bill Killed by S.D. House Committee," *Catholic Bulletin* (St. Paul, MN), February 8, 1963, 10; Susan Stocking, "Liberal Abortion Bill Draws Strong Opponents," *Minneapolis Tribune*, January 28, 1967.

29. Alan F. Guttmacher to Diane E. Falini, April 17, 1963, folder 10: "Correspondence—Abortion—F, 1962–1969," box 1, Alan Frank Guttmacher Papers, Countway Library of Medicine, Harvard University.

30. Lucie Prinz to Joshua M. Morse, October 24, 1967, folder 17: "Correspondence—Abortion—M, 1959–1969," box 1, Guttmacher Papers; Mary S. Calderone to J. David Wyles, March 13, 1963, folder 7: "Correspondence—Abortion—C, 1960–1969," box 1, Guttmacher Papers; Hazel Sagoff to Alan F. Guttmacher, December 13, 1966, folder 23: "Correspondence—Abortion—S, 1961–1969," box 1, Guttmacher Papers.

31. Morris Kaplan, "Abortion and Sterilization Win Support of Planned Parenthood," *New York Times*, November 14, 1968; Donald T. Critchlow, "Birth Control, Population Control, and Family Planning: An Overview," in *The Politics of Abortion and Birth Control in Historical Perspective*, ed. Donald T. Critchlow (University Park: Pennsylvania State University Press, 1996), 10.

32. Garrow, *Liberty and Sexuality*, 296–300; Sylvia Bloom to Alan Guttmacher, September 28, 1964, folder 7: "Correspondence—Abortion—C, 1960–1969," box 1, Guttmacher Papers. Within a year of its founding, the Committee for a Humane Abortion Law changed its name to the Association for Humane Abortion, and then to the Association for the Study of Abortion.

33. Alan F. Guttmacher to Mrs. Andrew G. Townsend, April 12, 1965, folder 24: "Correspondence—Abortion—T, 1959–1969," box 1, Guttmacher Papers; Alan F. Guttmacher to G. L. Timanus, March 28, 1962, folder 24: "Correspondence—Abortion—T, 1959–1969," box 1, Guttmacher Papers.

34. Anthony Beilenson to Dorothy Zoller, November 16, 1965, folder 1, box 514, Beilenson Papers; "Assemblyman Sees Abortion Act Passage," *Los Angeles Times*, September 30, 1964.

35. Transcript of hearings on the Humane Abortion Act (AB 2310), Assembly Interim Committee on Criminal Procedure, September 29, 1964, folder: "Abortion: Assembly Interim Committee on Criminal Procedure, 1964 Sep. 29," box 509, Beilenson Papers; James W. Fifield, "Dr. Fifield Says" column, *Los Angeles Times*, August 30, 1964; "Abortion Foes Open Campaign Here," *San Francisco Chronicle*, April 20, 1967.

36. Jack S. McDowell, "Liberalized Abortions Bill Voted," *San Francisco News Call-Bulletin*, May 26, 1965.

37. Transcript of hearings on the Humane Abortion Act (AB 2310).

38. Transcript of hearings on the Humane Abortion Act (AB 2310), 26.

39. Transcript of hearings on the Humane Abortion Act (AB 2310), 20–26; Lester Kinsolving, "Therapeutic Abortion—Past and Current Views," *San Francisco Chronicle*, April 2, 1966.

40. Jack Odom to Anthony C. Beilenson, June 14, 1967, folder 16, box 511, Beilenson Papers.

41. "Abortion Is Murder," *Tidings* (Los Angeles), October 2, 1964, 12.

42. "Wide Opposition Voiced to New Abortion Bill," *Tidings*, October 2, 1964, 13; Transcript of hearings on the Humane Abortion Act (AB 2310), 118; "The Newsmakers," *California News Reporter*, May 15, 1967.

43. Ruth Roemer to William T. Dalessi, May 13, 1965, folder 2, box 511, Beilenson Papers; "Abortion Law Repealer is Dead in Committee," *Sacramento Bee*, June 4, 1965; Anthony Beilenson to Dorothy Zoller, November 16, 1965, folder 1, box 514, Beilenson Papers; Alden J. Bell to James McIntyre, June 4, 1965, and McIntyre to Bell, June 9, 1965, folder: "Abortion: 1962–1965," Archives of the Archdiocese of Los Angeles.

CHAPTER 3

1. Leslie Woodcock Tentler, *Catholics and Contraception: An American History* (Ithaca, NY: Cornell University Press, 2004), 122–129, 162–172.

2. For Vatican II, see John W. O'Malley, *What Happened at Vatican II* (Cambridge, MA: Harvard University Press, 2010); and Colleen McDannell, *The Spirit of Vatican II: A History of Catholic Reform in America* (New York: Basic Books, 2011). For changes in the American Catholic Church during the 1960s, see Mark S. Massa, *The American Catholic Revolution: How the Sixties Changed the Church Forever* (New York: Oxford University Press, 2010).

3. Peter Kihss, "Bill for Liberalizing New York Statute Goes to the State Senate," *New York Times*, June 8, 1965; Philip Denvir, "Cardinal Asks Change in Birth Control Law," *Boston Globe*, June 23, 1965; AP, "Birth Control Data Backed by Cushing, *New York Times*, March 3, 1965.

4. Ronald Sullivan, "Albany Kills Bill to Repeal Law against Birth Control," *New York Times*, May 6, 1965; Sydney H. Schanberg, "Legislature Voids Birth Control Ban, In Effect 84 Years," *New York Times*, June 17, 1965; "Birth Control Help Legalized in State," *New York Times*, July 10, 1965.

5. Evert Clark, "Catholics Reaffirm Birth Control Bans in Reply to Johnson," *New York Times*, January 9, 1965; Tentler, *Catholics and Contraception*, 220.

6. Tentler, *Catholics and Contraception*, 240–241; American Institute of Public Opinion, "Majority of Catholics Think Church Will Change Stand on Birth Control," August 20, 1965, folder 8, box 86, collection 010, National Catholic Welfare Conference (NCWC) Papers, Catholic University of America Archives, Washington, DC; "Cushing Softens Birth Curb Stand," *New York Times*, June 24, 1965.

7. Tentler, *Catholics and Contraception*, 228–229.

8. Tentler, *Catholics and Contraception*, 266–267; Patrick Allitt, *Catholic Intellectuals and Conservative Politics in America, 1950–1985* (Ithaca, NY: Cornell University Press, 1993), 169–177.

9. For liberal Protestant views on birth control during the 1960s, see Tom Davis, *Sacred Work: Planned Parenthood and Its Clergy Alliances* (New Brunswick, NJ: Rutgers University Press, 2005); and "Promoting Family Planning," *Christian Century*, August 11, 1965, 980. For evangelical support of contraception, see M. O. Vincent, "A Christian View of Contraception," *Christianity Today*, November 8, 1968, 14–15. For further discussion of the shift in evangelical views on contraception (and abortion) in the 1960s, see Daniel K. Williams, "Sex and the Evangelicals: Gender Issues, the Sexual Revolution, and Abortion in the 1960s," in *American Evangelicals and the 1960s*, ed. Axel R. Schäfer (Madison: University of Wisconsin Press, 2013), 97–118.

10. Chalmers M. Roberts, "First White House Sanction Given for World Birth Control Efforts," *Washington Post*, January 6, 1965; John D. Morris, "U.S. to

Increase Birth Control Aid," *New York Times*, March 4, 1966; Nan Robertson, "Unwed to Receive Birth Control Aid," *New York Times*, April 2, 1966; AP, "Catholics Decry Aid for Birth Control," *New York Times*, July 10, 1966.

11. "Poverty War Birth Control Role Rapped," *Wanderer* (St. Paul, MN), March 17, 1966, 1; "Catholic Prelate Hits OEO Birth-Control Stand," *Wanderer*, July 14, 1966, 1; National Catholic Welfare Conference, "On the Government and Birth Control," November 14, 1966, folder 10, box 86, collection 010, NCWC Papers.

12. Lawrence Lader, "Abortion: Let's Attack the Core of the Problem," *Sexology*, May 1966, 700–701; Joan Lamb Ullyot, "Abortion Laws Should Be Repealed," Testimony before the Judiciary Committee of the California State Assembly, October 22, 1970, folder: "Reprints, 1963–1970," box 3, Society for Humane Abortion (SHA) Records, Schlesinger Library, Harvard University.

13. "For Abortion Law Reform," *New York Post*, June 24, 1966; Austin C. Wehrwein, "Abortion Reform Supported in Poll," *New York Times*, April 24, 1966; Lawrence Lader, "Abortion Reform Legislation as a Political Issue," draft article manuscript, n.d. [1966], box 2, Lawrence Lader Papers, Countway Library of Medicine, Harvard University.

14. William B. Ball to Paul V. Harrington, folder: "Abortion, 1965–1967," box 1, Rev. Paul V. Harrington Papers, Archives of the Archdiocese of Boston.

15. Alan F. Guttmacher, Statement on racial disparity in abortion deaths [April 21, 1965], folder 17: "Correspondence—Abortion—M, 1959–1969," box 1, Alan Frank Guttmacher Papers, Countway Library of Medicine; Alicia Armstrong, "Updated Abortion Laws Asked," *Milwaukee Journal*, May 5, 1961.

16. For examples of the *New York Times'* sympathetic coverage of the campaign to liberalize abortion laws, see Editorial, "A New Abortion Law," *New York Times*, February 13, 1965; and Lawrence Lader, "The Scandal of Abortion: Laws— Abortion Laws," *New York Times*, April 25, 1965.

17. Grisez, *Abortion*, 240. For popular media coverage of abortion, see Alan Guttmacher, "The Law That Doctors Often Break," *Redbook*, August 1959; Lawrence Lader, "Let's Speak Out on Abortion," *Reader's Digest*, May 1966; and Jack Starr, "The Growing Tragedy of Illegal Abortion," *Look*, October 19, 1965.

18. CBS, "Abortion and the Law," April 5, 1965, CBS online video archive, http://www.cbsnews.com/videos/public-eye-abortion-in-1965/; "Lessons from Before Roe: Will Past Be Prologue?" *Guttmacher Report on Public Policy*, March 2003, http://www.guttmacher.org/pubs/tgr/06/1/gr060108.html. The percentage of abortions that were obtained by married women in the mid-1960s is difficult to determine, since reliable statistics do not exist for a procedure that was still mostly illegal, but at the time, supporters of abortion law reform claimed that the vast majority of abortions were obtained by married women. For instance, in 1967, Alice Rossi, a supporter of liberalized abortion laws and a member of the Committee on Human Development at the University of Chicago, estimated that "between 85 and 90 percent of the illegal abortions involve married women"

(Alice S. Rossi, "Public Views on Abortion," in *The Case for Legalized Abortion Now*, ed. Alan F. Guttmacher (Berkeley, CA: Diablo Press, 1967), 27. But officially reported statistics from hospitals and abortion clinics in the early 1970s cast doubt on these estimates. In 1972, the first year for which official statistics are available, married women obtained 29.4 percent of the nation's 514,000 legal abortions and unmarried women accounted for the remaining 69.6 percent (with an additional 1 percent of abortions performed on women of unknown marital status). In 1975, when legal abortion was available everywhere in the United States, the percentage of abortions obtained by married women was only 25.6 percent (Richard S. Krannich, "Abortion in the United States: Past, Present, and Future Trends," *Family Relations* 29 (1980): 370. This suggests that either there was a massive change in abortion demographics between the mid-1960s and the early 1970s or else—as is more likely—the claim that 80 percent or more of abortions (legal or illegal) in the early 1960s were obtained by married women was erroneous and the actual percentage was probably considerably lower.

19. "Demand Grows for Legalizing Some Abortions," *Rodale's Health Bulletin*, June 18, 1966, 4; Victor Cohn, "Medicine Today," *Ladies' Home Journal*, April 1965; Walter Goodman, "Abortion and Sterilization: The Search for Answers," *Redbook*, October 1965, 148; "Abortion's Toll," *Colorado Springs Gazette Telegraph*, May 29, 1966; "Illegal Baby Surgery Put at 1.2 Million Yearly," *Los Angeles Times*, August 5, 1962; John Sibley, "Abortion Reform Urged in Albany," *New York Times*, March 8, 1966.

20. Alan F. Guttmacher to George R. Metcalf, September 13, 1961, folder 17: "Correspondence—Abortion—M, 1959–1969," box 1, Guttmacher Papers.

21. For liberal Protestant ministerial advocacy of civil rights and social reform in the mid-1960s, see James F. Findlay, *Church People in the Struggle: The National Council of Churches and the Black Freedom Movement, 1950–1970* (New York: Oxford University Press, 1993); and Michael B. Friedland, *Lift Up Your Voice Like a Trumpet: White Clergy and the Civil Rights and Antiwar Movements, 1954–1973* (Chapel Hill: University of North Carolina Press, 1998). For the *Christian Century*'s championship of the civil rights movement, see Elesha J. Coffman, *The Christian Century and the Rise of the Protestant Mainline* (New York: Oxford University Press, 2013), 218.

22. "Bishop Asks for State Change of Abortion Law," *Citizen-News* (Hollywood, CA), January 16, 1965; Kerry N. Jacoby, *Souls, Bodies, Spirits: The Drive to Abolish Abortion since 1973* (Westport, CT: Praeger, 1998), 3; Alfred L. Severson to Lester Kinsolving, March 30, 1966, folder 23: "Correspondence—Abortion—S, 1961–1969," box 1, Guttmacher Papers.

23. "Clergymen Offer Abortion Advice," *New York Times*, May 22, 1967; Susan Brownmiller, "Abortion Counseling: Service Beyond Sermons," *New York*, August 4, 1969, 27–31; Miriam Alburn, "Clergymen Advise on Abortion," *Minneapolis Tribune*, February 27, 1969.

24. Lawrence Lader, *Abortion* (Indianapolis: Bobbs-Merrill, 1966), 9, 13, 111–116; Austin C. Wehrwein, "Abortion Reform Supported in Poll"; George Dugan, "Foes of Abortion Assailed by Rabbi," *New York Times*, February 12, 1967.

25. Jerome F. Politzer, "Abortion at Issue," *Christianity Today*, September 2, 1966, 50–53; Paul L. Sadler, "The Abortion Issue within the Southern Baptist Convention, 1969–1988" (Ph.D. diss., Baylor University, 1991), 11–33.

26. William D. Freeland, "Inter-Faith Debate on Easing Abortion Laws," *Christianity Today*, April 28, 1967, 43; "A Protestant Affirmation on the Control of Human Reproduction," *Christianity Today*, November 8, 1968, 18. For examples of evangelical editorials reflecting a cautious approach to abortion, see: S. I. McMillen, "Abortion: Is It Moral?" *Christian Life*, September 1967, 50, 53; Nancy Hardesty, "Should Anyone Who Wants Abortion Have One?" *Eternity*, June 1967, 32–34; Paul K. Jewett, "The Relation of the Soul to the Fetus," *Christianity Today*, November 8, 1968, 6–9; Robert D. Visscher, "Therapeutic Abortion: Blessing or Murder?" *Christianity Today*, September 27, 1968, 6–8; and "Capital Consistency," *Christianity Today*, June 20, 1969, 21.

27. Immanuel Jakobovits, "Jewish Views on Abortion," in *Abortion and the Law*, ed. David T. Smith (Cleveland, OH: Western Reserve University, 1967), 124–143; News item on 1967 Greek Orthodox Yearbook, *Christianity Today*, May 12, 1967, 53–54; William D. Freeland, "Inter-Faith Debate on Easing Abortion Laws," *Christianity Today*, April 28, 1967, 43.

28. Lester Kinsolving, "Therapeutic Abortion—Past and Current Views," *San Francisco Chronicle*, April 2, 1966.

29. David J. Garrow, *Liberty and Sexuality: The Right to Privacy and the Making of* Roe v. Wade, 2nd ed. (Berkeley: University of California Press, 1998), 302; "Liberalization of Abortion," *Wanderer*, February 23, 1967, 1.

30. "Growing Consensus on Abortion," *America*, February 12, 1966, 219.

31. "The Drama of Life before Birth," *Life*, April 30, 1965; Iconic Photos, "How Life Begins," http://iconicphotos.wordpress.com/2009/10/19/how-life-begins/; William E. Tinsley, Address, Transcript of panel on "Communications," Society for Humane Abortion conference, January 9, 1966, folder: "Conference on Abortion, Jan. 9, 1966," box 2, SHA; Christine Nestler to Kenneth J. Merkel, May 15, 1971, folder 2: "Abortion, 1971–72," box 1, Kenneth J. Merkel Papers, Wisconsin Historical Society, Madison.

32. "Abortion Drive Warning Sounded," *Register* (Denver, CO), December 19, 1965.

33. Obituary for Msgr. Paul V. Harrington, *Boston Globe*, June 9, 1991; Paul V. Harrington to Russell Shaw, March 9, 1966, folder: "Abortion, 1965–1967," box 1, Harrington Papers; Paul V. Harrington to Nancy Parker, March 19, 1971, folder: "Abortion, 1971–72," box 1, Harrington Papers; Paul V. Harrington to Mr. and Mrs. James McGill, February 26, 1971, folder: "Abortion, 1971–72," box 1, Harrington Papers; Paul V. Harrington to Richard Cushing, January 23, 1969, folder: "Abortion Legislation, 1968–9," box 1, Harrington Papers; Paul

V. Harrington to W. N. Bergin, July 21, 1966, folder: "Abortion, 1965–1967," box 1, Harrington Papers; William B. Ball to Paul V. Harrington, March 16, 1966, folder: "Abortion, 1965–1967," box 1, Harrington Papers; Paul V. Harrington to Robert N. Byrn, October 30, 1967, folder: "Abortion, 1965–1967," box 1, Harrington Papers.

34. Thomas O'Toole, "A.M.A. Puts Off Abortion Stand," *New York Times*, December 2, 1965.

35. Frank J. Ayd Jr., "Liberal Abortion Laws: A Psychiatrist's View," February 3, 1967, folder 1: "Abortion," box 1, Chancery Office Records, Archives of the Diocese of Harrisburg, PA; O'Toole, "A.M.A. Puts Off Abortion Stand."

36. Harrington to Mr. and Mrs. James McGill, February 26, 1971.

37. Robert N. Karrer, "The National Right to Life Committee: Its Founding, Its History, and the Emergence of the Pro-Life Movement Prior to *Roe v. Wade*," *Catholic Historical Review* 97 (2011): 533; Harrington to Shaw, March 9, 1966.

38. "German Measles and Pregnancy: Current U.S. Epidemic Will Damage up to 20,000 Babies," *Life*, June 4, 1965; "Abortion Hearings," *Monitor* (San Francisco, CA), May 27, 1965, 20; Sagar C. Jain and Steven Hughes, "California Abortion Act 1967: A Study in Legislative Process" (Chapel Hill: Carolina Population Center, 1969), 25. For an analysis of the impact of the rubella epidemic on the abortion law reform movement, see Leslie J. Reagan, *Dangerous Pregnancies: Mothers, Disabilities, and Abortion in Modern America* (Berkeley: University of California Press, 2010).

39. Frank Martinez, "Abortion Probe at GG Hospital, *Santa Ana Register*, March 24, 1965; Joe Kassis and Monica Hayden, "Dr. Richard A. Hayden '37," Website for alumni of Brooklyn Preparatory School, August 16, 2005, http://legacy.fordham.edu/TESTING_SITE/Photos_1/1930/hayden.asp.

40. Martinez, "Abortion Probe at GG Hospital."

41. Editorial, "Abortion Hearings," *Monitor* (San Francisco, CA), May 27, 1965, 20; "German Measles and Pregnancy."

42. William R. Burke, Memo to Roman Catholic Bishops of California, Report on A.B. 2614, Therapeutic Abortion Hearings, San Diego, December 17–18, 1962, folder: "Abortion, 1962–1965," Archives of the Archdiocese of Los Angeles; Reagan, *Dangerous Pregnancies*, 147–149.

43. Peter Bart, "California Faces Abortion Debate," *New York Times*, June 19, 1966; Reagan, *Dangerous Pregnancies*, 153.

44. Bart, "California Faces Abortion Debate"; Jain and Hughes, "California Abortion Act, 1967," 36; Alan F. Guttmacher to Sheldon L. Gutman, April 6, 1966, folder 11: "Correspondence—Abortion—G, 1963–1968," box 1, Guttmacher Papers.

45. Melvin D. Field, "Poll Finds Majority Favors Liberalization of State Abortion Laws," Press Release from the California Poll, July 26, 1966, folder 7: "Social Action: Health & Medicine: Abortion, 1966," box 87, collection 010, NCWC Papers.

46. "Abortion Bill Still in Limbo," *California News Reporter*, May 15, 1967; Jain and Hughes, "California Abortion Act 1967," 42–43.

47. Leo Maher to Alden J. Bell, February 11, 1966, folder: "Abortion: 1966," Archives of the Archdiocese of Los Angeles.

48. Alden J. Bell to Paul F. Tanner, June 20, 1966, folder 7: "Social Action: Health & Medicine: Abortion, 1966," box 87, collection 010, NCWC Papers, Catholic University of America Archives; Minutes of NCWC Meeting on Abortion, June 23, 1966, folder 7: "Social Action: Health & Medicine: Abortion, 1966," box 87, collection 010, NCWC Papers.

49. NCWC, list of readings on abortion, June 24, 1966, folder 7, box 87, collection 010, NCWC Papers; Minutes of NCWC Meeting on Abortion, June 23, 1966. The booklet on abortion policy that the NCWC published in February 1966 was Russell Shaw's "Abortion and Public Policy."

50. NCWC, Report on Results of Survey on Abortion, August 25, 1966; James T. McHugh to Paul F. Tanner, "Re: Response to Abortion Questionnaire," August 18, 1966; Paul F. Tanner to Alden J. Bell, June 25, 1966 (all materials from folder 7, box 87, collection 010, NCWC Papers).

51. Alden J. Bell to Timothy Manning, August 19, 1966, folder: "Abortion—1966," Archives of the Archdiocese of Los Angeles; "Bishops to Press Abortion Battle," *New York Times*, April 14, 1967. For more information about the background to this vote and Fr. James McHugh's role in mobilizing this campaign as director of the Family Life Bureau, see chapter 4.

52. William R. Johnson to James McIntyre, "Re: The Meeting in Sacramento to Coordinate Plans for Opposing Liberalization of the Abortion Law," September 28, 1966, folder: "Abortion—1966," Archives of the Archdiocese of Los Angeles.

53. Statement of Catholic Bishops of California, "Thou Shalt Not Kill," December 8, 1966, folder: "Abortion—1966," Archives of the Archdiocese of Los Angeles; "State's Roman Catholic Bishops Amplify Stand against Abortion," *Los Angeles Times*, December 9, 1966.

54. See, for example, the 1942 resolution of the National Federation of Catholic Physicians' Guilds, in "Catholic Physicians Meet," *New York Times*, June 11, 1942.

55. For examples of the use of the phrase "right to life" in testimony against abortion bills in the early 1960s, see Timothy E. O'Brien, Testimony on A.B. 2614, Therapeutic Abortion Hearings, San Diego, CA, December 1962, and Vaughan, Brandlin, Robinson, and Roemer, "Legal Objections to Pending Bill Permitting Therapeutic Abortion (Assembly Bill No. 2614)," December 1962, both in folder: "Abortion, 1962–1965," Archives of the Archdiocese of Los Angeles.

56. James McIntyre, letter to California's bishops, December 9, 1966, folder: "Abortion—1966," Archives of the Archdiocese of Los Angeles; Obituary for Elizabeth Murphy Goodwin Peacock, *Orange County Register*, December 1, 2011.

57. James McIntyre, letter to priests in Los Angeles archdiocese, January 27, 1967, folder: "Abortion—1967," Archives of the Archdiocese of Los Angeles; James McIntyre to Joseph T. McGucken, January 26, 1967, folder: "Abortion—1967," Archives of the Archdiocese of Los Angeles; Description of Right to Life League [January or February 1967], folder: "Abortion—1967," Archives of the Archdiocese of Los Angeles.

58. "Suggestions for Parochial Support of the 'Right to Life League'" [spring 1967], folder: "Abortion—1967," Archives of the Archdiocese of Los Angeles.

59. "Abortion Foes Open Campaign Here," *San Francisco Chronicle*, April 20, 1967; "Abortion Foes' Crash Program," *San Francisco Chronicle*, April 19, 1967.

60. James McIntyre to John J. Brandlin, December 12, 1966, folder: "Abortion—1966," Archives of the Archdiocese of Los Angeles; "Catholics Get Letter on Abortion Bill," *Oakland Tribune*, April 26, 1967; David H. Tomshany, direct mail on behalf of Right to Life League [spring 1967], folder 16, box 511, Anthony C. Beilenson Papers, University of California, Los Angeles.

61. Jerry Gillam, "Anti-Abortion Bill Letters Flood Capital," *Los Angeles Times*, April 28, 1967.

62. Adele Vezeau to Anthony C. Beilenson, April 30, 1967, folder 4, box 520, Beilenson Papers. Other examples of similar letters include Margaret Mary Murphy to Anthony C. Beilenson, March 30, 1967, folder 5, box 520, Beilenson Papers; Lucy A. Van Buskirk to Beilenson, March 26, 1967; Maria K. Wagner to Beilenson, April 2, 1967; Eileen King to Beilenson, April 17, 1967; Ann Honsowetz to Beilenson, May 1, 1967; and Esther Boyer to Beilenson, May 9, 1967 (all in folder 4, box 520, Beilenson Papers).

63. Anthony C. Beilenson to Mary Kay Rennard, March 28, 1967, folder 4, box 520, Beilenson Papers; Rosalie M. Reardon and Frank A. Solomon Jr. to John Morrison, April 25, 1967, folder 10, box 514, Beilenson Papers; "Wider Abortion Laws Endorsed," *Washington Post*, March 25, 1966; Jain and Hughes, "California Abortion Act 1967," 48–49.

64. Jain and Hughes, "California Abortion Act 1967," 57; "Cardinal Condemns Abortion Legalization," *Wanderer*, June 22, 1967, 1.

65. Transcript of Press Conference of Governor Ronald Reagan, April 25, 1967, 19, folder: "Research File—Legal Affairs—Abortion," box GO 188, Governor's Papers, Ronald Reagan Library, Simi Valley, CA; Transcript of Press Conference of Governor Ronald Reagan, May 9, 1967, 2–3, folder: "Research File—Legal Affairs—Abortion," box GO 188, Governor's Papers; Martin Smith, "Reagan Balks on Deformity Abortion Issue," *Sacramento Bee*, May 24, 1967.

66. Transcript of Press Conference of Governor Reagan, February 28, 1967, folder: "Research File—Legal Affairs—Abortion," box GO188, Governor's Papers, Reagan Library; Transcript of Press Conference of Governor Ronald Reagan, May 23, 1967, Folder: "Research File—Legal Affairs—Abortion," box GO188,

Governor's Papers; Transcript of Press Conference of Governor Ronald Reagan, May 9, 1967, 4–5.

67. Transcript of Press Conference of Governor Ronald Reagan, May 23, 1967, 11–13; Richard Rodda, "Tuesday, June 13, Was Gov. Reagan's Unlucky Day," *Sacramento Bee*, June 18, 1967.

68. Transcript of Press Conference with Governor Ronald Reagan, May 2, 1967; George Skelton, "Assembly OKs Abortion Bill; Reagan Says He'll Sign It," *Sacramento Union*, June 14, 1967.

69. John Vasconcellos, statement against the Therapeutic Abortion Bill, April 24, 1967, folder 1, box 511, Beilenson Papers; "Abortion Bill Still in Limbo," *California News Reporter*, May 15, 1967; Jain and Hughes, "California Abortion Act 1967," 81–82.

70. UPI, "Colorado Said Near Liberal Abortion Bill," *Evening News-Independent* (Orange County, CA), April 7, 1967; "Colorado Is Split on Abortion Law," *New York Times*, April 30, 1967; UPI, "Colorado Senate Passes Abortion Bill," *Evening News-Independent* (Orange County, CA), April 9, 1967; AP, "Where the Abortion Seekers Aren't," *Sacramento Union*, May 1, 1967; Fred P. Graham, "Colorado Pioneers on Legal Abortions," *New York Times*, April 30, 1967; "Colorado Easing Curb on Abortion," *New York Times*, April 26, 1967.

71. "New Grounds for Abortion," *Time*, May 5, 1967, 95; Graham, "Colorado Pioneers on Legal Abortions."

72. UPI, "Governor Reagan Suggests Legislature Shelve Abortion Bill for Further Study," *Evening News-Independent* (Orange County, CA), May 10, 1967.

73. Transcript of Press Conference with Governor Ronald Reagan, June 13, 1967, 2–5, folder: "Research File—Legal Affairs—Abortion," box GO 188, Governor's Papers, Reagan Library; Skelton, "Assembly Oks Abortion Bill; Reagan Says He'll Sign It"; Rodda, "Tuesday, June 13, Was Gov. Reagan's Unlucky Day."

74. Elizabeth Goodwin to James McIntyre, June 5, 1967, folder: "Abortion—1967," Archives of the Archdiocese of Los Angeles.

75. Cheree Briggs, "Art Jones Bowing Out," *Observer* (Raleigh, NC), February 15, 1970; "Extra Messages," *Christianity Today*, July 17, 1970, 31; L. Nelson Bell, "An Alternative to Abortion," *Christianity Today*, June 18, 1971, 17; Johanna Schoen, *Choice and Coercion: Birth Control, Sterilization, and Abortion in Public Health and Welfare* (Chapel Hill: University of North Carolina Press, 2005), 180-184; "House in Carolina Backs Bill Easing Curbs on Abortion," *New York Times*, May 6, 1967.

76. William F. Powers, *Tar Heel Catholics: A History of Catholics in North Carolina* (Lanham, MD: University Press of America, 2003).

77. "3 Catholic Bishops Fight Abortion Bill," *New York Times*, February 22, 1967; Richard Homan, "Md. Legislators to Seek Wider Abortion Bills," *Washington Post*, March 14, 1967; Richard Homan, "Agnew Supports Abortion Bill,"

*Washington Post*, March 10, 1967; Richard Homan, "Assembly Committee Rejects Abortion Bill," *Washington Post*, March 25, 1967.

78. "Rockefeller Urges Abortion Review," *New York Times*, December 22, 1966; Sydney H. Schanberg, "Abortion Change Killed in Albany by Vote of 15 to 3," *New York Times*, March 8, 1967; Sydney H. Schanberg, "Javits Calls on Legislature to Pass Abortion Reform," *New York Times*, February 20, 1967; James R. Sikes, "Kennedy Predicts Abortion Reform," *New York Times*, February 18, 1967; "Impetus for Reform," *New York Times*, February 21, 1967.

79. Schanberg, "Javits Calls on Legislature to Pass Abortion Reform"; Sydney H. Schanberg, "Albany Bill on Abortion Reform Attacked by Protestant Senator," *New York Times*, February 23, 1967; Schanberg, "Abortion Change Killed in Albany by Vote of 15 to 3."

80. NC, "Catholic Welfare Leaders Urged to Fight Abortion Bills," *National Catholic Reporter*, May 5, 1967.

81. "Catholics to Prepare Statement on Abortion," *Minneapolis Star*, February 16, 1967.

82. Robert F. Drinan, "The Inviolability of the Right to Be Born," in *Abortion and the Law*, ed. David T. Smith (Cleveland, OH: Western Reserve University, 1967), 123; Daniel Callahan, *Abortion: Law, Choice and Morality* (New York: Macmillan, 1970), 436; Robert F. Drinan, "The Morality of Abortion Laws," *Catholic Lawyer* 14 (Summer 1968); Robert F. Drinan, "The State of the Abortion Question," *Commonweal*, April 17, 1970.

83. "Direct Abortion Opposed to God's Law," *Catholic Bulletin* (St. Paul, MN), March 3, 1967.

## CHAPTER 4

1. James T. McHugh, "Report of Meeting of Theologians," March 25, 1967, folder 1: "Abortion," box 1, Chancery Office Records, Archives of the Diocese of Harrisburg, PA.

2. Austin C. Wehrwein, "Abortion Reform Supported in Poll," *New York Times*, April 24, 1966.

3. James T. McHugh, "Pope Gave Guide for Sex Education of Young Persons," *Catholic Witness*, July 23, 1970, 4; Randy Engel, *The McHugh Chronicles* (self-published, 1997), i–10, http://uscl.info/edoc/doc.php?doc_id = 71&action = inline; Shaila K. Dewan, "Bishop of Long Island, James T. McHugh, Is Dead at 68," *New York Times*, December 12, 2000; Family Life Bureau, "Guidelines for the Formation of a Program of Sex Education," *Sex Education Bulletin*, March 28, 1969, folder: "Committee for Population and Pro-Life Activities, NCCB, Msgr. James T. McHugh, Director (1975)," box 141, collection 76, Catholic Charities USA Papers, Catholic University of America Archives.

4. Alden J. Bell to Paul F. Tanner, June 20, 1966, folder 7, box 87, collection 010, National Catholic Welfare Conference Papers, Catholic University of America Archives.

5. McHugh, "Report of Meeting of Theologians"; James T. McHugh, Letter to American bishops, June 10, 1968, folder 1: "Abortion," box 1, Chancery Office Records, Diocese of Harrisburg; UN General Assemblies Resolution 1386, "Declaration of the Rights of the Child," December 10, 1959, http://www1.umn.edu/humanrts/instree/k1drc.htm.

6. Richard A. McCormick, "Abortion," *America*, June 19, 1965, 877–881.

7. McHugh, "Report of Meeting of Theologians."

8. Germain Grisez, direct mail to American Catholic bishops, October 30, 1968, folder 1: "Abortion," box 1, Chancery Office Records, Diocese of Harrisburg; Germain Grisez, *Abortion: The Myths, the Realities, and the Arguments* (New York: Corpus Books, 1970), 424.

9. Charles E. Rice, *The Vanishing Right to Live: An Appeal for a Renewed Reverence for Life* (Garden City, NY: Doubleday, 1969); Paul Marx to Marge Wilson, November 11, 1971, folder 10, box 2, Fr. Paul Marx Papers, Saint John's University, Collegeville, MN; Randy Engel to Paul Marx, May 12, 1972, folder 40, box 3, Marx Papers; Paul Marx to Randy Engel, May 19, 1972, folder 40, box 3, Marx Papers; Engel, *The McHugh Chronicles*, 16–19.

10. Eugene F. Diamond, "Contraception and Abortifacients," *Linacre Quarterly* 38 (May 1971): 126.

11. John T. McGreevy, *Catholicism and American Freedom: A History* (New York: W. W. Norton, 2003), 241–245, 266–268; Leslie Woodcock Tentler, *Catholics and Contraception: An American History* (Ithaca, NY: Cornell University Press, 2004), 266–270.

12. One good example of this common approach in the early 1970s is John C. and Barbara Willke's *Handbook on Abortion* (Cincinnati, OH: Hiltz, 1971), which was the most widely distributed pro-life book of the era. In the late 1960s, the Willkes, who were Catholic, had given public presentations for college students on the need to delay sex until marriage, and they were opponents of the sexual revolution (John C. and Barbara Willke, *Sex—Should We Wait?* [Cincinnati, OH: Hiltz, 1969]). Yet in their *Handbook on Abortion*, they said nothing against contraception or sex outside of marriage, and instead focused solely on human rights arguments for the value of fetal life. Similarly, the *National Right to Life News* (published by the NRLC) rarely discussed issues of sexual morality in the 1970s, and on the few occasions when it did so, it suggested that abortion was a far worse evil than homosexuality or illicit sex between consenting adults (see, for instance, Anne Stewart Connell, "Homosexual Ruling Inconsistent," *National Right to Life News*, May 1976, 10).

13. McHugh, "Report of Meeting of Theologians"; Robert N. Karrer, "The National Right to Life Committee: Its Founding, Its History, and the Emergence of

the Pro-Life Movement Prior to *Roe v. Wade*," *Catholic Historical Review* 97 (2011): 527. For more discussion of this expenditure and the California bishops who encouraged the NCCB to take this step, see chapter 3.

14. UPI, "Georgia Approves Bill Liberalizing Abortion," *New York Times*, February 27, 1968; "Maryland Adopts Abortion Law," *Washington Post*, March 27, 1968.

15. James T. McHugh, letters to American bishops, June 10, 1968, and July 25, 1968, folder 1: "Abortion," box 1, Chancery Office Records, Diocese of Harrisburg.

16. Fred C. Shapiro, "'Right to Life' Has a Message for New York State Legislators," *New York Times*, August 20, 1972; Karrer, "The National Right to Life Committee," 538–539.

17. Karrer, "The National Right to Life Committee," 537–539; Author's telephone interview with Juan Ryan, June 4, 2012.

18. James T. McHugh, letter to American bishops, June 10, 1968; Diocese of Harrisburg, Memo, Re: Human Life Committee, July 21, 1970, folder 2: "Abortion—Right-to-Life Programs," box 1, Chancery Office Records, Diocese of Harrisburg; John Warren to James McHugh [November 13, 1970], folder: "Correspondence, 1970–1971," box 2, North Dakota Right to Life Association (NDRLA) Records, State Historical Society of North Dakota, Bismarck; Joseph A. Lampe to Robert Lynch and William Cox, August 12, 1974, folder: "MCCL, 1974," box 11, American Citizens Concerned for Life (ACCL) Records, Gerald R. Ford Library, Ann Arbor, MI.

19. James T. McHugh, letters to American bishops, July 25, 1968, and January 20, 1969, folder 1: "Abortion," box 1, Chancery Office Records, Diocese of Harrisburg.

20. Cheriel M. Jensen to NARAL, December 23, 1969, folder: "CA, Oct.–Dec., 1969," carton 2, MC 313, NARAL Records, 1968–1976, Schlesinger Library, Harvard University; Joseph A. O'Connor to Paul Ramsey, October 9, 1968, folder: "Joseph A. O'Connor," box 21, Paul Ramsey Papers, Duke University; John Warren to Edwin C. Becker, November 24, 1970, folder: "Correspondence, 1970–1971," box 2, NDRLA; Edwin C. Becker to Athanasius Buccholz, January 14, 1974, folder: "Correspondence, 1974," box 2, NDRLA; NDRLA, "Report to the North Dakota Catholic Conference," February 23, 1971, folder: "Miscellaneous Information and Handouts," box 5, NDRLA; "Right to Life Committee Largest of Groups Supporting Amendment," *National Catholic Reporter*, August 3, 1973.

21. William H. Keeler to Paul M. Hemler, February 9, 1971, folder 2: "Abortion—Right-to-Life Programs," box 1, Chancery Office Records, Diocese of Harrisburg; Jane Muldoon to Joseph Bernardin, July 7, 1976, folder: "Correspondence & Press Relations—Correspondence, 1973–1977," box 2, Right to Life of Michigan Records, Bentley Historical Library, Ann Arbor, MI; Minutes of Board Meeting of Michigan Citizens for Life, December 3, 1975, folder: "Administrative—Board of Directors—Minutes, 1975," box 1, Right to Life of Michigan Records; Douglas J. Kreutz, "A Dead Issue?" *Olé: The Tuscon*

*Daily Citizen Magazine*, undated clipping [1974], folder: "Arizona," carton 1, Pr-3, NARAL Printed Materials Collection, Schlesinger Library, Harvard University; NC, "Chicago Clergy Organize Own Anti-Abortion Group," *Michigan Catholic*, August 23, 1972.

22. McHugh, letter to American bishops, January 10, 1969; James T. McHugh, "Abortion: Some Theological and Sociological Perspectives," Family Life Bureau publication, December 1968, folder 1: "Abortion," box 1, Chancery Office Records, Diocese of Harrisburg.

23. William B. Ball to Paul V. Harrington, March 16, 1966, folder: "Abortion, 1965–1967," box 1, Rev. Paul V. Harrington Papers, Archives of the Archdiocese of Boston; Michael Taylor to NRLC Board of Directors, December 1, 1972, folder: "NRLC 1972," box 4, ACCL.

24. James T. McHugh to George Leech, November 6, 1967, folder 1: "Abortion," box 1, Chancery Office Records, Diocese of Harrisburg.

25. Examples of Protestant doctors who took leadership positions in state pro-life organizations in the early 1970s included, among others, Albert Forman (North Dakota), Carolyn Gerster (Arizona), Mildred Jefferson (Massachusetts), Richard Jaynes (Michigan), and Fred Mecklenburg (Minnesota).

26. Charles Carroll, "Abortion Without Ethics? The Legal Becomes Moral," n.d. [c. 1972], folder 7, box 15, George Huntston Williams Papers, Harvard Divinity School; Sagar C. Jain and Steven Hughes, *California Abortion Act 1967: A Study in Legislative Process* (Chapel Hill: Carolina Population Center, 1969), 79–80; Paul Marx to Paul Anderson, September 16, 1969, folder 26, box 3, Marx Papers; Maurice J. Dingman to Paul Marx, July 11, 1969, folder 26, box 3, Marx Papers; Paul Marx to Maurice J. Dingman, July 16, 1969, folder 26, box 3, Marx Papers.

27. Paul Ramsey, "The Sanctity of Life: In the First of It," *Dublin Review*, Spring 1967, 1–21; George Huntston Williams, "The Sacred Condominium," in *The Morality of Abortion: Legal and Historical Perspectives*, ed. John T. Noonan Jr. (Cambridge, MA: Harvard University Press, 1970), 146–171; George H. Williams to Gerard S. Garey [1974], folder 9, box 11, Williams Papers; Richard John Neuhaus, "The Dangerous Assumptions," *Commonweal*, June 30, 1967, 408–413.

28. For instance, numerous articles from the *New York Times* in the late 1960s and early 1970s treated opposition to abortion as primarily a Catholic cause. For one of the many examples of this phenomenon, see "Opposition Growing in Wisconsin to U.S. Court Legalization of Early Abortions," *New York Times*, March 15, 1970, which portrayed the opposition to abortion legalization in Wisconsin as coming mainly from Catholics, and especially from Catholic clerics.

29. Paul Ramsey to Rev. Thomas F. Dentici, October 3, 1969, folder: "Right to Life," box 24, Ramsey Papers; Paul Ramsey to Joseph A. O'Connor, November 8, 1968, folder: "Joseph A. O'Connor," box 21, Ramsey Papers; George H. Williams, "Creatures of a Creator, Members of a Body, Subjects of a Kingdom," sermon

preached at Memorial Church, Harvard University, February 27, 1972, folder 5, box 8, Williams Papers; Charles E. Rice to George Williams, February 10, 1972, folder 4, box 6, Williams Papers; Neuhaus, "The Dangerous Assumptions," 411. In 1990, Neuhaus, after becoming more politically conservative and more outspoken in his opposition to abortion, converted to Catholicism.

30. Raymond Tatalovich, *The Politics of Abortion in the United States and Canada: A Comparative Study* (New York: M. E. Sharpe, 1997), 29.

31. "Impetus for Reform," *New York Times*, February 21, 1967; "Rockefeller Urges Abortion Review," *New York Times*, December 22, 1966; Sydney H. Schanberg, "Rockefeller Asks Abortion Reform," *New York Times*, January 10, 1968; Sydney H. Schanberg, "Javits Calls on Legislature to Pass Abortion Reform," *New York Times*, February 20, 1967; UPI, "Abortion Laws Seen Fading," *New York Times*, April 4, 1970; Robert O. Self, *All in the Family: The Realignment of American Democracy since the 1960s* (New York: Hill and Wang, 2012), 256; Lee Edwards, *Goldwater: The Man Who Made a Revolution* (Washington, DC: Regnery Books, 1995), 420–421; Mary S. Melcher, *Pregnancy, Motherhood, and Choice in Twentieth-Century Arizona* (Tucson: University of Arizona Press, 2012), 120; Arnold H. Lubasch, "Goldwater Hails Young People, Agrees with 'Much' of New Left," *New York Times*, February 21, 1970.

32. "Gov. Agnew Backs Legalized Abortions," *Washington Post*, January 10, 1968; "Maryland Adopts Abortion Law," *Washington Post*, March 27, 1968; "Delaware Eases Its Abortion Code," *New York Times*, June 22, 1969.

33. Dr. and Mrs. Robert M. Derman to Donald A. Bell, March 23, 1969, folder: "Abortion, 1969 (file #3)," box 1, MS 74–15, Donald A. Bell Papers, Wichita State University; Donald A. Bell to Clara Lee, April 17, 1969, folder: "Abortion, 1969 (file #1)," box 1, MS 74–15, Bell Papers; Biddy Hurlbut, "Politics and Abortion," November 15, 1970, folder: "KS, 1969–1970," carton 3, NARAL Records; Donald A. Bell to Mrs. L. J. Antonelli, March 18, 1969, folder: "Abortion, 1969 (file #1)," box 1, MS 74–15, Bell Papers; Mary Ellen Lipke to Donald A. Bell, March 3, 1969, folder: "Abortion, 1969 (file #3)," box 1, MS 74–15, Bell Papers; James E. Skahan to Donald A. Bell, March 19, 1969, folder: "Abortion, 1969 (file #2)," box 1, MS 74–15, Bell Papers.

34. Gallup Poll, Abortion, November 1969, in Gallup Organization, *America's Opinion on Abortion, 1962–1992* (Princeton, NJ: Gallup Organization, 1992), unpaginated; Bernard Weinraub, "Unrest Spurs Growth of Conservative Student Groups," *New York Times*, October 12, 1969; AP, "Young Republicans Urge Liberalized Abortion Law," *New York Times*, February 2, 1969.

35. Donald T. Critchlow, *Intended Consequences: Birth Control, Abortion, and the Federal Government in Modern America* (New York: Oxford University Press, 1999), 50–54.

36. "Abortion Reform Rejected," *New York Times*, April 8, 1971; "Abortion Reform Defeated," *New York Times*, April 8, 1971; Sydney H. Schanberg, "Abortion

Change Killed in Albany by Vote of 15 to 3," *New York Times*, March 8, 1967; John Kifner, "Abortion Reform Dies in the Assembly," *New York Times*, April 4, 1968.

37. K. D. Whitehead, "The Maryland Abortion Law—'An Abomination in the Sight of the Lord,'" *Wanderer*, June 11, 1970, 5.


CHAPTER 5

1. Paul V. Harrington to Robert Byrn, December 7, 1967, folder: "Abortion, 1965–1967," box 1, Rev. Paul V. Harrington Papers, Archives of the Archdiocese of Boston.

2. "Reform Favored," *New York Times*, March 7, 1966.

3. "Colorado Is Split on Abortion Law," *New York Times*, April 30, 1967.

4. Paul V. Harrington to Roy Heffernan, June 9, 1966, folder: "Abortion, 1965–1967," box 1, Harrington Papers; Harrington to W. N. Bergin, July 21, 1966, folder: "Abortion, 1965–1967," box 1, Harrington Papers.

5. William J. Robinson, *The Law against Abortion: Its Perniciousness Demonstrated and Its Repeal Demanded* (New York: Eugenics Publishing Co., 1933); A. J. Rongy, *Abortion: Legal or Illegal?* (New York: Vanguard Press, 1933), 85–98; Frederick J. Taussig, *Abortion: Spontaneous and Induced, Medical and Social Aspects* (St. Louis, MO: C. V. Mosby, 1936), 317–321, 422.

6. Susan Berman, "The Abortion Crusader," *San Francisco*, July 1970, 16–17.

7. CCHAL, Chronological Events of Citizens Committee for Humane Abortion Laws [late 1964], folder: "Citizens' Committee for Humane Abortion Laws, 1961–1964," box 1, MC 289, Society for Human Abortion (SHA) Records, Schlesinger Library, Harvard University; Eloise Dungan, "Trying to Break Silence Barrier on Abortion Laws," *San Francisco News Call-Bulletin*, August 28, 1964; Pat Maginnis to Alan Guttmacher, March 28, 1962, folder 17, box 1, Alan Frank Guttmacher Papers, Countway Library of Medicine, Harvard University; SHA Newsletter, May 9, 1965, folder: "SHA Newsletters, 1965–1973 (scattered)," box 1, MC 289, SHA Records; Staff Report of California State Assembly Committee on Criminal Procedure, "On Therapeutic Abortion," n.d. [late 1963 or early 1964], folder 9, box 509, Anthony C. Beilenson Papers, University of California, Los Angeles; Citizens Committee for Humane Abortion Laws Resolution [December 1964], folder: "Citizens' Committee for Humane Abortion Laws, 1961–1964," box 1, MC 289, SHA Records.

8. Louise Butler, "The Society for Humane Abortion," unpublished paper, May 21,1965, 14–15, 39, folder: "Butler, Louise: 'The Society for Human Abortion,' May 21, 1965," box 1, MC 289, SHA Records; "Drive to Legalize Abortion Gathering Steam, Backers Say," *San Jose Mercury*, August 29, 1965.

9. David J. Garrow, *Liberty and Sexuality: The Right to Privacy and the Making of Roe v. Wade*, 2nd ed. (Berkeley: University of California Press, 1998), 284–308; Pat Maginnis to Richard Bowers, December 6, 1969, folder: "CA, Oct.–Dec.,

1969," carton 2, MC 313, NARAL Records, 1968–1976, Schlesinger Library, Harvard University.

10. McKinney, "A Step toward Legality"; Rowena Gurner, LTE, *San Francisco Chronicle*, May 5, 1967; Berman, "The Abortion Crusader," 16; "Critic of Abortion Laws," *Golden Gator*, San Francisco State University, November 21, 1967; Mildred Schroeder, "One Woman's Abortion Crusade," *San Francisco Examiner*, September 26, 1966.

11. *Society for Humane Abortion Newsletter*, January/February 1967, 3; Woman Plans Abortion Test on Self," *Redwood City (CA) Tribune*, May 20, 1967.

12. "Woman Tells of Techniques and Lists Places to Go," *New York Times*, December 3, 1966; Berman, "The Abortion Crusader," 18; "Drive to Legalize Abortion Gathering Steam, Backers Say," *San Jose Mercury*, August 29, 1965.

13. Lawrence Lader, *Abortion* (Indianapolis: Bobbs-Merrill, 1966); Harold Rosen, Afterword, in *Abortion in America: Medical, Psychiatric, Legal, Anthropological, and Religious Considerations*, ed. Harold Rosen (Boston: Beacon Press, 1967), 320.

14. National Organization for Women, "The Right of a Woman to Control Her Own Reproductive Process," 1967, http://www.feminist.org/research/chronicles/early3.html; Alan F. Guttmacher to Miss F. Thomas, September 17, 1968, folder 24, box 1, Guttmacher Papers; "N.A.R.L. [*sic*] Is Born," *Society for Humane Abortion Newsletter*, April 1969, folder: "SHA Newsletters, 1965–1973 (scattered)," box 1, MC 289, SHA Records; "New Group Will Seek Changes in Abortion Laws," *New York Times*, February 17, 1969; Donna Adler to Carol Radcliffe, August 19, 1971, folder: "CO, 1969–10/71," box 2, NARAL Records; Lee Gidding to Kathleen McElroy, May 25, 1971, folder: "MD, 1971–72," box 3, NARAL Records; Leigh Ann Wheeler, *How Sex Became a Civil Liberty* (New York: Oxford University Press, 2013), 128–131. NARAL changed its name in 1973 to the National Abortion Rights Action League and then became NARAL Pro-Choice America in 2003.

15. Robert D. McFadden, "Flaws in Abortion Reform Found in an 8-State Study," *New York Times*, April 13, 1970; Hawaii State Legislature Conference Committee Report No. 3–70, February 19, 1970, folder 13, box 509.

16. Jane E. Brody, "Eased Laws on Abortion Failing to Achieve Goals," *New York Times*, June 8, 1970.

17. U.S. Department of Health, Education, and Welfare, "Abortion Surveillance Report: Hospital Abortions—Annual Summary, 1969," April 1, 1970, "National Right to Life Meeting, 7/31–8/2/70" folder, box 4, American Citizens Concerned for Life (ACCL) Records, Gerald R. Ford Library, Ann Arbor, MI.

18. "Public Evenly Divided on Abortion in Early Stage of Pregnancy," in Gallup Organization, *America's Opinion on Abortion, 1962–1992* (Princeton, NJ: Gallup Organization, 1992), unpaginated.

19. Unitarian Universalist Association, General Resolution on Reform of Abortion Statutes, 1963, http://www.uua.org/statements/statements/13423.shtml; Unitarian

Universalist Association, General Resolution on Abortion, 1968, http://www. uua.org/statements/statements/14441.shtml; American Baptist Convention, Resolution on Abortion, May 1968; United Presbyterian Church in the USA, Resolution on Abortion, 1970; General Conference of the United Methodist Church, Resolution on Abortion, April 1970; Episcopal Diocese of New York, Resolution on Abortion, February 1969. Copies of all resolutions come from folder: "Orgzl. Pos. on abortion, 1970–73," carton 8, MC 313, NARAL Records.

20. United Nations, "The World at Six Billion" [1999], http://www.un.org/esa/population/publications/sixbillion/sixbilpart1.pdf; Mollie Orshansky, "The Shape of Poverty in 1966," *Social Security Bulletin*, March 1968, 7–9, http://www.un.org/esa/population/publications/sixbillion/sixbilpart1.pdf.

21. "Singles Group to Hear Talk on Abortion," *Riverdale (NY) Press*, January 5, 1967; Garrett Hardin, "Parenthood: Right or Privilege?" *Science*, July 31, 1970; California Committee to Legalize Abortion, fundraising letter, n.d. [late 1960s?], folder: "Citizens' Committee for Humane Abortion Laws, 1961–1964," box 1, MC 289, SHA Records; Lana Clarke Phelan, "Abortion Laws: The Cruel Fraud," speech presented at CA Conference on Abortion in Santa Barbara and reprinted by Society for Humane Abortion, February 10, 1968, folder 12, box 509, Beilenson Papers; Frank E. McCoy to Anthony C. Beilenson, April 28, 1967, folder 14, box 514, Beilenson Papers.

22. Paul R. Ehrlich, *The Population Bomb* (New York: Ballantine Books, 1968), 44–45, 139; Donald T. Critchlow, *Intended Consequences: Birth Control, Abortion, and the Federal Government in Modern America* (New York: Oxford University Press, 1999), 90.

23. Statement of Senator Anthony C. Beilenson, March 9, 1970, folder 34, box 166, Beilenson Papers; Voice for the Unborn (Oakland, CA), Open Letter to Senator Anthony C. Beilenson, May 21, 1970, folder 11, box 514, collection 391, Beilenson Papers.

24. Statement on Population Issued by the Bishops of the United States, 1959, folder 7, box 86, National Catholic Welfare Conference Papers, Catholic University of America; U.S. Department of Health, Education, and Welfare, *Vital Statistics of the United States 1965* (Washington, DC: US Public Health Service, 1967), vol. 1, I–22, http://www.nber.org/vital-stats-books/nat65_1.CV.pdf; Anthony Zimmerman, *The Catholic Viewpoint on "Overpopulation"* (Techny, IL: Divine Word Publications, 1959), 14–16; Robert D. McFadden, "In 3 Countries with Legal Abortion, Debate Goes On," *New York Times*, April 15, 1970; Randy Engel, *A Pro-Life Report on Population Growth and the American Future* (self-published, 1972), 50–51; Russ Wilhelm to Gordon Anderson, October 20, 1972, folder: "Wilhelm, Russ, 1972," box 8, North Dakota Right to Life Association (NDRLA) Records, State Historical Society of North Dakota, Bismarck.

25. Renew America, "Randy Engel Column," http://www.renewamerica.com/columns/engel; United States Coalition for Life, "Minority Report Challenges

Objectivity of Rockefeller Population Commission" [1972], folder: "Miscellaneous Reference Materials (4)," box 3, ACCL; Engel, *A Pro-Life Report on Population Growth and the American Future*, 35; Agenda for National Right to Life Convention Annual Meeting, June 16–18, 1972, folder: "Convention, National, 1972," box 2, NDRLA. The charge that birth control promotion programs in poorer nations were a form of elite control—and perhaps even a new "imperialism"—eventually became a common leftist or liberal critique that was accepted in pro-choice, as well as pro-life, circles. For examples of this critique, see Dorothy Roberts, *Killing the Black Body: Race, Reproduction, and the Meaning of Liberty* (New York: Random House, 1997); and Matthew Connelly, *Fatal Misconception: The Struggle to Control World Population* (Cambridge, MA: Harvard University Press, 2008).

26. Bruce Schulman, *The Seventies: The Great Shift in American Culture, Society, and Politics* (New York: Free Press, 2001), 33; Felicia Kornbluh, *The Battle for Welfare Rights: Politics and Poverty in Modern America* (Philadelphia: University of Pennsylvania Press, 2007), 93; James T. Patterson, *Grand Expectations: The United States, 1945–1974* (New York: Oxford University Press, 1996), 698; Dan T. Carter, *The Politics of Rage: George Wallace, the Origins of the New Conservatism, and the Transformation of American Politics*, 2nd ed. (Baton Rouge: Louisiana State University Press, 2000), 458.

27. Legislative Analyst's Report to the Ways and Means Committee of the California State Assembly [spring 1970], folder: "Abortion, 1970–1972," Archives of the Archdiocese of Los Angeles; NARAL, "Facts of Life in California—1973," folder: "CA, 1973," carton 2, MC 313, NARAL Records; Wayne H. Davis, Statement to House Judiciary Subcommittee Hearings on Abortion, Franklin, KY, February 14, 1972, folder: "KY: 1969–75," carton 3, MC 313, NARAL Records.

28. John T. Noonan Jr., Statement before California Assembly Committee on Judiciary, October 22, 1970, folder: "National Right to Life Committee, 1970–1972," box 5, NDRLA.

29. Lader, *Abortion*, 166; NARAL, "Abortion: Questions and Answers," brochure, n.d. [c. 1971 or 1972], folder: "Miscellaneous Information and Handouts, 1971-1972," box 5, NDRLA; John C. Willke and Barbara Willke, *Handbook on Abortion*, 3rd ed. (Cincinnati, OH: Hiltz, 1973), 51–53; Juan J. Ryan, Press Release on Behalf of the National Right to Life Committee, March 17, 1972, folder: "National Right to Life Committee, 1972," box 5, NDRLA.

30. Lon Daniels, "Foes of Abortion Demonstrate Here," *San Francisco Examiner*, October 15, 1973; Miami ZPG Newsletter, November 1971, folder: "Florida," carton 1, Pr-3, NARAL Printed Materials, Schlesinger Library, Harvard University; Margot Sheahan, LTE, *Arizona Republic*, January 27, 1977; Thomas W. Hilgers, "Abortion: Is It Really the Best We Have to Offer?: The Philosophy of Involvement," SOUL, n.d. [c. 1971–1972], folder: "Speeches and Articles, 1968–1971," box 7, NDRLA.

While it was certainly true, as Hilgers suggested, that it was more difficult to find adoptive homes for minority and handicapped children than it was to find placements for healthy white babies, the number of white families adopting black children rapidly increased in the late 1960s. In 1968, 23 percent of black children placed for adoption were adopted by white families; in 1970, 35 percent were (Gordon Scott Bonham, "Who Adopts: The Relationship of Adoption and Social-Demographic Characteristics of Women," *Journal of Marriage and Family* 39 (1977): 299).

31. Penelope L. Maza, "Adoption Trends, 1944–1975," Adoption History Project, University of Oregon, http://darkwing.uoregon.edu/~adoption/archive/MazaAT. htm. From 1965 to 1972, an average of 19.3 percent of white women who gave birth out of wedlock put their child up for adoption, but from 1973 to 1981, only 7.6 percent did so—a statistic that suggests that in the 1970s, a rapidly increasing percentage of single white women were choosing to raise their children themselves, and that single parenthood may have been losing some of its traditional stigma among whites. The percentage of single black women giving their children up for adoption had always been low, but the practice became even less common in the 1970s; only 1.5 percent of black women who gave birth out of wedlock between 1965 and 1972 gave their children up for adoption, and only 0.2 percent did so between 1973 and 1981 (Christine A. Bachrach et al., "Relinquishment of Premarital Births: Evidence from National Survey Data," *Family Planning Perspectives* 24 (1992): 29).

32. Thomas Hilgers claimed that 800,000 couples had applied to adopt in 1970, but that only 11 percent had been given a child (Hilgers, "Abortion: Is It Really the Best We Have to Offer?"). I have not been able to determine the validity of Hilgers's statistics, but regardless of whether or not his statement of the number of couples who had applied to adopt was fully accurate, he was correct in his general claim that the number of couples interested in adopting exceeded the number of children available for adoption, as later data showed. In 1988, for instance, the National Survey of Family Growth found that more than two million women had contacted an agency or lawyer at some point in the past to begin the adoption application process, but only 620,000 had ever been given a child (Kathy S. Stolley, "Statistics on Adoption in the United States," *Future of Children* 3 (1993): 37).

33. Sidney Callahan, "Talk of 'Wanted Child' Makes for Doll Objects," *National Catholic Reporter*, December 3, 1971.

34. *Gleitman v. Cosgrove*, 49 N.J. 22, New Jersey Supreme Court (1967). For a discussion of earlier court decisions in favor of fetal rights, see chapter 2.

35. "Are Abortion Laws an Invasion of Privacy?" *SHA Newsletter*, April/May 1966, folder: "SHA Newsletters, 1965–1973 (scattered)," box 1, MC 289, SHA Records; Jean Faust, testimony in support of abortion law repeal at a hearing of the New York State Joint Legislative Committee on the Problems of Public Health, Medicare, Medicaid, and Compulsory Health and Hospital Insurance,

February 13, 1969, folder 2, box 56, National Organization for Women (NOW) Records, Schlesinger Library, Harvard University.

36. *People v. Belous*, 71 Cal.2d 954 (1969), http://scocal.stanford.edu/opinion/people-v-belous-22692.

37. *People v. Belous*; Garrow, *Liberty and Sexuality*, 377–382.

38. J. J. Brandlin to James McIntyre, April 9,1969; J. J. Brandlin to Thomas J. Arata and other attorneys, January 23, 1969; J. J. Brandlin to John F. Duff, October 3, 1969; J. J. Brandlin to James McIntyre, September 17, 1969 (all in folder: "Abortion: 1968–1969," Archives of the Archdiocese of Los Angeles); NC, "Foes of Abortion Lose Attempt to Get Supreme Court Involved," *Catholic Witness* (Harrisburg, PA), March 5, 1970, 5; "Court Cases Pose Urgent Challenge," NRLC Newsletter, December 1969, folder: "Abortion Legislation and Litigation (3 of 7)," box 23, Harrington Papers.

39. Press release from Senator Anthony C. Beilenson, January 31, 1969, folder 6, box 167, Beilenson Papers; Al Antaczak, NC, "California Abortion Survey," *Nevada Register*, July 13, 1972; "Court in California, 4–3, Makes Possible Abortion on Demand," *New York Times*, November 23, 1972; Alice Hartle, "Reagan Likes HLA, Gives Views on Abortion, Euthanasia," *National Right to Life News*, December 1975, 1.

40. Statement of Senator Anthony C. Beilenson, March 9, 1970, folder 34, box 166, Beilenson Papers.

41. Alan F. Guttmacher to Miss F. Thomas, September 17, 1968, folder 24, box 1, Guttmacher Papers; American Civil Liberties Union, Policy Statement on Abortion, July 1968, and American Humanist Association, Resolution on Abortion, April 28, 1966, reproduced in Thomas M. Hart, Compilation of Statements of Organizations in Favor of Repeal of Abortion Laws, October 1, 1968, folder 6, box 1, Guttmacher Papers; Lee Gidding to Joyce C. Kahn, April 1, 1970, folder: "DE, 1969–75," carton 2, MC 313, NARAL Records.

42. Garrett Hardin, "A Scientist's Case for Abortion," *Redbook*, May 1967, 124.

43. Ti-Grace Atkinson, Refutation of Catholic position on abortion [1967], folder 3, box 23, NOW Records; Alicia Armstrong, "Updated Abortion Laws Asked," *Milwaukee Journal*, May 5, 1961; Thomas P. O'Neill to Abortion Task Force, NOW, December 8, 1971, folder 12, box 1, Patricia Gold Papers, Schlesinger Library, Harvard University.

44. Ashley Montagu, unpublished letter to the *New York Times*, March 3, 1967, box 2 (no separate folder), Lawrence Lader Papers, Countway Library of Medicine; Lucile Newman, "Between the Ideal and Reality: Values in American Society," in *The Case for Legalized Abortion Now*, ed. Alan F. Guttmacher (Berkeley, CA: Diablo Press, 1967), 63; Ti-Grace Atkinson, Refutation of Catholic position on abortion [1967], folder 3, box 23, NOW Records.

45. Paul Harrington to W. N. Bergin, July 21, 1966, folder: "Abortion, 1965–1967," box 1, Harrington Papers.

46. NARAL, "Portrait of the Opposition," February 1972, folder: "Opposition, 1972," carton 8, MC 313, NARAL Records.

47. Germain Grisez, *Abortion: The Myths, the Realities, and the Arguments* (New York: Corpus Books, 1970), 270.

48. Grisez, *Abortion*, 2–4.

49. Harrington to Bergin, 21 July 1966, folder: "Abortion, 1965–1967," box 1, Harrington Papers; Patricia G. Steinhoff and Milton Diamond, *Abortion Politics: The Hawaii Experience* (Honolulu: University of Hawaii Press, 1977), 16; Nancy D. Morrison to Vicki Kaplan, May 5, 1974, folder: "Hawaii: 1969–75," carton 3, MC 313, NARAL Records; "Anti-Abortion Law Gains in Hawaii," *New York Times*, February 11, 1970.

50. Laurence Wiig to Lee Gidding, December 12, 1969, folder: "Hawaii, 1969–75," carton 3, MC 313, NARAL Records; "Support Repeal of Abortion Law," flyer [1970], folder: "Hawaii, 1969–75," carton 3, MC 313, NARAL Records; Steinhoff and Diamond, *Abortion Politics*, 8–17; John A. Burns to Mrs. Auray Stewart, July 20, 1970, folder: "Legislation—Various States', 1964–1971," box 4, NDRLA; Hawaii State Legislature Conference Committee Report No. 3–70, February 19, 1970, folder 13, box 509, Beilenson Papers.

51. Hawaii State Legislature Conference Committee Report No. 3–70.

52. Hawaii State Legislature Conference Committee Report No. 3–70; "Plans Cemetery for Aborted Children," *Wanderer* (St. Paul, MN), May 21, 1970, 1.

53. "Anti-Abortion Law Gains in Hawaii," *New York Times*, February 11, 1970; "Bill to Legalize Abortions Clears Hawaii Legislature," *New York Times*, February 25, 1970.

54. Paul M. Weyrich, "An Open Letter to Gov. Burns of Hawaii," *Wanderer*, March 26, 1970, 4.

55. "Plans Cemetery for Aborted Children"; William Helton, AP, "Abortion Foe Gives Alternative," *Bismarck Tribune*, June 5, 1972.

56. AP, "Liberalized Abortion Vetoed in Alaska," *New York Times*, April 19, 1970; AP, "Abortion Reform Veto Overridden in Alaska," *New York Times*, May 1, 1970.

57. Sydney H. Schanberg, "Assembly Blocks Abortion Reform in Sudden Switch," *New York Times*, April 18, 1969.

58. "Brydges Easing Opposition to New Abortion Law," *New York Times*, February 19, 1970; Bill Kovach, "Brydges Sees Governor Backed on Budget Cuts," *New York Times*, January 28, 1970; Francis X. Clines, "State Senate to Act on Abortion Reform," *New York Times*, March 11, 1970.

59. William E. Farrell, "Opponents of the Abortion Law Gather Strength in Legislature," *New York Times*, January 26, 1970; Stacie Taranto, "Defending 'Family Values': Women's Grassroots Politics and the Republican Right, 1970–1980" (Ph.D. diss., Brown University, 2010), 41–46; Statement of Constance Cook, December 16, 1968, folder: "NY, 1968–Dec. 1969," carton 4, MC 313, NARAL Records; Bill Kovach, "Abortion Reform Beaten in the Assembly by 3 Votes," *New York Times*, March 31, 1970.

60. "Bishops Oppose Abortion Law," *Catholic News* (New York), March 12, 1970, 1; Dick Dowd, "Latest Abortion Bill Seen as No Different from Rest," *Catholic News*, March 12, 1970, 14; "Abortion Reform Has Only a Fighting Chance," *New York Times*, March 22, 1970; "Position on Abortion," *Catholic News*, April 9, 1970, 3.

61. Francis X. Clines, "State Senate to Act on Abortion Reform," *New York Times*, March 11, 1970; Bill Kovach, "Albany G.O.P. Leaders Appear Split on Legislation," *New York Times*, March 12, 1970; Bill Kovach, "Albany to Open Abortion Debate," *New York Times*, March 17, 1970; Bill Kovach, "Abortion Reform Approved, 31–26, by State Senate," *New York Times*, March 19, 1970; Bill Kovach, "New Vote Due Next Week," *New York Times*, April 1, 1970. For a discussion of Brydges's probable motives in endorsing an abortion law repeal bill that he later opposed, see Lawrence Lader, *Abortion II: Making the Revolution* (Boston: Beacon Press, 1973), 132–133.

62. Dick Dowd, "Statewide Opposition Mounts against Abortion Repeal Bill," *Catholic News*, March 26, 1970, 1; "Position on Abortion," *Catholic News*, April 9, 1970, 3; Bill Kovach, "Abortion Reform: How Victory Was Turned into Defeat," *New York Times*, April 5, 1970.

63. "Catholic Bishops' Statement," *Catholic News*, March 26, 1970, 1; "Abortion Narrowly Defeats Abortion Repeal—But," *Catholic News*, April 2, 1970, 1; "Permissive Abortion in Maryland; Loses in New York," *Wanderer*, April 9, 1970, 1; AP, "Man Who Cast Key Vote on Abortion Is Rebuffed," *New York Times*, April 20, 1970.

64. "N.Y. Now on Abortion Bandwagon," *Wanderer*, April 23, 1970, 1; Bill Kovach, "Abortion Reform Is Voted by the Assembly, 76 to 73; Final Approval Expected," *New York Times*, April 10, 1970; Bill Kovach, "Final Approval of Abortion Bill Voted in Albany," *New York Times*, April 11, 1970.

65. Editorial, "Foundation of Human Life," *Catholic News*, April 16, 1970, 1; Dick Dowd, "Governor Signs Abortion Law," *Catholic News*, April 16, 1970, 1.

66. Deirdre Carmody, "Catholic Bishops Assail Abortion Bill," *New York Times*, April 11, 1970; "Notes Excommunication Penalty for Abortion," *Wanderer*, June 25, 1970, 1; Dick Dowd, "N.Y. Bishops Call Abortion 'Tragic Chapter in History,'" *Catholic News*, July 2, 1970, 1.

67. Catherine Willis, "Abortion: Theory and Reality," *Wanderer*, November 26, 1970, 5.

68. Thomas J. Riley to Paul V. Harrington, June 9, 1970, folder: "Cushing, Cardinal Richard re Abortion, 1970," box 3, Harrington Papers.

69. Fred C. Shapiro, "'Right to Life' Has a Message for New York State Legislators," *New York Times*, August 20, 1972.

70. "Legal Abortion: Who, Why, and Where," *Time*, September 27, 1971.

71. Thomas A. Connolly to priests in Seattle, April 14, 1970, and Connolly to priests in Seattle, September 29, 1970, folder: "Opposition, 1972," carton 8, MC 313, NARAL

Records; "Heated Campaign Fought in Washington State over Abortions," *New York Times*, October 25, 1970; UPI, "Abortion Referendum Stirring Bitter Debate," *Reading (PA) Eagle*, October 21, 1970; NC, "Seattle Archbishop Protests Passage of Abortion Measure," *New World* (Chicago), November 20, 1970.

72. K. D. Whitehead, "The Maryland Abortion Law—'An Abomination in the Sight of the Lord,'" *Wanderer*, June 11, 1970, 5; "Abortion: Whose Right to Decide?" *Washington Post*, March 6, 1970.

73. Kirk Scharfenberg, "Liberalized Abortion Bill Up to Mandel," *Washington Post*, April 1, 1970; "Liberalized Abortion Bill Is Vetoed in Maryland," *New York Times*, May 27, 1970.

74. Ruth Steel to Lee Gidding, November 5, 1970, folder: "CO, 1969–10/71," carton 2, MC 313, NARAL Records; JoinCalifornia, Election History for the State of California, Results of the November 3, 1970, General Election, http://www.join-california.com/election/1970-11-03; Bill Roy, "No Issue Has Affected Politics Like This One," *Topeka Capital-Journal*, February 17, 2007, http://cjonline.com/stories/021707/opi_148881415.shtml; Dennis Hevesi, "Constance E. Cook, 89, Who Wrote Abortion Law, Is Dead," *New York Times*, January 24, 2009.

75. Gallup Poll, "Legal Abortions," January 1966, in Gallup Organization, *America's Opinion on Abortion*, unpaginated; Louis Harris, "Poll on Abortion," *Washington Post*, June 22, 1970.

76. Judy Edinger, "Court Must Decide Legality of Abortion, Attorneys Told," *Catholic News*, May 7, 1970, 11.

CHAPTER 6

1. Paul Marx to George Speltz, April 29, 1970, folder 2, box 2, Fr. Paul Marx Papers, Saint John's University, Collegeville, MN.

2. Paul Marx to Charles Carroll, February 9, 1970, folder 26, box 3, Marx Papers.

3. James McIntyre to Robert D. Wood, July 8, 1966, folder: "Abortion—1966," Archives of the Archdiocese of Los Angeles; Charles E. Rice, *The Vanishing Right to Live: An Appeal for a Renewed Reverence for Life* (Garden City, NY: Doubleday, 1969); Russell B. Shaw, *Abortion on Trial* (Dayton, OH: Pflaum Press, 1968).

4. Tom Pawlick, "'After about 10 to 12 Weeks . . . the Child Inside Is Cut into Pieces and Pulled or Scooped Out,'" *Catholic Witness* (Harrisburg, PA), April 16, 1970, 4; NC, "Live, Aborted Babies Reported Sold for Tests," *Catholic Witness*, May 28, 1970, 8; "Today My Mother Killed Me: The Distressing Diary of an Aborted Child," *Catholic Witness*, May 21, 1970, 4.

5. A. J. Matt Jr., "Murderous and Ghastly," *Wanderer* (St. Paul, MN), February 26, 1970.

6. Mary Ann Knight, Editorial Rebuttal for KHJ radio station, Hollywood, CA, November 3, 1970, folder 12, box 509, Anthony C. Beilenson Papers, University of California, Los Angeles.

7. For a clinical description of these abortion techniques, see Malcolm Potts et al., *Abortion* (Cambridge: Cambridge University Press, 1977), 184–203.

8. "What Nurses Think about Abortion," *RN*, June 1970, 41; Gallup Poll, Abortion, November 1969, in Gallup Organization, *America's Opinion on Abortion, 1962–1992* (Princeton, NJ: Gallup Organization, 1992), unpaginated.

9. US Census Bureau, "Percentage of Nurses Who Are Men from 1970 to 2011" (2013), http://www.census.gov/newsroom/releases/img/cb13-32_figure1-hi.JPG; Nancy Groves, "From Past to Present: The Changing Demographics of Women in Medicine," *Ophthalmology Times*, February 2008; "Abortion: A Stormy Subject," *RN*, September 1970, 56.

10. Doris Revere Peters, "New York Nurses Start Shunning Abortion Hospitals," *Catholic Witness*, November 5, 1970, 10.

11. Ronald Kotulak, "New Law Goes Too Far, Angry Doctors Charge," *Chicago Tribune*, December 18, 1970; Ronald Kotulak, "A.M.A. 'Violently Opposes' Legal Late-Term Abortions," *Chicago Tribune*, December 19, 1970.

12. Kotulak, "New Law Goes Too Far."

13. "N.Y. Doctor Says 4,000 Aborted Live," *Michigan Catholic*, May 10, 1972.

14. Right to Life League of Southern California, Advertisement for "Post-Abortion Slide Studies of Fetuses" [c. 1971], folder: "National Right to Life Committee, 1970–1972," box 5, North Dakota Right to Life Association Records (NDRLA), State Historical Society of North Dakota, Bismarck; Right to Life of Palos Verdes Estates, CA, order form for postcards, n.d. [1972?], folder: "Miscellaneous Reference Materials (4)," box 3, American Citizens Concerned for Life Records (ACCL), Gerald R. Ford Library, Ann Arbor, MI; Charlotte Robinson, "Respect for Life: The Fight for the Unborn," *Detroit Free Press*, June 4, 1974. For examples of fetal photographs of the early 1970s, see John C. and Barbara Willke, *Handbook on Abortion*, 3rd ed. (Cincinnati, OH: Hiltz, 1973), photo insert, 27–28; and John C. and Barbara Willke, with Marie Willke Meyers, *Abortion and the Pro-Life Movement: An Inside View* (West Conshohocken, PA: Infinity, 2014), 41, 44, 60–61, 73–74. For examples of more recent fetal photographs distributed by the Willkes and their associates, see Life Issues Institute, "New Fetal Development Pictures," 2001, http://www.lifeissues.org/2001/04/new-fetal-development-pictures/.

15. Paul Marx to Margie Montgomery, November 28, 1972, folder 21, box 1, Marx Papers; Paul Marx, Christmas letter, December 1968, folder 19, box 1, Marx Papers.

16. "Teaching Pro-Life Story Is Subject of Newest Willke Book," *National Right to Life News*, November 1973, 13.

17. "Teaching Pro-Life Story Is Subject of Newest Willke Book," 13.

18. Willke and Willke, *Abortion and the Pro-Life Movement*, 44–75.

19. J. C. Willke to Paul Marx, March 5, 1971, folder 45, box 2, Marx Papers.

20. J. C. Willke to Paul Marx, December 18, 1970, folder 45, box 2, Marx Papers; "N.Y. Doctor Says 4,000 Aborted Live."

21. Willke and Willke, *Handbook on Abortion*, photo insert, 27–28; Richard Cohen, "200 Attend Assembly Unit Hearing on New Maryland Abortion Bill," *Washington Post*, January 29, 1971; Lawrence Meyer, "Md. Abortion Bill Loses in House," *Washington Post*, March 25, 1971.

22. Missouri Citizens for Life, "Important Information for Adults," direct mail, n.d. [1972?], folder 7.2, box 148, R. Sargent Shriver Papers, John F. Kennedy Library, Boston.

23. Missouri Citizens for Life, "Important Information for Adults."

24. "Abortion—Pro or Con?" *Here and Now* (Newsletter of the greater Kansas City chapter of NOW), August 1973, folder 39, carton 53, MS 496, National Organization for Women (NOW) Records, Schlesinger Library, Harvard University.

25. Grace Lichtenstein, "Abortion Laws Opposed at Rally," *New York Times*, March 29, 1970.

26. "Why Do the Rockefellers Push Abortion So Hard?" Minnesota Citizens Concerned for Life (MCCL) Newsletter, June–July 1972, 8, folder: "Miscellaneous Information and Handouts, 1970–1972," box 5, NDRLA; Roy Gibbons, "Abortion Rate Is Enormous, Doctor Warns," *Chicago Tribune*, June 17, 1960; Statement by Constance Cook, December 16, 1968, folder: "NY, 1968—Sept. 1969," carton 4, MC-313 NARAL Records, 1968–1976, Schlesinger Library, Harvard University; "Lessons from Before *Roe*: Will Past Be Prologue?" *Guttmacher Report on Public Policy*, March 2003, http://www.guttmacher.org/pubs/tgr/06/1/gr060108.html.

27. "Teaching Pro-Life Story Is Subject of Newest Willke Book," *National Right to Life News*, November 1973, 13; "Dr. Willke Elected as NRLC President," *National Right to Life News*, July 7, 1980; Willke and Willke, *Handbook on Abortion*, 4 (emphasis in original).

28. "Handbook on Abortion: Ideas for its More Effective Use," n.d. [c. 1972], folder: "Michigan Right to Life Committee—Promotional & Campaign Literature, 2 of 2," box 1, Elizabeth Lemmer Papers, Bentley Historical Library (BHL), University of Michigan, Ann Arbor.

29. "Reform Favored," *New York Times*, March 7, 1966; Gallup poll on abortion, November 1969, in Gallup Organization, *America's Opinion on Abortion*, unpaginated; Jack Rosenthal, "Survey Finds 50% Back Liberalization of Abortion Policy," *New York Times*, October 28, 1971; National Organization for Women, press release, "NOW's Adoption of Bill of Rights," November 20, 1967, https://350fem.blogs.brynmawr.edu/1968/11/20/press-release-nows-adoption-of-bill-of-rights/.

30. AP, "N.Y. Says Three Died after Abortions," *Washington Evening Star*, July 22, 1970; Jane E. Brody, "City's Year-Old Abortion Record Hailed," *New York Times*, June 30, 1971.

31. Michael Taylor, direct mail on behalf of NRLC, March 13, 1971, folder: "National Right to Life Committee, 1970–1972," box 5, NDRLA; "Throng Cheers Abortion Defeat," *Alton (IL) Evening Telegraph*, March 17, 1971; "Committee Kills Abortion Bill," *Mississippi Today*, January 24, 1971; Michael Taylor, direct mail on behalf of NRLC, February 12, 1971, folder: "National Right to Life Committee, 1970–1972," box 5, NDRLA; William Willoughby, "The Easy Abortion Trend: Has Its Course Changed?" *Washington Evening Star*, March 13, 1971; Michael Taylor, direct mail on behalf of NRLC, May 7, 1971, folder: "Legislation, Various States', 1964–1971," box 4, NDRLA.

32. Fred C. Shapiro, " 'Right to Life' Has a Message for New York State Legislators," *New York Times*, August 20, 1972; Robert D. McFadden, "Lobbying on Abortion Increases at Capitol," *New York Times*, May 8, 1972.

33. NRLC Newsletter, June 1970, 2–3, folder: "Newsletters, Outside, 1970," box 5, NDRLA.

34. "The War on the Womb," *Christianity Today*, June 5, 1970, 24–25; Willoughby, "The Easy Abortion Trend."

35. Carl F. H. Henry, "Is Life Ever Cheap?" *Eternity*, February 1971, 20–21.

36. L. Nelson Bell, "An Alternative to Abortion," *Christianity Today*, June 18, 1971, 17–18.

37. "Extra Messages," *Christianity Today*, July 17, 1970, 31.

38. "The Vatican on Birth Control," *Christianity Today*, August 16, 1968, 28–29; "Social Action Aborning," *Christianity Today*, May 7, 1971, 26.

39. Paul L. Sadler, "The Abortion Issue within the Southern Baptist Convention" (Ph.D. diss., Baylor University, 1991), 25–26; Southern Baptist Convention, Resolution on Abortion, June 1971, http://www.sbc.net/resolutions/13/resolution-on-abortion.

40. John Lear, "Women Lead Opposition to Abortion," *Washington Evening Star-News*, April 17, 1973. The public opinion survey was conducted by political scientists at the University of Michigan's Institute for Social Research.

41. Gallup polls on abortion, January 1966 and November 1969, in Gallup Organization, *America's Opinion on Abortion*, unpaginated; Mary K. Stine, LTE to *Pilot* (Boston), March 7, 1969, folder: "Abortion Symposium, 'Right to Life of the Unborn,' 1969," box 1, Rev. Paul V. Harrington Papers, Archives of the Archdiocese of Boston.

42. Paul V. Harrington to Mary K. Stine, March 12, 1969, folder: "Abortion Symposium, 'Right to Life of the Unborn,' 1969," box 1, Harrington Papers.

43. Valerie Vance Dillon, "In Defense of Life: A Handbook for Those Who Oppose the Destruction of the Unborn" (New Jersey Right to Life Committee, December 1970), 12, folder: "Miscellaneous Reference Materials (10)," box 3, ACCL.

44. Evidence of women's early pro-life lobbying efforts comes from a wide variety of sources, including North Dakota Right to Life Association, "Report to the North Dakota Catholic Conference," February 23, 1971, folder: "Miscellaneous

Information and Handouts," box 5, NDRLA; MCCL Newsletter, May 1971, folder: "Newsletters, Outside, 1971," box 5, NDRLA; David H. Tomshany to Richard A. Clark, February 8, 1968, folder: "Abortion, 1968–1969," Archives of the Archdiocese of Los Angeles.

45. David J. Garrow, *Liberty and Sexuality: The Right to Privacy and the Making of Roe v. Wade*, 2nd ed. (Berkeley: University of California Press, 1998), 348; Stacie Taranto, "Defending 'Family Values': Women's Grassroots Politics and the Republican Right, 1970–1980" (Ph.D. diss., Brown University, 2010), 66.

46. Dolores Dvorak, "She Speaks for the Unborn" [1974?], unidentified clipping, single folder in Mary Winter Papers, Schlesinger Library, Harvard University; Mary Winter, speech, West Virginians for Life Annual Banquet, October 1982, single folder in Winter Papers.

47. Dvorak, "She Speaks for the Unborn."

48. Mary Winter, "Abortion—The Abandonment of Women and Children," testimony given to the Shapps Abortion Commission Hearings, Pennsylvania, 1972, single folder in Winter Papers.

49. For an example of criticisms of women who obtained abortions as "guilty" and "personally responsible" for their pregnancies, see Paul V. Harrington, "Abortion," *Linacre Quarterly* 32 (1965): 341–342. For an example of the new compassionate approach that became popular among pro-lifers in the early 1970s, see Willke and Willke, *The Abortion Handbook*.

50. Mary Winter, speech, October 1982.

51. Mary Winter, testimony on behalf of H.B. 71, January 12, 1978, single folder in Winter Papers; Winter, speech, October 1982.

52. "Liberal Plan Approved," *New York Times*, April 1, 1970.

53. Sidney Callahan, "Abortion: Abandoning Women and Children," Minnesota Citizens Concerned for Life publication [1970], folder: "Miscellaneous Information and Handouts, 1971–1972," box 5, NDRLA; Jason DeParle, "Beyond the Legal Right," *Washington Monthly*, April 1989.

54. Sidney Callahan, "Feminist as Antiabortionist," *National Catholic Reporter*, April 7, 1972, 11.

55. Cindy Osborne, "Pat Goltz, Catherine Callaghan, and the Founding of Feminists for Life," in *Pro-Life Feminism: Yesterday and Today*, ed. Mary Krane Derr et al., 2nd ed. (Kansas City, MO: Feminism and Nonviolence Studies Association, 2005), 219–221; Pat Goltz, "Equal Rights," in *Pro-Life Feminism*, 224–226; Sharon Abercrombie, "Pro-Life Begins Boycott," *Columbus Citizen Journal*, June 19, 1974.

56. Carolyn Gerster, testimony before the Senate Judiciary Committee, September 10, 1981, http://www.gpo.gov/fdsys/pkg/GPO-CHRG-OCONNOR/pdf/GPO-CHRG-OCONNOR-4-7-2.pdf; Helen Fogel, "'Abortion Isn't Personal Thing,'" *Detroit Free Press*, February 28, 1971; "Gloria Klein Given Power of 1 Person G.R.I. 1973 Award," unidentified, undated clipping [June 1973], folder 1: "Clippings,"

box 1, Lifespan, Inc. Records, BHL; Gloria Klein, Chairman, Wayne County Lifespan, to "Candidate for Public Office" [July 1974], folder 1: "Clippings," box 1, Lifespan, Inc. Records.

57. Michael A. Taylor, "Birthright," *Catholic Family Leader*, October–November 1970, 1.

58. Louise Summerhill, *The Story of Birthright: The Alternative to Abortion* (Kenosha, WI: Prow Books, 1973), 117, 128–134.

59. Birthright, Membership Statement, 1985, folder: "Birthright, Inc.," Wilcox Collection of Contemporary Political Movements, University of Kansas, Lawrence; "An Ordinary Person Who Did Something Extraordinary for God," *Interim*, September 3, 1991, http://www.theinterim.com/issues/an-ordinary-person-who-did-something-extraordinary-for-god/; Birthright International, "About Birthright," http://www.birthright.org/htmpages/about.htm; Program for NRLC conference, Barat College, Chicago, July 31–August 2, 1970, folder: "National Right to Life Meeting, 7/31–8/2/70," box 4, ACCL; Memo from Paul V. Harrington, October 3, 1973, folder: "Birthright—Boston, 1973–78," box 2, Harrington Papers; AP, "Anti-Abortion Help Offered," *Detroit Free Press*, April 12, 1971.

60. Ruth Ann Burns, "Abortion Opponents Active," *New York Times*, June 11, 1972.

61. Eunice Kennedy Shriver, "The 'Unwanted Children,'" *Los Angeles Times*, July 19, 1972.

CHAPTER 7

1. Minnesota Citizens Concerned for Life, Pamphlet, n.d. [early 1971], folder: "Correspondence, 1970–1972", box 2, North Dakota Right to Life Association Records (NDRLA), North Dakota Historical Society, Bismarck.

2. "Catholics to Prepare Statement on Abortion," *Minneapolis Star*, February 16, 1967; "Minnesota Bishops Score Effort to Relax Abortion Law," National Catholic News Service press bulletin, March 2, 1967, Archives of the Archdiocese of St. Paul and Minneapolis; "Abortion Change Hearings Slated," *Catholic Bulletin* (St. Paul, MN), February 28, 1969, 3; Minnesota House of Representatives Judiciary Committee, Report of Subcommittee on Abortion Laws, December 1968, folder: "Testimony, 1968–1971," box 8, NDRLA.

3. Arlene Doyle, "Do You Need Permission to Save an Unborn Baby?" (1977), http://uscl.info/edoc/doc.php?doc_id = 88&action = inline-; Robert N. Karrer, "The National Right to Life Committee: Its Founding, Its History, and the Emergence of the Pro-Life Movement Prior to *Roe v. Wade*," *Catholic Historical Review* 97 (2011): 540–541.

4. Karrer, "The National Right to Life Committee," 540–541; Peter Vaughan, "The Vocal 'Minority' Is Growing," *Minneapolis Star*, April 16, 1971; Minnesota

Citizens Concerned for Life, Inc. (MCCL), Articles of Incorporation, June 7, 1968, folder: "Minnesota Citizens Concerned for Life, 1968," box 4, NDRLA.

5. Karrer, "The National Right to Life Committee," 541; Marjory Mecklenburg, "Developing Alternatives to Abortion," testimony given to Pennsylvania Abortion Law Commission, Pittsburgh, PA, March 14, 1972, folder: "Convention, National, 1972," box 2, NDRLA; Gordon Slovut, "9-year Debate Goes on as Friendly Foes Argue on Abortions," *Minneapolis Star*, September 25, 1973.

6. Karrer, "The National Right to Life Committee," 540–541; Vaughan, "The Vocal 'Minority' Is Growing," *Minneapolis Star*, April 16, 1971; Marjory Mecklenburg, "Developing Alternatives to Abortion," testimony given to Pennsylvania Abortion Law Commission, Pittsburgh, PA, March 14, 1972, folder: "Convention, National, 1972," box 2, NDRLA.

7. Minnesota Citizens Concerned for Life Newsletter, June–July 1972, folder: "Miscellaneous Information and Handouts, 1970–1972," box 5, NDRLA; MCCL Newsletter, May 1971, folder: "Newsletters, Outside, 1971," box 5, NDRLA; Alice Hartle, Editorial, MCCL Newsletter, November–December 1972, folder: "Miscellaneous Information and Handouts, 1972–1973," box 5, NDRLA; J. H. Adams and Associates, MCCL Area Chapter Manual, n.d. [c. late 1970 or 1971], folder: "Miscellaneous Information and Handouts, 1970–1973," box 5, NDRLA.

8. MCCL, Articles of Incorporation.

9. Fred Mecklenburg, Testimony in Opposition to Minnesota Senate File #998, March 31, 1969, folder: "ACCL Admin File: People—General—Dr. Fred Mecklenburg (2)," box 24, American Citizens Concerned for Life (ACCL) Records, Gerald R. Ford Library, Ann Arbor, MI; "Abortion Chaplain's Subject," *Catholic Bulletin* (St. Paul, MN), February 28, 1969, 8; Gordon Slovut, "Abortion Fighters on Offensive," *Minneapolis Star*, March 19, 1971.

10. NARAL, Office Memo, "Re: Minnesota Situation (Phone conversation with Robert McCoy)," July 28, 1970, folder: "MN, 1969–70," carton 3, MC 313 NARAL Records, 1968–1976, Schlesinger Library, Harvard University; "Abortion Becomes Campaign Issue," National Right to Life Committee Newsletter, October 1970, 1, folder: "Newsletters, Outside, 1970," box 5, NDRLA.

11. Slovut, "Abortion Fighters on Offensive"; Vaughan, "The Vocal 'Minority' Is Growing."

12. Vaughan, "The Vocal 'Minority' Is Growing"; Fred Mecklenburg, direct mail to MCCL members, March 1971, folder: "Correspondence, 1970–1972," box 2, NDRLA; *Guardian* (MCCL newsletter), January 1971, folder: "Newsletters, Outside, 1971," box 5, NDRLA.

13. John XXIII, *Pacem in Terris*, April 11, 1963, http://w2.vatican.va/content/john-xxiii/en/encyclicals/documents/hf_j-xxiii_enc_11041963_pacem.html. For the transformation of American liberalism during the 1960s, see Allen J. Matusow, *The Unraveling of America: A History of Liberalism in the 1960s*,

2nd ed. (Athens: University of Georgia Press, 2009); John D. Skrentny, *The Minority Rights Revolution* (Cambridge, MA: Harvard University Press, 2002); and James T. Patterson, *Grand Expectations: The United States, 1945–1974* (New York: Oxford University Press, 1996). For the religious dimension of American liberals' Cold War foreign policy and its close connection with Catholic values, see William Inboden, *Religion and American Foreign Policy, 1945–1960: The Soul of Containment* (New York: Cambridge University Press, 2008).

14. Mark S. Massa, *The American Catholic Revolution: How the '60s Changed the Church Forever* (New York: Oxford University Press, 2010), 103–128; Daniel Callahan, "America's Catholic Bishops," *Atlantic Monthly*, April 1967, http:// www.theatlantic.com/past/docs/issues/67apr/callahan.htm; Wallace Turner, "Death Row Cases Upset Gov. Brown," *New York Times*, December 24, 1966; Paul Hofmann, "Bishop Sheen's Vitality Startles and Delights Rochester," *New York Times*, August 7, 1967.

15. Wilson D. Miscamble, "Francis Cardinal Spellman and 'Spellman's War,'" in *The Human Tradition in the Vietnam Era*, ed. David L. Anderson (Wilmington, DE: Scholarly Resources, 2000), 3–21; Callahan, "America's Catholic Bishops."

16. Callahan, "America's Catholic Bishops"; "Bishop Sheen Urges Vietnam Pullout," *Wanderer* (St. Paul, MN), August 3, 1967, 1; "3 US Bishops Join Peacenik Front," *Wanderer*, August 3, 1967, 1.

17. Daniel Berrigan, "An Inkling of a Life Being Snuffed Out," *Sojourners*, November 1980, 25; Phyllis Schlafly, "What's Wrong with Equal Rights for Women?" (1972); Rosemary Radford Ruether, *Christianity and the Making of the Modern Family* (Boston: Beacon Press, 2000), 161–162; Richard John Neuhaus, "The Dangerous Assumptions," *Commonweal*, June 30, 1967, 408–413.

18. For the contrast between Catholic and evangelical voting patterns during the 1960s and 1970s, see Lyman Kellstedt et al., "Faith Transformed: Religion and American Politics from FDR to George W. Bush," in *Religion and American Politics: From the Colonial Period to the Present*, ed. Mark A. Noll and Luke E. Harlow, 2nd ed. (New York: Oxford University Press, 2007), 272–273.

19. James T. McHugh, letter to US bishops, January 10, 1969, and sermon outline on human life issues [January 1969], folder 1: "Abortion," box 1, Chancery Office Records, Diocese of Harrisburg, PA; Author's telephone interview with Juan Ryan, June 4, 2012.

20. Norman St. John-Stevas, "The Muddled Issue of Abortion," *National Catholic Reporter*, November 3, 1972, 7; Germain Grisez, *Abortion: The Myths, the Realities, and the Arguments* (New York: Corpus Books, 1970), 323–325, 337–339.

21. Patrick Joyce, "'Choose Life,' Speakers Singers Tell Youth Rally," National Catholic News Service, September 5, 1972, folder: "Series 7.2: 1972 Campaign Subject File—Health: Abortion [Ahmann] (2 of 3)," R. Sargent Shriver Papers, John F. Kennedy Library, Boston.

22. Charles E. Rice, *The Vanishing Right to Live: An Appeal for a Renewed Reverence for Life* (Garden City, NY: Doubleday, 1969); Tom Riley, "Prelate Calls Abortion Crime, But Defends Death Penalty," *Boston Herald Advertiser*, May 6, 1973.

23. "Abortion Issues Aired at Meeting," *Bismarck Tribune*, April 17, 1972; Anna Lawler and Angela Wozniak, direct mail on behalf of MCCL, February 24, 1971, folder: "Legislation, Various States', 1964–1971," box 4, NDRLA.

24. "Majority Still Oppose Abortion on Demand," National Right to Life Committee Newsletter, July 1970, 2, folder: "Newsletters, Outside, 1970," box 5, NDRLA; Frederick B. Currier, "Abortion Reform Favored by Wide Margin in Poll," *Detroit News*, September 14, 1972.

25. Joyce M. Dwyer to Paul V. Harrington, April 14, 1971, folder: "Abortion, 1971–72," box 1, Rev. Paul V. Harrington Papers, Archives of the Archdiocese of Boston.

26. Minutes of Diocesan Human Life Task Force Meeting, Harrisburg, PA, September 23, 1970, folder: "Abortion—Right-to-Life Programs," box 1, Chancery Office Records, Diocese of Harrisburg.

27. "Two 'U' Students Push 'Liberal' Drive against Abortion," *Minneapolis Star*, October 2, 1971; Suzanne Perry, "Students Join Anti-Abortion Cause," *Minnesota Daily* (St. Paul), December 6, 1971.

28. Thomas W. Hilgers, "Abortion: Is It Really the Best We Have to Offer? The Philosophy of Involvement," SOUL, n.d. [c. 1971–1972], folder: "Speeches and Articles, 1968–1971," box 7, NDRLA; Delores Lutz, "Only One Side Heard at U, New Group Claims," *Minnesota Daily* (St. Paul), May 19, 1971.

29. Lutz, "Only One Side Heard at U"; "Two 'U' Students Push 'Liberal' Drive against Abortion"; "SOUL 'Mushrooms' into Mighty Fortress," *St. Cloud (MN) Visitor*, February 17, 1972; Louise Lague, "Youth Pro-Life Rally Has Anti-Abortion Theme," *Washington Evening Star-News*, September 4, 1972.

30. "Students on Tour for Unborn," *Catholic Universe Bulletin* Cleveland, OH, September 3, 1971, 13; Pennsylvanians for Human Life Newsletter, April 1972, folder: "Miscellaneous Reference Materials (4)," box 3, ACCL.

31. Michael Taylor, direct mail on behalf of NRLC, November 11, 1971, folder: "1971 Correspondence," Value of Life Committee Records, Sisters of Life Archive, New York, NY.

32. Michael Taylor, direct mail on behalf of NRLC, April 14, 1972, 3–4, folder: "National Right to Life Committee, 1970–1972," box 5, NDRLA.

33. Norman McCarthy, "Monument Rally Stresses Rights of the Unborn," *Catholic Standard* (Washington, DC), September 7, 1972; Frank Lynn, "Delegates in 3 States Say Eagleton Should Quit Race," *New York Times*, July 30, 1972.

34. National Youth Pro-Life Coalition, direct mail, "Re: National Rally for Human Life, September 3, 1972" [summer 1972], folder: "Miscellaneous Information and Handouts, 1971–1972," box 5, NDRLA; Ruth Dean, "1,800 'Born and Left to Die,'" *Washington Evening Star-News*, September 2, 1972.

35. Michael Taylor, direct mail on behalf of NRLC, September 8, 1972, folder: "Miscellaneous Information and Handouts, 1972–1973," box 5, NDRLA.

36. Hiley H. Ward, "Dearden Ties War Protest to Fight against Abortion," *Detroit Free Press*, September 29, 1972.

37. James T. McHugh, direct mail explaining Respect Life Week, August 3, 1972, folder: "Series 7.2: 1972 Campaign Subject File—Health: Abortion [Ahmann] (2 of 3)," box 148, Shriver Papers; Cletus F. O'Donnell to members of the Diocese of Madison, WI, September 26, 1972, folder: "Series 7.2: 1972 Campaign Subject File—Health: Abortion [Ahmann] (1 of 3)," box 148, Shriver Papers.

38. Edward M. Kennedy to Mrs. Edward J. Barshak, August 3, 1971, folder 31: "MORAL (Mass. Organization to Repeal Abortion Laws), 1970–1974," box 2, Patricia Gold Papers, Schlesinger Library, Harvard University.

39. William Willoughby, "O'Boyle Charges Genocide," *Washington Evening Star-News*, August 7, 1972; Editorial, "Crying Genocide," *Washington Evening Star-News*, August 10, 1972; James T. McHugh, LTE, *Washington Evening Star-News*, August 19, 1972. For a conservative Catholic critique of coerced sterilization, see William F. Buckley Jr., "Sterilize That Woman!" *Wanderer*, June 30, 1966, 7.

40. "Abortion and the Poor," Louisiana Right to Life Association Newsletter, April–May 1972, folder: "Miscellaneous Reference Materials (7)," box 3, ACCL.

41. Women for the Unborn, "The Disposable Humans?," 1972, folder: "Miscellaneous Reference Materials (7)," box 3, ACCL; Donald Granberg and Beth Wellman Granberg, "Abortion Attitudes, 1965–1980: Trends and Determinants," *Family Planning Perspectives* 12 (1980): 254; Larry R. Petersen and Armand L. Mauss, "Religion and the 'Right to Life': Correlates of Opposition to Abortion," *Sociological Analysis* 37 (1976): 248–249.

42. Erma Craven, LTE, *Minneapolis Star*, March 13, 1971. Craven had good reason to be suspicious of the motivations of at least some (though not all) proponents of abortion law liberalization in the South. For the role that eugenics and a desire to reduce welfare expenditures played in generating support for abortion law liberalization in North Carolina, see Johanna Schoen, *Choice and Coercion: Birth Control, Sterilization, and Abortion in Public Health and Welfare* (Chapel Hill: University of North Carolina Press, 2005), 183–191.

43. Jennifer Nelson, *Women of Color and the Reproductive Rights Movement* (New York: New York University Press, 2003), 106–107; Jesse L. Jackson, "How We Respect Life is Over-riding Moral Issue," *National Right to Life News*, January 1977.

44. "Liberal-Left Position Emerging against Abortion, Pacifist Says," *National Right to Life News*, December 1975, 16; Minutes of Meeting of Board of Directors of Americans United for Life, November 19–20, 1971, 10, folder: "bMS 404 /4 (3) Americans United for Life, Correspondence, Board of Directors, 1971," box 4, George Huntston Williams Papers, Harvard Divinity School; Eleanor

Roberts, "Dr. Mildred F. Jefferson Knew What She Wanted," *Boston Post*, July 15, 1951.

45. Dennis Hevesi, "Mildred Jefferson, 84, Anti-Abortion Activist, Is Dead," *New York Times*, October 18, 2010; Paul V. Harrington to Mildred Jefferson, July 28, 1970, folder: "Abortion, 1968–70," box 1, Harrington Papers.

46. Hevesi, "Mildred Jefferson, 84, Anti-Abortion Activist, Is Dead"; Charles B. Fancher Jr., "Much in Common but Worlds Apart," *Philadelphia Inquirer*, April 23, 1978; "A New Iconoclast," *Chicago Tribune*, July 22, 1990.

47. Hevesi, "Mildred Jefferson, 84, Anti-Abortion Activist, Is Dead"; Testimony of Mildred F. Jefferson, in *Jane Doe v. Mother & Unborn Baby Care of North Texas, Inc. et al.*, District Court of Tarrant County, TX, August 29, 1986, folder 6, box 16, Mildred Jefferson Papers, Schlesinger Library, Harvard University; Mildred F. Jefferson to Paul V. Harrington, September 14, 1970, folder: "Abortion, 1968–70," box 1, Harrington Papers.

48. "Positive Approach to Life Needed: MD," *Ottawa Citizen* (Ontario), November 5, 1973.

49. "Positive Approach to Life Needed"; Program for Witness for the Unborn at State House in Massachusetts, May 20, 1973, folder: "Massachusetts Citizens for Life, 1972," box 3, RG III.G.02, Birth Control and Abortion Records, Archives of the Archdiocese of Boston; Michael Taylor, direct mail on behalf of NRLC, July 30, 1973, folder 8: "Abortion—1973," box 18, MSS 636, Joanne Duren Papers, Wisconsin Historical Society, Madison.

50. Vera Glaser, "The Doctor Has No Question It's Morally Wrong," *Philadelphia Inquirer*, October 1, 1980.

51. National Right to Life Committee, Agenda for NRLC Annual Meeting, June 16–18, 1972, folder: "Convention, National, 1972," box 2, NDRLA.

52. Fred C. Shapiro, "'Right to Life' Has a Message for New York State Legislators," *New York Times*, August 20, 1972; Robert D. McFadden, "Lobbying on Abortion Increases at Capitol," *New York Times*, May 8, 1972.

53. James F. Clarity, "Governor Urges Change to 16-Week Abortions," *New York Times*, April 26, 1972; William E. Farrell, "Governor Offers an Abortion Bill," *New York Times*, May 6, 1972.

54. William E. Farrell, "Abortion Repeal Gains in Albany," *New York Times*, May 3, 1972; "Thousands Here Urge Repeal of Abortion Statute," *New York Times*, April 17, 1972; Alfonso A. Narvaez, "Abortion Repeal Urged in Albany," *New York Times*, April 18, 1972.

55. McFadden, "Lobbying on Abortion Increases at Capitol."

56. Alfonso A. Narvaez, "Abortion Repeal Passed by Senate, Sent to Governor," *New York Times*, May 11, 1972; William E. Farrell, "Assembly Votes to Repeal Liberalized Abortion Law," *New York Times*, May 10, 1972.

57. Westchester Right to Life Newsletter, June 1972, folder: "Miscellaneous Reference Materials (4)," box 3, ACCL; William Kennedy, "The Lobsterman

Who Runs the Assembly," *New York Times*, April 23, 1972; Francis X. Clines, "Abortion Dispute in State Accented by Nixon's Letter," *New York Times*, May 8, 1972.

58. Lee Gidding to George W. Kellogg, May 18, 1972, folder: "CA, 1972," carton 2, MC 313 NARAL Records.

59. Michael Taylor, direct mail on behalf of NRLC, "New York State Repeal Drive," May 19, 1972, folder: "Abortion in New York (1 of 3)," box 23, Harrington Papers.

CHAPTER 8

1. Robert O. Self, *All in the Family: The Realignment of American Democracy since the 1960s* (New York: Hill and Wang, 2012), 189–247; Harold T. Christensen and Christina F. Gregg, "Changing Sex Norms in America and Scandinavia," *Journal of Marriage and Family* 32 (1970): 619–621; George Gallup, "College Freshmen, Seniors Differ Sharply on Marijuana, Sex, Abortion," Gallup Poll, May 18, 1975, in Gallup Organization, *America's Opinion on Abortion, 1962–1992* (Princeton, NJ: Gallup Organization, 1992), unpaginated.

2. Christopher Tietze, "Unintended Pregnancies in the United States, 1970–1972," *Family Planning Perspectives* 11 (1979): 186–187; Alfred M. Mirande and Elizabeth L. Hammer, "Premarital Sexual Permissiveness and Abortion: Standards of College Women," *Pacific Sociological Review* 17 (1974): 485–503; Gene Currivan, "Poll Finds Shift to Left among College Freshmen," *New York Times*, December 20, 1970.

3. For the sexual revolution in television during the early 1970s, see Elana Levine, *Wallowing in Sex: The New Sexual Culture of 1970s American Television* (Durham, NC: Duke University Press, 2007).

4. Thomas Robertson, *The Malthusian Moment: Global Population Growth and the Birth of American Environmentalism* (New Brunswick, NJ: Rutgers University Press, 2012), 170; Catherine S. Chilman, "Public Social Policy and Population Problems in the United States," *Social Service Review* 47 (1973): 513.

5. Eileen Shanahan, "Equal Rights Amendment Is Approved by Congress," *New York Times*, March 23, 1972; Gilbert Y. Steiner, *Constitutional Inequality: The Political Fortunes of the Equal Rights Amendment* (Washington, DC: Brookings Institution, 1985), 54–55; Charlotte Curtiss, "Modest Gains Please Republican Feminists," *New York Times*, August 21, 1972; Catherine Rymph, *Republican Women: Feminism and Conservatism from Suffrage through the Rise of the New Right* (Chapel Hill: University of North Carolina Press, 2006), 188–211; Nan Robertson, "Democrats Feel Influence of Women's New Power," *New York Times*, July 15, 1972; Laurie Johnston, "Abortion Forces Prepare for Foes," *New York Times*, September 27, 1972; Betty Friedan, "Abortion: A Woman's Civil Right," speech, National Conference for the Repeal of Abortion Laws, Chicago, February 14, 1969, folder 12, box 1, Patricia Gold Papers, Schlesinger

Library, Harvard University; "Abortion and Child-Care Planks to Be Proposed to the G.O.P.," *New York Times*, August 11, 1972; John Herbers, "McGovern Forces Shape Planks to Suit Candidate," *New York Times*, July 13, 1972.

6. Self, *All in the Family*, 3–14.

7. Jack Rosenthal, "Survey Finds Majority, in Shift, Now Favors Liberalized Laws," *New York Times*, August 25, 1972.

8. Mary Ziegler, *After Roe: The Lost History of the Abortion Debate* (Cambridge, MA: Harvard University Press, 2015), 37; John C. and Barbara Willke, *Handbook on Abortion*, 3rd ed. (Cincinnati, OH: Hiltz, 1973), 143.

9. Richard Reeves, *President Nixon: Alone in the White House* (New York: Simon and Schuster, 2001), 265.

10. Richard Nixon, "Special Message to the Congress on Problems of Population Growth," July 18, 1969, http://www.population-security.org/09-CH1.html; Donald T. Critchlow, "Birth Control, Population Control, and Family Planning: An Overview," in *The Politics of Abortion and Birth Control in Historical Perspective*, ed. Donald T. Critchlow (University Park: Pennsylvania State University Press, 1996), 13; UPI, "Abortions Provided at Military Bases," *New York Times*, August 18, 1970; "Judge Rejects Suit to Halt Abortions by the Air Force," *New York Times*, January 21, 1971.

11. Joseph Stanton to Richard Nixon, November 15, 1970, and memo from James T. McHugh, March 26, 1971, folder: "National Right to Life Committee, 1970–1972," box 5, North Dakota Right to Life Association (NDRLA) Records, North Dakota State Historical Society, Bismarck.

12. James Reston, "Nixon and Muskie on Abortion," *New York Times*, April 7, 1971.

13. "Nixon Abortion Statement," *New York Times*, April 4, 1971; "Nixon Orders End to Eased Abortions in Armed Services," *New York Times*, April 3, 1971.

14. Michael Taylor, direct mail on behalf of NRLC, "Re: President Nixon's Statement on Abortion," April 5, 1971, and NRLC, press release, April 5, 1971, folder: "National Right to Life Committee, 1970–1972," box 5, NDRLA; James T. McHugh, press release on behalf of Family Life Division of the United States Catholic Conference, April 5, 1971, folder: "Miscellaneous Reference Materials (3)," box 3, American Citizens Concerned for Life (ACCL) Records, Gerald R. Ford Library, Ann Arbor, MI.

15. Memo from Charles Colson to Peter Flanigan, "Catholic Voting Attitudes," February 18, 1972, folder: "February 1972," box 131, Charles Colson Files, White House Staff Files (WHSF), Richard Nixon Presidential Library, Yorba Linda, CA; Tape recording of conversation between Richard Nixon and Charles Colson, April 5, 1972, EOB 330–17, White House Tapes, Nixon Library; Tape recording of conversation between Richard Nixon and H. R. Haldeman, April 10, 1972, Oval 705–3, White House Tapes, Nixon Library; Robert B. Semple Jr., "President Bars Birth Curb Plans," *New York Times*, May 6, 1972.

16. "Has Humphrey Changed Stand?" Minnesota Citizens Concerned for Life Newsletter, November 1971, folder: "Newsletters, Outside, 1971," box 5, NDRLA; Michael Taylor, direct mail on behalf of NRLC, May 19, 1972, folder: "National Right to Life Committee, 1970–1972," box 5, NDRLA.

17. Michael Taylor, direct mail on behalf of NRLC, May 19, 1972, folder: "National Right to Life Committee, 1970–1972," box 5, NDRLA; Mary Russell, "McGovern's 'Radical' Views Attacked," *Washington Post*, May 6, 1972.

18. Don Oberdorfer, "'Radical' Issue Hits McGovern," *Washington Post*, May 9, 1972; Anthony Ripley, "McGovern Victor over Humphrey in Nebraska Vote," *New York Times*, May 10, 1972; John Herbers, "McGovern Forces Shape Planks to Suit Candidate," *New York Times*, July 13, 1972; Carol Greitzer to Harriet Van Horne, July 25, 1972, folder: "Opposition, 1972," carton 8, MC 313, NARAL Records, 1968–1976, Schlesinger Library, Harvard University.

19. Michael Taylor, direct mail on behalf of NRLC, May 19, 1972, folder: "National Right to Life Committee, 1970–1972," box 5, NDRLA.

20. Greitzer to Van Horne, July 25, 1972.

21. Christina Wolbrecht, *The Politics of Women's Rights: Parties, Positions, and Change* (Princeton, NJ: Princeton University Press, 2000), 35–37; "How McGovern Lost a Delegate's Vote," *New York Times*, July 23, 1972; Herbers, "McGovern Forces Shape Planks to Suit Candidate"; Michael Taylor, direct mail on behalf of NRLC, June 30, 1972 folder: "National Right to Life Committee, 1970–1972," box 5, NDRLA; Michael Taylor, direct mail on behalf of NRLC, "Re: Democratic National Convention—Defeat of Minority Report #7," July 19, 1972, folder: "National Right to Life Committee, 1970–1972," box 5, NDRLA.

22. Eunice Kennedy Shriver, "Life: The Other Choice," *Our Sunday Visitor*, July 16, 1972, 6–7; Rick Casey, "McGovern Seeks Catholic Support," *National Catholic Reporter*, September 1, 1972; Matt Ahmann to Tersh Boasberg and Bill Josephson, August 18, 1972, folder: "Series 7.5—1972 Campaign—Issues and Research Division—Issue Files: Catholics," box 193, R. Sargent Shriver Papers, John F. Kennedy Library, Boston. Evidence of Eagleton's support for the pro-life cause in the early 1970s comes from Montana Right to Life Association Newsletter, July 21, 1972, folder: "Miscellaneous Information and Handouts, 1972," box 5, NDRLA; and Vivian Western and David H. Klassen to Tom Eagleton, October 18, 1973, folder 38, box 53, MC 496, National Organization for Women (NOW) Records, Schlesinger Library, Harvard University. Eagleton remained committed to the pro-life cause even in the 1980s, long after most other Democratic senators had become pro-choice. In 1983, he cosponsored Senator Orrin Hatch's anti-abortion constitutional amendment proposal (Douglas Johnson, "Eagleton Proposes Amendment to Repeal Roe v. Wade Decision," *National Right to Life News*, March 10, 1983, 1).

23. Tersh Boasberg to Judy Bianco and Ginger Tille, October 19, 1972, folder 7.2, box 148, Shriver Papers; Marion K. Sanders, "Enemies of Abortion," *Harper's*,

March 1974; Mrs. Paul Schaefer to Sargent Shriver, September 26, 1972, folder 7.2, box 148, Shriver Papers; Paul Marx to John McEneaney, October 26, 1972, folder 20, box 1, Fr. Paul Marx Papers, Saint John's University, Collegeville, MN; Paul Marx to Clara Purcell, February 12, 1972, folder 9, box 2, Marx Papers.

24. [Patrick Buchanan], "Abortion" [1972], folder: "Abortion," box 11, Patrick J. Buchanan Files, WHSF, Nixon Library.

25. Charles Colson to Clark MacGregor, July 13, 1972, folder: "July 1972," box 132, Colson Files, WHSF, Nixon Library; Joshua M. Glasser, *The Eighteen-Day Running Mate: McGovern, Eagleton, and a Campaign in Crisis* (New Haven, CT: Yale University Press, 2012), 38. That senator, it was later disclosed, was Thomas Eagleton.

26. Richard Nixon to Terence Cooke, May 5, 1972, folder: "John Ehrlichman [2 of 2]," box 7, Colson Files; Robert B. Semple Jr., "Nixon Aides Explain Aims of Letter on Abortion Law," *New York Times*, May 11, 1972.

27. Charlotte Curtis, "Draft Abortion-Reform Plank Being Written at White House," *New York Times*, August 6, 1972; "Abortion and Child Care Planks to be Proposed to the G.O.P.," *New York Times*, August 11, 1972; Sally Quinn, "The Republican Women's Attempt at Semi-Activism," *Washington Post*, August 24, 1972; Rita E. Hauser to John Ehrlichman, August 28, 1972, folder: "Abortion," box 28, Colson Files.

28. S. J. Adamo, "No Real Difference," *Catholic Star Herald* (Camden, NJ), October 6, 1972.

29. AP, "Abortion Foes Go to High Court," *Detroit Free Press*, August 8, 1972; "Abortion Vote Assured But—," *Detroit News*, August 12, 1972; Frederick B. Currier, "Abortion Reform Favored by Wide Margin in Poll," *Detroit News*, September 14, 1972.

30. Hiley H. Ward, "Churches Move to 'Education' on Abortion," *Detroit Free Press*, August 26, 1972; Jim Stackpoole, "Drs. Fedeson, Jaynes OK'd by Judge Kaufman: Name 2 Doctors Guardians of Unborn," *Michigan Catholic*, January 19, 1972.

31. Paul M. Branzburg, "Liberalized Abortion Loses by 3–2 Margin," *Detroit Free Press*, November 8, 1972; Ward, "Churches Move to 'Education' on Abortion"; "Pro-Life Group to Fight Easy Abortion Campaign," *Michigan Catholic*, September 6, 1972; Nancy Manser, "Anti-Abortion Drive to Begin," *Detroit News*, September 29, 1972.

32. Branzburg, "Liberalized Abortion Loses by 3–2 Margin"; Judy Diebolt, "Christ Billboards Can Stay," *Detroit Free Press*, November 1, 1972.

33. Branzburg, "Liberalized Abortion Loses by 3–2 Margin"; Al Sandner, "Abortion Reform Loss Leaves Issue Up to Court," *Detroit News*, November 8, 1972; Voice of the Unborn flyer, "Be the Voice of the Unborn. Vote No on B" [October 1972], folder 3: "Printed Material," box 1, Lifespan, Inc., Records, Bentley Historical Library (BHL), Ann Arbor, MI; Rosetta Ferguson, Voice of the Unborn, "Is

Abortion Black Genocide?" [October 1972], folder 3, box 1, Lifespan, Inc., Records.

34. Corinne Smith, "Who Are Our Seven Women in the State Legislature?" *Ann Arbor News*, April 12, 1970; Rosetta Ferguson, Voice of the Unborn, "Is Abortion Black Genocide?" [October 1972], and Voice of the Unborn flyer, "Have You Considered?" [October 1972], folder 3, box 1, Lifespan, Inc., Records, BHL.

35. "Proposal B Makes Abortion Individual, Medical Matter," *Detroit Free Press*, November 3, 1972; William Mitchell, "Abortion Foes Reverse Trend in 2 Months," *Detroit Free Press*, November 9, 1972; Sandner, "Abortion Reform Loss Leaves Issue up to Court."

36. AP, "6,000 Sign Liberalized N.D. Abortion Law Proposal," *Grand Forks (ND) Herald*, March 12, 1972; "Easy Abortion Loses in Two States," *National Catholic Reporter*, November 24, 1972.

37. "Abortion Issues Aired at Meeting," *Bismarck Tribune*, April 17, 1972; Doug Manbeck, "Controversial Abortion Reform Measure Heads for State Ballot," *Mandan (ND) Morning Pioneer*, August 27, 1972; Gary W. Clark, "Abortion Measure Seen as Major Voter Magnet," *Bismarck Tribune*, November 6, 1972.

38. A. H. Fortman, "Presentation on Positive Alternatives to Abortion," speech to Legislative Committee of the North Dakota Conference of Churches, August 7, 1972, folder: "Miscellaneous Information and Handouts, 1971–1972," box 5, NDRLA; Edwin C. Becker to Athanasius Buccholz, January 14, 1974, folder: "Correspondence, 1974," box 2, NDRLA; Don Effenberger, "Anti-Abortion Victory Held Proof of Values," *Catholic Bulletin* (St. Paul, MN), November 24, 1972.

39. Forrest C. Stevenson Jr., mass mailing to members of Voice of the Unborn, November 16, 1972, folder: "Correspondence, 1971–1978," box 1, Elizabeth Lemmer Papers, BHL; Willmar Thorkelson, "Defeat of Abortion Measure Spurs N.D. 'Life Rights' Push," *Minneapolis Star*, November 18, 1972.

40. *Babbitz v. McCann*, 310 F. Supp. 293, Dist. Court, E.D. Wisconsin (1970), http://www.leagle.com/decision/1970603310FSupp293_1550.xml/BABBITZ%20v.%20McCANN; National Right to Life Committee Newsletter, October 1970, 1, "Newsletters, Outside, 1970," box 5, NDRLA; Al Sandner, "Fetus Is Person, Court Rules," *Detroit News*, July 10, 1971; *O'Neill v. Morse*, 385 MICH 130 (1971), http://www.micourthistory.org/wp-content/uploads/verdict_pdf/oneill/oneill_maj.pdf.

41. *United States v. Vuitch*, 402 U.S. 62 (1971), http://caselaw.lp.findlaw.com/scripts/getcase.pl?court=us&vol=402&invol=62; Michael Taylor, direct mail on behalf of NRLC, "Re: Supreme Court Decision," April 23, 1971, folder: "National Right to Life Committee, 1970–1972," box 5, NDRLA.

42. Jerry M. Flint, "Abortion Backers Hopeful of Gains," *New York Times*, October 9, 1972; UPI, "Florida High Court Voids 103-Year-Old Abortion Law," *New York Times*, February 15, 1972; UPI, "Court in California, 4–3, Makes Possible Abortion on Demand," *New York Times*, November 23, 1972; "Connecticut

Takes Ruling on Abortion to U.S. High Court," *New York Times*, September 22, 1972; Sandner, "Abortion Reform Loss Leaves Issue up to Court."

43. Memo from Germain G. Grisez, "A Strategy for an Effective Attack on the Anti-Life Movement" [spring 1971], folder: "Schmitz—Abortion, 1971 (file #1)," box 1, John G. Schmitz Papers, Wichita State University; Michael Taylor to William J. Rogers, April 12, 1971, folder: "NRLC, 1971," box 4, ACCL.

44. John G. Schmitz to Raymond L. Weiland, July 14, 1972, folder: "Schmitz, Abortion, 1972," box 2, Schmitz Papers; Steve Garger, Memo on Right to Life Amendment to the Constitution of the United States" [1972], folder: "Schmitz, Abortion, 1972," box 2, Schmitz Papers.

45. Capitol Region Life Line, July 15, 1972, folder: "Newsletters, Outside, 1971–1972," box 6, NDRLA; South Dakota Right to Life Newsletter, October 1972, folder: "Miscellaneous Information and Handouts, 1972," box 5, NDRLA.

46. Paul Marx to Marge Wilson, May 19, 1971, folder 10, box 2, Marx Papers.

47. Transcript of Oral Arguments in *Roe v. Wade* (1973), December 13, 1971, http://www.scribd.com/doc/68497248/Transcript-Roe-v-Wade-1st-Oral-Dec-13-1971; Transcript of Oral Arguments in *Doe v. Bolton*, 410 U.S. 179 (1973), December 13, 1971, http://www.scribd.com/doc/68497230/Transcript-Doe-v-Bolton-1st-Argument-Dec-13-1971.

48. "High Court Abortion Debate Relaxed, Decorous," *American Medical News*, December 20, 1971; Transcript of Oral Arguments in *Roe v. Wade* (1973), December 13, 1971; Transcript of Oral Arguments in *Doe v. Bolton*, 410 U.S. 179 (1973), December 13, 1971.

49. J. J. Brandlin to James McIntyre, September 17, 1969, folder: "Abortion, 1968–1969," Archives of the Archdiocese of Los Angeles.

50. Charles E. Rice, Amicus Curiae Brief Submitted to US Supreme Court on Behalf of Americans United for Life in *Roe v. Wade* and *Doe v. Bolton*, October 1971, folder: "bMS 404 / 12 (3) U.S. Court Briefs and Proceedings on Abortion, 1971," box 12, George Huntston Williams Papers, Harvard Divinity School; Transcript of Oral Arguments in *Roe v. Wade*, December 13, 1971.

51. Dennis J. Horan et al., Amicus Curiae Brief Submitted to US Supreme Court in *Roe v. Wade* and *Doe v. Bolton*, October 1971, folder: "bMS 404 / 12 (3) U.S. Court Briefs and Proceedings on Abortion, 1971," box 12, George Huntston Williams Papers, Harvard Divinity School.

52. Women for the Unborn, Amicus Curiae Brief Submitted to US Supreme Court in *Roe v. Wade*, October 1971, folder 2, box 730, Harry A. Blackmun Papers, Library of Congress.

53. Juan Ryan et al., Amicus Curiae Brief Submitted on Behalf of the National Right to Life Committee to the US Supreme Court in *Roe v. Wade*, October 8, 1971, folder 2, box 730, Blackmun Papers.

54. "Abortion Landmark Unlikely," *American Medical News*, December 20, 1971; "Lineup on Abortion," *American Medical News*, December 6, 1971; Lee Gidding

to Richard D. Lamm, August 12, 1971, folder: "CO, 1969–10/71," carton 2, MC 313, NARAL Records.

55. *Eisenstadt v. Baird*, 405 U.S. 438 (1972), http://caselaw.lp.findlaw.com/scripts/getcase.pl?court = US&vol = 405&invol = 438; Transcript of Re-argument in *Roe v. Wade*, October 11, 1972, http://www.scribd.com/doc/68497271/Transcript-Roe-v-Wade-Re-Argument-Oct-1972.

56. Transcript of Re-Argument in *Roe v. Wade*.

57. Transcript of Re-Argument in *Roe v. Wade*.

58. Transcript of Re-Argument in *Roe v. Wade*.

59. *Roe v. Wade*, 410 U.S. 113 (1973), http://caselaw.lp.findlaw.com/scripts/getcase.pl?court = us&vol = 410&invol = 113.

60. Harry A. Blackmun to conference of Supreme Court justices, November 21, 1972, folder 8, box 151, Blackmun Papers; Blackmun to Lewis Powell, December 4, 1972, folder 4, box 151, Blackmun Papers; Thurgood Marshall to Blackmun, December 12, 1972, folder 4, box 151, Blackmun Papers; Lewis Powell to Blackmun, November 29, 1972, folder 8, box 151, Blackmun Papers; Blackmun to conference of Supreme Court justices, December 15, 1972, folder 4, box 151, Blackmun Papers; *Roe v. Wade*, 410 U.S. 113 (1973), http://caselaw.lp.findlaw.com/scripts/getcase.pl?court = us&vol = 410&invol = 113.

61. Harry A. Blackmun, Statement from the Bench Re: *Roe v. Wade* and *Doe v. Bolton*, January 22, 1973, folder 3, box 151, Blackmun Papers.

62. Germain Williams to Harry A. Blackmun, January 23, 1973, folder 3, box 71, Blackmun Papers; "Reaction to Abortion Ruling Is Mixed," *Rochester (MN) Post-Bulletin*, January 23, 1973.

63. Dale L. Kratzer to Harry A. Blackmun, January 25, 1973, folder 3, box 71, Blackmun Papers; Victoria R. Nichols to Blackmun, January 23, 1973, folder 3, box 71, Blackmun Papers; Robert R. Soltis to Blackmun, January 24, 1973, folder 3, box 71, Blackmun Papers; Harry A. Blackmun to Joseph H. Pratt, January 31, 1973, folder 1, box 68, Blackmun Papers.

64. Michael T. Malloy, "Despite Court's Ruling, Abortion Fight Goes On," *National Observer* (Washington, DC), February 3, 1973.

65. Malloy, "Despite Court's Ruling, Abortion Fight Goes On."

CHAPTER 9

1. Program for First Annual North Dakota Right to Life Convention, January 11–12, 1973, folder: "Miscellaneous Information and Handouts, 1970–1973," box 5, North Dakota Right to Life Association (NDRLA) Records, North Dakota State Historical Society, Bismarck.

2. J. P. McFadden, direct mail on behalf of Ad Hoc Committee in Defense of Life, October 23, 1973, folder: "Opposition, 1973," MC 313, NARAL Records, 1968–1976, Schlesinger Library, Harvard University (emphasis in original).

3. "Abortion Ruling Praised, Rapped," *Lancaster (PA) New Era*, January 24, 1973; "30,000 at Life Rally in St. Louis," *National Right to Life News*, November 1973, 2.

4. Minnesota Citizens Concerned for Life, draft of ad copy, 1973, folder: "MCCL—1973," box 11, American Citizens Concerned for Life (ACCL) Records, Gerald R. Ford Library, Ann Arbor, MI.

5. National Conference of Catholic Bishops, Statement of the Committee for Pro-Life Affairs, January 24, 1973, http://www.usccb.org/issues-and-action/ human-life-and-dignity/abortion/upload/Statement-of-the-Committee -for-ProLife-Affairs.pdf.

6. Ray Ruppert, "Knights of Columbus: Topics: Abortion, Smut, School Funds," *Seattle Times*, August 23, 1973.

7. "Abortion and the Court," *Christianity Today*, February 16, 1973, 32–33.

8. Judith Blake, "The Supreme Court's Abortion Decisions and Public Opinion in the United States," *Population and Development Review* 3 (1977): 48–54; Gallup Poll, "Abortion Ruling," March 1974, in Gallup Organization, *America's Opinion on Abortion* (Princeton, NJ: Gallup Organization, 1992), unpaginated.

9. Eileen Foley, "The Abortion Battle's Not Over," *Detroit Free Press*, May 3, 1973; Paul M. Branzburg, "Liberalized Abortion Loses by 3–2 Margin," *Detroit Free Press*, November 8, 1972; Pam Dillon, testimony on behalf of Michigan Citizens for Life before Senate Municipalities and Elections Committee, n.d. [May 1, 1975], folder: "Topical Files—Government Agencies—Michigan Women's Commission, 1973–1979," box 1, Right to Life of Michigan Records, Bentley Historical Library (BHL), Ann Arbor, MI; Jane Muldoon to Joseph Bernardin, July 7, 1976, folder: "Correspondence & Press Relations—Correspondence, 1973–1977," box 2, Right to Life of Michigan Records, BHL; "Abortion Foes Shift Fight on Court Decisions to Congress," *Hospital Practice*, October 1973, 201.

10. David J. Garrow, *Liberty and Sexuality: The Right to Privacy and the Making of Roe v. Wade*, 2nd ed. (Berkeley: University of California Press, 1998), 327–330, 347–348, 853; Raymond Tatalovich, *The Politics of Abortion in the United States and Canada: A Comparative Study* (New York: M. E. Sharpe, 1997), 28; Mary C. Segers and Timothy A. Byrnes, "Introduction: Abortion Politics in American States," in *Abortion Politics in American States*, ed. Segers and Byrnes (New York: M. E. Sharpe, 1995), 3.

11. "Committee Kills Abortion Bill," *Mississippi Today*, January 24, 1971.

12. Warner Stough, "Abortion Coalition Forms to Set Strict Guidelines," *Birmingham News*, August 1, 1973; Judith Helms, "Alabama's Abortion Law Declared Unconstitutional," *Montgomery Journal*, May 17, 1974; "Abortion in the South," *Daily News* (Middlesborough, KY), July 4, 1989.

13. "Abortions, Legal for Year, Performed for Thousands," *New York Times*, December 31, 1973; "Abortions Legal in South Carolina," *Spartanburg (SC) Herald-Journal*, September 15, 1974; "House Committee Will Report Out Abortion Measure," *Greenville (SC) News*, January 25, 1974.

14. "Abortions, Legal for Year, Performed for Thousands"; Lawrence Lader to Alan Reitman, April 23, 1973, folder: "Orgz. Corr., 1973," carton 8, NARAL Records; Roy Reed, "In the South, Road to Equal Rights Is Rocky and Full of Detours," *New York Times*, March 20, 1975.

15. "Abortion Repeal Sought in Senate," *Topeka Daily Capital*, January 17, 1973; Laura Scott Divin, "Kansas Abortion Bill Killed," *Kansas City Star*, February 27, 1973; AP, "'Right to Life Group' against Abortion Law," *Lawrence (KS) Daily Journal-World* [1973], folder: "Kansas," carton 2, NARAL Printed Materials Collection, Schlesinger Library, Harvard University.

16. Mary Vandemark, "Despite Ruling, Hospitals Continue Abortion Policy," *Minot (ND) Daily News*, December 11, 1974.

17. Rachelle Patterson, "Citizens for Life Replace Catholic Church as Leader in Mass. Abortion Battle," *Boston Globe*, May 15, 1974.

18. Merrill R. Bailey, "Abortions: The Clamor Belies Tide," *Providence Evening Bulletin*, January 23, 1974; Merrill R. Bailey, "Abortion Bill Filed," *Providence Journal*, January 19, 1974; Hamilton F. Allen, "Abortion Law Ruled Illegal," *Providence Evening Bulletin*, June 10, 1975.

19. "Parade to Mark Opposition to Abortion," *Providence Journal*, September 29, 1973; William K. Gale, "March for Life is Columbus Day Parade Theme," *Providence Journal*, October 6, 1973; "Bishop Calls Abortion 'Most Heinous Sin,'" *Providence Journal*, October 8, 1973; Simone Caron, *Who Chooses? American Reproductive History since 1830* (Gainesville: University Press of Florida, 2008), 205.

20. Helen Morris, "Diocese Studying Ramifications of Non Compliance on Abortion Rule," *Huntington (WV) Herald-Dispatch*, February 19, 1974; J. Roy Bardsley, "Utahans Favor Abortions in Some Circumstances," *Salt Lake City Tribune*, October 7, 1973; Marjorie Hyer, "Suits Attack Abortion Rules," *Washington Post*, September 1, 1973.

21. "Abortions, Legal for Year, Performed for Thousands."

22. Edwin F. Daily et al., "Repeat Abortions in New York City, 1970–1972," *Family Planning Perspectives* 5 (1973): 89; Jane E. Brody, "New Abortion Rules Take Effect, Complicating Confused Picture," *New York Times*, October 20, 1970; "Abortions, Legal for Year, Performed for Thousands"; David Anable, "Abortion Question Revives Pro, Con Demonstrations," *Christian Science Monitor*, January 28, 1974; ZPG, "The Right to Choose: Facts on Abortion" [1976?], folder: "Abortion," box 128, Carter/Mondale 1976 Campaign Files, Jimmy Carter Library, Atlanta, GA; Alan Guttmacher Institute, "The Unmet Need for Abortion Services in the U.S.," *Family Planning Perspectives* 7 (1975): 225–226; "U.S. Court Annuls an Abortion Curb," *New York Times*, July 15, 1974; Edward Weinstock et al., "Abortion Needs and Services in the United States," *Family Planning Perspectives* 8 (1976): 59; Ellen Sullivan et al., "Legal Abortion in the United States, 1975–1976," *Family Planning*

*Perspectives* 9 (1977): 116; Isabel Wilkerson, "North Dakota a Hostile Landscape for Abortion," *New York Times*, May 6, 1990; "Most Insurers are Paying for Abortions," *American Medical News*, March 26, 1973, 7; AP, "Cost of Abortions, Vasectomies and Pills Ruled Tax Deductible," *New York Times*, April 11, 1973.

23. Rachel K. Jones and Kathryn Kooistra, "Abortion Incidence and Access to Services in the United States, 2008," *Perspectives on Sexual and Reproductive Health* 43 (2011): 43; Guttmacher Institute, "Trends in Abortion in the United States, 1973–2008," January 2011, http://www.guttmacher.org/presentations/trends.pdf; US Centers for Disease Control and Prevention, "Live Births, Birth Rates, and Fertility Rates, by Race, 1909–2003" [2003], http://www.cdc.gov/nchs/data/statab/natfinal2003.annvol1_01.pdf. In 1980, there were 3.6 million live births in the United States, according to statistics compiled by the US Centers for Disease Control, and, according to the Guttmacher Institute, there were 1.55 million abortions that year—a 7:3 ratio.

24. Charles E. Rice, Statement on Supreme Court Decision and Human Life Amendment, January 30, 1973, folder 1: "Abortion," box 1, Chancery Office Records, Archives of the Diocese of Harrisburg, PA.

25. Charles E. Rice, "Overruling *Roe v. Wade*: An Analysis of the Proposed Constitutional Amendments," *Boston College Law Review* 15 (December 1973): 322.

26. Editorial, "An Old Law Is Being Broken," *Presbyterian Journal*, March 24, 1971.

27. "Buckley Pushes Curb on Abortion," *New York Times*, June 1, 1973; Rice, "Overruling *Roe v. Wade*," 323–330.

28. NC, "Deluge of Letters to Hit Congress," *Anchor* (Fall River, MA), June 6, 1974, 8; Gilbert Durand to Humberto Medeiros, January 18, 1974, folder: "Correspondence, 1974," box 2, RG III.G.02—Birth Control and Abortion Records, Archives of the Archdiocese of Boston; Committee of Ten Million, Promotion for "Operation Avalanche" [1974], folder: "Correspondence, 1974," box 2, RG III.G.02—Birth Control and Abortion Records, Archives of the Archdiocese of Boston; Planned Parenthood, "Could the Supreme Court 'Abortion' Decisions Be Lost? Yes!" April 1973, folder 12, box 11, Wilda Scott Heide Papers, Schlesinger Library, Harvard University.

29. Gallup Poll, "Anti-Abortion Constitutional Amendment," February 27–March 1, 1976, in Gallup Organization, *America's Opinion on Abortion*, unpaginated.

30. "Abortion Foes Shift Fight on Court Decisions to Congress," *Hospital Practice*, October 1973, 200; Rice, "Overruling *Roe v. Wade*," 321–322; Lawrence Lader to Robert L. Webber, April 11, 1973, folder: "CA, 1973," carton 2, NARAL Records; National Right to Life Committee, Resolution #8, July 10, 1973, folder: "NRLC—1973 (3)," box 4, ACCL.

31. Albert H. Fortman, direct mail to candidates for North Dakota state legislature, October 1, 1974, folder: "Correspondence, 1974," box 2, NDRLA.

32. Marion K. Sanders, "Enemies of Abortion," *Harper's*, March 1974; Saul Friedman, "Survey Surprises Pro-Life Group," *Detroit Free Press*, March 10, 1975.

33. Rick Casey, "Congress Faces Abortion Battle," *National Catholic Reporter*, August 3, 1973; Eunice Kennedy Shriver, address to the National Right to Life Committee, Boston, June 26, 1976, folder: "ACCL Admin File—People—General—Shriver," box 25, ACCL; "Mrs. Shriver on Rights and Wrongs," *Washington Star*, June 23, 1975.

34. Marjory Mecklenburg to Kenneth Van Derhoeff, July 18, 1974, folder: "Correspondence, 1974," box 2, NDRLA; Robert M. Lynch, Memo to All State Catholic Conference Directors; Members of the Board of Directors, MCHLA, "Re: American Citizens Concerned for Life," August 23, 1974, folder: "Correspondence, 1974," box 2, NDRLA; "1 in 12 Enters Plea on Fraud Charges," *Deseret News*, May 25, 1974; Marjory Mecklenburg to David L. Cornwell, April 10, 1978, folder: "Correspondence, 1978 (2)," box 14, ACCL.

35. Warren Schaller, testimony before the Senate Subcommittee on Constitutional Amendments, August 21, 1974, folder: "Correspondence, 1974," box 2, NDRLA; Marjory Mecklenburg to Denyse Handler, April 18, 1980, folder: "General Correspondence, 1980 (1)," box 14, ACCL.

36. Mecklenburg to Cornwell, April 10, 1978.

37. Betty Wilson, "Abortion Factions Gird for Caucus Showdown," *Minneapolis Star*, February 20, 1976; Judy Klemesrud, "Abortion in the Campaign: Methodist Surgeon Leads the Opposition," *New York Times*, March 1, 1976; Ann Baker, "Squeal Rule," *St. Paul Pioneer Press*, March 9, 1983; Marjory Mecklenburg to Judy Fink, September 30, 1978, folder: "Correspondence, 1978 (2)," box 14, ACCL.

38. Robert N. Lynch, "The National Committee for a Human Life Amendment, Inc.: Its Goals and Origins," *Catholic Lawyer* 20 (1974): 303; John Krol to Joseph T. Daley, March 1, 1974, folder 1: "Abortion," box 1, Chancery Office Records, Archives of the Diocese of Harrisburg, PA; Richard L. Rashke, "Abortion: Key Issue in '76?" *National Catholic Reporter*, May 30, 1975.

39. "4 Cardinals Urge U.S. Abortion Ban," *New York Times*, March 8, 1974; "Abortion and the Law," *New Republic*, May 18, 1974.

40. *Commonweal* editorial quoted in "Abortion and the Law," *New Republic*, May 18, 1974; James J. Diamond, "The Troubled Anti-Abortion Camp," *America*, August 10, 1974.

41. National Conference of Catholic Bishops, "Pastoral Plan for Pro-Life Activities," November 20, 1975, www.priestsforlife.org/magisterium/bishops/75-11-20past oralplanforprolifeactivitiesnccb.htm.

42. "Liberal-Left Position Emerging against Abortion, Pacifist Says," *National Right to Life News*, December 1975, 16; Jack Willke, "Finally—a Vote on a Human Life Amendment," *National Right to Life News*, June 9, 1983, 3.

43. Peter Steinfels, "Roman Catholics and American Politics, 1960–2004," in *Religion and American Politics: From the Colonial Period to the Present*, ed. Mark A. Noll and Luke E. Harlow, 2nd ed. (New York: Oxford University Press, 2007), 357; Statement of Wilma Scott Heide on Abortion, Fall 1971, folder 12, box 11, Wilma Scott Heide Papers, Schlesinger Library, Harvard University; Edward M. Kennedy to Mrs. Edward J. Barshak, August 3, 1971, folder 31, box 2, Patricia Gold Papers, Schlesinger Library, Harvard University.

44. "J.D." to "Bishop," June 11, 1975, folder: "Correspondence, 1975," box 2, Birth Control and Abortion Records, Archives of the Archdiocese of Boston; Robert E. Burns, "Dr. Jefferson and the Politicians," *Wanderer* (St. Paul, MN), December 4, 1975.

45. Robert E. Burns, "Dr. Jefferson and the Politicians," *Wanderer*, December 4, 1975; Marjory Mecklenburg to Edward M. Kennedy, October 24, 1978, folder: "Correspondence, 1978 (2)," box 14, ACCL.

46. Jim Castelli, "Senate Committee Defeats Pro-Life Bill," *Michigan Catholic*, September 24, 1975.

47. Marjory Mecklenburg to Larry De Santo, October 28, 1975, folder: "ACCL Admin File: Kennedy Foundation Proposal—Shriver Campaign Committee (1)," box 30, ACCL; John T. Noonan Jr. to Marjory Mecklenburg, November 11, 1975, folder: "ACCL Admin File—People—General—Shriver," box 25, ACCL.

48. Transcript of Sargent Shriver's interview on *Meet the Press*, September 21, 1975, folder: "1980 Elections (3)," box 43, ACCL; Lucinda Franks, "Shriver Stressing 'Kennedy Connection,'" *New York Times*, December 31, 1975.

49. James M. Perry, "Shriver Falls Victim to His Own Church," *National Observer* (Washington, DC), January 31, 1976.

50. Marjory Mecklenburg to C. Thomas Bendorf, August 25, 1975, folder: "ACCL Admin File: Kennedy Foundation Proposal—Shriver Campaign Committee (3)," box 30, ACCL; "Action Summary," *ACCL Update*, September 26, 1975.

51. James M. Perry, "Shriver Falls Victim to His Own Church"; "The Kennedy Who Could Be President (If She Weren't a Woman)," *Ladies Home Journal*, March 1976.

52. Dexter Duggan, "Still Waiting for Shriver," *National Right to Life News*, December 1975, 8; Marjory Mecklenburg to Shriver Campaign Leaders and Friends, February 19, 1976, folder: "ACCL Admin File: Kennedy Foundation Proposal—Shriver Campaign Committee (2)," box 30, ACCL.

53. Warren Weaver Jr., "Bayh Accuses Carter of Raising 'False Hopes' of Abortion Foes," *New York Times*, January 30, 1976; Charles Mohr, "Abortion Dispute Troubling Bayh," *New York Times*, February 12, 1976; "Prayer Vigil Held at Notre Dame as Bayh Speaks," *National Right to Life News*, December 1975, 13.

54. R. W. Apple Jr., "Carter and Bayh Favored in Iowa," *New York Times*, January 19, 1976.

55. Weaver, "Bayh Accuses Carter of Raising 'False Hopes' of Abortion Foes," *New York Times*, January 30, 1976; Birch Bayh, Fact Sheet on Alternatives to

Abortion Package and speech in support of the legislation, September 17, 1975, folder: "Miscellaneous Reference Materials (3)," box 3, ACCL; Christopher Lydon, "Abortion Is Big Issue in the Primaries in Massachusetts and New Hampshire," *New York Times*, February 4, 1976; Roy Reed, "Wallace Pressing the Abortion Issue," *New York Times*, March 3, 1976.

56. Pro-Life Action Committee, "Right to Life TV Commercials—1976 Ellen McCormack Presidential Campaign," n.d. [1975 or 1976], folder: "1980 Elections (1)," box 43, ACCL.

57. D. J. Horan to National Right to Life Committee executive committee, September 7, 1973: "NRLC 1973 (7)," box 5, ACCL; Pro-Life Action Committee, "Right to Life TV Commercials—1976 Ellen McCormack Presidential Campaign"; "Reagan Declares Opposition to Abortion, Euthanasia," *Wanderer*, December 4, 1975.

58. Pro-Life Action Committee, "Right to Life TV Commercials—1976 Ellen McCormack Presidential Campaign."

59. Douglas Martin, "Ellen McCormack, Anti-Abortion Presidential Candidate, Dies at 84," *New York Times*, March 29, 2011; Pro-Life Action Committee, "Right to Life TV Commercials—1976 Ellen McCormack Presidential Campaign."

60. Martin, "Ellen McCormack, Anti-Abortion Presidential Candidate, Dies at 84"; "Ellen McCormack Endorses Buckley," *New York Times*, October 14, 1976; Phyllis Bernstein, "Anti-Abortion Candidate for President," *New York Times*, November 30, 1975.

61. William Delaney, "Pro-Life's McCormack—Another Lawrence of Arabia?" *Washington Star*, February 27, 1976.

62. Christopher Lydon, "Carter and Ford Victors in the Vermont Primaries," *New York Times*, March 3, 1976; R. W. Apple Jr., "Bayh and Shriver Expected to Quit Democratic Race," *New York Times*, March 4, 1976; "Ellen McCormack Delegates Set for Democratic National Convention," *National Right to Life News*, July 1976, 2; Alice Hartle, "What Made the Difference? A Tale of Three Cities," *National Right to Life News*, July 1976, 3.

63. Marjory Mecklenburg to Democratic National Convention Platform Committee, April 29, 1976, folder: "ACCL Political File: Political—1980 Elections (2)," box 43, ACCL.

64. George Gallup Jr., "Public Closely Divided on Abortion Issue," *Gallup Poll*, March 18, 1976.

65. "Former Speaker McCormack Sends Pro-Life Message to Democrat Platform Committee," *Wanderer*, April 15, 1976.

66. Democratic Party Platform of 1976, http://www.presidency.ucsb.edu/ws/index. php?pid = 29606; Les Ledbetter, "Coast Democrats Play Down Controversy in Platform Proposals," *New York Times*, March 22, 1976; David E. Rosenbaum, "Democrats Adopt a Platform Aimed at Uniting Party," *New York Times*, June 16, 1976.

67. Marjory Mecklenburg to Democratic Platform Drafting Task Force, June 15, 1976, folder: "1980 Elections (2)," box 43, ACCL.

68. Peter Kihss, "10,000 Antiabortionists Attend a Protest Rally," *New York Times,* July 12, 1976.

69. Andrew Mollison, "Do Catholics Cut Carter Chances?," *Atlanta Constitution,* July 13, 1976; Fran Watson, direct mail, August 10, 1976, folder: "Abortion Issue (1)," box C25, President Ford Committee Records, 1975–76, Ford Library; Willmar Thorkelson, "Religion Issue Enters Presidential Campaign," *Minneapolis Star,* July 17, 1976.

70. "Anti-Abortion Measure Is Killed as Senate Refuses to Debate It," *New York Times,* April 29, 1976; "Ford Is Firm for an Amendment to Let States Act on Abortions," *New York Times,* September 6, 1974; Catherine E. Rymph, *Republican Women: Feminism and Conservatism from Suffrage through the Rise of the New Right* (Chapel Hill: University of North Carolina Press, 2006), 205; Tanya Melich, *The Republican War against Women: An Insider's Report from behind the Lines* (New York: Bantam Books, 1996), 53; UPI, "Betty Ford Would Accept 'An Affair' by Daughter," *New York Times,* August 11, 1975; "Monthly Picketing Set at White House," *National Right to Life News,* December 1975, 1.

71. Transcripts of press conferences with Ronald Reagan, May 9, 1967, April 16, 1968, and June 8, 1972, folder: "Research File—Legal Affairs—Abortion," box GO 188, Governor's Papers, Ronald Reagan Library; Ronald Reagan, direct mail to California residents [1970], folder: "Research File—Legal Affairs—Abortion," box GO 188, Governor's Papers; author's telephone interview with Mary Vanis, April 2, 2012; Jackson Doyle, "Reagan Cool to New Abortion Bill," *San Francisco Chronicle,* April 17, 1968.

72. Alice Hartle, "Reagan Likes HLA, Gives Views on Abortion, Euthanasia," *National Right to Life News,* December 1975, 1.

73. Ronald Reagan to Henry J. Hyde, July 27, 1979, folder: "Right to Life (2/3)," box 135, Series III: Ed Meese Files, Ronald Reagan 1980 Campaign Papers, Reagan Library; Martin Tolchin, "Age Issue Hampering Goldwater Effort," *New York Times,* October 28, 1980; Douglas E. Kneeland, "Bush Is Growing More Cautious as Stock in Party Rises," *New York Times,* February 16, 1980.

74. Jim Reichley to Dick Cheney, June 25, 1976, folder: "Constituency Analysis," box 2, A. James Reichley Files, Ford Library; George Van Cleve to Michael Duval, July 23, 1976, folder: "Republican Party Platform—Issue Papers (5)," box 29, Michael Raoul-Duval Files, Ford Library; Alice Hartle, "GOP to Focus on Abortion," *National Right to Life News,* September 1976; Melich, *Republican War against Women,* 63–64; William A. Link, *Righteous Warrior: Jesse Helms and the Rise of Modern Conservatism* (New York: St. Martin's Press, 2008), 176–177; Republican Party Platform of 1976, http://www.presidency.ucsb.

edu/ws/?pid=25843; Jim Reichley to Dick Cheney, September 15, 1976, folder: "Abortion," box 1, Reichley Files, Ford Library.

75. Americans against Abortion, press release [Sept. 1976], folder: "ACCL Political File: '76 Presidential Campaign—NRL Project," box 46, ACCL.

76. Mike Leary, "A Hard Look—'Pro-Life' Army: Organized, Tough," *San Francisco Examiner*, September 16, 1976; New Jersey Right to Life, press release, October 12, 1976, folder: "Abortion Issue (1)," box C25, President Ford Committee Papers, 1975–76, Ford Library; Karen Mulhauser, direct mail on behalf of NARAL, October 5, 1976, folder: "Abortion—General (1)," Sarah C. Massengale Files, Ford Library; Marjory Mecklenburg to Bill Russo [1976], folder: "Abortion Issue (1)," box C25, President Ford Committee Papers, 1975–76, Ford Library.

77. George G. Higgins, "The Prolife Movement and the New Right," *America*, September 13, 1980, 109; statement of Peter B. Gemma Jr. on SJR 110, December 7, 1981, folder: "National Pro-Life Action Committee: POTUS— Pro-Life Coalition—Cabinet Room—01/23/1984 (2 of 2)," box OA9079, Morton Blackwell Files, Reagan Library; *National Pro-Life PAC Newsletter*, January 1979, folder: "National Pro-Life Action Committee: POTUS—Pro-Life Coalition—Cabinet Room—01/23/1984 (2 of 2)," box OA9079, Morton Blackwell Files, Reagan Library; Peter B. Gemma Jr. to Ronald Reagan, May 24, 1979, folder: "National Pro-Life," box 86, Charles Black Files, Ronald Reagan 1980 Campaign Papers, Reagan Library; *Pro-Life Political Reporter*, September 1979, folder: "Pro-Life," box 87, Black Files, Reagan 1980 Campaign Papers; "We Mean Business!" *Pro-Life Political Reporter*, June 1979, folder: "National Pro-Life Action Committee: POTUS—Pro-Life Coalition—Cabinet Room—01/23/1984 (2 of 2)," box OA9079, Morton Blackwell Files; National Pro-Life PAC, press release, March 13, 1979, box 22, Paul M. Weyrich Papers, American Heritage Center, University of Wyoming, Laramie; Charles C. Fiore, "Democrats for Life . . . or Death?," *Pro-Life Political Reporter*, September 1980, folder: "National Pro-Life Political Action Committee," box OA9079, Morton Blackwell Files.

78. Sara Diamond, *Roads to Dominion: Right-Wing Movements and Political Power in the United States* (New York: Guilford Press, 1995), 170; Paul M. Weyrich, "Blue Collar or Blue Blood? The New Right Compared with the Old Right," in *The New Right Papers*, ed. Robert W. Whitaker (New York: St. Martin's Press, 1982), 60.

79. Diamond, *Roads to Dominion*, 170; Nathaniel Sheppard Jr., "Group Fighting Abortion Planning to Step up Its Drive," *New York Times*, July 3, 1978; Douglas E. Kneeland, "Clark Defeat in Iowa Laid to Abortion Issue," *New York Times*, November 13, 1978.

80. Life Amendment Political Action Committee, press release, June 7, 1978, folder 10, box 15, Mildred Jefferson Papers, Schlesinger Library, Harvard University;

Scott Sherry, "Political Action Committee Formed," *National Right to Life News*, September/October 1979, 4; "Pro-Life Activists Will Play Major Role in Elections," *National Right to Life News*, September/October 1979, 4.

81. "Hyde Amendment: An Unlooked-for Light in 1976," *National Right to Life News*, July 7, 1980; Kevin P. Phillips, "The Life Issue That Won't Die," *Boston Herald*, August 2, 1976; Rachel Benson Gold, "After the Hyde Amendment: Public Funding for Abortion in FY 1978," *Family Planning Perspectives* 12 (1980): 131–134; Janet Grant, "Pro-Life Strength Shown in Hyde Amendment Vote," *National Right to Life News*, September 1976, 1; Martin Tolchin, "Age Issue Hampering Goldwater Effort." For the role of the abortion funding issue in creating a Republican pro-life consensus and limiting abortion availability, see William Saletan, *Bearing Right: How Conservatives Won the Abortion War* (Berkeley: University of California Press, 2003).

82. Gallup Poll, "When Human Life Begins," May 1981, in Gallup Organization, *America's Opinion on Abortion*, unpaginated; Donald Granberg, "The Abortion Activists," *Family Planning Perspectives* 13 (1981): 158–160.

83. Francis A. Schaeffer, *How Should We Then Live?: The Rise and Decline of Western Thought and Culture* (Old Tappan, NJ: Fleming H. Revell, 1976), 223; Francis A. Schaeffer and C. Everett Koop, *Whatever Happened to the Human Race?* (Old Tappan, NJ: Fleming H. Revell, 1979), 194–195.

84. Jerry Falwell, *How You Can Help Clean Up America* (Lynchburg, VA: Liberty, 1978), 9–32; Brad Kutrow, "Falwell Takes Aim at Freeze," *Lynchburg (VA) News*, March 16, 1983; Richard Halloran, "Bishops Joining Nuclear Arms Debate," *New York Times*, October 4, 1982.

85. Southern Baptist Convention, Resolution on Abortion, June 1980, http://www.sbc.net/resolutions/amResolution.asp?ID = 19; Paul D. Simmons, "Religious Approaches to Abortion," in *Abortion, Medicine and the Law*, ed. J. Douglas Butler and David F. Walbert, 5th ed. (Martinsville, IN: Fideli, 2011), ch. 31; "Report of the Ad Interim Committee on Abortion," Sixth General Assembly of the Presbyterian Church in America, 1978, http://pcahistory.org/pca/2-015.pdf.

86. For more analysis of the place of abortion and other cultural issues in the evangelical political mobilization of the 1970s, see Daniel K. Williams, *God's Own Party: The Making of the Christian Right* (New York: Oxford University Press, 2010), 105–185.

87. Granberg, "The Abortion Activists," 162; Democratic Party Platform of 1980, http://www.presidency.ucsb.edu/ws/?pid = 29607.

88. Numan V. Bartley, *The New South, 1945–1980* (Baton Rouge: Louisiana State University Press, 1995), 455; "E.R.A. Means Abortion and Population Shrinkage," *Phyllis Schlafly Report*, December 1974; "Readers Argue Abortion Effects of Equal Rights Amendment," *National Right to Life News*, April 1977, 8; Juli Loesch, "Feminists for Life Author Says No Abortion Link," *National Right to Life News*, January 1979, 9; "The ERA—Be Ready to Fight!" *A.L.L. about*

*Issues*, September 1983; George Gallup, "Evangelicals' Views on Issues Are Similar to Other Voters'," *Washington Post*, September 8, 1980; Granberg, "The Abortion Activists," 157–162.

89. Reagan to Hyde, July 27, 1979; Henry J. Hyde, direct mail to pro-life activists, August 27, 1979, folder: "Right to Life (2/3)," box 135, Ed Meese Files, Ronald Reagan 1980 Campaign Papers, Reagan Library.

90. "Reagan Goofs!" *Pro-Life Political Reporter*, August 1981, 3; Patrick Buchanan, "Reagan's Run-In with the Right-to-Lifers," *New York Daily News*, August 11, 1981; memo from Thomas M. McMurray to James Lake, Re: Pro-Life Letter to Senator Humphrey, January 6, 1980, folder: "Right to Life (2/3)," box 135, Ed Meese Files, Ronald Reagan 1980 Campaign Papers, Reagan Library; "Iowa Pro-Lifers Blast Kennedy's Campaign Tactics," *Arlington (VA) Catholic Herald*, January 10, 1980.

91. Draft for Senator Schweiker's Remarks at the March for Life Rally on the Capitol Steps [January 1980], folder: "Right to Life (2/3)," box 135, Ed Meese Files, Ronald Reagan 1980 Campaign Papers, Reagan Library; Leslie Bennetts, "Thousands March in Capital, Seeking Abortion Ban," *New York Times*, January 23, 1980; Ronald Reagan to Nellie J. Gray, February 7, 1980, Gray to Reagan, February 8, 1980, and statement of Nellie J. Gray, February 9, 1980, folder: "Pro-Life II (5 of 6)," box OA9081, Morton Blackwell Files, Reagan Library; Emily Langer, "Nellie Gray, March for Life Founder, Dead at 88," *Washington Post*, August 14, 2012.

92. Memo from Communications Broadcast Services to RFP Staff—D.C./L.A., Pete McPherson, Iowa, January 21, 1980, folder: "Abortion," box 553, Ronald Reagan 1980 Campaign Papers, Reagan Library; "Reagan Meets with NRLC Presidents," *National Right to Life News*, July 7, 1980; J. C. Willke, "Dr. Willke to Retire as NRLC President," *National Right to Life News*, April 23, 1991, 3.

93. Catholics in the Public Square, "Marlene Elwell, Founder of CPS," http://www. catholicsinthepublicsquare.org/aboutus_founder.html.

94. Right to Life of Michigan, Board Meeting Minutes, April 2, 1980, June 14, 1980, and July 23, 1980, folder: "Administrative—Board of Directors—Minutes, 1980," box 1, Right to Life of Michigan Records, BHL; "NRL PAC Statement on Bush," *National Right to Life News*, July 21, 1980.

95. Bill Peterson, "In Her Farewell, Mary Crisp Blasts GOP 'Sickness,'" *Washington Post*, July 10, 1980; Leslie Bennetts, "Mrs. Crisp, Former G.O.P. Aide, Will Direct Anderson Campaign," *New York Times*, August 15, 1980; Lydia Saad, "Republicans', Dems' Abortion Views Grow More Polarized," Gallup Politics, March 8, 2010, http://www.gallup.com/poll/126374/republicans-d ems-abortion-views-grow-polarized.aspx; Rowland Evans and Robert Novak, "Why It Probably Won't Be Baker," *Washington Post*, May 9, 1980; "NRL PAC Statement on Bush," *National Right to Life News*, July 21, 1980.

EPILOGUE

1. Alan Sears, "Overwhelming Turnout of Young People at March for Life Is Encouraging," *American Thinker*, February 14, 2013, http://www.american-thinker.com/blog/2013/02/overwhelming_turnout_of_young_people_at_march_for_life_is_encouraging.html; Carol Morello and James Arkin, "March for Life in Front of Supreme Court Decries *Roe v. Wade* on 40th Anniversary," *Washington Post*, January 25, 2013; Marjorie Hyer, "Abortion Issue Foes March," *Washington Post*, January 23, 1974.

2. Gallup Poll, Abortion, data for May 2013, http://www.gallup.com/poll/1576/abortion.aspx; Pam Belluck, "Pregnancy Centers Gain Influence in Anti-Abortion Arena," *New York Times*, January 4, 2013; Pew Research Religion and Public Life Project, "Public Opinion on Abortion Slideshow," January 16, 2013, http://www.pewforum.org/2013/01/16/public-opinion-on-abortion-slideshow/.

3. Morello and Arkin, "March for Life in Front of Supreme Court Decries *Roe v. Wade* on 40th Anniversary"; Lydia Saad, "Generational Differences on Abortion Narrow," Gallup, March 12, 2010, http://www.gallup.com/poll/126581/generational-differences-abortion-narrow.aspx.

4. See, for instance, Laura Bassett, "Anti-abortion Laws Take Toll on Clinics Nationwide," *Huffington Post*, August 26, 2013, http://www.huffingtonpost.com/2013/08/26/abortion-clinic-closures_n_3804529.html; and Kate Pickert, "What Choice?" *Time*, January 14, 2013, http://content.time.com/time/magazine/article/0,9171,2132761,00.html.

5. Jack Willke, "The Prolife Movement Has Cause for Hope," *National Right to Life News*, July 21, 1980, 9; Robert M. Byrn, Memorandum in Opposition to S.J. Res. 110 [fall 1981], folder: "Pro-Life (continued—#2) (2 of 5)," box OA9081, Morton Blackwell Files, Ronald Reagan Library, Simi Valley, CA; "Down the Hatch!" *A.L.L. About Issues*, January 1982, 3; "Marchers Were of One Mind," *Our Sunday Visitor*, February 7, 1982; "Anti-Abortion Group Backs Hatch Proposal," *New York Times*, December 13, 1981; David Shribman, "Foes of Abortion Beaten in Senate on Amendment Bid," *New York Times*, June 29, 1983.

6. Conference Program, Reversing *Roe v. Wade* through the Courts: A Strategic National Pro-Life Conference, March 31, 1984, folder: "Americans United for Life Legal Defense Fund (Letters n.d., misc.) RH WL Eph 543.3," Wilcox Collection, Spencer Research Library, University of Kansas, Lawrence.

7. Dave Andrusko, "A Court out of Control," *National Right to Life News*, June 30, 1983, 2; David N. O'Steen and Darla St. Martin, "The Road to Reversing *Roe v. Wade*: Facing the Challenges of 1988," *National Right to Life News*, January 22, 1988, 23; Dave Andrusko, "Bursting with Pride," *National Right to Life News*, November 17, 1988, 3; Carol Long, "The Challenge of 1992: Everyone Is Responsible, Everyone Is Needed," *National Right to Life News*, January 1992, 1; Dave Andrusko, "America on the Couch," *National Right to Life News*, July 21,

1992, 2; Wanda Franz, "A Confused and Arrogant Supreme Court Reaffirms the 'Right' to Abortion," *National Right to Life News*, July 21, 1992, 3.

8. Jesse L. Jackson, "How We Respect Life is Over-riding Moral Issue," *National Right to Life News*, January 1977; "More HLAs Sponsored in House," *National Right to Life News*, March 1977, 1, 12; Richard L. Berke, "Now, Democrats Take a Turn at Abortion Fight," *New York Times*, January 30, 2000; Excerpts from Press Conference of Rev. Jesse Jackson, Washington, DC, November 3, 1983, folder 3, box 9, Mildred F. Jefferson Papers, Schlesinger Library, Harvard University; Charlotte Grimes, "Gephardt's Switch on Abortion May Be Costly," *St. Louis Post-Dispatch*, May 18, 1986; David E. Rosenbaum, "On the Issues: George Bush," *New York Times*, March 24, 1980; J. C. Willke, "We Won the Big One," *National Right to Life News*, November 17, 1988, 3, 10, 14.

9. Dave Andrusko, "Pro-Life Democrats Fight Uphill Battle in Congress," *National Right to Life News*, April 28, 1992, 4; National Right to Life Committee, Federal NRLC Scorecard—113th Congress, 2014, https://nrlc.capwiz.com/nrlc/scorecard.xc?chamber = S&session = 113.

10. Robert O. Self, *All in the Family: The Realignment of American Democracy since the 1960s* (New York: Hill and Wang, 2012), 3–7; John T. McGreevy, *Catholicism and American Freedom: A History* (New York: W. W. Norton, 2003), 153–165, 277–281.

11. Michael Sean Winters, *Left at the Altar: How the Democrats Lost the Catholics and How the Catholics Can Save the Democrats* (New York: Basic Books, 2008) (see page 93 for a brief discussion of O'Boyle's civil rights activism).

12. For an analysis of the way in which individualistic thinking pervaded both conservatism and liberalism in the postwar era, see Daniel T. Rodgers, *Age of Fracture* (Cambridge, MA: Harvard University Press, 2011).

13. Marjory Mecklenburg to Eunice Kennedy Shriver, January 25, 1979, folder: "ACCL Admin File—People—General—Shriver," box 25, American Citizens Concerned for Life (ACCL) Files, Gerald R. Ford Library, Ann Arbor, MI; Juli Loesch to Burke Balch, February 15, 1978, folder 11, box 4, John Cavanaugh-O'Keefe Papers, Wisconsin Historical Society, Madison.

14. Jim Wallis, "Lift Every Voice," *Sojourners*, July–August 1996, 7; Julie Polter, "Outrage over the Abortion Veto," *Sojourners*, July–August 1996, 9.

15. Irvin Molotsky, "Former Gov. Robert P. Casey Dies at 68; Pennsylvania Democrat Opposed Abortion," *New York Times*, May 31, 2000; Wanda Franz, "The Decline of the Democratic Party," *National Right to Life News*, February 4, 1992, 3.

16. Dave Andrusko, "Abortion-on-Demand Losing Proposition for Democrats," *National Right to Life News*, June 2, 1992, 13; Dave Andrusko, "Pro-Life Democrats Fight Uphill Battle in Congress," *National Right to Life News*, April 28, 1992, 4.

17. National Conference of Catholic Bishops, "The Challenge of Peace: God's Promise and Our Response," May 3, 1983, http://www.usccb.org/upload/challenge-peace-gods-promise-our-response-1983.pdf; Kenneth A. Briggs, "Bernardin Asks Catholics to Fight Both Nuclear Arms and Abortion," *New York Times*, December 7, 1983; Mary E. Bendyna, "JustLife Action," in *Risky Business? PAC Decisionmaking in Congressional Elections*, ed. Robert Biersack et al. (New York: M. E. Sharpe, 1994), 195–199; David R. Swartz, *Moral Minority: The Evangelical Left in an Age of Conservatism* (Philadelphia: University of Pennsylvania Press, 2012), 246–247; Marvin L. Krier Mich, *Catholic Social Teaching and Movements* (Mystic, CT: Twenty-Third Publications, 1998), 213–216; Tom Squitieri, "Jefferson Announces Senate Candidacy," *Boston Herald*, August 17, 1989.

18. Kenneth A. Briggs, "Religious Leaders Assail Reagan Policies," *New York Times*, December 2, 1981; Kenneth A. Briggs, "Roman Catholic Bishops Toughen Stance against Nuclear Weapons," *New York Times*, May 3, 1983; NCCB, "The Challenge of Peace."

19. "Archbishop Contends Abortion Is Key Issue," *New York Times*, June 25, 1984; Kenneth A. Briggs, "Catholics Urged to Press Views Held by Church," *New York Times*, August 10, 1984; United States Conference of Catholic Bishops, "Catholics in Political Life," June 2004, http://www.usccb.org/issues-and-action/faithful-citizenship/church-teaching/catholics-in-political-life.cfm; Vatican II, *Gaudium et Spes* ("The Church in the Modern World"), December 7, 1965, sect. 51, http://www.vatican.va/archive/hist_councils/ii_vatican_council/documents/vat-ii_const_19651207_gaudium-et-spes_en.html; John Paul II, *Evangelium Vitae* ("The Gospel of Life"), March 25, 1995, http://www.vatican.va/holy_father/john_paul_ii/encyclicals/documents/hf_jp-ii_enc_25031995_evangelium-vitae_en.html; John Thavis, "Cardinal Ratzinger Lays out Principles on Denying Communion, Voting," Catholic News Service, July 6, 2004, http://www.catholicnews.com/data/stories/cns/0403722.htm; Eusebius J. Beltran, "The Most Important Issue," October 5, 2008, http://www.priestsforlife.org/magisterium/bishops/beltran-oklahoma-city.htm.

20. United States Conference of Catholic Bishops, "The Challenge of Faithful Citizenship: A Catholic Call to Political Responsibility," 2004, http://www.usccbpublishing.org/client/client_pdfs/bulletininsert.pdf.

21. David N. O'Steen, "Welfare 'Reforms' Pose Threat to Unborn Babies," *National Right to Life News*, February 22, 1995, 1, 4–5; Charles E. Curran, *The Social Mission of the U.S. Catholic Church: A Theological Perspective* (Washington, DC: Georgetown University Press, 2011), 157–170; Jonathan V. Last, "Weekly Standard: Obamacare vs. the Catholics," National Public Radio, February 7, 2012, http://www.npr.org/2012/02/07/146511839/weekly-standard-obamacare-vs-the-catholics.

22. Laurie Goodstein, "Rev. R. J. Neuhaus, Political Theologian, Dies at 72," *New York Times*, January 8, 2009; Richard John Neuhaus, "Iraq and the Moral Judgment," *First Things*, October 2005, http://www.firstthings.com/article/2005/10/iraq-and-the-moral-judgement; UPI, "Ouster Asked for Author of Birth Control Rule," *New York Times*, February 25, 1983.

23. James Risen and Judy L. Thomas, *Wrath of Angels: The American Abortion War* (New York: Basic Books, 1998); William Martin, *With God on Our Side: The Rise of the Religious Right in America* (New York: Broadway Books, 1996), 174–200.

24. "Anti-Abortion Group Spreads Anti-Semitic, Theocratic Message," *Church and State*, September 1994, 20; James Ridgeway, "The Prolife Juggernaut," *Voice*, July 16, 1985, 28–29.

25. Paul M. Weyrich, "Blue Collar or Blue Blood? The New Right Compared with the Old Right," in *The New Right Papers*, ed. Robert W. Whitaker (New York: St. Martin's Press, 1982), 60.

26. Transcript of Jerry Falwell's *Old Time Gospel Hour* broadcast, October 19, 1980, 14–15, folder: "Moral Majority—Old Time Gospel Hour (1980–81)," People for the American Way Archives, Washington, DC.

27. Charles E. Rice, *The Vanishing Right to Live: An Appeal for a Renewed Reverence for Life* (Garden City, NY: Doubleday, 1969); Mark O. Hatfield, Address to National Right to Life Convention, Detroit, June 9, 1973, folder: "Correspondence, 1974," box 2, North Dakota Right to Life Association Records, State Historical Society of North Dakota, Bismarck.

28. Death Penalty Information Center, Executions by Year, 1976–2014, http://www.deathpenaltyinfo.org/executions-year; Guttmacher Institute, "Trends in Abortion in the United States, 1973–2008," January 2011, http://www.guttmacher.org/presentations/trends.pdf.

29. Natasha Zaretsky, *No Direction Home: The American Family and the Fear of National Decline, 1968–1980* (Chapel Hill: University of North Carolina Press, 2007), 11–17; George H. Gallup Jr., "Current Views on Premarital, Extramarital Sex," Gallup Organization, June 24, 2003, http://www.gallup.com/poll/8704/current-views-premarital-extramarital-sex.aspx.

30. Rachel K. Jones et al., "Patterns in the Socioeconomic Characteristics of Women Obtaining Abortions in 2000–2001," *Perspectives on Sexual and Reproductive Health* 34 (2002): 228; Sally C. Curtin et al., "Pregnancy Rates for US Women Continue to Drop," NCHS Data Brief, December 2013, 5, http://www.cdc.gov/nchs/data/databriefs/db136.pdf; Lawrence B. Finer and Stanley K. Henshaw, "Abortion Incidence and Services in the United States in 2000," *Perspectives on Sexual and Reproductive Health* 35 (2003): 6.

31. Fred E. Mecklenburg, "Building Bridges Instead of Walls" [1977], folder: "ACCL Admin File: People—General—Dr. Fred Mecklenburg (2)," box 24, ACCL; Charles E. Rice, "New Mandate for the Pro-Life Movement," *Triumph*, May 1972, 12; Judy Fink to Ed Golden et al., "Re: Policy Statement of the NRLC

Concerning 'Birth Control,'" May 15, 1973, folder: "NRLC, 1973 (2)," box 4, ACCL.

32. For evangelical views of birth control in the late twentieth and early twenty-first centuries, see Daniel K. Williams, "Sex and the Evangelicals: Gender Issues, the Sexual Revolution, and Abortion in the 1960s," in *American Evangelicals and the 1960s*, ed. Axel R. Schäfer (Madison: University of Wisconsin Press, 2013), 97–120; Allan Carlson, *Godly Seed: American Evangelicals Confront Birth Control, 1873–1973* (New Brunswick, NJ: Transaction, 2012), 113–160; Amy DeRogatis, *Saving Sex: Sexuality and Salvation in American Evangelicalism* (New York: Oxford University Press, 2015), 93–128.

33. Juli Loesch, "Unmarried Couples Shouldn't Live Together," *U.S. Catholic*, July 1985, 16–17; Molly Kelly, "Education: Not Condoms and Clean Needles," *Living*, Fall 1990, 21; Matthew Habiger, direct mail on behalf of Human Life International [October 1995], folder: HH361: [Human Life International], box 1–4, Hall-Hoag Collection, John Hay Library, Brown University, Providence, RI; John F. Kippley, "Teaching Adult Chastity through Natural Family Planning," *A.L.L. about Issues*, March 1989, 30.

34. Jeff Gardner, "Twenty-Five Years of Love and Life at the Pope Paul VI Institute," *Celebrate Life*, January–February 2011, http://www.clmagazine. org/article/index/id/ODkzNg/; Paul Marx, *"The Gospel of Life* Crowns My Life," *HLI Reports*, May 1995, 3; Sam and Bethany Torode, "Make Love and Babies," *Christianity Today*, November 12, 2001; Karen Swallow Prior, "The Pill: Contraceptive or Abortifacient?" *Atlantic*, December 31, 2012, http:// www.theatlantic.com/sexes/archive/2012/12/the-pill-contraceptive-or-abortifacient/266725/; Randall Patterson, "Students of Virginity," *New York Times*, March 30, 2008; Stanford Anscombe Society, "Pro-Life, Pro-Family Reception," May 26, 2012, https://anscombe.stanford.edu/content/pro-l ife-pro-family-reception-0.

35. Guttmacher Institute, "Trends in Premarital Sex in the United States, 1954–2003," *Public Health Reports*, January–February 2007, 73–78, http://www.ncbi. nlm.nih.gov/pubmed/17236611; Guttmacher Institute, "Contraceptive Use in the United States," June 2015, http://www.guttmacher.org/pubs/fb_contr_use. html.

36. Rachel's Vineyard Ministries, "History of Rachel's Vineyard," http://www. rachelsvineyard.org/aboutus/ourstory.htm; Steven Ertelt, "Woman Behind *Roe v. Wade*: 'I'm Dedicating My Life to Overturning It,'" LifeNews, January 22, 2013, http://www.lifenews.com/2013/01/22/woman-behind-roe-v-wade-im-dedicating-my-life-to-overturning-it/; Wonderfully Made Ministry, biography of Sandra Cano, http://www.wonderfullymadeministry.com/; Feminists for Life website, www.feministsforlife.org.

37. Wendy Simonds, *Abortion at Work: Ideology and Practice in a Feminist Clinic* (New Brunswick, NJ: Rutgers University Press, 1996), 229.

38. Margot Anne Sheahan to Eva S. Moseley, October 12, 1986, folder 1, 86-M215, Margot Anne Sheahan Papers, Schlesinger Library, Harvard University; David C. Reordan et al., *Victims and Victors: Speaking out about Their Pregnancies, Abortions, and Children Resulting from Sexual Assault* (Springfield, IL: Acorn Books, 2000); Rebecca Kiesling, professional website, http://www.rebeccakiessling.com/index.html.

39. Jennifer S. Bryson, "Stanford, Marriage and Abortion Controversies, and the Mission of a University," *Public Discourse*, March 19, 2014, http://www.thepublicdiscourse.com/2014/03/12913/. For more on the contrast between pro-lifers' and pro-choicers' views of motherhood and womanhood, see Kristin Luker, *Abortion and the Politics of Motherhood* (Berkeley: University of California Press, 1984).

40. Donald Granberg, "The Abortion Activists," *Family Planning Perspectives* 13 (1981): 158.

41. John Cavanaugh-O'Keefe, "No Cheap Solutions," (1984), 39, folder 1, box 4, John Cavanaugh-O'Keefe Papers, Wisconsin Historical Society, Madison.

42. Risen and Thomas, *Wrath of Angels: The American Abortion War* (New York: Basic Books, 1998); Williams, *God's Own Party*, 222–225; Holly Morris, "Reluctant Couple Converts to Activism," *Washington Post*, February 2, 1989; Charles E. Shepard, "Operation Rescue's Mission to Save Itself," *Washington Post*, November 24, 1991.

43. Memo from John C. Willke to All Pro-Life Friends, "Re: Convention '86 and Public Witness," May 27, 1986, folder 5, box 2, Cavanaugh-O'Keefe Papers; John C. Willke, "Statement against Violence at Abortion Facilities," July 6, 1984, folder 5, box 2, Cavanaugh-O'Keefe Papers; National Abortion Federation, "History of Violence," https://www.prochoice.org/about_abortion/violence/history_violence.html; Patricia Baird-Windle and Eleanor J. Badle, *Targets of Hatred: Antiabortion Terrorism* (New York: Palgrave Macmillan, 2001); Jerry Reiter, *Live from the Gates of Hell: An Insider's Look at the Antiabortion Underground* (Amherst, NY: Prometheus Books, 2000), 124; Risen and Thomas, *Wrath of Angels*, 339–372; Alesha Doan, *Opposition and Intimidation: The Abortion Wars and Strategies of Political Harassment* (Ann Arbor: University of Michigan Press, 2007), 108; Army of God Manual, 3rd ed. [c. 1993], http://www.armyofgod.com/AOGhistory.html; "Reaction to Abortion Clinic Violence: Pro-Choice Hysteria Dominates the Debate," *Lifelines*, Winter 1995, 4.

44. For one of the many expositions of this argument, see Lewis M. Killian, foreword to *Religious Violence and Abortion: The Gideon Project*, by Dallas A. Blanchard and Terry A. Prewitt (Gainesville: University Press of Florida, 1993), ix–xii.

45. "National Right to Life Committee Statement concerning Abortion Clinic Violence," *National Right to Life News*, August 5, 1994, 22; Doan, *Opposition and Intimidation*, 86–89; Risen and Thomas, *Wrath of Angels*, 301–314; "A Victory for Abortion Rights," *New York Times*, May 14, 1994; "Protestors to Be Kept

Farther from Clinics," *New York Times*, April 16, 1999; "Abortion Harassers as Racketeers," *New York Times*, April 23, 1998; James Risen, "Abortion Clinic Slayings May Kill Operation Rescue," *Los Angeles Times*, August 10, 1994.

46. "After *Gonzales v. Carhart*: The Future of Abortion Jurisprudence," Pew Research Religion and Public Life Project, June 14, 2007, http://www. pewforum.org/2007/06/14/after-gonzales-v-carhart-the-future-of-abortion-jurisprudence/; "Louisiana Abortion Law Is Halted in U.S. Court," *New York Times*, August 8, 1991; Pam Belluck, "Complex Science at Issue in Politics of Fetal Pain," *New York Times*, September 16, 2013; Erik Eckholm, "Ultrasound: A Pawn in the Abortion Wars," *New York Times*, February 25, 2012; AP, "Mississippi: Governor Signs Abortion Restriction," *New York Times*, April 24, 2014; Louise Radnofsky, "Survey Shows Abortions Decline to Lowest Point Since 1970s," *Wall Street Journal*, February 3, 2014; Laura Bassett, "Anti-Abortion Laws Take Toll on Clinics Nationwide," *Huffington Post*, August 26, 2013, http://www. huffingtonpost.com/2013/08/26/abortion-clinic-closures_n_3804529.html; US Census Bureau, "Abortions—Number and Rate by State of Occurrence: 2000 to 2008," table 103 in *Statistical Abstract of the United States*, 2012, 76, https:// www.census.gov/compendia/statab/2012/tables/12s0103.pdf.

47. James Viciney, "Judge Upholds Embryonic Stem Cell Research Funds," *Washington Post*, July 28, 2011; Editorial, "Stem Cell Research Gets a Reprieve," *New York Times*, January 20, 2013; Rob Stein, "As Abortion Rate Drops, Use of RU-486 Is on Rise," *Washington Post*, January 22, 2008; "Group Leaders Meet with HEW Officials over In Vitro Funding," *National Right to Life News*, September/October 1979, 1, 9; Kristan Hawkins, "Pro-Life Concerns about IVF Include Abortion, Exploitation," LifeNews.com, September 6, 2011, http:// www.lifenews.com/2011/09/06/pro-life-concerns-about-ivf-include-abortion-exploitation/; Denise Grady, "Medical Nuances Drove 'No' Vote in Mississippi," *New York Times*, November 14, 2011.

48. Guttmacher Institute, "Abortion Rate Increasing among Poor Women, Even as It Decreases among Most Other Groups," May 23, 2011, http://www.gutt-macher.org/media/nr/2011/05/23/ab.html; Rachel K. Jones and Megan L. Kavanaugh, "Changes in Abortion Rates between 2000 and 2008 and Lifetime Incidence of Abortion," *Obstetrics and Gynecology* 117 (2011): 1358–1366; Richard M. Doerflinger, "What Ever Happened to 'Reducing Abortions'?" *On Faith*, February 21, 2013, http://www.faithstreet.com/onfaith/2013/02/21/ how-to-reduce-abortions/11312.

49. Doerflinger, "What Ever Happened to 'Reducing Abortions'?"

50. Williams, *God's Own Party*, 239–242, 266, 274.

# Index